개정판

International

Incoterms® 2020 수록

Trade Practice

무역실무영어

이신규 저

도서출판 두남

REVISED PREFACE

The international trade environment has undergone dramatic changes during the past few years not only in terms of volume but in complexity as well. I would like to thank the professors who adopted this book as a textbook and also thank all the readers for adopting this book to study international trade practice.

The main objective of this edition of this book is to present a comprehensive, up-to-date and clear explanation of Incoterms® 2020 that entered into force on January 1, 2020.

International Chamber of Commerce (ICC) has launched Incoterms® 2020 set that contains the rules for use of the 11 Incoterms® trade rules. It takes into account the latest developments in commercial practice, and updates the rules to make them more accessible and easier to use.

The characteristics of Incoterms® 2020 can be summarized as follows;

- The Incoterms® FCA (Free Carrier) now provides the additional option to make an on-board notation on the Bill of Lading prior loading of the goods on a vessel.
- The costs now appear centralized in A9/B9 of each Incoterms® rule.
- CIP now requires at least an insurance with the minimum cover of the Institute Cargo Clause (A) (All risk, subject to itemized exclusions).
- CIF requires at least an insurance with the minimum cover of the Institute Cargo Clause (C) (Number of listed risks, subject to itemized exclusions).

- The Incoterms® rules Free Carrier (FCA), Delivered at Place (DAP), Delivered at Place Unloaded (DPU) and Delivered Duty Paid (DDP) now take into account that the goods may be carried without any third-party carrier being engaged, namely by using its own means of transportation.
- The rule Delivered at Terminal (DAT) has been changed to Delivered at Place Unloaded (DPU) to clarify that the place of destination could be any place and not only a "terminal".
- The Incoterms® 2020 now explicitly shifts the responsibility of security-related requirements and ancillary costs to the seller.

I would like to express my gratitude to the president of Dunam Publishing Company and all the editorial staff of the company.

February, 2020
Shinkyuo, Lee

PREFACE

Globalization requires professionals to deal with their counterparts in countries with different business environments. There have been a lots of books and researches on international business english and trade practice. As those materials have been published in Korean mostly, there have been some problems that even people who acquired great deal of knowledge on international trade have hard time carrying out their international trade efficiently due to lack of communication and negotiation skills which are key factors to succeed in conducting international trade.

In order to meet the requirements of traders and students studying international business, the author decided to publish "International Business English" which covers the fundamental techniques and procedures of international trade in English only. This book provides a clear framework to guide international business people and students interested in international business. This book will help traders in trading companies and students interested in international business and students preparing for the examinations of all kinds of trade related licences acquire a basic knowledge on international trade practice and develop communication skills that are indispensible in carrying out international business.

This book covers the methods of doing market researches for developing international markets and also covers main contents in international trade such as offer and acceptance, trade contract, order and acknowledgement, letter of credit, international cargo transport and insurance, documents, claims and arbitration, etc.

This book could not have been completed without the assistance of many other people. I would like to thank many authors and professors who made it possible to cover a broad range of issues related to international trade. My grateful appreciation goes to Jeon, Doo Pyo, President of Dunam Publishing Co., Ltd. Finally, I am thankful to my wife and two daughters, Naeun and Jiwon for their graceful support and inspiration in countless ways.

May, 2014
Shinkyuo, Lee

Contents

Chapter 1

Export and Import Procedures

Chapter

1 Export and Import Procedures

1.1 Export Procedures

1. Contract of Sale

Through market researches, a seller can get information on a buyer and starts business negotiations by exchanging circular letters, trade inquiries, offer and acceptance. Terms and conditions such as quality, quantity, price, payment, shipment, packaging, insurance, dispute settlement, etc. need to be agreed by the parties concerned before drawing up a contract of sale. A contract of sale is a voluntary legal agreement between two or more parties that outlines each party's rights and obligations.

2. Receipt of Letter of Credit

If payment is to be made by Letter of Credit(L/C), the buyer will ask a bank, issuing bank, to issue a L/C in favor of the seller. The issuing bank issues a letter of credit as a way to ensure the seller that the issuing bank guarantees to pay the complying presentation.

After receiving the L/C, the seller should examine the L/C if the terms and conditions in the L/C correspond to those in their contract of sale. If there is any discrepancy in the L/C, the seller should ask the buyer to amend the L/C.

3. Export Approval(If necessary)

A seller can export freely without getting an export approval. However, there are some items the seller has to get export licence for some reasons. If an export licence is needed, the seller must obtain an export licence from the government.

4. Arrangement of Goods for Export

1) Arrangement of Goods

A seller must get the goods ready for shipment before the stipulated delivery time. The quality, quantity, packaging and marking of the goods and the delivery date must strictly follow the stipulations in the contract. There are two ways to arrange the goods for export as follows;

① The seller produces the goods directly
② The seller purchases the finished goods from other suppliers

First, the seller should purchase the raw and sub-materials or parts for the goods from other suppliers in both domestic and overseas markets to produce the goods directly. Second, if the seller doesn't have any manufacturing facilities and can't produce the goods, they have to purchase the finished goods from other manufacturers in both domestic and overseas markets as well.

2) Inspection of Goods

If the goods need to be inspected before shipment, inspection should be carried out in time and appropriate inspection certificates should be obtained. The methods of inspection of the goods are as follows;

① inspection by the seller
② inspection by the buyer
③ inspection by the authorities of the exporting country
④ inspection by the authorities of the importing country

3) Export Packaging

The goods need to be marked correctly to ensure a speedy and smooth transport. There is a wide variety of shipping marks depending on specific national regulations, customs, type of goods and individual exporter and importer specifications. Shipping marks contained are ① main mark, ② destination port/place mark, ③ case(box) number mark, ④ country of origin mark, ⑤ care mark, etc. The purpose of shipping marks is consequently to identify the cargo and help to move goods rapidly and safely without delay to the final destination.

5. Export Clearance

Export Clearance is a regulatory customs procedure that enforces the seller to declare to Customs not only the nature of goods they intend to export, but also their quantity, price and any other particulars. The seller should declare the goods for export to the customs by submitting appropriate documents such as commercial invoice, a copy of sales contract and so on. An export declaration must be made under the names of customs brokers, customs broker corporations or exporters.

6. Contracts of Carriage and Insurance

Unless otherwise agreed between the parties concerned, the party which is responsible for making contracts of carriage or insurance is decided according to the rules of Incoterms® 2020.

As for contract of carriage under the rules of Carriage Paid To(CPT), Carriage and Insurance Paid to(CIP), Delivered At Place(DAP), Delivered At Place Unloaded(DPU), Delivered Duty Paid(DDP), Cost and Freight(CFR) and Cost, Insurance and Freight(CIF), the seller must contract or procure a contract for the carriage of goods. Under the rules of Ex Works(EXW), Free Carrier(FCA), Free Alongside Ship(FAS) and Free on Board(FOB), the buyer must contract for the carriage of goods.

As for contract of insurance under the rules of CIP, CIF, the seller must obtain, at its own expense, cargo insurance. Under the rules of EXW, FCA, CPT, FAS, FOB and CFR, however, the buyer must make a contract of insurance at its own expense for himself.

7. Shipment of Goods

Transport in international trade will be performed by sea, air, land, rail, inland waterway or combination of them. Shipment is made according to the contract terms. For ocean transport under the rules of CFR and CIF, for example, the carrying vessel will issue a bill of lading. Upon completion of the shipment, the seller should give the buyer a shipping advice to enable him to arrange insurance, payment, etc.

8. Payment

After shipment is made, if L/C is used, the seller should present a negotiating bank or the nominated bank the documents required in the L/C. All documents such as draft(bill of exchange), commercial invoice, bill of lading, insurance policy, packing list, country of origin, etc. must be made out in accordance with the terms and conditions of the L/C. Documentation should be completed with absolute accuracy and clarity. If documentary collection is used, the documents should be sent to the buyer through banks for payment.

9. Customs Refund

If the seller has produced goods using raw materials, sub-materials or parts imported and have exported the finished goods, there is a possibility the seller can get a refund of the duty. Drawback is a mechanism that Customs enables importers in exporting country to get a refund of duty paid on imported goods after the finished goods are exported.

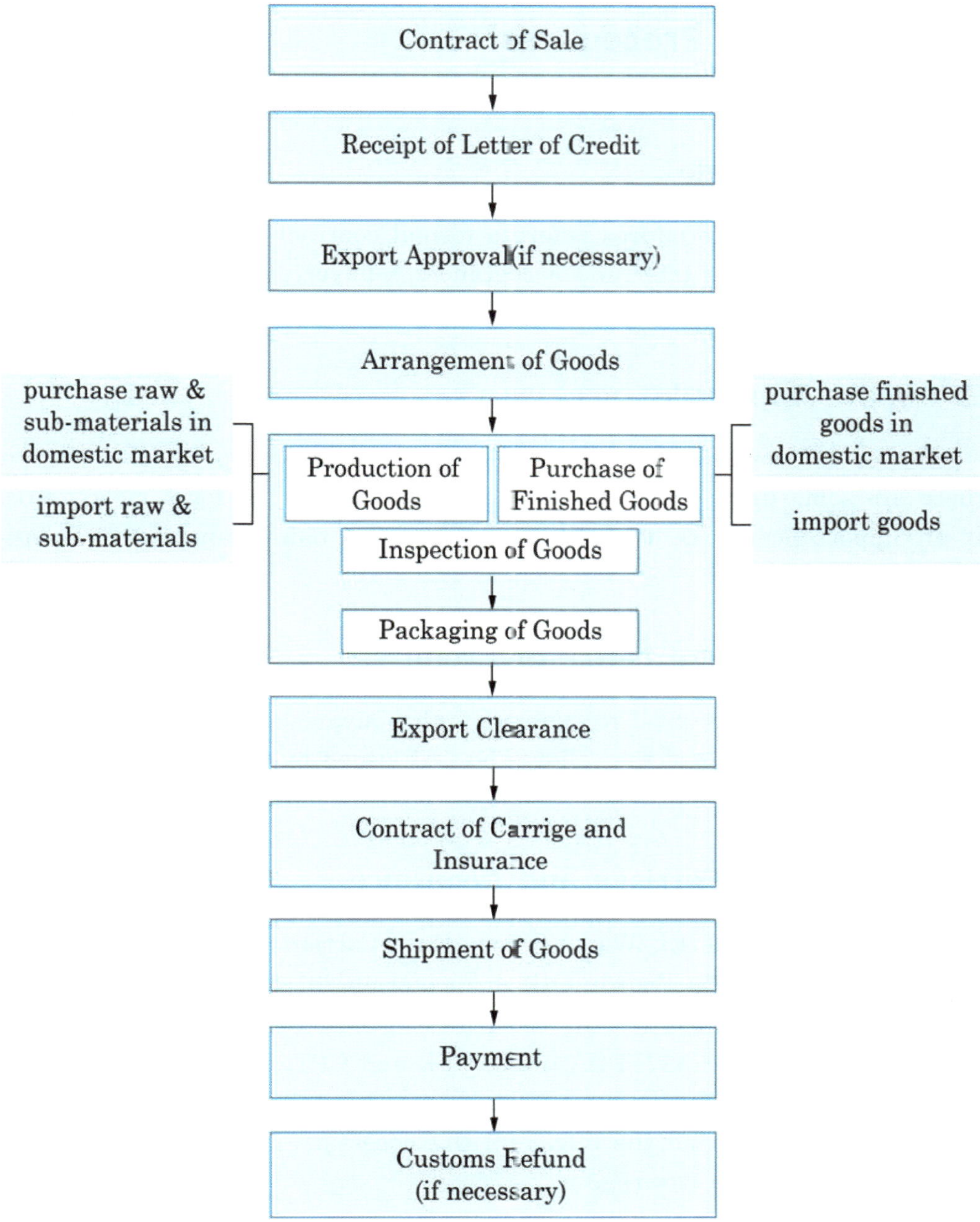

Figure 1.1 Export Procedure

1.2 Import Procedures

1. Contract of Sale

There are many procedures before a formal contract is drawn up such as inquiry, offer, counter offer and acceptance. A buyer should draw up a contract with a seller to import the goods.

2. Import Approval(If necessary)

A buyer can import freely without getting an import approval. However, there are some items the buyer has to get import licence for some reasons. If an import licence is needed, the buyer must obtain an import license from the government.

3. Issue and advise Letter of Credit

If letter of credit is used for payment, the buyer should issue a letter of credit in time in favor of the seller. The L/C issued by the issuing bank will be advised to the beneficiary through an advising bank in seller's country.

4. Contracts of Carriage and Insurance

Under the rules of Ex Works(EXW), Free Carrier(FCA), Free Alongside Ship(FAS) and Free on Board(FOB) in Incoterms 2010, the buyer must contract at its own expense for the carriage of goods.

Under the rules of EXW, FCA, FOB, CFR and CPT, the buyer must make a contract of insurance at its own expense for himself as agreed. The seller should in due time send the buyer all the necessary information the buyer needs to arrange the coverage.

5. Document Examination and Payment

After the shipment, the seller will present the relevant documents to the negotiating bank or the nominated bank. In consequence, the issuing bank will honour the complying presentation. If there is not any discrepancy, the buyer should make the payment.

Under documentary collection, the buyer should examine the documents presented by the seller to confirm if they meet the requirements of the sales contract. If there is not any problem, payment should be made.

6. Import Clearance

The goods for import must be cleared the Customs. Documents such as commercial invoice, bill of lading(B/L), country of origin(C/O), etc. required for customs clearance should be submitted.

Korea maintains an import declaration system that allows for the immediate release of goods upon acceptance of an import declaration filed without defect. With the exception of high-risk items related to public health and sanitation, national security, and the environment, which often require additional documentation and technical tests, goods imported by the companies with no record of trade law violations are released upon the acceptance of the import declaration without customs inspection. The Korea Customs Service's(KCS) Electronic Data Interchange(EDI) system for paperless import clearance allows importers to make an import declaration by computer without visiting the Customs Service.

7. Taking Delivery and Inspection

With the shipping documents, the buyer can take delivery of the goods from the carrier after paying import duty. Then, an inspection should be carried out to confirm if the goods delivered are in conformity with the terms and conditions stipulated in the sales contract.

8. Claims and Adjustments

If problems such as weight shortage, inferior quality or wrong shipment are found and attributed to the seller, the buyer should make claims against the seller. If the loss or damage is due to the negligence of the carrier, the claim should be made against the carrier. If the loss or damage has been caused by the risks that are covered by insurance, the claim should be made against the underwriter.

Claims should be filed within the time limit stipulated in the contract of sale. Necessary documents like an official inspection report should be presented to the relevant party. Claims which can not be amicably settled between the parties concerned shall be submitted to arbitration according to their contract of sale.

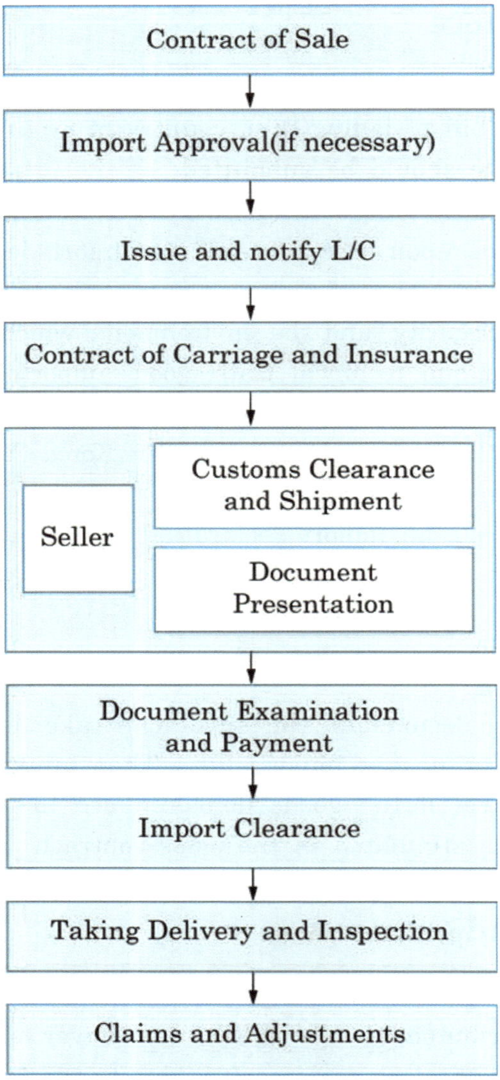

Figure 1.2 Import Procedure

Chapter **2**

Establishing Business Relations

Chapter

2 Establishing Business Relations

2.1 Overseas Market Research

1. Definition of Overseas Market Research

Overseas market research is the process of gathering, analyzing and interpreting information about products, services or organizations in the overseas market using statistical and analytical methods and techniques of the applied social science to gain insight or support decision making. Through market researches, a seller will select a target market and make a thorough credit inquiry to select a proper buyer.

2. Contents of Overseas Market Research

Based on basic understanding about the target market, an assessment of the competitors, prices, customers and distribution structures, etc. should be made.

1) Target market

The target market is the particular market segment on which a marketing activity is focused. Essentially, this is the market the goods are intended to be sold. Particulars of the contents of the target market include :

① selection of target areas : understanding commercial practices of target countries

② current situation of import and export of products
③ climate and geographical conditions
④ import management systems(item management system, customs clearance, tariffs, foreign exchange, etc.)
⑤ stability of currency and economic situation
⑥ transportation and communication(especially logistics facilities such as harbors and airports), etc.

2) Market demand

Demand is a need or desire for a certain goods or services supported by the capacity to purchase them. A demand analysis is an aspect of research that studies the sales generated by goods or services to determine the factors for its success or failure. Particulars of demand analysis are included:
① research into market potential : situation of supply and demand of the products(its own production, import quantity, and demand)
② estimate of market growth rates
③ research into market development, etc.

3) Consumer research

Consumer research is conducted to assess the preferences, motivations, and buying behavior of the target market through observation, surveys and interviews. A pushcart refers to the test-selling of one's intended product by tentatively exporting only a small amount of the item to be sold to verify the response. Considerations in consumer research include:
① population, its preferences and living standards
② distribution of consumers by area and demographics such as age and income
③ purchasing motivation, place, means, time, quantity and ability
④ satisfaction of goods and future change of consumers' tastes, etc.

4) Competitors

Analyzing competitors in the same line of business is one of the important factors in success. Considerations in researching competitors include :
① marketing strategies of competitors
② advantages and disadvantages of competitors

③ export prices of competitors, export quantity, and advantages of export competition, etc.

5) Products(goods)

To conduct a systematic research into products, the characteristics of the goods or services must be examined to determine the qualities that make those goods or services desirable. Considerations in research into products include:

① kinds, quality, and size of demanded products

② yield of local country, selling quantity, and ratio of exports and imports

③ quality comparison between local products and imported products

④ research of color, design, size, style, function, and packing of major local imports, etc.

6) Distribution channels

The distribution route or channel is the path through which goods and services flow from the seller to the consumer. The flow of the goods in its simplest path is directly from a distributor to a consumer. More commonly, there are intermediaries along the way such as wholesalers, distributors, agents and retailers. At each stage in the transaction, the cost increases so that each player can receive a cut for his efforts. Considerations in researching distribution routes are as follows :

① distribution structure of the products(distribution type, market leader, margin rate by step)

② research into trade practices of the products; research into the distribution area

③ research into seasonality, that is, high-demand season and low-demand season of the products(some products are more susceptible to seasonality than others), etc.

7) Pricing

The market value or exchange value of products is largely determined by supply and demand. Considerations in researching price are as follows :

① research into the price of exports and imports within the area

② price comparisons between local products and imports; trends in price fluctuation by season

③ price differences between the high-demand and low-demand season, etc.

2.2 Establishing Business Connections

The most daunting challenge any seller faces is to find buyers for the goods. Selling in international market has never been simple to any seller due to diverse language, geographical distance, cultural difference and lack of market knowledge, etc. There are many ways one can find one's potential counterparts in overseas countries.

1. Internet

International business people should think of an effective strategy to utilize internet resources. Today, the internet has emerged as the most effective, low cost solution for global marketing. Various internet websites allow business people to post the goods or services online so that prospective buyers can contact them. Due to the internet, it is easier to get products directly to the final customers than in the past, allowing the exporter or producer to avoid the costs of the middlemen who often force them to sell their products at lower prices.

2. Business Directory

Business directory is a website or printed listing of information which lists all businesses within some categories. Businesses can be categorized by type of business, location, activity or size.

The details provided in a business directory vary from business to business. They may include the company names, addresses, telephone numbers, e-mail addresses, location, type of service or products the business provides, number of employee, service region and any professional associations. Some directories include a section for user reviews, comments and feedback.

Business Directory

A business directory is a website or printed listing of information which lists all businesses within some categories

① Kellysearch.co.uk http://www.kellysearch.co.uk
② Dun & Bradstreet http://www.dnb.com/us
③ Tomas Register http://www.thomasnet.com
④ Standard Trade Index of Japan http://www.cin.or.jp/trade
⑤ World Business Bridge Serving America, Asia, Africa, Oceania and Europe http://www.aaaoe.com
⑥ Diredtory for International Trade http://www.importers-exporters.com
⑦ World Trade Point Federation http://www.tradepoint.org
⑧ Trade Lead Zone http://www.tradezon.com
⑨ Wyzen Trade Network http://wyzen.com/tradeportals
⑩ Kapitol http://www.infobel.com/en/world/index.aspx

3. Trade Related Organizations

International business people can take advantage of trade related organizations in Korea such as Korea International Trade Association (KITA), Korea Trade-Investment Promotion Agency(KOTRA), Korea Chamber of

Commerce and Industry(KCCI), etc. and other trade associations in foreign countries. Korean business people can contact trade related organizations in overseas countries such as New York Chamber of Commerce, Japan External Trade Organization(JETRO), etc. Business people can also contact foreign embassies in Korea to get some information on foreign markets, products and companies.

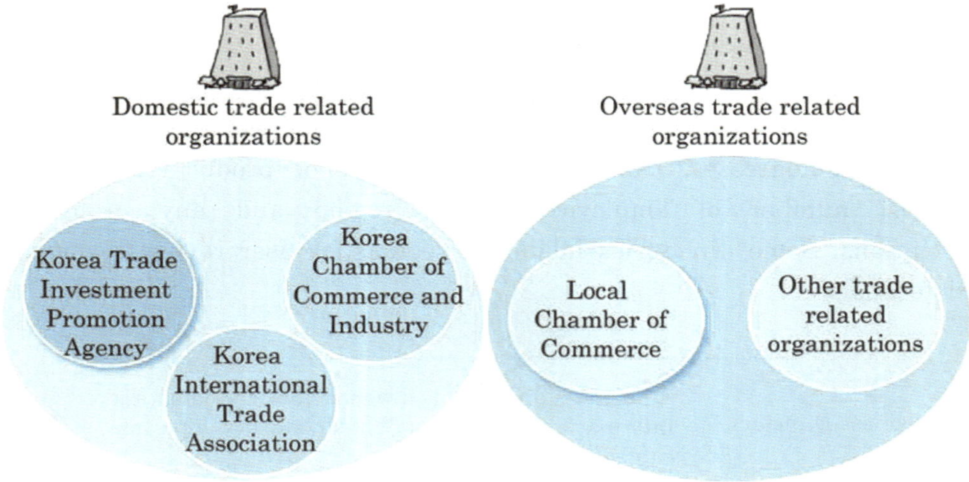

4. Trade Fair

Trade fair(overseas exhibition or trade show) is an event at which goods and services in a specific industry are exhibited and demonstrated. One of the most effective ways to find buyers is to attend trade fairs because an exporter can interact face-to-face with many potential buyers at once, and easily promote their companies and items based on general catalogues, presentations and a strong first impression.

Overseas trade fairs are sponsored by trade associations for specific industries and there are many associations running shows every year. Exhibiting at a trade show is an excellent way to find customers to help one's business grow. Trade fairs are also economical ways of getting sales. Also, trade fairs are popular, and it's easy to find one that fits one's industry and one's company's needs.

2.3 Business Proposal and Inquiry

The first step in international trade is to seek the new promising customers to whom circular letters are sent with a view to opening an account with them. As this business proposal is the first letter introduced to the foreign traders, it is far better to be courteous and polite when writing it. If the counterpart is interested in doing business with the partner who sent the circular letter, they inquire about price, quality, quantity, shipment of the goods, etc.

1. Business Proposal

A business proposal is a solicited or unsolicited submission by one party to supply(or buy) certain goods or services to(or from) another. Unlike an offer, a proposal is not a promise or commitment but, if accepted by the other party, its proposer is expected to follow through and negotiate for a business contract.

When writing a business proposal, the seller needs to discover what the customer needs and then presents a proposal in the customer's perspective. A business proposal should be about what matters to the customer and not just what the seller wants to tell them. Business proposals are sent to the promising partners collected through market researches in form of circular letters.

A circular letter is a written document that is addressed to a group of business people to open an account with them.

Like advertisements in newspapers and magazines, circular letters are addressed to many, but more usually they are sent only to selected readers who are likely to be interested in. Names and addresses can be obtained from many different sources. The following rules should be observed.

- keep the letter short, otherwise it may not be read.
- catch the reader's interest in the opening paragraphs.
- give the letter an attractive look and make it as personal as possible.
- create the impression of personal interest.

A Circular Letter

① an opening clause (information on how the proposer got the counterpart's e-mail address)
② introduce the company and main line of business briefly
③ introduce the company's products and business reputation
④ mention the seller can supply the counterpart with information required later
⑤ inform the counterpart of a trade reference
⑥ a closing clause

Dear Sirs,

Your company has been recommended to us by the Korean Embassy in Beijing, China as a major importer and distributor of electronic products. We are, therefore, writing you with a keen desire of opening an account with you.

We, Daehan Trading Co., Ltd. are one of the companies producing high quality electronic products and exporting them to many countries. We have been enjoying a good reputation from our customers having extensive and close connections with us due to excellent quality, reasonable prices and prompt delivery.

Having been engaged in this line of business for more than 20 years, we dominate the biggest market share in Korea and we established two overseas manufacturing companies in both New York in the U.S.A and London in England to meet the requirements of our overseas customers.

For more objective information, please e-mail me or visit our web site, http://www.daehan.com. You can find a brief company profile of ours and digital catalogues more easily. Also you can contact the KEB Hana Bank in Beijing for our credit rating.

We look forward to receiving your affirmative reply soon.

Yours truly,

2. Business Inquiry

A business inquiry is a letter written by the receiver of the circular letter to get information on certain products or services. Potential customers will send their inquires to ask for the terms of transaction. The parties who are interested in the circular letters send business inquiries by asking for terms and conditions such as price, quality, quantity, shipment, payment, etc.

In a business inquiry, it is advisable for the writer to ask for price, quality, quantity, delivery, payment and other terms and conditions together with some catalogues and samples, if possible.

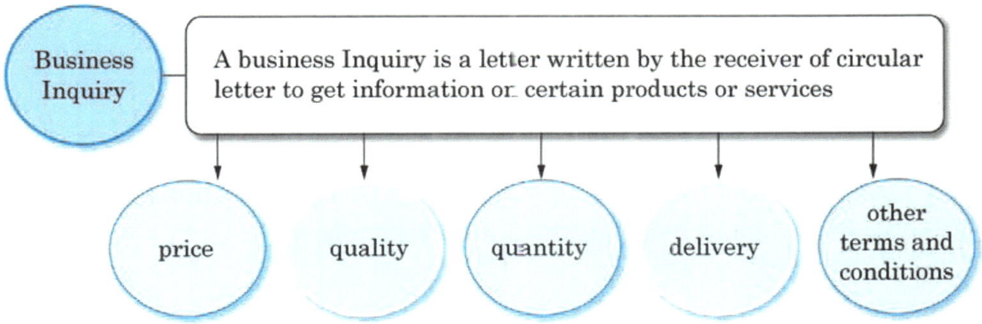

A business inquiry

① an opening clause
② introduce the company briefly
③ ask for terms and conditions together with some catalogues and samples
④ others
⑤ a closing clause

Dear Mr. Lee,

Thank you for your e-mail and for your interest in our company. We visited your home page and we are interested in entering into business relations with you. We have been importing and distributing some different kinds of products from the U.S.A., and the products are selling well in our market.

We are prepared to accept your proposal as long as your products prove suitable for our market in price and quality. As the products made in Korea are welcomed by our domestic customers, the demand for this line of products is estimated to increase steadily in the near future.

We have a desire of adding new products in that line and we shall be obliged if you will send us your illustrated catalogues and quotations with all information so that we can take a feasibility study through our local agents.

Thank you for your cooperation and we remain,

Very truly yours,

3. Reply to Business Inquiry

The receiver of a business inquiry needs to respond without delay in the usual form of a quotation, an offer, or a bid. A response must be sent immediately in the same way as the inquiry is sent.

2.4 Sample Letters of Business Proposals

1. Business Proposal concerning Cellular Phones

1) A business proposal

Dear Sirs,

Through the courtesy of your Korean partner for computer parts, Young Industrial Co., Ltd., we have learned that you are one of the best firms having nationwide distribution channels for cellular phones.

We have been exporting various kinds of cellular phones to many countries including the United States and Canada, and acquiring a good reputation from our customers. It is our keen desire to supply you with our quality products on favorable terms.

Our products have proved highly successful wherever they have been introduced and we are confident that you will be able to build up a good market sooner or later.

Please find the digital brochure outlining some of the major products along with a quotation attached to this e-mail. If you have any questions, please feel free to give me a call or drop me a line via e-mail so that we can follow you up everything you need immediately.

You may ask your partner, Young Industrial Co., Ltd. or refer to the KEB Hana Bank in your city for our business ability.

We look forward to your favorable reply soon.

Yours very truly,

2) A business inquiry(reply)

Dear Mr. Lee,

It is indeed gratifying to know that you are interested in establishing a business connection with us. We heard from our business partner, Young Industrial Co., Ltd. that you are the most reliable company in the line of cellular phones in Korea. We would like to take the cordial advice of our partner for the reputation you are enjoying and for your business experience accumulated for a few decades.

We have been importing and marketing various products and have succeed in building up a considerable number of well-established connections showing excellent business results.

We should appreciate it if you could send us your latest catalogues, prices and the terms of payment together with some samples.

We are looking forward to your early and favorable reply soon.

Yours very truly,

2. Business Proposal for Medical Equipments

1) A business proposal

Dear Sirs,

We have learned your name through the Korea Chamber of Commerce and Industry in Seoul as a promising importer handling various medical equipments.

We have been established for more than 10 years as an exporter of medical equipments and we enjoy an advantageous position specially in the same line of business as we have wide and direct connections with the customers in Korea.

For the last few years, we have done our independent market surveys in European countries to find out a reliable business partner which can distribute our good quality products made in Korea. As we still don't have any proper representative in your area, we may be able to get an opportunity of making better business arrangements with you for the above-mentioned products.

You may be assured that any orders you may give us later will be executed at the lowest market prices and on the best terms possible.

You can see full ranges of products on our web site, http://www.eckorea.net, and we really would like to hear from you if you are interested in our proposal. Our Bank, Kookmin Bank, will give you any information regarding our credit standing.

Yours very truly,

2) A business inquiry(reply)

Dear Mr. Whang,

We thank you for your inquiry of May 15 and for your intention to establish business connections with us concerning medical equipments.

We are very much interested in introducing your quality products through our considerable number of organized business connections. We regret to inform you, however, that we can not handle additional line of products you inquired about as we are the sole agent of a company in the U.S.A.

Please understand that we will bear your proposal in mind and will get in touch with you when we are allowed to.

Very truly yours,

3. Business Proposal for Electronic Appliances

1) A business proposal

Dear sirs,

We owed your name to a Consul at the Korean Embassy in Paris as one of the most reliable and leading exporters of electronic appliances in France.

We have been selling various kinds of products to large wholesalers and retailers in Korea for a few years, and we have a considerable number of customers.

Until recently, we had not been in a position to handle additional lines as we had been concentrating our effort on strengthening our marketing activities in our market.

However, we have now enough facilities to extend our business activities and please let us have your quotation on your products together with your catalogues. If your prices are reasonable and other terms and conditions are satisfactory, we shall devote our full attention to sell your products.

We are convinced that there is an enormous potential market in Korea and you can be sure of increasing your turnover considerably if you allow us to promote sales of your products.

You can visit our internet home page for more information on our sales organization, and please refer to the KEB Hana Bank in Paris regarding our credit rating.

Your cooperation on the above matter would be highly appreciated and we look forward to receiving an early reply.

Very truly yours,

2) A business inquiry(reply)

Dear Mr. Boucher,

We thank you for your kind e-mail of December 11 showing your intention to deal with our products.

Even though we have already done some business in your country, we have not had any proper representative so far. The illustrated catalogues and terms and conditions for the models in which you are especially interested are attached to this e-mail.

We have an excellent organization for conducting export business and our wide and close connections with the best sources of supply give us confidence that we can meet any requirements. We have long been exporting electronic appliances to all parts of the world and the products have been commanding excellent sales. Because of their excellent quality and low prices, you can be sure our products will no doubt help you expand your market sooner or later.

We thank you again for your proposal and we wish you to refer to the KEB Hana Bank in your city regarding our credit standing.

Awaiting to hear from you, we remain.

Yours faithfully,

4. Business Proposal for Setting up a Joint Venture Company

1) A business proposal

Gentlemen :

We have learned from "International Business News", a monthly magazine issued by the Institute for International Business in Paris, France that you are one of the leading firms producing industrial robots and would like to set up a joint venture company in France to manufacture robots.

We are a company having some excellent sales networks in France for the products you are dealing with.

For some time now, we have been thinking about the idea of forming a joint venture company with a Korean company having an advanced technology in the same industry.

It is going to be difficult for you to export Korean products to France under the Korean brand names. You'd better take advantage of country of origin to cover European countries.

We have extensive sales networks for this line of products and there is no doubt that our sales volume would naturally increase as a result of access to our sales networks.

If you are interested in this promising project, please let us know by e-mail so that we can move on to our details.

Very truly yours,

2) A business inquiry(reply)

Dear, Mr. Denang,

Thank you for your e-mail of October 5, 20×× proposing us to participate in making a joint venture company with you together.

Even before you came up with this proposal, we had been discussing the possibility of setting up a manufacturing company abroad, particularly in France. As you mentioned, we feel that it is going to be increasingly difficult in the future to export Korean-made products directly to France.

We were thinking of establishing our own manufacturing company in your country on the basis of independent surveys which we have conducted up to this time. All this was already in progress when we received your proposal.

However, there will be a possibility of working on this project with you if your master plans for this business are pretty much agreeable to us.

Therefore, please present your written proposal containing all the details such as the ratio of capital and investment, the composition of staff, the jurisdictional role of the company and planning for facilities.

Basically, we would like to propose you that we supply you with our technology and that we want an equal partnership between our two companies.

We look forward to your favorable reply.

Very truly yours,

2.5 Credit Inquiry

1. Definition of Credit Inquiry

A credit inquiry means that a seller investigates the financial status and responsibility of a prospective customer who proposes to open an account with the seller. Before entering into business relations with a foreign buyer, the first step to be taken on the part of the seller is a credit inquiry.

As the parties engaged in international trade are so distantly separated from each other, it is essential to have a reliable and up-to-date information about the credit standing and responsibility of the counterpart before entering into business relations.

International trade comes with the added difficulties of differences in language, customs, culture and law, and therefore it is often difficult to determine whether a potential trade partner will be faithful in honoring the agreement. One of the methods in determining whether the deal will go through as planned is to run a credit inquiry.

2. Factors of Credit Inquiry

1) Character

The first aspect to review is the potential partner's character. It is the most difficult part of making an assessment of the partner's credit. If a firm fails to properly determine the partner's character, it can face detrimental results. Character refers to the sense of morality, faithfulness, reputation, and overall attitude of the counterpart.

Therefore, sellers need to investigate personality, integrity, honesty, attitude toward business, reputation, willingness to meet obligations of the counterpart.

2) Capital

No matter how the counterpart is credible, a sound financial status plays an import role in meeting the obligations. Financial status, sound financial structure and other assets of the counterpart need to be investigated.

The second aspect to review is the potential partner's capital ability, which verifies whether or not the company has enough funds to make the contracted payments. The buyer does not have to be rich himself, but his company needs to have the ability to make payments through capital on-hand and projected cash flows.

Character	Capital	Capacity
personality	financial status	turn-over
integrity	ratio of capital	type of business
reputation	financial structure	business experience
attitude toward business	other assets	business ability
willingness to meet obligation		

3) Capacity

The third aspect to review is the potential partner's capacity to activate the trade. This is a measure of the importer's ability to sell the seller's products successfully. It is done by analyzing the company's history, annual sales, the type of corporation, experience and so on. It is important to make sure that the buyer has successfully been growing and developing, or is equipped with sufficient capacity.

Annual sales turnover, type of business, business experience, business capability, etc. should be investigated for transaction capacity.

3. Credit Reference

A credit reference is an information that can provide details about an organization's past track record with credit. To ensure getting a reliable information on the buyer, the seller needs to ask banks, business partners or other references that can supply information on the company's credibility or credit. Sometimes, special agencies such as Dun & Bradstreet Information Service can be used.

1) Bank reference

It is a credit reference written by a bank which would provide basic information about how long the customer has held an account, what type of account it was, and whether or not there were any overdrafts or late payments noted. A bank reference generally includes ① number of years of a customer's relationship with the bank, ② financial status of the customer, ③ its opinion whether the customer is credible, etc. Banks usually are under no obligation to seek the customer's approval or to reveal the identity of the recipient for releasing such information.

Generally speaking, it is usual for international business people to obtain information from the bank reference given by the counterpart. The credit file of the bank is one of the valuable assets.

2) Trade reference

It is a reference in which one trader gives his opinion as to the credit worthiness of another trader in the same line of business. A seller can get a credit information on the counterpart from the seller's branch offices, representatives or agents abroad.

3) Mercantile Agency

A mercantile agency is a specialized organization that collects and supplies information on the financial credit standing of individuals and companies. The famous international Mercantile Agencies are Dun & Bradstreet, Inc. in the U.S.A,[1] Bradstreet British Ltd. in England, Auskunft W. Schimmelpfeng in Germany, La Societe du Commerce in France, and Tyoko Mercantile Agency in Japan. Specialized organizations in Korea are Korea Trade-Investment Promotion Agency(KOTRA) and Korea Trade Insurance Corporation.

Mercantile agencies may provide information on all types of business firms or may limit their investigations to firms in a particular line of trade or a particular region. Credit files should be kept strictly up to date, not only by securing annual confirmation of previous information, but by utilizing every opportunities for obtaining information from new sources.

1) Dun & Bradstreet(DNB, D&B) in New Jersey, USA is a public company which supplies information on businesses and corporations for use in credit decisions, B2B marketing and supply chain management.

2.6 Sample Letters of Credit Inquiry

1. Credit Inquiry through a Trader

1) A credit inquiry

Dear Sirs,

Dae Young Woolen Textile Co., Ltd. is anxious to make a joint venture company with us to manufacture clothes in Kazakhstan.

They would like to procure raw and sub-materials from Korea and to take advantage of low labor costs here. We expect this business to be feasible and we want to enter into our business if they can meet our requirements.

Our particular interest is to know in what line they have been mainly engaged and, if possible, your candid opinion on their financial rating, credibility and reputation. We shall, of course, treat any information you may give us as strictly confidential and we would be pleased to perform a service for you should an opportunity arise later on.

Please let us know any expense in connection with this inquiry so that we can pay you right away and thank you for your kind cooperation.

Very truly yours,

2) A reply

In reply to your inquiry of April 13, we would like to make the following comments on them without any responsibility and prejudice on our part free of charge.

The company was established in 2000 as a manufacturer of clothes in Korea and they have accumulated a credibility from local business concerns by providing superior quality products and resonable prices.

Their business manners such as prompt delivery, payment on time and etc. have assured the companies and the banks both in Korea and abroad that they are the best company in the line of clothing industry.

Our opinion is that we can safely trust them for the amount of business you mentioned. However, this is just our personal opinion based on our business relations with them and we can not guarantee any business that you are going to enter into.

We hope you can just take this information into deep consideration and we can have a further opportunity to serve you later.

2. Credit Inquiry through a Bank

1) A credit inquiry

Dear Mr. Boucher,

Monte Carlo Co., Ltd. which wants to import and distribute our products in France has given your name as a trade reference saying that they have been doing business with you for a long time.

We should be very grateful to you for any information you can give us about their business activities and the scope of their transactions.

As we are not acquainted with that company, we will be thankful if you will inform us of their financial standing, the way of doing business, reputation and other information that may be helpful to us.

Any other information which you could supply would be appreciated and would of course be treated as strictly confidential.

Yours faithfully,

2) A favorable reply

Dear Mr. Han,

As for the company you inquired about, we are glad to inform you that they have now a sound business standing with an excellent business turnover. We can dare to say that they can be rated as one of the reliable firms and we would like to enter into business with them if we were in your place.

We are glad to be of help, but ask you to ensure that the information we give you is treated as strictly confidential.

Yours faithfully,

3) An unfavorable reply

Dear, Mr. Han,

In reply to your e-mail inquiry of March 7 about Monte Carlo Co., Ltd., we regret that we are unable to give you a favorable information on the said company.

They have been said to be slow in settling their payments, and there are rumors going around that their financial standing is very poor for which we can not verify.

For the past two years, the company has been the defendant in two court cases involving claims for non-payment of sums due, although payment was subsequently made in each instance.

It is true that we did business with them, but the amount involved was not large and accounts were not always satisfactorily kept.

We want you to use this confidential information with every discretion and we do not have any responsibility on this matter.

Yours faithfully,

Chapter 3

Offer and Acceptance

Chapter 3

Offer and Acceptance

3.1 Offer

1. Definition of Offer

An offer is the expressed or implied expression of one party, called an offeror, to enter into a definite and legally binding contract on certain terms with another party, called an offeree.

A proposal for concluding a contract addressed to one or more specific persons constitutes an offer if it is sufficiently definite and indicates the intention of the offeror to be bound in case of acceptance. A proposal is sufficiently definite if it indicates the goods and expressly or implicitly fixes or makes provision for determining the quantity and the price.[1]

A proposal other than one or more specific persons is to be considered merely as an invitation to make offers, unless the contrary is clearly indicated by the person making the proposal.[2]

Like an inquiry, an offer can be made either by a seller or by a buyer. The offer made by the seller is customarily called a selling offer while the offer made by the buyer is called a buying offer. In general, it is the seller, the offeror, who offers the sale of certain goods to the buyer, the offeree.

1) United Nations Convention on Contracts for the International Sale of Goods (Vienna Convention, 1980), Article 14(1).
2) United Nations Convention on Contracts for the International Sale of Goods (Vienna Convention, 1980), Article 14(2).

It is an expressed offer when an offer is made orally by telephone or in writing. It is an implied offer when an offer is made impliedly such as goods with price tags in a store.

In international business, an offer usually is made in writing and it contains terms and conditions such as packing method, country of origin, shipment, payment, inspection, validity, price, etc.

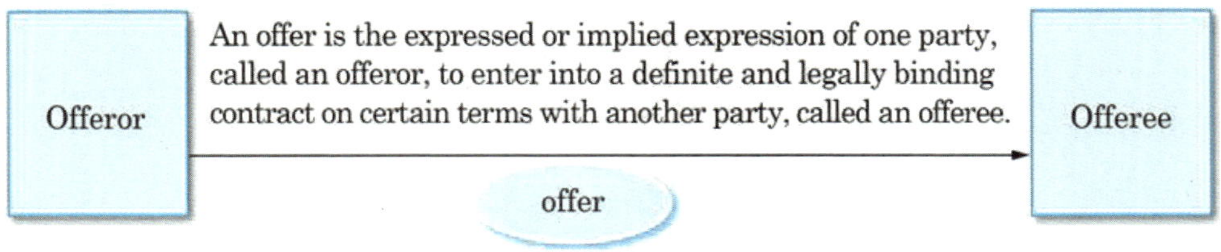

2. General Rules of Offer

1) Offer must be communicated

No offer becomes effective until it has been communicated to the offeree. A mere desire to enter into an agreement can never constitute an offer. A letter embodying a definite proposal will be futile unless the letter reaches the offeree.

An offer must be communicated by the offeror or his duly authorized agent through the medium or channel selected by the offeror.

2) Offer must be legally definite

An offer must be legally definite. A mere quotation of price does not constitute an offer. Something which indicates a willingness to contract with a particular party at the terms and conditions quoted must accompany the quotation of them.

3. Types of Offer

1) Firm offer

A firm offer is an offer in writing which states it may not be withdrawn, revoked or amended for a specific period of time. An offer containing the words like 'firm' or 'irrevocable' or a phrase that it will not be revoked within reasonable time is regarded as a firm offer even though it does not contain validity.

Until the time specified expires or until the possible acceptor of the firm offer refuses the option, the offer cannot be withdrawn. If the offer is not accepted within the time specified, it is understood to be withdrawn.

A firm offer, however, may be revoked or withdrawn by the offeror within the time stipulated, but the revocation must reach the offeree before he dispatches his acceptance. The majority of export transaction is executed on the firm offer.

The time limit of the firm offer should be indicated in either each offer or general agreement as :

- Validity : This offer is valid until September 30, 20××.
- We offer you firm subject to your acceptance reaching us by September 30, 20×× as follows;

A firm offer is an offer in writing which states it may not be withdrawn, revoked or amended for a specific period of time.

If an offer does not contain validity,

An offer containing the words like 'firm' or 'irrevocable' or a phrase that it will not be revoked within reasonable time is a firm offer

① Validity : This offer is valid until September 30, 20××

② We offer you firm subject to your acceptance reaching us by September 30, 20×× as follows;

2) Free offer

A free offer is an offer open for a reasonable time in which the offeror merely states the terms and conditions of the goods without binding the offeree to accept it within a specified period.

A free offer is an offer open for a reasonable time in which the offeror merely states the terms and conditions of the goods without binding the offeree to accept within a specified period.

① We offer you the following goods on the terms and conditions mentioned hereunder

② We are pleased to offer you without engagement as follows

3) Counter offer

A counter offer is an offer made by an offeree to an offeror accepting some terms and adding or revising other terms. If the offeree cannot accept a firm offer tendered, the offeree may propose an alternative at once setting forth some revised terms and conditions.

A reply to an offer which purports to be an acceptance but contains additions, limitations or other modifications is a rejection of the offer and constitutes a counter offer.

A counter offer, in fact, is a rejection of the original offer. Hence, it is a new offer and at the same time, the original offer lapses. It is rather rare that an acceptance is made just correspondingly in reply to an initial firm offer.

A counter offer is an offer mde by an offeree to an offeror accepting some terms and adding or revising other terms.

The original offer is rejected and becomes a new offer → The original offer is lapsed by a counter offer

"Your offer dated March 10 is too high. We can accept the offer at USD 5.00 per piece CIF Long Beach, CA, U.S.A."

DAEHAN TRADING CO., LTD.
C. P. O BOX, 203, SEOUL, KOREA

O F F E R S H E E T

Messrs. : GEOSYSTEM
New York, USA

Date : August 11, 20××
Ref. No. Euro 20××

Dear Sirs,
We are pleased to offer you as follows :

Packing : Export Standard Packing
Origin : Republic of Korea(R.O.K)
Shipment : Within 60 days from the date of contract
Payment : By an irrevocable L/C at sight in our favor
Inspection : Manufacturer's inspection is final
Validity : By the end of November, 20××
Remarks : Minimum order requirement - 1,000pcs above per item

H. S.	Item#	Description	Quantity	Unit Price	Amount
		Cosmetics		CIF New York/pc	
3304.99.2000	20	Make-up Base 30gr	1,000pcs	@U$3.00	U$3,000.00
3304.20.9000	79	Mascara 5ml	1,000pcs	@U$2.50	U$2,500.00
		Total :	2,000pcs		U$5,500.00

Yours very truly,

(signed)
S. K. Lee
Director
Daehan Trading Co., Ltd.

4) Conditional offer

(1) Offer without engagement or offer subject to market fluctuation

An offer without engagement is an offer that the offeror can change the prices offered without giving a prior notice to the offeree according to market situations. This offer is used for the goods liable to market fluctuation. This offer is understood as a free offer, but it is not an offer in a strict sense.

> We offer the goods USD 5.00 per piece CIF Long Beach, CA, U.S.A. subject to market fluctuation

(2) Offer subject to prior sale

An offer subject to prior sale is an offer that creates a binding contract when there are stocks available by the time the acceptance of the offeree reaches the offeror. It is called an offer subject to being unsold. This offer means the person who comes first, gets the goods first. This offer is a free offer.

> We offer the goods at USD 5 per piece CIF Long Beach, CA, U.S.A. subject to being unsold

(3) Offer on approval

An offer on approval is an offer permitting that the offeree can pay the goods delivered together with the offer and the offeree also can return the offeror the goods within the resonable time when he doesn't want to buy. This offer is a firm offer.

> We offer the goods on approval at USD 5 per piece CIF Long Beach, CA, U.S.A.

(4) Offer on sale or return

An offer on sale or return is an offer that the offeree sells the goods delivered together with the offer for reasonable time and can return the offeror the goods left. This offer is a firm offer.

> We offer the goods on sale or return at USD 5 per piece CIF Long Beach, CA, U.S.A.

(5) Offer subject to our final confirmation

An offer subject to our final confirmation is an offer that requires the final confirmation of the offeror for the acceptance of the offeree for the offer to legally bound. Actually, it not an offer but an invitation to offer.

> We offer the goods at USD 5.00 per piece CIF Long Beach, CA, U.S.A. subject to our final confirmation

4. Time at which an offer becomes effective

According to United Nations Convention on Contracts for the International Sale of Goods(Vienna Convention, 1980), an offer becomes effective when it reaches the offeree.

> An offer becomes effective when it reaches the offeree.

5. Termination of Offer

1) Withdrawal of offer

The withdrawal of an offer is an expression of an offeror to terminate the offer intentionally before the offer becomes effective. An offer, even if it is irrevocable, may be withdrawn if the withdrawal reaches the offeree before or at the same time as the offer.[3)]

2) Revocation of offer

An offer becomes effective when it reaches the offeree. Until a contract is concluded, an offer may be revoked if the revocation reaches the offeree before he dispatches an acceptance.

However, an offer cannot be revoked ;

① if it indicates, whether by stating a fixed time for acceptance or otherwise, that it is irrevocable; or

② if it is reasonable for the offeree to rely on the offer as being irrevocable and the offeree has acted in reliance on the offer.

3) Rejection of offer

An offer, even if it is irrevocable, is terminated when a rejection reaches the offeror. Rejection of an offer must be communicated to the offeree and it is not effective until it reaches the offeree.

4) Counter offer

A counter offer, in fact, is a rejection of the offer. Hence, it is a new offer and at the same time, the original offer is terminated.

5) Lapse of validity

If an offer stipulates the period during which it is to continue, it automatically lapses at the end of that period. An attempted acceptance after that period could only amount to a new offer.

A free offer in which no definite time for acceptance is stated can be accepted within a reasonable time. Reasonableness of time depends on the circumstances of each particular case.

6) Death or insanity of the party

The death or insanity of either the offeror or the offeree, before accept-

---

3) United Nations Convention on Contracts for the International Sale of Goods (Vienna Convention, 1980), Article 15.

ance of the offer, causes an offer to be terminated. No notice of the death to the other party is necessary. If one of the parties dies or become insane, it is impossible to enter into the agreement. It should be emphasized, however, that the death or insanity of one of the parties does not cause a rescission of a contract which has previously been formed.

3.2 Acceptance

1. Definition of Acceptance

An acceptance is a statement made by or other conduct of the offeree indicating assent to an offer. An acceptance can only be made orally, in writing or by act by the offeree. Either a verbal or a written statement is good for the purpose. It is upon acceptance that a contract comes into existence. To be effective, an acceptance must absolutely meet all the terms and conditions contained in the offer. It is necessary that an offeree should make an acceptance within the period of time.

Definition of Acceptance	A statement made by the offeree or other conduct of the offeree indicating assent to an offer
Methods of Acceptance	An acceptance can be made orally, in writing or by act by the offeree

2. General Rules of Acceptance

The general rules in connection with the acceptance are as follows;

① The contents of acceptance must be complied with those in the offer
② Acceptance must be absolute, final and unconditional
③ Acceptance must be made within the validity in the offer
④ Acceptance must be made by an offeree, the particular person or a group of persons who are clearly stipulated in the offer

⑤ Acceptance must be made by the same mode of communication stipulated in the offer

3. Types of Acceptance

1) Acceptance which forms a contract

(1) Absolute and unconditional acceptance

If the offeree wishes to accept an offer, he must comply strictly with the terms and conditions stated in the offer. That is to say, acceptance must be absolute and unconditional. It is the offeror who makes the offer and he is free to dictate the terms of the offer. The offeror is privileged to include any terms and conditions he wishes in the offer irrespective of how unreasonable they may be.

The offeree is under no obligation to give any attention to the offer, and if the offeree thinks the conditions in the offer are unreasonable, he is free to ignore the offer. However, if he wishes to accept the offer, his acceptance must correspond with all the conditions specified in the offer. As has already been discussed, if the acceptance contains any new terms or conditions, or if it varies in any manner the terms of the offer, it becomes a counter offer and therefore rejects the original offer.

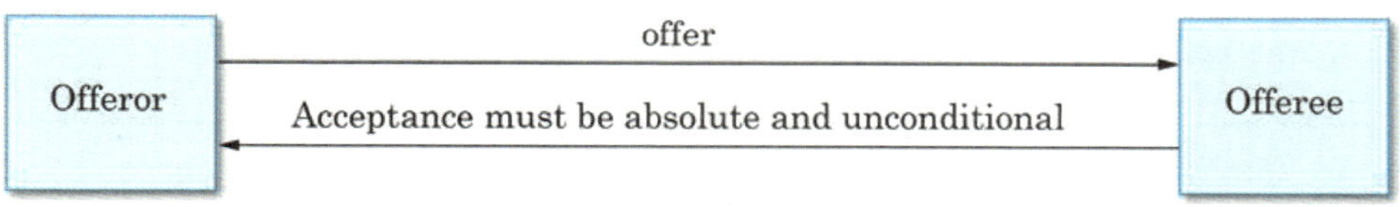

(2) Acceptance by act

The conduct the buyer(offeree) pays the seller(offeror) for the goods offered or the seller(offeree) delivers the goods to the buyer(offeror) without giving any notice is also an acceptance forming a contract. However, silence or inactivity does not in itself amount to acceptance.

If, by virtue of the offer or as a result of practice which the parties have established between themselves or of usage, the offeree indicates an assent by performing an act that the offeror dispatches the offeree the goods and the offeree pays the offeror without notice, the acceptance is effective at the moment the act is performed provided that the act is performed within the period of time.

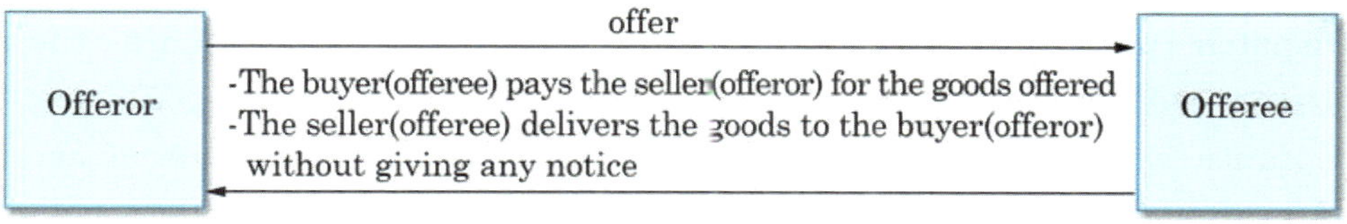

2) Acceptance which doesn't form a contract

(1) Delayed acceptance

An acceptance must be made within the time limited in the offer, or, if no time is limited, within a reasonable time. An acceptance reached the offeror after the time limit can not form a contract. Should the offeror make the offer subject to receipt of the acceptance, there can be no contract until the acceptance is communicated to the offeror and actually received by him.

An acceptance beyond this time would be a late acceptance and then it is up to the offeror to inform the offeree if the offeror wants to take the late acceptance as an effective acceptance. Or the late acceptance can be taken as a new offer.

A delayed acceptance is effective as an acceptance if, without delay, the offeror orally so informs the offeree or dispatches a notice to that effect.

(2) Conditional acceptance

A conditional acceptance is the one that offeree changes or adds some terms and conditions in the original offer. As this becomes a counter offer, it doesn't constitute a contract without acceptance by the offeror.

(3) Partial acceptance

A partial acceptance is the one that offeree just accepts part of terms and conditions in the offer. This also can be regarded as a counter offer.

(4) Acceptance by silence or inactivity

Silence or inactivity does not constitute an acceptance. Silence can be an acceptance only when the parties so agree.

4. Time at which an Acceptance becomes Effective

1) Dispatch rule

Dispatch rule is that an acceptance would become valid as soon as the acceptance is dispatched by the offeree. Under the law of some countries, an acceptance begins to function at the moment the letter or cable of acceptance is posted or dispatched. A contract is thus formed at this very moment.

2) Receipt rule

Receipt rule is that an acceptance would become valid when it is received by the offeror(by civil law system). An acceptance, as a rule, takes effect when it reaches the offeror. If the letter or cable may be lost in the mail or transmission, the offeror knows nothing about the acceptance until it is found later. To avoid subsequent dispute or confusion in this respect, it is the practice to clarify the offeree that an acceptance would not be valid unless the letter or cable is received before the time limit.

According to the "United Nations Convention on Contracts for the International Sale of Goods", an acceptance becomes effective when it is received and a contract is concluded at the moment when an acceptance of an offer becomes effective.

Table 3-1 Time at which an acceptance becomes effective

<table>
<tr><th colspan="3">governing law / mode of communication</th><th>Korea</th><th>Japan</th><th>England</th><th>U.S.A</th><th>Germany</th><th>Vienna Convention</th></tr>
<tr><td colspan="3">General rule of communication</td><td>receipt</td><td>receipt</td><td>receipt</td><td>receipt</td><td>receipt</td><td>receipt</td></tr>
<tr><td rowspan="6">Acceptance</td><td rowspan="4">between inter-locutors</td><td>face to face</td><td>receipt</td><td>receipt</td><td>receipt</td><td>receipt</td><td>receipt</td><td>receipt</td></tr>
<tr><td>telephone</td><td>receipt</td><td>receipt</td><td>receipt</td><td>receipt</td><td>receipt</td><td>receipt</td></tr>
<tr><td>telex</td><td>receipt</td><td>receipt</td><td>receipt</td><td>receipt</td><td>receipt</td><td>receipt</td></tr>
<tr><td>EDI
e-mail</td><td>receipt</td><td>receipt</td><td>receipt</td><td>receipt</td><td>receipt</td><td>receipt</td></tr>
<tr><td rowspan="2">between persons in remote places</td><td>air mail</td><td>dispatch</td><td>dispatch</td><td>dispatch</td><td>dispatch</td><td>receipt</td><td>receipt</td></tr>
<tr><td>telegram</td><td>dispatch</td><td>dispatch</td><td>dispatch</td><td>dispatch</td><td>receipt</td><td>receipt</td></tr>
</table>

* 'receipt' means receip rule and 'dispatch' means dispatch rule.

5. Mode of Communication

1) Mode of communication designated in the offer

If an offeror designates a mode of communication in an offer, an offeree should use the means authorized by the offeror to communicate an acceptance. Thus, if the offeror designates that an acceptance should be sent by post, the offeree should send an acceptance using the same mode of communication designated in the offer. Under such circumstances, the placing of a correctly addressed stamped letter of acceptance with the post office or depositing it in the postbox will consumate the contract. If a telegraphic mode of communication is designated, the message of acceptance is handed to the telegraph office for delivery to the offeror. In either case, a contract results as soon as the acceptance is made, not at the time when the offeror receives the letter or the telegram.

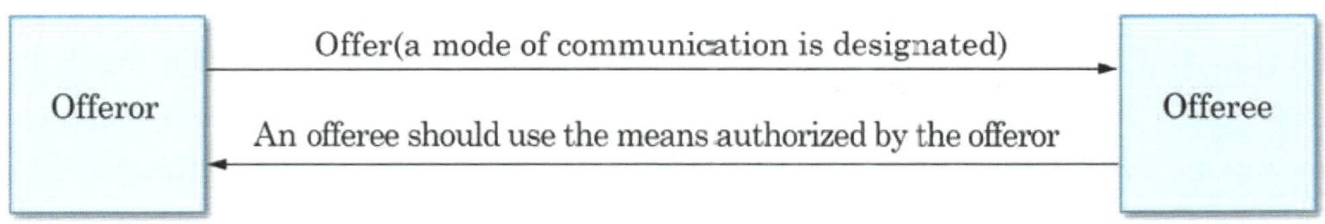

2) Mode of communication not designated in the offer

If an offeror doesn't designate any mode of communication in an offer, the offeror impliedly requests the offeree to employ the same medium used in the offer. For example, if a letter of acceptance is posted in response to an offer received by the post, it is an effective expression of assent to contract even though the letter is delayed or lost in transit.

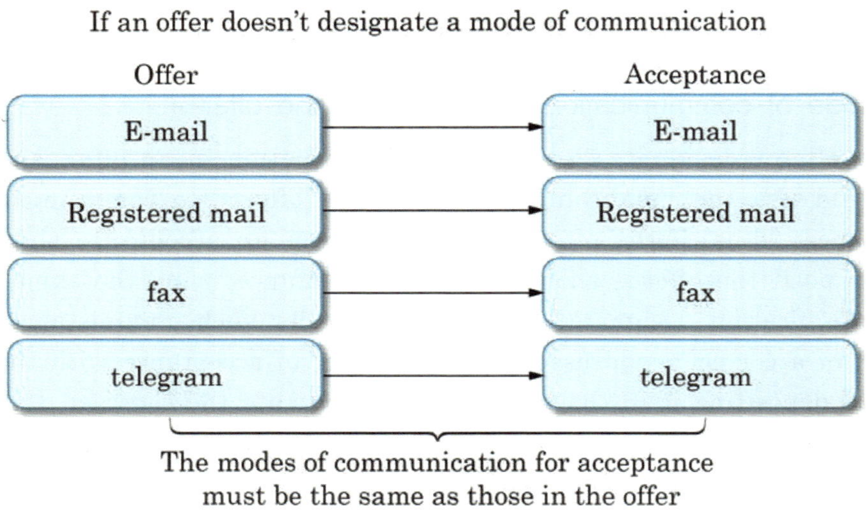

3) Withdrawal of an acceptance

Can the offeree withdraw the acceptance after he sent an acceptance? If the rule that an acceptance begins to function at the moment the mail, letter or cable of acceptance is posted or dispatched is adopted, the acceptance can not be withdrawn. If the rule that an acceptance begins to function the moment the mail, letter or cable of acceptance is delivered to the offeror is adopted, an acceptance can be withdrawn if the withdrawal reaches the offeror before or at the same time with the acceptance.

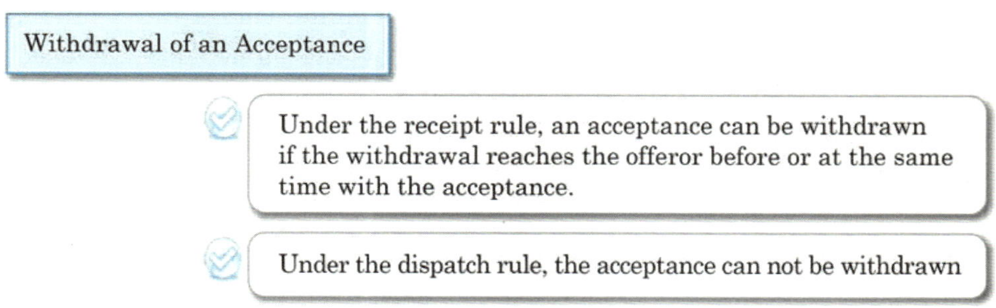

4) Revocation of an acceptance

Revocation of an acceptance is impossible as the contact is formed at the very moment the acceptance comes into effect.

3.3 Sample Letters of Offer and Acceptance

1. Offer for Cosmetics and Counter Offer

1) A firm offer

To : bronco@simpati.com
From : sklee@chung.co.kr
Date : July, 20, 20××.
Subject : A firm Offer for Cosmetics

Dear Sirs,
We take much pleasure in offering you as follows:
Packing : Manufacturer's Export Standard Packing
Origin : Republic of Korea
Shipment : Within 60 days after the date of contract
Payment : By an irrevocable L/C at sight in our favor or T/T
Inspection : Manufacturer's inspection is final
Validity : This offer is valid until the end of September, 20××

H.S.	Description		Quantity	Price/pc	Amount
	Nagrand Brand Cosmetics		CIF New York, USA		
3304.99.2000	Make-up Base No.10	30gr	500pcs	@U$2.55	U$1,275
	Liquid Foundation No.13	30gr	300pcs	@U$2.35	U$705
3304.91.1000	Compact No.13	12gr	100pcs	@U$2.35	U$235
	Pressed Powder No.13	25gr	250pcs	@U$3.10	U$775
3304.20.1000	Tripple Shadow No.31	5gr	200pcs	@U$2.76	U$552
3304.20.9000	Mascara No.79	5ml	1,000pcs	@U$2.05	U$1,540
	Total :		2,350pcs		U$5,082

Very truly yours,

2) A counter offer for extending shipment time

Dear Sirs,

Thank you for your offer of July 20 and we are pretty much satisfied with the terms and conditions you mentioned. The samples and your terms and conditions are quite up to our expectation. Although your quotation is satisfactory, we regret this business can not be successful at your present delivery date.

In case we receive the products almost 3 months later from now, we may lose our market opportunity as make-up products will be out of season. Under these circumstances, we would like to ask for your earliest shipment available next month to get a leg up on the market.

Your products have to be exhibited together with clothes for women supplied by Wooyoung Mulsan Co., Ltd. by the end of next month.

We will be able to issue an irrevocable L/C at sight in your favor immediately if you agree with us. Otherwise, it will not be possible for us to place an order with you this time.

We trust you will make every effort to advance your delivery time.

Very truly yours,

3) A counter offer for price reduction

Dear Sirs,

We examined the samples and patterns you sent us and also investigated your terms and conditions with interest.

While we appreciate the good quality of your products, we find your prices rather high considering quotations ruling in this market. There is no doubt that the prospective customers will refuse to accept your offer as the prices offered are not competitive enough to tempt them to deal with. Actually your competitors are making endeavors to get our business by offering much lower prices than those of yours.

As have been stated in our previous e-mails, competition in this line is very fierce. Owing to a growing demand for this line, however, the market here shows signs of strength.

We will be able to work on this business if you consider decreasing your prices by 15% each, which is not even competitive here.

Consequently, we are sure that you will revise the prices for our long term business and we look forward to receiving your reply.

Very truly yours,

2. Offer and Counter Offer for Cellular Phones

1) A firm offer

Dear Sirs,

We thank you very much for your inquiry of July 1, and we are glad to make the following firm offer subject to your acceptance reaching here by July 31, 20××.

1. Commodity : Cellular Phone, Galaxy S5
2. Quantity : 1,000 pcs
3. Price : @U$200.00 per piece.- CIF New York, USA.
4. Shipment : Within 60 days after receipt of your L/C.
5. Packing : Export standard packing
6. Payment : By an irrevocable and confirmed L/C at sight in our favor only.

The quotation we offer is the best we can give you and the price, we believe, will enable you to realize a large profit. Now, large orders are rushing in from your country and the market here is very strong. Under the circumstances, there is an indication that the price will rise soon.

We trust that pleasant business relations will soon be established between us.

Very truly yours,

2) A counter offer

Dear Sirs,

Thank you for your offer of April 6 for 1,000pcs of cellular phone, Galaxy S5. We have given our careful consideration to your firm offer and tried to meet your terms and conditions.

There is a steady demand for high quality range and fashionable design. We have been receiving a number of inquires from our trade connections for the same products.

Your offer is basically acceptable to us except payment terms. We are suffering from some financial difficulties for the time being and we are pretty much interested in Usance L/C for our business this time.

As this will be a banker's usance L/C, there will not be any problem for you to negotiate the documents with a negotiating bank just as you do with L/C at sight.

If you agree with our proposal without changing other conditions, we will place an initial order for 1,000pcs of products with you immediately.

We look forward to receiving your response.

Sincerely yours,

3. Offer and Counter Offer for Digital Camera

1) An offer

Gentlemen :

We have received your offer dated February 8 asking us to quote the price for digital camera and we are glad to offer you under the terms and conditions mentioned below subject to your acceptance reaching us by March 31, 20××.

Description : Digital Camera
Price : @US$250.25 per piece, CIF Piraeus, Greece.
Quantity : 1,000 pieces

Packing : 10 pieces in each outer box.
Shipment : April 30, 20××.
Payment : Draft at sight under an irrevocable Letter of Credit.

We can guarantee our perfect combination of durability and softness for the products. Please note that the price we offer is the most attractive one you can receive from us and the price will inevitably be raised in the future because the prices of raw materials and the wages are on a steady rise. We are quite sure that our offer will meet your entire satisfaction.

Looking forward to your reply, we remain.

Yours faithfully,

2) A counter offer

Dear Sirs,

We thank you for your offer of digital camera and we would like to draw your attention that there is every indication of the price reduction soon here as the competition in the same type of products is very heavy.

We receive many offers from your competitors abroad and your price is rather stiff in view of the quotation ruling in the market.

Your competitors are making attempts to get our business by offering lower prices than that of yours. If you come down the price by 10% per piece, we are prepared to give you a trial order. Unless you can accept this price, our business will fall through.

Your deep consideration to this matter would be appreciated.

Yours faithfully,

3) A reply to the counter offer

Gentlemen :

We received your counter offer requesting us to reduce the price and we regret that our price is not low enough to meet your requirements.

We believe that our competitive price will surely ensure steady sales due to our excellent design and quality. We find it difficult to allow any further discount on our products as the price has been put to the absolute minimum.

The price we offered is the best one we can give you at present and the high quality of our product can't be maintained at lower prices.

Insead, we are prepared to grant you a credit of US$10,000 for an initial advertisement. We think this is a more practical way to meet your requirement.

We look forward to having your reply soon.

Very truly yours,

4. Offer and Counter Offer for Automobile Parts

1) A counter offer

Dear Sirs,

Our promising distributors have done their market surveys with your quotation and samples. They informed us that the patterns and functions are acceptable in the market, but the price is on the high side, which they wouldn't even make a counter offer.

The price is not competitive enough for the market here and we want you to contact the manufacturer in your country and see if they can sharpen the pencil a little bit more to reduce the price by 5% at least.

All other terms and conditions seem reasonable and please bear in mind that once your offer is successful in securing a foothold with that item, you will receive substantial orders from our customers in the future.

Very truly yours,

2) A reply to the counter offer

Dear Sirs,

With your counter offer of November 12 on hand, we conducted our negotiations with the supplier and tried to induce them to reduce the price as you suggested.

As the prices of automobile parts go up day by day, they won't be able to accept your counter offer basically.

In consideration of the very pleasant business relationship we have had with you for several years, we have decided to agree to your suggestion and we are quite sure that you will realize this is a special occasion.

We want you to send us your order sheet together with a notice that you instructed your bank to issue a letter of credit in our favor right away.

Sincerely yours,

Chapter 4

Basic Terms of Business Contract

Chapter

4 Basic Terms of Business Contract

There are many kinds of terms and conditions which need to be considered before drawing up a contract. Basic terms of business contract are ① terms of quality, ② terms of quantity, ③ terms of price, ④ terms of shipment, ⑤ terms of payment, ⑥ terms of packaging, ⑦ terms of insurance, ⑧ terms of dispute settlement, ect. These terms are indispensable factors in preparing an agreement between the parties.

In making an offer or before entering into the contract of sale, the parties concerned should state these matters explicitly and come to an agreement each other.

4.1 Terms of Quality

Some quality standards that are in frequent use in a country or a specific industry may not be known or may be interpreted differently in other countries or industries. Usually different goods have different qualities, but even the same goods have different qualities. Therefore, a great care needs to be taken to specify terms of quality to avoid any dispute.

In international trade, the seller and the buyer are usually far apart in different countries. The buyer is unable to see the goods until they reach the buyer. But, he should know the quality of goods before he decides to buy them. Then, how could the seller have the quality of the goods on sale made known to the buyer? The parties need to agree on ① method of deciding quality, ② time of deciding quality and ③ methods of proving quality

1. Method of Deciding Quality

1) Sale by sample

Sale by sample is a sale that quality of the goods is decided according to that of the sample. The buyer buys the goods on the condition that they are of the same quality as the one shown to the buyer as sample.

When writing a business contract, however, it is desirable to add an elastic clause like "Quality should be about equal to the sample" or "Quality should be similar to the sample" instead of clauses like "Quality should be fully equal to the sample" or "Quality should be the same as the sample" to avoid the possible disputes.

The buyer, when receiving the sample, knows what kind of goods and in particular, what quality of the goods he is buying. Industrial products, light industry products, etc. are generally sold by this method.

In practice, representative samples, called original samples or type samples, are usually sent by the seller to the buyer, and at the same time, duplicate samples are always kept by the seller for later reference. When the samples are accepted by the buyer, the seller is responsible for the delivery of the goods of the same quality as shown in the sample. Such a transaction is called a Sale by Seller's Sample[1]. In case the quality of the goods delivered is not identical with the sample, the buyer is entitled to claim a compensation for loss or reject the goods.

Sometimes the buyer may send a sample to the seller who is asked to supply the goods in accordance with it. The transaction held is called a Sale by Buyer's Sample[2]. When possible, the seller may send the buyer a sample in similar quality, called a return sample or a counter sample, as a proposal for the buyer's consideration.

---

1) A seller's sample is the sample which is submitted by the seller to a buyer. In case of the seller's sample, it must be observed that the overseas buyer is, of course, not bound to take delivery of the goods supplied if they are not equal in quality to the sample on which the order was given.

2) A buyer's sample is the sample which is sent from the buyer accompanied by his/her inquiries or orders. Inquiries or orders from overseas customers are often accompanied by samples of goods required. The seller submits such samples to likely manufacturers and obtains from them counter samples of similar or nearly similar goods. The seller sends these counter samples to overseas customers in order to obtain their orders.

2) Sale by brand or trademark

Sale by brand or trademark is a sale that quality of the goods is decided according to brand or trademark which identifies products or services of a particular source from those of others.

Most industrial goods are represented by brands or trade marks. Goods of the same brand or trademark are of the same quality. Their quality remains unified and unchanged. So, from the brand or trademark, people can tell what quality the goods possess. It is more convenient to name the brand or trademark of the product to indicate its quality than to enumerate so many specifications one by one. Occasionally, the place of origin of the goods is also used for this purpose

Some goods are offered under certain well-known brand or trademark as, for example, 'Nikon Camera', 'Omega Wrist Watch', 'Lipton's Tea'. etc. The brand or mark signifies the quality of the goods and such goods do not usually require to be represented by samples.

3) Sale by specification

Sale by specification is a sale that quality of the goods is decided by detailed specifications, blueprints, drawings or diagrams of the goods.

Machines, apparatuses, instruments, furniture, vessels, complete set of equipments, etc. are apt to sell by this method. It is difficult to indicate their quality in detail by merely presenting samples because of their structures and functions are complicated and their installation, application and maintenance are subject to specified rules. Consequently, relevant technical manuals, booklets of directions, drawings or diagrams will serve the purpose.

4) Sale by type or grade

Sale by type or grade is a sale that quality of the goods is decided according to the type or grade of certain goods regulated by countries or commercial organizations such as International Organization for Standardization (ISO), Korean Standards(KS), Japanese Industrial Standards(JIS), British Standards(BS), etc. In case of sale by type or grade, what the parties concerned have to do with the terms of the quality of the goods is just simply to state its type or grade.

5) Sale by inspection

Sale by inspection is a sale that the buyer inspects the goods delivered for deciding the quality before drawing up a contract. Cash on Delivery (COD), Cash Against Document(CAD), Bonded Warehouse Transaction (BWT), Offer On Approval, Offer On Sale or Return, etc. are used for deciding quality by this method.

6) Sale by standard

Sale by standard is a sale that standard quality of agricultural and fishery products, etc. which are to be cropped is decided as the quality of goods to be delivered.

Agricultural products such as grain, cotton, wheat, tobacco, sugar, tea, etc. are sold for future delivery on type and subject to crop. A type or standard or sometimes a type sample is not a part of the lot offered for sale, but represents a 'norm' that the quality of the products may be expected to approximately close. The type may be taken from the product cropped in the previous year. Sometimes, it may be even several years old. Sale by standard is divided into two quality terms as follows;

(1) Fair Average Quality(FAQ)

Fair Average Quality(FAQ) denotes a quality of the product that is offered not on a particular quality specification but on the basis that is equal to the average quality of the current group, recent shipment, etc. It is used to decide the quality of grains, tea, fruits and so on.

(2) Good Merchantable Quality(GMQ)

Good Merchantable Quality(GMQ) refers to the sound quality that is free from defects and is sufficiently good enough to be sold in the market. It is used to decide the quality of logs, fishery products, etc.

FAQ and GMQ terms are rather too general and sweeping. When in use, therefore, they are usually supplemented by some concrete specifications.

Table 4-1 Method of deciding quality

<table>
<tr><th colspan="2">division</th><th>contents</th><th>remarks</th></tr>
<tr><td colspan="2">Sale by sample</td><td>a sale that quality of the goods is decided according to that of the sample</td><td>Industrial products</td></tr>
<tr><td colspan="2">Sale by brand or trademark</td><td>a sale that quality of the goods is decided according to brand or trademark which identifies products or services of a particular source from those of others.</td><td>Nikon Camera, Omega Watch, etc.</td></tr>
<tr><td colspan="2">Sale by specification</td><td>a sale that quality of the goods is decided by detailed specifications, blueprints, drawings or diagrams of the goods</td><td>Machines, equipment, vessel, automobiles</td></tr>
<tr><td colspan="2">Sale by type or grade</td><td>a sale that quality of the goods is decided according to the type or grade of certain goods regulated by countries or commercial organizations</td><td>KS, JIS, BS. ISO</td></tr>
<tr><td colspan="2">Sale by inspection</td><td>a sale that the buyer inspects the goods delivered for deciding the quality before drawing up a contract</td><td>CAD, COD, BWT</td></tr>
<tr><td rowspan="3">Sale by standard</td><td colspan="3">a sale that standard quality of agricultural and fishery products, etc. which are to be cropped is decided as the quality of goods to be delivered</td></tr>
<tr><td>F.A.Q</td><td>a quality of the product that is offered not on a particular quality specification but on the basis that is equal to the average quality of the current group, recent shipment, etc.</td><td>Grains, Tea, etc.</td></tr>
<tr><td>G.M.Q</td><td>a sound quality that is free from defects and is sufficiently good enough to be sold in the market</td><td>Logs,
Fishery products</td></tr>
</table>

2. Time of Deciding Quality

1) Shipped quality terms

Shipped quality terms means that the quality of products is decided at the time of shipment. The seller is not responsible for any defect or damage in transit. The buyer doesn't have any right to claim any damage except in those cases where it can be proved that the ship was not in condition to carry the goods or that they were shipped in a negligent manner. The contract on tale quale(TQ) for grains usually contains a clause providing the goods for shipment in good condition.

Tale Quale(TQ), EXW, FCA, FAS, COB, CFR, CIF, CPT, CIP rules and Fair Average Quality(FAQ) belong to shipped quality terms.

2) Landed quality terms

Landed quality terms means that the quality of products is decided at the time of arrival. The contract on landed quality terms is the most favorable one for the buyer as the seller guarantees the quality of products on arrival. It indicates that damages may be claimed when the products delivered are not up to the standard on account of damage above a certain percentage that can ordinarily be expected. The seller, therefore, assumes the risks in transit. Ray Terms(RT), DAP, DPU, DDP rules and Good Merchantable Quality(GMQ) belong to landed quality terms.

Time of deciding quality

shipped quality terms	• The quality of products is decided at the time of shipment • EXW, FCA, FAS, FOB, CFR, CIF, CPT, CIP, FAQ and Tale Quale(TQ)
landed quality terms	• The quality of products is decided at the time of arrival • DAP, DPU, DDP, GMQ and Rye Terms(RT)

3. Method of Proving Quality

The method of proving quality is to prove whether the quality of products delivered corresponds to that of the products contracted.

1) Shipped quality terms

Under shipped quality terms, the seller has to prove that the quality of the products at the time of shipment corresponds to the quality contracted. The seller is responsible for supplying the buyer with a certificate of inspection or a certificate of quality issued by an authorized surveyor at the port of shipment before the goods are shipped. Therefore, the seller is not responsible for any quality after shipment.

2) Landed quality terms

Under landed quality terms, the seller has to prove that the quality of the products at the time of arrival corresponds to the quality contracted. The seller is responsible for the quality of goods until they reach the final destination port or place. Should there be any discrepancy found, which is not in conformity with the contract of sale, the seller, provided that the insurers or the carriers are supposed not to be liable for such discrepancies, is responsible for the reimbursement in case the buyer loges claims against the seller.

Method of proving quality

shipped quality terms	• The seller has to prove that the quality of the products at the time of shipment corresponds to the quality, contracted.
landed quality terms	• The seller has to prove that the quality of the products at the time of arrival corresponds to the quality, contracted.

4.2 Terms of Quantity

The quantity of goods is expressed in various ways according to the nature of the goods or trade customs. In particular, the business laws of certain countries stipulate that the quantity of the goods delivered should be identical to that called for in the contract. The buyer has the right to reject the goods if their quantity delivered is less than the quantity agreed upon. The buyer is also entitled to reject the whole lot or that portion of the goods excessive in quantity. Therefore, a due attention should be paid to the quantity terms during business negotiations.

1. Quantity Unit

Weight, measurement, piece, length, etc. applicable in international trade for quantity are different according to countries. The difference lies not only in the names of the unit but also in the actual quantity involved. The units of quantity generally used in international trade are as follows;

Table 4-2 Quantity Units

		Unit
Weight		• Long ton(English ton : Gross ton : LT=2,240lbs=1,016.1kgs(England) • Short ton(American ton : Net ton : S/T=2,000lbs=907.2kgs(America) • Metric ton(French ton : Kilo ton : M/T=2,204lbs=1,000kgs(Germany) • Gross Weight(aggregate weight including the package) • Net Weight(a weight that tare is deducted from gross weight)
Measurment	timber	• Cubic Meter : CBM, Cubic Feet : cft • Sufer Feet(sf)=1 square foot × 1 inch
	liquid	• Barrel : 31.5gallons(America), 36gallons(England) • Gallon(gal) : American gallon(wine gallon)=4,456 liters=4 quarts English gallon(imperial gallon)=3,785 liters=4 quarts • Quart(qt) : 1/4gallon=2 pints=0.95 liter(America)=1.14 liter(England) • Liter(lit) : 1,000 cc • Pint : 0.47 liter(America) = 0.57 liter(England)
	grain	• Bushel= 8 gallons = 35 liters(America) = 36 liters(England)
	vessel	• Measurement ton(M/T)=1CBM(m3)=40입방피트=480sf
piece		• Dozen : 12pcs • Gross : 144pcs(12pcs × 12pcs), Small Gross=120pcs(12×10pcs) Great Gross : 1,728pcs(12×12×12pcs)
length		• Meter, Yard, Inch, Foot
packaging		• TEU : Twenty Feet Equivalent Unit • Case, Bale, Bag, Sack, Keg, Drum, Bundle, etc.

2. More or Less Clause(M/L Clause)

The quantity clause in a sale of contract should always be stated clearly and definitely. Such an expression as "About 1,000 metric tons" is not advisable. Raw materials such as oil, coal or cereals, agricultural and mineral goods which are liable to lose weight in transit because of leakage or evaporation, wastage, shrinkage or the like may be delivered not in exact conformity with the quantity contracted.

1) A contract which doesn't stipulate M/L clause

A tolerance not to exceed 5% more or 5% less than the quantity of the goods is allowed, provided the credit does not state the quantity in terms of a stipulated number of packing units or individual items and the total amount of the drawings does not exceed the amount of the credit.

This tolerance does not apply when the credit stipulates the quantity in terms of a stated number of packing units or individual items.

2) A contract which stipulates M/L clause

More or Less Clause is used, particularly, in the transaction of agricultural or mineral goods which are liable to lose weight in transit. The followings are some examples of M/L clause

① "Quantity shall be subject to a variation of 3% more or less at seller's option"
② "Seller has the option of delivering 3% more or less on the quantity contracted"
③ "Seller has the option of shipment with a variation of 3% more or less on the quantity contracted, unless otherwise agreed"

3) Approximate quantity terms

The words "about" or "approximately" used in connection with the amount of the credit or the quantity or the unit price stated in the credit are to be construed as allowing a tolerance not to exceed 10% more or 10% less than the amount, the quantity or the unit price to which they refer.

Table 4-3 Quantity

<table>
<tr><th>Division</th><th>Expression</th><th>Goods</th><th colspan="2">Meaning</th></tr>
<tr><td rowspan="3">A contract which doesn't stipulate M/L clause</td><td rowspan="3">stipulate exact quantity</td><td>• packing unit cargo
• individual items</td><td colspan="2">deliver exact quantity according to a contract of sale</td></tr>
<tr><td rowspan="2">• bulk cargo</td><td>L/C transaction</td><td>allow 5% more or less</td></tr>
<tr><td>other transactions</td><td>there is no regulation on M/L clause</td></tr>
<tr><td>A contract which stipulates M/L clause</td><td>stipulate M/L clause(ex: x% more or less)</td><td>• packing unit cargo
• individual items
• bulk cargo</td><td>every transactions</td><td>allow a tolerance of x% more or less agreed</td></tr>
<tr><td rowspan="2">Approximate quantity terms</td><td rowspan="2">stipulate words like 'about', 'approximately'</td><td rowspan="2">• packing unit cargo
• individual items
• bulk cargo</td><td>L/C transaction</td><td>allow 10% more or less</td></tr>
<tr><td>other transactions</td><td>there is no regulation on M/L clause</td></tr>
</table>

3. Time of Deciding Quantity

1) Shipped quantity terms

Shipped quantity terms means that the quantity of goods at the time of shipment should be the same as the quantity contracted. The seller is not responsible for any partial loss of quantity in transit. FCA, CPT, CIP, FAS, FOB, CFR and CIF rules under Incoterms® 2010 belong to shipped quantity terms.

2) Landed quantity terms

Landed quantity terms means that the quantity of goods at the time of arrival should be the same as the quantity contracted. The seller is responsible for any partial loss of quantity in transit. DAP, DPU and DDP rules under Incoterms® 2020 belong to landed quantity terms.

4. Method of Proving Quantity

1) Shipped quantity terms

Under shipped quantity terms, the seller has to prove that the quantity of goods at the time of shipment corresponds to the quantity contracted. The seller is responsible for supplying the buyer with a certificate of inspection or a certificate of quantity issued by an authorized surveyor at the port of shipment before the goods are shipped. Therefore, the seller is not responsible for any quantity after shipment.

2) Landed quantity terms

Under landed quantity terms, the seller has to prove that the quantity of goods at the time of arrival corresponds to the quantity contracted. The seller is responsible for the quantity of goods until they reach the final destination port or place. Should there be any discrepancy found, which is not in conformity with the contract of sale, the seller, provided that the insurers or the carriers are supposed not to be liable for such discrepancies, is responsible for the reimbursement in case the buyer loges a claim against the seller.

4.3 Terms of Price

When quoting prices to the overseas buyer, the seller will naturally consider various expenses involved in getting the goods from the factory or the warehouse in the seller's country to the buyer's premises.

1. Cost structure

1) Export price structure

The factors affecting export price are ① manufacturing costs, ② profit, ③ packing charges, ④ inspection charges, ⑤ inland freight, ⑥ storage, ⑦ CFS charges, ⑧ export clearance cost, ⑨ shipping and stowing charges, ⑩ ocean freight or carriage, ⑪ insurance premium, etc.

2) Import price structure

The factors affecting import price are ① ocean freight or carriage, ② insurance premium, ③ unloading charges, ④ port duties or wharfage charge, ⑤ import clearance cose and import duties, ⑥ storage and godown, etc.

2. Incoterms

Incoterms rules are international rules that are accepted by government, legal authorities and practitioners worldwide for the interpretation of the most commonly used terms in international trade. It either reduces or removes uncertainties arising from different interpretations of such terms in different countries. The purpose of incoterms is to alleviate or reduce confusion over price terms by outlining exactly who is obliged to take control of the goods at a particular point in the shipping process. Further, the terms will outline the obligations for the clearance of the goods for export or import.

The contents of Incoterms® 2010 will be explained in Chapter 5.

4.4 Terms of Shipment

When negotiating a transaction, the buyer and the seller should reach an agreement on ① time of shipment, ② method of shipment, ③ exemption clause of delayed shipment and specify them in the contract of sale. A clear stipulation of shipment clause is an important condition for the smooth execution of the contract.

1. Time of Shipment

Time of shipment is the time period or the deadline by which the seller makes shipment of the contracted goods. When stipulating the time of shipment, both parties should consider the availability of goods, carriers and shipping space, etc.

1) Shipment within a specified date

It is a condition that the seller has to effect a shipment within the date specified. According to the following examples, the seller can make a shipment within May 20, 20××. This method is most widely used in international trade.

- Shipment : May 20, 20××.
- Shipment : Not later than May 10, 20××.
- Shipment by May 10, 20××.
- Shipment should be made not later than May 10, 20××.

2) Shipment within a specified month

There are two methods for this mode as follows;

(1) Shipment during a specified one month

It is a condition that the seller should make a shipment during May, 20×× at one time if partial shipments are not allowed.

- May shipment.
- Shipment during May, 20××.
- Shipment shall be made during May, 20××.

(2) Shipment during consecutive specified months

It is a condition that the seller should make shipments during May and June, 20×× and the seller can make shipments partially.

- Shipment during May and June, 20××.
- May/June, 20×× shipment.

3) Shipment within a specified period of time

(1) "On or About" of a month

The expression "on or about" or similar will be interpreted as a stipulation that an event is to occur during a period of five calendar days before until five calendar days after the specified date, both start and end dates included. Therefore, the seller can ship the goods between May 5 and May 15, 20××.

- Shipment on or about May 10, 20××.

(2) "First half" and "Second half" of a month

The terms "first haft" and "second half" of a month shall be construed respectively as the 1st to the 15th and the 16th to the last day of the month, all dates inclusive.

- Shipment : first half of May, 20××.
- Shipment : second half of May, 20××.

(3) "Beginning", "Middle" and "End" of a month

The terms "beginning", "middle" and "end" of a month shall be construed respectively as the 1st to the 10th, the 11th to the 20th and the 21st to the last day of the month, all dates inclusive.

- Shipment : beginning of May, 20××.
- Shipment : middle of May, 20××.
- Shipment : end of May, 20××.

(4) Immediate shipment and others

"Prompt shipment", "Immediate shipment", "Shipment as soon as possible", "Shipment by the first vessel available" or "Shipment by the first opportunity" are vague and open to misunderstanding. Expressions such as "prompt", "immediately", "as soon as possible" and the like should not be used. It is recommended that when the seller and the buyer use these terms in their transactions, they should come to mutual understanding as to the interpretation of the terms. Unless required to be used in a document, words such as "prompt", "immediately", or "as soon as possible" will be disregarded.

2. Method of Shipment

1) Partial Shipment

Partial shipment means the goods under one contract are shipped by more than two lots. The shipment clause must specify whether partial shipments are allowed by using a phrase such as "Partial shipments are allowed" or "Partial shipments are prohibited." Partial shipments are allowed unless the credit stipulates otherwise.

- Partial shipments : Not allowed = Partial shipments : Prohibited
- Partial shipments are not allowed = Partial shipments are prohibited
- Partial shipments : Allowed = Partial shipments : Not prohibited
- Partial shipments are allowed = Partial shipments are not prohibited

2) Instalment Shipment

Installment shipment means that the time and quantity of each shipment should be specified such as "shipment during March to June in four equal monthly lots". The seller should strictly follow the regulation. Otherwise, the buyer has a right to reject the goods. If the shipments by instalments with given period are specified, each instalment shall be treated as a separate transaction. If an instalment is not shipped within the given period, the credit ceases to be available for that and any subsequent instalments.

- Shipment during March to June in four equal monthly lots
- Equal monthly shipments during March, April, May and June
- May and June shipments are equally divided

3) Transhipment

Transhipment means unloading from one vessel and reloading to another vessel during the carriage from the port of loading to the port of discharge stated in the credit.[3)]

When there is no direct vessel between the port of shipment and the port of destination, or no suitable vessels available at that particular period, the goods have to be transferred from one vessel to another at an intermediate port. The clause must also specify whether "Transhipment is(or is not) allowed".

If transhipment is carried out in order to reach the agreed destination, the seller would have to pay the costs arising from the transhipment. If, however, the carrier exercised his rights under a transhipment or similar clause in order to avoid unexpected hindrances(such as ice, congession, labor disturbances, government orders, war or warlike operations), then any additional costs would be on the buyer's account.

- Transhipment : Not allowed = Transhipment : Prohibited
- Transhipment is not allowed = Transhipment is prohibited
- Transhipment : Allowed = Transhipment : Not prohibited
- Transhipment is allowed = Transhipment is not prohibited

Even if the credit prohibits transhipment, the following documents are acceptable.

(1) Transport document covering at least two different modes of transport

A transport document indicating that transhipment will or may take place is acceptable even if the credit prohibits transhipment.

(2) Bill of lading

A bill of lading indicating that transhipment will or may take place is acceptable, even if the credit prohibits transhipment, if the goods have been shipped in a container, trailer or LASH barge as evidenced by bill of lading.

(3) Non-negotiable sea waybill

Non-negotiable sea waybill indicating that transhipment will or may take

3) In combined transport, transhipment means unloading from one means of conveyance and reloading to another means of conveyance(whether or not in different modes of transport) during the carriage from the place of dispatch, taking in charge or shipment to the place of final destination stated in the credit.

place is acceptable, even if the credit prohibits transhipment, if the goods have been shipped in a container, trailer or LASH barge as evidenced by non-negotiable bill of lading.

(4) Air transport document

An air transport document indicating that transhipment will or may take place is acceptable, even if the credit prohibits transhipment.

(5) Road, Rail or Inland Waterway transport documents

A road, rail or inland waterway transport document indicating that transhipment will or may take place is acceptable, even if the credit prohibits transhipment.

Table 4-4 Time and methods of shipment

division	subjects	expressions
time of shipment	Shipment within a specified date	Shipment : May 20, 20××. Shipment : Not later than May 10, 20××. Shipment by May 10, 20××. Shipment should be made not later than May 10, 20××.
	Shipment within a specified month	Shipment during May, 20××..
		Shipment during May and June, 20××.
	Shipment within a specified period of time	Shipment on or about May 10, 20××.
		Shipment : first half of May, 20××.
		Shipment : beginning of May, 20××.
		Immediate shipment
methods of shipment	Partial shipment	Partial shipments are allowed(not prohibited). Partial shipments are not allowed(prohibited).
	Instalment shipment	Shipment during March to June in four equal monthly lots.
	Transhipment	Transhipment is allowed(not prohibited). Transhipment is not allowed(prohibited).

3. Proof of Shipment Date

1) Transport document covering at least two different modes of transport

The date of issuance of the transport will be deemed to be the date of dispatch, taking in charge or shipped on board, and the date of shipment. However, if the transport document indicates, by stamp or notation, a date of dispatch, taking in charge or shipped on board, this date will be deemed to be the date of shipment.

2) Ocean bill of lading, Non-negotiable sea waybill, Charter party bill of lading

The date of issuance of the bill of lading(non-negotiable sea waybill, charter party bill of lading) will be deemed to be the date of shipment unless the bill of lading(non-negotiable sea waybill, charter party bill of lading) contains an on board notation indicating the date of shipment, in which case the date stated in the on board notation indicating the date of shipment, in which the date stated in the on board notation will be deemed to be the date of shipment.

3) Air transport document

The date of issuance will be deemed to be the date of shipment unless the air transport document contains a specific notation of the actual date of shipment, in which case the date stated in the notation will be deemed to be the date of shipment.

4) Road, rail or inland waterway transport document

The date of shipment or the date the goods have been received for shipment, dispatch or carriage at the place stated in the credit. Unless transport document contains a dated reception stamp, an indication of the date of receipt or a date of shipment, the date of issuance of the transport document will be deemed to be the date of shipment.

5) Courier Receipt, Post Receipt or Certificate of Posting

The date of pick-up or of receipt or wording to this effect will be deemed to be the date of shipment.

Table 4-5 The date of shipment

transport documents	date of shipment
combined(multimodal) transport document	•the date of issuance •the date of dispatch, taking in charge or shipped on board
bill of lading	•the date of issuance •the date stated in the on board notation
non-negotiable sea waybill	•the date of issuance •the date stated in the on board notation
charter party bill of lading	•the date of issuance •the date stated in the on board notation
air transport document	•the date of issuance •the actual date of shipment
road, rail or inland waterway transport document	•the date of shipment •the date the goods have been received for shipment, dispatch or carriage •the date of issuance
courier receipt, post receipt or certificate of posting	•the date of pick-up or of receipt or wording to this effect

4. Exemption of Delayed Shipment

It goes without saying that the seller must hold himself responsible for the delay in shipment caused by their neglect, fault or carelessness. Frequently, however, the seller is hindered by a number of accidents beyond their control from shipping the goods within the time stipulated in the contract. The provision which exempts the seller from fulfillment of a contractual obligation in the case of accidents and fortuitous circumstances is usually embodied in the contract.

> "If the shipment of the contracted goods is prevented or delayed in whole or in part by reason of war, earthquake, floods, fire, storm, heavy snow or other causes of force majeure, the seller shall not be liable for non-shipment or late shipment of the goods or non-performance of this contract. However, the seller shall notify the buyer by fax or e-mail and furnish the relevant documents by registered airmail."

5. Port of Shipment and Port of Destination

Port of shipment is the port where goods are shipped while port of destination is the port at which goods are ultimately discharged. Both of them should be specified in the contract. Normally, one specific port of shipment and one specific port of destination are stipulated, but sometimes two or more of each are stated to meet special requirements. In case a decision cannot be made, several alternatives should be listed such as "One port out of London /Hamburg /Rotterdam as the port of destination at the buyer's location" or perhaps a general scope is stated such as "EMP(European Main Port)", "Korea Port". As "EMP" or "Korea Port" is too vague, we'd better try to avoid using them. In choosing port of shipment and port of destination, it's better to specify them as clearly as possible.

4.5 Terms of Payment

To effect payments in international trade, the parties involved need to discuss the method of payment, the price and time of payment and so on. The payment methods chiefly include ① Method of payment, ② Means of payment and ③ Time of payment.

1. Method of payment

1) Remittance

Remittance refers to the transfer of funds from one party to another in different country through banks. In remittance, there are four parties involved; ① remitter, ② payee, ③ remitting bank, ④ paying bank. From the legal point of view, the remitter remits money to the payee as it is required by the contract concluded between them. And when the remitter comes to the remitting bank, he fills out an application form to effect the payment, which upon acceptance will be binding upon the remitting bank. And the paying bank pays the payee(seller) because it is the branch bank or correspondent bank of the remitting bank in the country of the seller.

Remittance is chiefly used for payment in advance, cash with order, delivery first and payment afterward for small quantity of goods, commission, sundry charges, etc. If it is used for payment in advance or cash with order, it will place the seller in an advantageous position. If it is used for delivery first and payment afterward, it will place the buyer in an advantageous position. Remittance uses commercial credit, and hence in adopting this method, the parties involved need to have trust each other.

(1) Means of Remittance

① **Mail Transfer**

The buyer makes the payment of the goods to the remitting bank that will authorize its branch bank or correspondent bank in the country of the payee(seller) by mail to make the payment to him.

② **Telegraphic Transfer**

Telegraphic Transfer(T/T) is a method of transferring funds by the telecommunication system such as telex or cable. SWIFT(Society for Worldwide Interbank Financial Telecommunication) members are able to transfer funds within their own telecommunication network at a much lower cost. This has made T/T very popular as most international banks are SWIFT members.

③ **Demand Draft**

The buyer will come to a local bank to buy a banker's bill and then deliver it to the seller or payee by mail. When the seller or the beneficiary receives it, he will come to the bank for cash. Apart from banker's bill, promissory notes or checks can also be used in this way.

Remittance refers to the transfer of funds from one party to another in different country through banks.

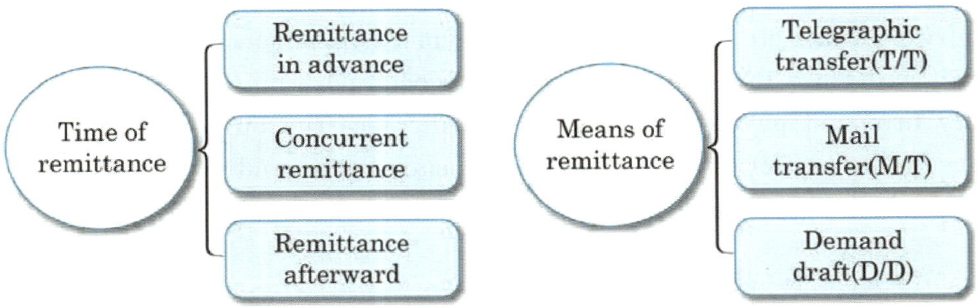

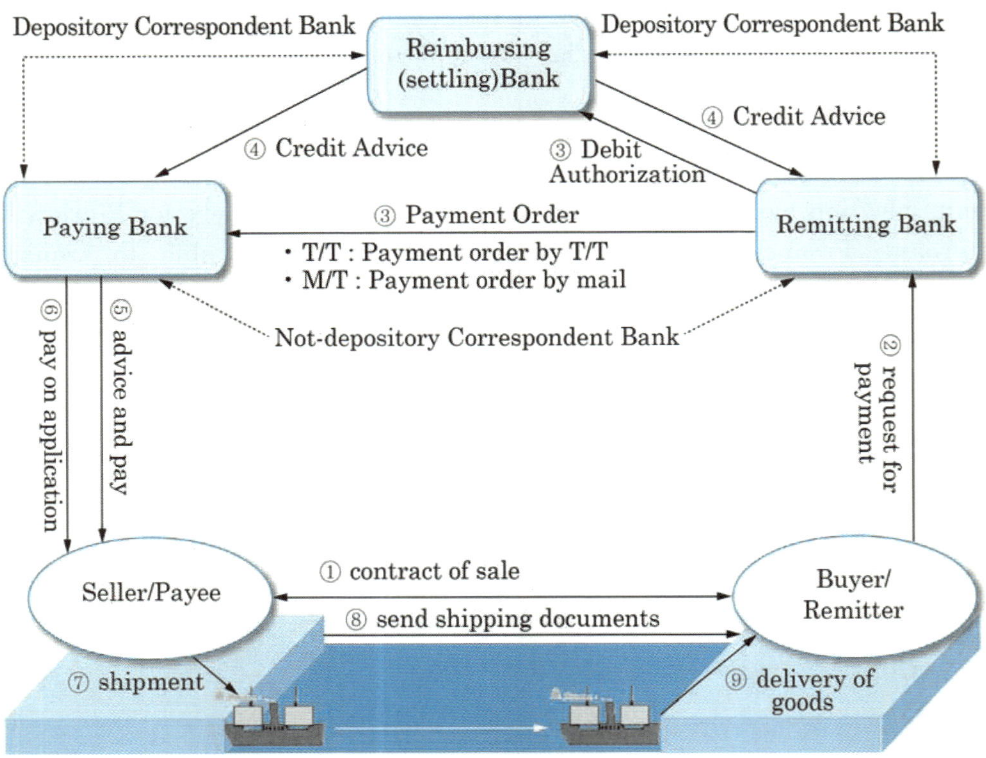

Figure 4.1 Workflow of Mail Transfer and Telegraphic Transfer

(2) Cash on Delivery(COD)

Cash on delivery(COD) means a transaction where the payment of goods and/or services received is done at the time of actual delivery rather than paid-for in advance. Payment is given at the time delivery is accomplished. Upon shipment, the seller sends the shipping documents to his agent or a correspondent bank in the buyer's country. The buyer inspects the goods arrived and receives the goods and the buyer pays for the goods at the same time.

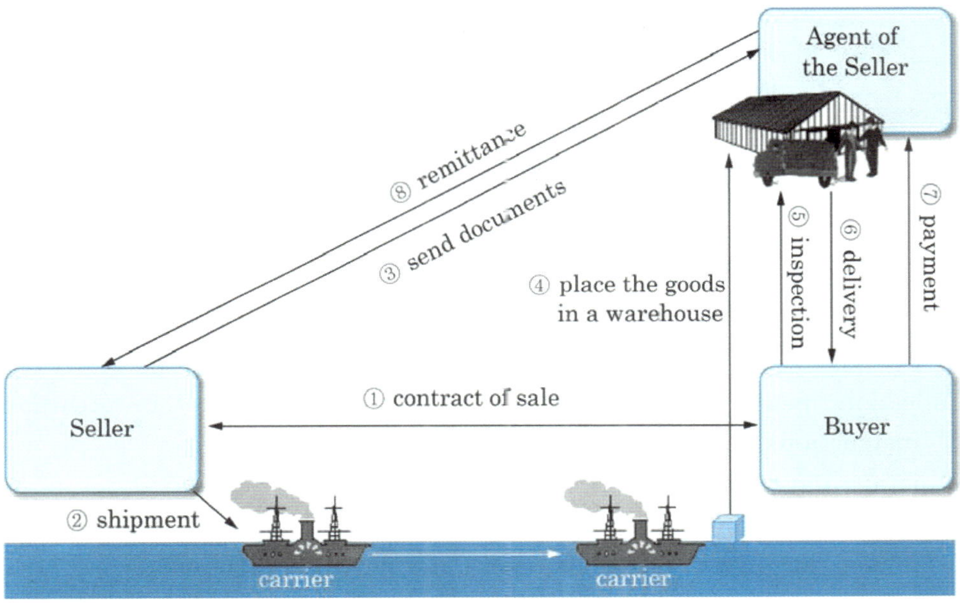

Figure 4.2 Workflow of Cash on Delivery(COD)

(3) Cash against Document(CAD)

Cash against document(CAD) means a type of transaction in which the documents of the goods are released to an agent of the buyer or a bank in seller's country after the seller gets paid. It is a payment method that the buyer must pay in cash before he gets shipping documents. The transaction involves a third party, which pays the seller on behalf of the buyer and sends the documents to the buyer.

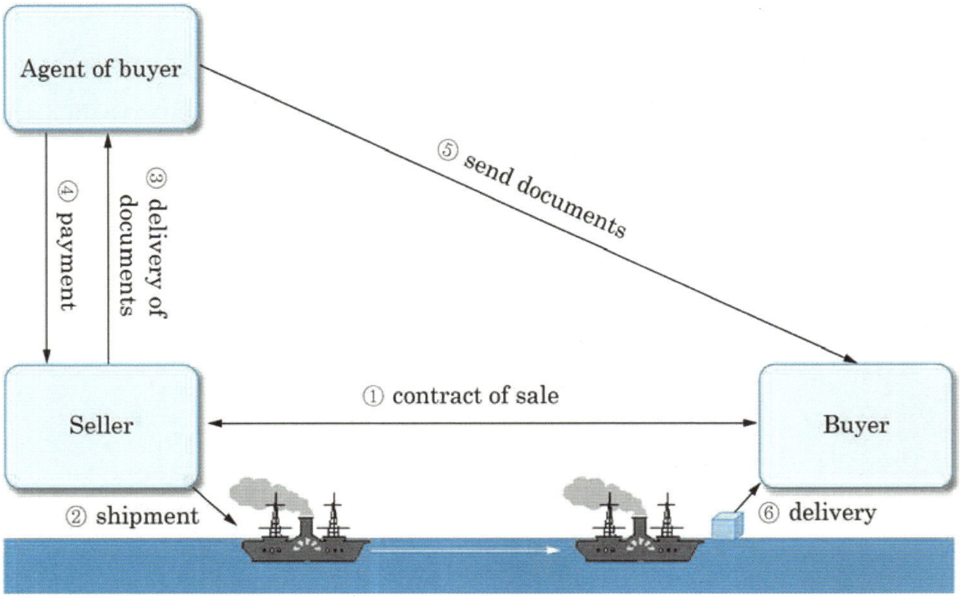

Figure 4.3 Workflow of Cash against Document(CAD)

2) Collection

Collection means the handling by banks of documents4) in accordance with instructions received in order to ;

① obtain payment and/or acceptance, or

② deliver documents against payment and/or against acceptance, or

③ deliver documents on other terms and conditions5)

Under collection, the seller takes the initiative to collect the payment from the buyer. Collection can be of either documentary collection or clean collection. Documentary collection has the relevant shipping documents attached to the draft, while in clean collection only draft is used. Documentary collection is a trade transaction in which the exporter hands over the task of collecting

---

4) "Documents" means financial documents and/or commercial documents. "Financial Documents" menas bills of exchange, promissory notes, cheques, or other similar instruments used for obtaining the payments of money. "Commercial Documents" means invoices, transport documents, documents of title or other similar documents, or any other documents whatsoever, not being financial documents(Uniform Rules for Collections, 1995, Article 2, b).

5) Uniform Rules for Collections, 1995, Article 2, a.

payment for goods supplied to his bank, which sends the shipping documents to the importer's bank together with payment instructions.

Upon the delivery of the goods, the seller draws bills of exchange on the buyer for the sum due, with or without relevant shipping documents attached, and authorizes his bank to effect the collection of the payment through a branch bank or a correspondent bank in the buyer's country.

Documentary collection is most used for payments in international trade while clean collection is occasionally used in the payment of payment balance, extra charges, or the like.

A key document in documentary collections is the bill of exchange or draft, which is a formal demand for payment from the exporter to importer. Documentary collections can be classified into two types, depending on when payment is sought by the exporter: ① Documents against Payment(D/P), which requires the importer to pay the face amount of the draft at sight, or ② Documents against Acceptance(D/A), which requires the importer to pay on a specified future date.

The collection cycle starts when the seller, having shipped the goods and obtained the necessary documents, presents the documents together with his instructions to his bank(remitting bank). The bank will send these to its branch/correspondent bank(collecting bank) in the buyer's country for payment.

The risk of the seller is much greater because the seller does not have a bank's guarantee unlike the case of a documentary credit.

The parties concerned in collection are as follows;

① Principal

The principal is the party entrusting the handling of a collection to a bank and it is the seller.

② Remitting Bank

The remitting bank is the bank to which the principal has entrusted the handling of a collection. Usually the remitting bank is a bank at the place of the seller.

③ Collecting Bank

The collecting bank is the bank authorized by the remitting bank to collect the payment from the drawee or the buyer of the goods. It is usually a bank, other than the remitting bank, involved in processing the collection.

④ **Presenting Bank**

The presenting bank is the collecting bank making presentation to the drawee. The presenting bank is the buyer's bank and it becomes the collecting bank.

⑤ **Drawee**

The drawee is the party to whom presentation is to be made according to the collection instruction. The drawee is usually the buyer of the goods who makes payment of the goods in time.

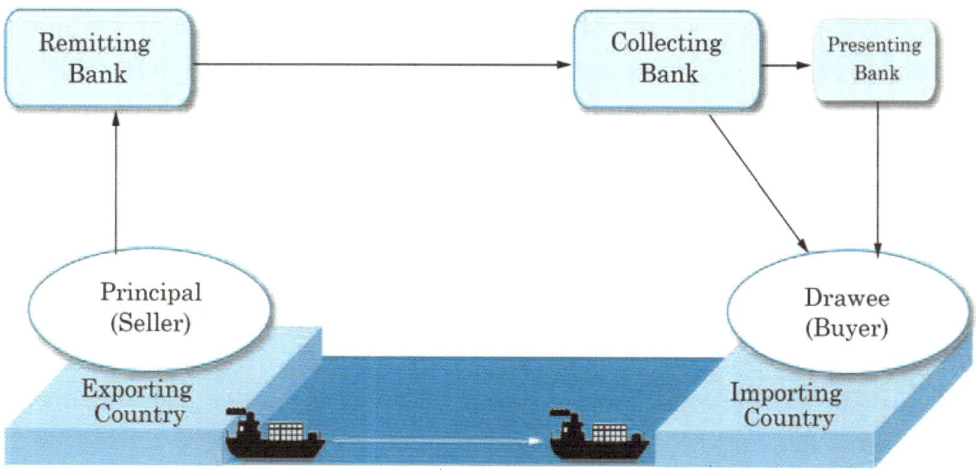

(1) Document Against Payment(D/P)

In D/P collection, the seller ships the goods and then gives the documents to his bank(remitting bank). The bank forwards these documents to the buyer's bank(collecting bank), which will only release the documents to the buyer on receipt of payment for the goods. The collecting bank then remits the funds to the exporter's bank for payment to the seller.

① **D/P at sight**

Under D/P at sight, the seller might either draw or not draw drafts on the buyer. He presents the documents together with drafts(or without drafts) to the remitting bank and the documents and the drafts will be forwarded to the collecting bank which will present the drafts to the buyer and ask him to make the payment at sight. The buyer, upon sight, should then make the payment and get the documents. When the collecting bank receives the payment from the buyer, it should immediately remit the payment received to the remitting bank and the remitting bank pays the seller.

Upon first presentation, the buyer shall pay against documentary draft drawn by the seller at sight. The documents are to be delivered against payment only.

Let's suppose the terms are as follows;

① Date of shipment at the port of shipment : May 1, 20××
② Date the documents are arrived at the collecting bank : May 10, 20××
③ Date the goods are arrived at the final destination port : May 30, 20××

① The seller and the buyer draw up D/P at sight contract
② The seller makes a shipment
③ The seller draws sight drafts on the buyer and asks the remitting bank for collection
④ The remitting bank sends the drafts and relevant documents to the collecting bank
⑤ The collecting bank notifies the buyer the arrival of the documents upon receipt of them
⑥ The buyer pays for the draft and documents
⑦ The collecting bank delivers the documents on payment
⑧ The collecting bank remits the payment received to the remitting bank
⑨ The remitting bank remits the payment to the seller
⑩ The buyer presents the shipping documents when the goods are arrived(The buyer bears the interests arising between the time he pays and the time the goods are arrived)
⑪ The carrier delivers the goods to the buyer

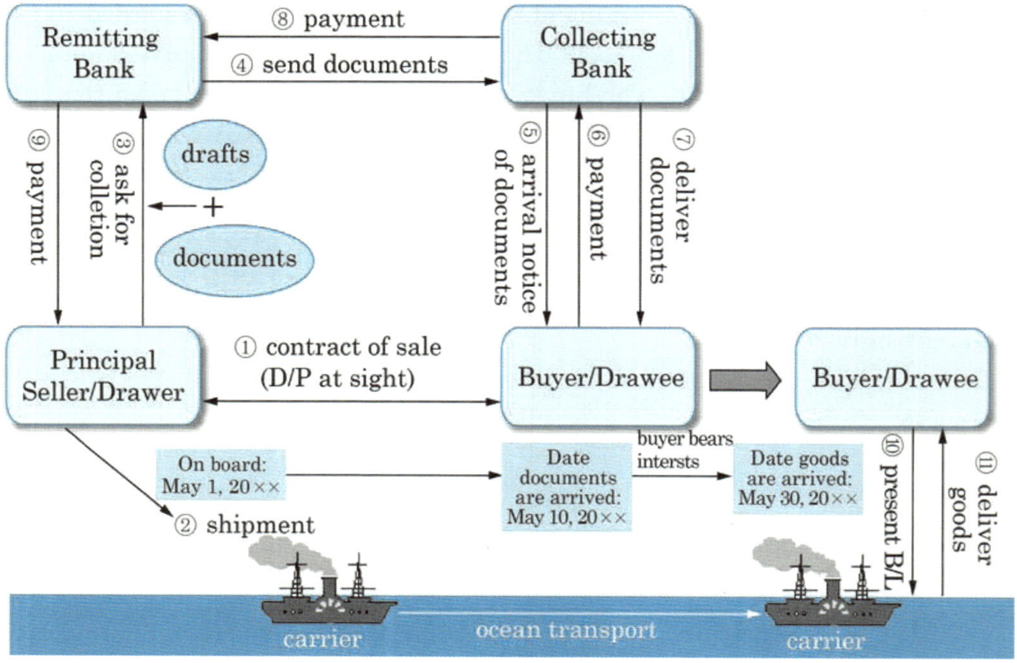

Figure 4.4 Workflow of Document Against Payment(D/P At Sight)

(2) D/P usance(at 30 days after B/L date)

D/P usance means that the collecting bank hands the documents received from the remitting bank over to the buyer after the collecting bank receives the payment from the buyer at maturity. Under D/P usance, the collecting bank receives the documents from the remitting bank and doesn't present the documents until it receives the payment from the buyer at maturity.

The collecting bank does not present the documents until the buyer has actually paid for them and the buyer is not responsible for paying the bill before its due date.

D/P usance can be used as follows;

① D/P 30 days after B/L date(shipment date)

The buyer shall pay against documentary draft, drawn by the seller at 30 days after date of B/L. The documents are delivered against payment only.

② D/P 30 days after date(of drafts)

The buyer shall pay against documentary draft drawn by the seller at 30 days after date of the draft. The documents are delivered against payment only.

③ D/P 30 days after sight

The buyer shall pay against the documentary draft drawn by the seller at 30 days after sight upon first presentation and make payment at maturity. The documents are delivered against payment only.

Let's suppose the payment term is '30 days after B/L date' and other conditions are as follows;

① Date of shipment at the port of shipment : May 1, 20××
② Date the documents are arrived at the collecting bank : May 10, 20××
③ Date the goods are arrived at the final destination port : May 30, 20××

① The seller and the buyer draw up D/P usance contract
② The seller makes a shipment
③ The seller draws usance drafts on the buyer and asks the remitting bank for collection
④ The remitting bank delivers the drafts and relevant documents to the collecting bank
⑤ The collecting bank keeps the documents and notifies the buyer the arrival of the documents on the due date(at maturity)
⑥ The buyer pays for the drafts and documents
⑦ The collecting bank delivers the documents on payment
⑧ The collecting bank remits the payment received to the remitting bank
⑨ The remitting bank remits the payment to the seller
⑩ The buyer presents the shipping documents
⑪ The carrier delivers the goods to the buyer

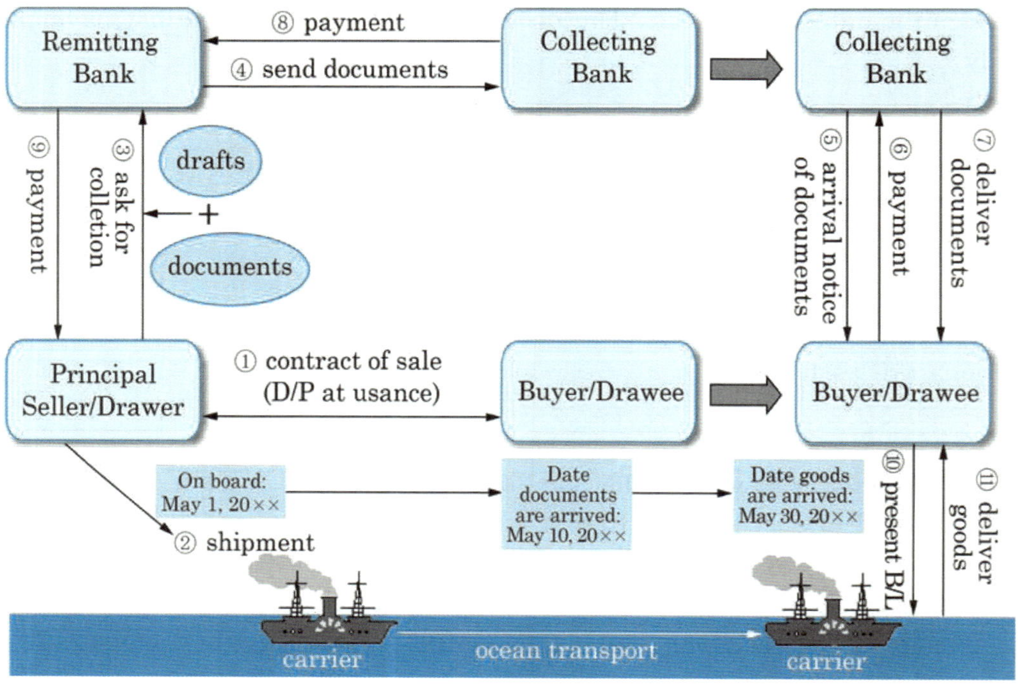

Figure 4.5 Workflow of Document Against Payment(D/P Usance)

(3) Document Against Acceptance(D/A)

D/A collection differs from D/P collection because the seller extends credit to the buyer through a time draft. Once the buyer signs the time draft which becomes a binding obligation to pay on the due date, the documents are released to the buyer. The collecting bank contacts the buyer on the due date for payment which upon receipt is remitted to the seller's bank for payment to the seller.

The seller's risk is obviously higher in the D/A collection process, since the seller has no control over the goods after the buyer's acceptance and may not get paid for them.

Document Against Acceptance is an arrangement in which the seller asks the remitting bank for collection and that bank forwards the drafts and related documents to the collectiong bank and the buyer accepts the documents guaranting that he will pay on the due date.

Under D/A, the buyer can get the documents from the collecting bank after he duly accepted the drafts. This is only applicable to time draft. This will greatly be convenient for the buyer, but it means much more risk for the seller, for once he has delivered the documents, he will lose title over the goods.

The buyer shall duly accept the documentary drafts drawn by the seller upon presentation and makes payment at ___ days after date of bill of lading(or after date of draft or after sight). The documents are to be delivered against acceptance.

Under Document Against Acceptance, the seller allows the period of credit called as usance period to the buyer. The buyer(drawee) is required to accept the draft to make a signed promise to pay the draft at a set date in the future.

① The seller and the buyer draw up D/A(30 days from B/L date) contract
② The seller makes a shipment
③ The seller draws usance drafts on the buyer and asks the remitting bank for collection
④ The remitting bank delivers the drafts and relevant documents to the collecting bank
⑤ The collecting bank presents the documents to the buyer upon receipt of them
⑥ The buyer accepts the documents after he signs them without payment
⑦ The collecting bank delivers the documents to the buyer
⑧ The buyer presents shipping documents to the carrier
⑨ The carrier hands the goods over to the buyer after receiving the shipping documents
⑩ The buyer pays the collecting bank on the due date(at maturity)
⑪ The collection bank remits the payment to the remitting bank
⑫ The remitting bank remits the payment to the seller

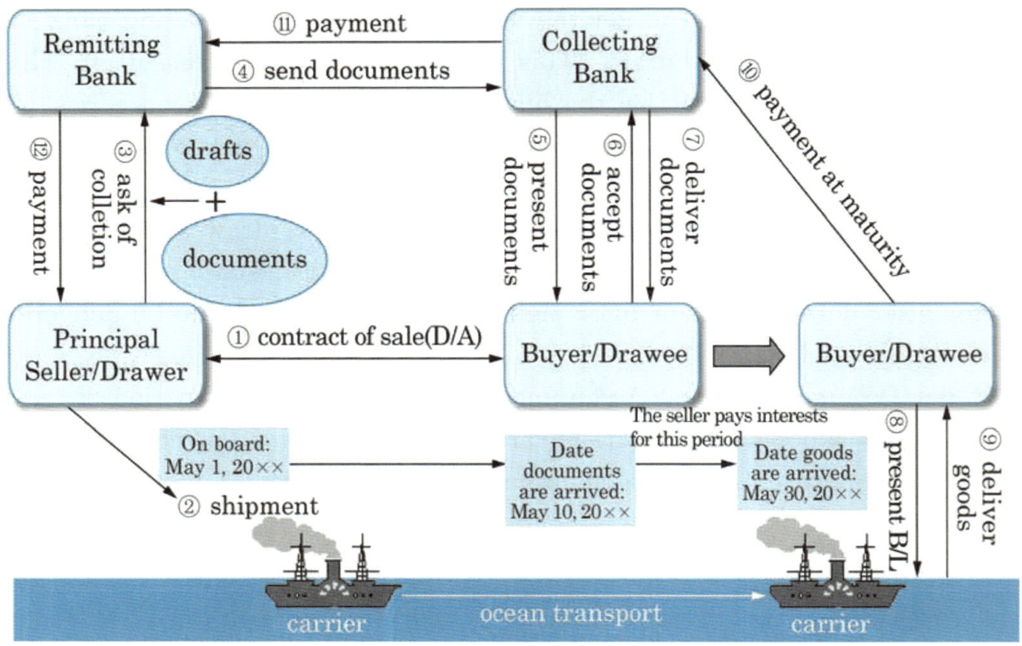

Figure 4.6 Workflow of Document Against Acceptance(D/A)

(4) Some particular remarks about collection

Undef collection such as D/P or D/A, the banks involved do not bear any risk if the payment of the goods is not made by the buyer. So, before adopting this method, the seller should be sure that the buyer is reliable and able to make the payment.

Under D/P, the buyer cannot get the documents if the buyer does not make the payment. Should this happen, the seller needs to negotiate with the buyer, and at the same time, he may consider if he can sell the goods to some others or to ship the goods back at his own expense and risk.

D/A means more risks for the seller because the buyer might refuse to pay after he has accepted the drafts and taken delivery of the goods.

To use collection, the seller needs to have a good understanding of the credit status of the buyer. It is advisable not to use collection if the importing country has a strict control over foreign exchanges. And under collection, the shipping documents should be "to order". Also, the deal should be done under CIF, so that when the goods have been damaged during transit and the buyer refuses to make the payment, the seller can claim against the insurer. Finally, the seller should stick to the contract and various export regulations so that he can produce various required documents in time to avoid possible excuses for the buyer to refuse to make payment.

Document Against Payment - D/P at sight - D/P usance	Document Against Acceptance : D/A

Under colletion, the banks involved do not bear any risk if the payment of the goods is not made by the buyer.

➡ the seller should be sure that the buyer is reliable and able to make the payment

"Payment Terms : Under D/P at sight in U.S. Dollars"
"Payment Terms : Under D/A at 60days after sight in U.S. Dollars"

2. Letter of Credit

Documentary letter of credit is defined as a letter or instrument issued by the bank(issuing bank) at the request of the buyer authorizing the seller to draw drafts on the bank or the buyer for an amount not exceeding the stipulated sum, and guaranteeing the payment and acceptance of those drafts if drawn in compliance with the terms set forth in the letter of credit.

In L/C transaction, the seller is beneficiary and the buyer is applicant. The bank that issues the L/C is referred as the issuing bank which is generally in the country of the buyer. The bank that advises the L/C to the seller is called as the advising bank which is often in the country of the seller.

Banks issue letters of credit as a way to ensure the sellers that they will get paid as long as they do what they've agreed to do. Letters of credit are common in international trade because the bank acts as an uninterested party between the seller and the buyer.

With the bank's involvement, the seller looks to the bank for payment instead of relying upon the ability or willingness of the buyer to pay, but the seller cannot obtain payment unless the documents presented are not complied with all the terms and conditions in the Letter of Credit.

Letter of Credit will be discussed in detail in Chapter 7.

3. Electronic Payment

Electronic payment systems promote international electronic trade by transferring value quickly and effectively and by imposing a minimum of additional costs or risks on the transacting parties. A payment system can be described in terms of liquidity, finality, transaction risk and systemic risk. The requisites of electronic payment systems are how to make payment electronically in manner that is economic, efficient, reliable and secure.

The payment systems such as Electronic Fund Transfers, TradeCard system and Electronic Letters of Credit issued by SWIFT system enable partly sellers, buyers and service providers to settle payment electronically. However, they have signigicant limitations for international electronic trade transactions.

For vitalization of electronic trade transactions, requisites and problems of electronic systems are acquiring information security such as authenticity, integrity, non-repudiation and confidentiality;

4. International Factoring

1) Definition

Factoring is a financial transaction in which the seller sells its accounts receivable to a third party called a factor at a discount. International factoring may be defined as the sale of assignments of short-term accounts receivable arising from an international sale of goods or services.

There are four parties involved in a transaction: the exporter(seller), the factor(export factor), the foreign factor(import factor) and the customer(debtor, buyer). Transactions are somewhat more complex than traditional domestic factoring since there are a number of parties, depending on how many countries there are in which the seller conducts business.

Arrangement is made typically with recourse, leaving the exporter ultimately liable for repaying the factor in the case of default. Some factors accept export receivables without recourse but require a large discount.

International factoring is a low value short term financing form. It involves the purchase of invoices for an amount less than US$100,000 and 90 ~120 days payment terms. After shipping the goods or services, the factor purchases the invoices and advances cash to the exporter.

The seller will sign a factoring agreement with the export factor. Under this agreement, the seller's accounts receivable are assigned to the export factor and the seller is covered against credit losses up to 100 percent of the approved credit.

2) Transaction flow of international factoring

① The seller and the buyer agree to do business on international factoring
② The seller and the export factor make an agreement on an international factoring transaction. The export factor makes an inquiry to the export factor about debtor's credit approval
③ The export factor inquires a credit approval to the import factor.
④ The import factor investigates the debtor's credit status and decides the credit amount
⑤ The import factor notifies the credit approval to the export factor
⑥ The export factor notifies the credit approval to the seller
⑦ The seller draws up a contract within the amount of credit approval
⑧ The seller makes a shipment
⑨ The seller transfers invoice and account receivable to the export factor.
⑩ The export factor purchases accounts receivable and makes payment accordingly
⑪ The export factor sends the invoice to the import factor and requests payment collection. The export factor sends the original invoice to the debtor and sends the copy of invoice to the import factor.
⑫ The import factor delivers the invoice to the debtor and requests the payment in timely manner.
⑬ The debtor pays the import factor at maturity
⑭ The import factor sends collected payment to the export factor
⑮ The export factor offsets the collected payment and purchasing payment(financed amount) and notifies the seller

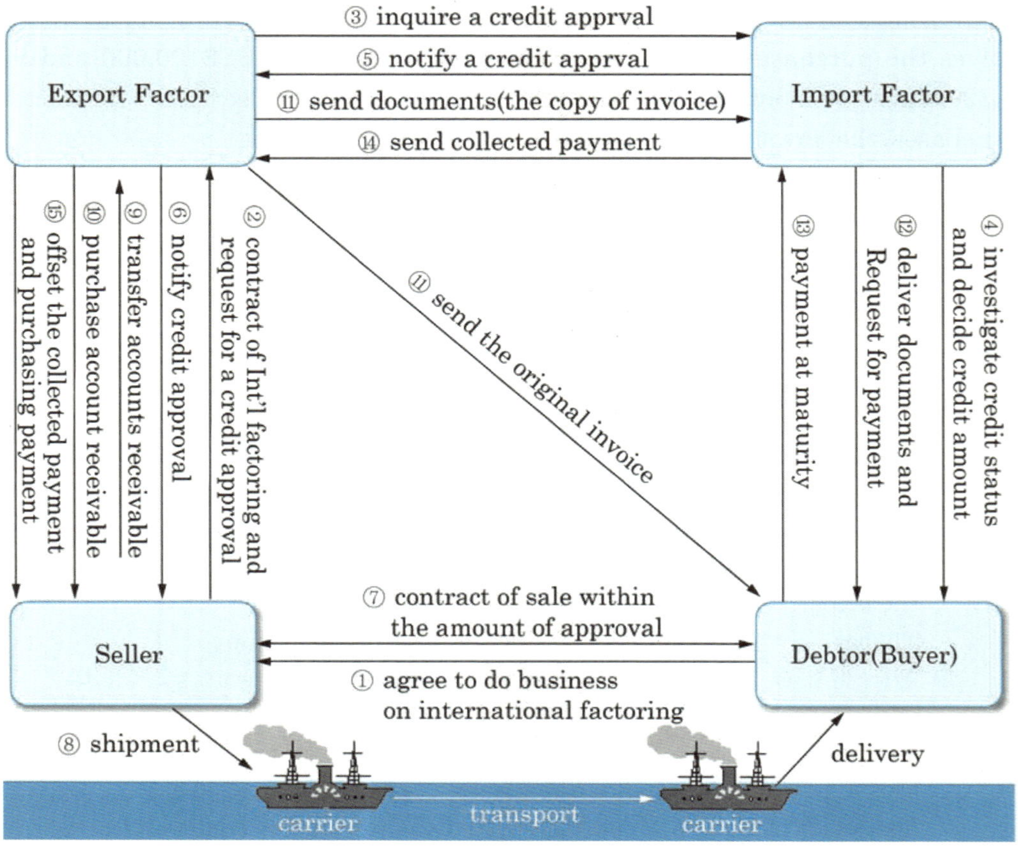

Figure 4.7 Workflow of International Factoring

3) The benefit of international factoring

(1) Benefit for the Seller

① Expanding scale of sale

The service can prevent insolvent bond even if the seller is on Open Account Credit Terms transaction with a debtor because the accounts payable is guaranteed. The service can dramatically reduce a debtor's capital burden so that the scale of sale can be expanded through the market expansion.

② Prevent insolvent bond

Unlike the current export bill, insurance policy, an anxiety of possible occurrence of payment default by the debtors can be dramatically reduced because the term is payment under guarantee for 100%. If a claim or a dispute occurs for products, the factoring companies that have a through knowledge about each country's commercial practice aggressively resolve such disputes by minimizing risks in payment delays.

③ Easy to raise operating fund

Finance assistance from the export factor is provided up to 100% within the credit approval amount of a debtor upon the purchasing of shipping documents. The seller can readily capitalize credit bonds based on the conditional sales on credit.

④ Reduce incidental expense

Doing business with export factor can reduce a credit inquiry expense because the service provides possibility for credit approval based on the latest credit information of the debtor.

⑤ Reinforce managing ability for open account term bond

Factoring companies offer sales management services such as original ledger processing, possible loan amount for open term account, accounts receivable collection status and delaying status per each month. Seller can focus on sales promotion and product manufacturing while expecting decrease in expense for accounts receivable management.

(2) Benefit for the Debtor

① Expect effect of usance import and interest margin profit

The debtor can avoid pressure with operating funds due to cash settlement because the debtor can make settlement after certain period when doing import on a deferred payment basis. Considering international margin and fund raising during differed payment period, the debtor can expect interest margin profit.

② Reduce incidental expenses

If the debtor goes through import factoring, there is no issuing service fee to issue a L/C. Security deposit for import will be reduced and absolutely no service fee in doing business with factoring is required.

When doing a factoring transaction, the seller must pay for the service fee for both the export and import factor(the same bank) deducting from payment for the purchase made.

③ **Guarantee quality of the goods imported**

If there is a problem with the goods imported or if the overseas seller breached the contract, the debtor has a right to delay the payment.

5. Forfaiting

1) Definition

Forfaiting means the purchasing of an exporter's receivables(the amount the importer owes the exporter) at a discount by paying cash. The forfaiter, the purchaser of the receivables, becomes the entity to whom the importer is obliged to pay its debt. Forfaiting is a financial transaction involving the purchase of receivables from exporters by a forfaiter without recourse. Without recourse means that if the buyer does not pay, the forfaiter can not recover the payment already made from the seller.

In ocean transport, the forfaiter provides the seller with cash at the time of shipment. In a typical fortaiting trade, the buyer pays the seller with bills of lading or promissory notes guaranteed by a leading bank in the buyer's country. The seller can sell those documents to a third party called as forfaiter at a discounted price from their face value for immediate cash. The sale is made under without recourse to the seller and the forfaiter takes all the risks and can not claim to the seller. The forfaiter takes on all the risks associated with the receivables but earns a margin. The discount rates can be different according to the buyer's creditworthiness and country, the quality of the guaranteeing bank.

Fortfaiting is a high value medium and long term financing form. It involves the purchase of negotiable instruments for more than US$100,000 and from six months to five years payment terms.

By purchasing these receivables which are usually guaranteed by the buyer's bank, the forfaiter frees the seller from credit and from the risk of not receiving payment from the buyer who purchased the goods on credit. While giving the seller a cash payment, forfaiting allows the buyer to buy goods for which it cannot immediately pay in full.

Its main characteristics are as follows;

- 100% financing without recourse to the seller
- Debt is normally evidenced by bills of exchange, promissory notes or a letter of credit
- The buyer's obligation is usually supported by a local bank's guarantee
- Documentation is very simple. The evidence of underlying transaction (copies of shipping documents) and certain confirmations from obligor/guaranteeing bank are required.
- Transactions can be concluded on a fixed or floating interest rate basis
- Exporter receives funds upon presentation of necessary documents, shortly after shipment

2) Transaction flow of Forfaiting(Usance credit)

① The seller and the buyer agree to do business on forfaiting
② The buyer instructs his bank to issue an usance credit
③ The issuing bank advises the credit to its corresponding bank(advising bank)
④ The advising bank advises the credit to the seller
⑤ The seller makes a shipment
⑥ The seller makes a forfaiting contract with forfaiter, his bank[the seller asks the forfaiter for a commitment to purchase the debt obligations(bills of exchange, promissory notes etc.) created under the export transaction. The forfaiter issues a commitment and it binds on both parties]
⑦ The seller presents drafts and documents related to the forfaiter
⑧ The forfaiter sends those documents to the issuing bank
⑨ The issuing bank informs the forfaiter of the acceptance of the drafts and documents.
⑩ The forfaiter pays the seller without recourse
⑪ The issuing bank presents the drafts and documents to the buyer
⑫ The buyer pays the issuing bank at maturity
⑬ The issuing bank remits collected payment to the forfaiter

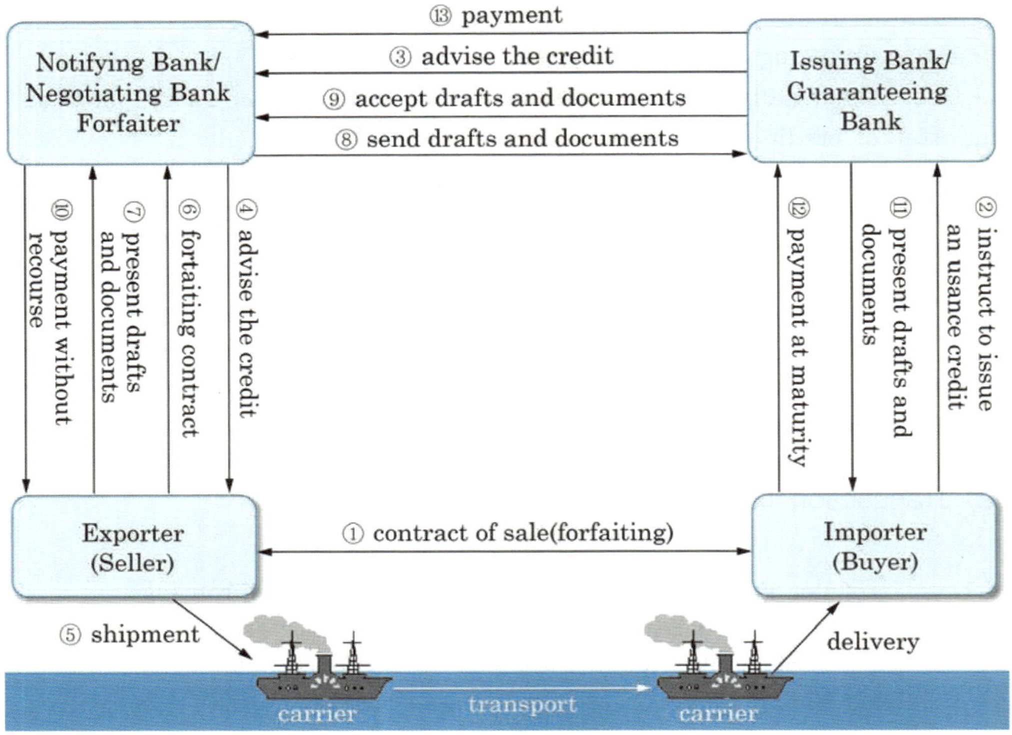

Figure 4.8 Workflow of Forfaiting

3) The benefit of forfaiting

(1) Eliminates Risks

- Removes political, transfer and commercial risk
- Provides financing for 100% of contract value
- Protects against risks of interest rate increase and exchange rate fluctuation

(2) Enhances Competitive Advantage

- Enables sellers of goods to offer credit to their customers, making their products more attractive
- Helps sellers do business in countries where the risk of non-payment would otherwise be too high

(3) Improves Cash Flow

- Forfaiting enables sellers to receive cash payment while offering credit terms to their customers
- Removes accounts receivable, bank loans or contingent liabilities from the balance sheet

(4) Increases Speed and Simplicity of Transactions

- Fast, tailor-made financing solutions
- Financing commitments can be issued quickly
- Documentation is typically concise and straightforward
- No restrictions on origin of export
- Relieves seller of administration and collection burden

6. Means of payment

1) Payment by Cash

Under this arrangement, the seller is paid by cash such as Cash In Advance(CIA), Cash With Order(CWO), Cash On Delivery(COD), Cash Against Document(CAD) and remittance

2) Payment by bill of exchange(draft)

A bill of exchange(bill or draft) is defined as an unconditional order in writing signed by a drawer and addressed to a drawee, typically a bank, ordering the drawee to pay stated sum of money to a payee, often a seller, on demand or at a fixed or determinable future time. The drawer uses a draft to instruct the drawee to pay a certain amount to a named person.

Two types of drafts are used. One is documentary bill and the other is clean bill. Documentary bill is the bill of exchange which the shipping documents such as bills of lading, insurance policy, invoice and necessary documents are attached. These documents become collateral securities when the seller negotiates the bill through the negotiating bank, then the bank becomes their lawful holder and acquires title to the goods they present.

Drafts are used in Letter of Credit(L/C) and collection such as Document against Payment(D/P) and Document against Acceptance(D/A).

7. Time of payment

1) Advance Payment

Advance payment(payment in advance) is a payment method in which the buyer pays for the goods before they are dispatched. It is used where the buyer is of unknown creditworthiness and it is unable to obtain a letter of credit.

Advance payment is that the seller is paid when the buyer places his order or when the goods are ready for shipment to the buyer. Examples of payment in advance are Cash in Advance(CIA), Cash with Order(CWO), Remittance in Advance and Red Clause L/C.

Table 4-6 Advance Payment

division	content
Cash in Advance	A buyer pays a seller in cash before a shipment is made
Cash with Order	Payment has to be made in cash when the order is placed.
Remittance in Advance	A buyer remits a seller by Telegraphic Transfer(T/T), Mail Transfer(M/T) or Demand Draft(D/D)
Red Clause L/C	It allows a beneficiary to receive funds for the purchase of the goods in advance

2) Concurrent Payment

Concurrent payment is that payment is made at the same time when the goods are delivered or when the documents related are delivered. Cash on Delivery(COD), Cash against Document(CAD) and Letter of Credit at sight(L/C at sight) belong to this method.

Table 4-7 Concurrent Payment

division	content
Cash on Delivery	A transaction in which payment for the goods is made at the time of delivery.
Cash Against Document	A transaction in which the title for the purchased goods is released to the buyer after payment is made
L/C at sight	A letter of credit that is paid upon presentation
D/P at sight	A collection method which requires the buyer to pay the face amount of the draft at sight
D/P Usance	A collection method that the collecting bank receives the documents from the remitting bank and doesn't present the documents until it receives the payment from the buyer at maturity.

3) Deferred Payment

Deferred payment is the opposite of payment in advance. The seller arranges with the buyer to allow him a credit for a certain period after the goods or relevant documents are delivered to him. The buyer does not make payment until the period of the credit is due. Usance L/C, Document against Acceptance(D/A) and Open Account(O/A) belong to deferred payment.

Table 4-8 Deferred Payment

division	content
Usance L/C	A letter of credit payable at a determined future date after presentation of conforming documents
Document against Acceptance(D/A)	A collection method which requires the buyer to pay on a specified future date
Open Account	Credit relationship in which the buyer pays upon the receipt of goods, or on deferred payment basis

Table 4-9 Method of payment and time of payment

Method of Payment		Time of payment		
		Advance Payment	Concurrent Payment	Deferred Payment
Payment by Cash		Cash in Advance(CIA) Cash with Order(CWO)	COD CAD	
Drafts	Letter of Credit	Red Clause L/C	L/C at sight	Usance L/C
	Collection		D/P at sight	D/A D/P usance
Remittance	T/T M/T D/D	Advance Payment	COD CAD	Deferred Payment
Electronic Payment		electronic check, TradeCard, electronic fund transfer, electronic L/C, electronic money, credit card etc.		
Others		International Factoring, Forfaiting, etc.		

4.6 Terms of Packaging

Packing normally refers to the process of packaging and labeling. Packaging is the science, art, and technology of enclosing or protecting goods for distribution, storage, sale, and use. Packaging also refers to the process of design, evaluation, and production of packages. Packaging can be described as a coordinated system of preparing goods for transport, warehousing, logistics, sale and end use.

1. Method of Packaging

1) Individual(item or unit) packaging

Individual packaging means a packaging of individual item with proper materials or containers to increase the value of goods or protect goods.

2) Inner packaging

Inner packaging means a packaging for which an outer packaging is required for transport. It does not include the inner receptacle which requires an outer packaging in order to perform its containment function.

3) Outer Packaging

Outer packaging means the outermost enclosure of a composite or combination packaging together with any absorbent materials, cushioning and any other components necessary to contain and protect inner receptacles or inner packagings.

2. Types of packaging

The followings are types of outer packaging used in international trade.

Table 4-10 Types of export packaging

type	packaging materials		goods
box, case, carton	• wooden case, box • carton • tin-lined case • crate skeleton case	W/B CTN C/S CRT	food, general merchandise canned food automobiles
bale	• hassian cloth, burlap • pressed bale • straw-mat	- - -	cotton yarn, wool raw cotton rice
bag	• gunny bag • sack • paper bag • polyethylene bag	BG SK BT BG	grain, minor cereals wheat cement, lime salt, feeds, powered drug
container	• barrel • cask • keg	BRL CSK KG	alcoholic drink, soy sauce dyestuff nail, bolt
special container	• drum • tin, can • jar, pot, carboy • basket, hamper • cylinder, iron flask	DR - - BKT -	chemical oil, canned food beverage fruit carbon
packaging without container	• roll, coil • bundle • ingot	RL, CL BDL -	iron plate, newspaper, wire steel bar steel, aluminum

1) Bale

A bale is a heap of material pressed together and tied with rope or metal wire. It is most suitable for paper, wool, cotton and carpet, etc. Bale is an effective, low-cost and easy to handle mode of packing, but it only offers limited protection to cargoes.

2) Bags

Bags can be made of cotton, plastic, paper or jute(fibre from the outer skin of certain plants). They are ideal for cement, fertilizer, flour, chemicals and many consumer products. Their advantage is low cost and the disadvantage is their vulnerability to damage by water, sweat, leakage and breakage.

3) Barrel or Drum

This type of container is made of wood, plastic or metal. It is used for liquid or greasy cargoes such as casing for sausage. The advantage is the resale value in some countries and the disadvantage is that a metal drum can get rusty and resulted in leakage if the container is not sealed properly.

4) Box or Case

A case is made of wood and varies in size. Some cases are lined to create airtight packaging. It is an expensive form of packing and has a certain resale value in some countries. This type of packing gives complete protection and lessens risk of pilferage plus an aid to handling. This form of packing is particularly prominent with surface transport and is used for much machinery and other items of expensive equipment. However, it is becoming less popular as the cost of timber has risen sharply in recent years and containerization has lessened the need for such elaborate robust packing in certain trades.

5) Glass Container

This type of packaging is often used for dangerous liquid cargoes such as acids. It protects workers and transport vehicles but requires more careful handling.

6) Carton

Cartons are a very common form of packaging with the development of containerization and palletization, particularly for consumer products. This form of packing is very much on the increase as it is relatively inexpensive, expandable, and aids marketing, handling and stowage. The disadvantage is their susceptibility to crushing and pilferage.

7) Create or Skeleton Case

This form of packaging is halfway between a bale and a case and has a wooden structure, It is often used for lightweight goods of large cubic capacity such as machinery and domestic appliances.

8) Palletization

Palletization is closely associated with packing. The pallet may be of steel or wooden construction. A typical size is 1,000 × 1,200mm, which has a capacity of two tons and, in appearance, is like a platform on which the cargo is placed. An aperture is provided at each side to enable the fork lift truck to mobilize or handle the pallet. Wooden pallets by which the cargo is anchored are very common in air freight, thereby facilitating cargo handling on a utilized basis. The pallet accompanies the cargo throughout the transit.

3. Shipping mark

A shipping mark is an identifying word, number, or symbol placed on cargo to designate the consignee, destination, weight, and related information. A shipping mark can be used to identify what the goods are or where they are being shipped from or to. A shipping mark consists of the name of the consignee or shipper, destination and packaging number, etc.

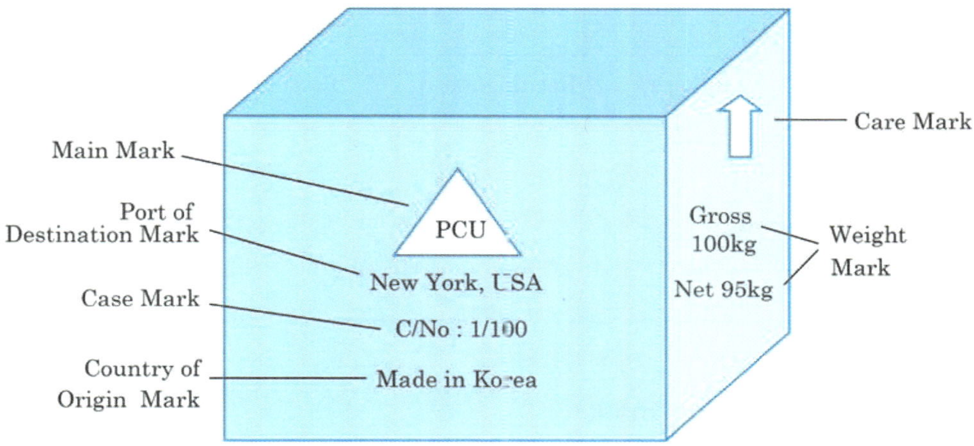

When an order is received from abroad, the seller gets the goods ready for shipment. It is most important for him to see that they are suitably packed. Associated with packaging is the marking of the goods. The outer packaging must be marked clearly with the identifying symbols and numbers in accordance with the instructions of the customer in order to enable the customs authorities, the steamship clerks and the customer to identify the packages an route or at the port of destination. Basically, the mark(or symbol) is vital in the correct identification of the shipment. In marketing and numbering packages, it is essential that the mark(or symbol) and numbers conform in every respects to those written in the commercial invoice, the consular invoice, the bill of lading and the other shipping documents used. Packages should not be marked with crayons, tags or cards. The best method of marking is to stencil the marks in the outside of the package. Marks should be permanent and easily read at a glance.

1) Main mark

Main mark is usually consisted of a particular shape such as a diamond shape and the company's or consignee's name is included as well. Usually, symbols with a simple identity with code or initials are often used instead of writing out the full name of the shipper or consignee.

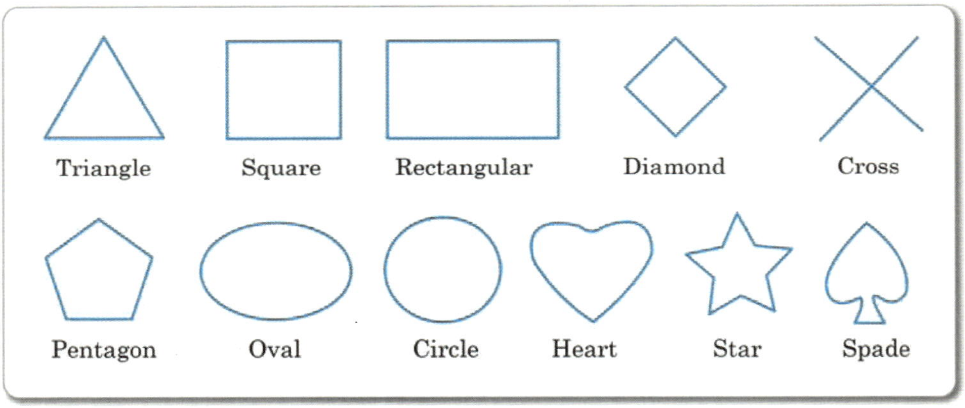

2) Port of destination mark

Port of destination mark is a mark showing the final destination of a shipping package.

3) Case number mark

Case number mark is a mark numbered consecutively in outer boxes to distinguish the numbers from other documents such as commercial invoice and other transport documents.

4) Country of origin mark

Country of origin mark is a mark showing the country the goods are produced.

5) Warning Mark(Care Mark)

To facilitate handling or to warn the dockers and crews against dangerous cargo or to overcome different language problems, recognized marking terms are used.

4.7 Terms of Insurance

Marine insurance is defined as a contract of insurance whereby the insurance company in return for premiums collected undertakes to indemnify the insured in a manner and to the extent thereby agreed against marine losses, that is to say, the losses incidental to marine adventure. Indemnity implies that the purpose of an insurance contract is to enable a party to cover the loss that it has suffered.

1. Scope of Insurance Coverage

There are mainly two types of insurance coverage, basic coverage and additional coverage. Basic coverage includes ICC(A), ICC(B) and ICC(C). Additional coverage includes general additional coverage.

1) Basic Coverage

(1) ICC(A)

ICC(A) is the most comprehensive coverage under which the insurer is responsible for all total or partial loss of or damage to the goods insured either arising from sea perils or general external causes. However, it does not cover loss, damage or expense caused by delay, inherent vice or nature of goods insured, or special external risks of war, strike, etc.

(2) ICC(B)

ICC(B) is a wider cover than ICC(C). It provides extensive cover against all loss or damage due to marine perils throughout the duration of the policy, including partial loss or damage which may be attributed to natural calamities like heavy weather.

(3) ICC(C)

ICC(C) is a limited form of cargo insurance cover under which no partial loss or damage is recoverable. It only provides coverage for total losses and general average emerging from the actual 'marine perils' like vessel being stranded, grounded or sunk.

2) Additional Coverage

General additional risks include TPND(Theft, Pilferage and Non-delivery), Fresh Water Rain Damage, Risk of Shortage, Risk of Intermixture and Contamination, Risk of Leakage, Risk of Clash and Breakage, Risk of Odor, Damage caused by Heating and Sweating, Hook Damage, Risk of Rust, etc. These additional risks cannot be covered independently and should go with ICC(A), ICC(B) and ICC(C).

2. Obligation of Marine Insurance

Obligation of marine insurance can be applied to Incoterms® 2020. Under the CIP rule, the seller is required to obtain extensive insurance cover complying with Institute Cargo Clauses(A). Under the CIF rule., however, the seller is required to obtain limited insurance cover complying with Institute Cargo Clauses(C).

For other rules of Incoterms® 2020, one party has no obligation to the other party. In case of EXW, FAS, FOB, CFR, CPT, DAP, DPU and DDP rules, the seller can obtain cargo insurance for himself until the risks are transferred to the buyer(until the goods are delivered to the buyer) and the buyer can obtain cargo insurance for himself after the risks are transferred to the buyer(after the goods are delivered to the buyer). The seller must provide the buyer, at the buyer's request, risk and expense(if any), with information that the buyer needs for obtaining insurance.

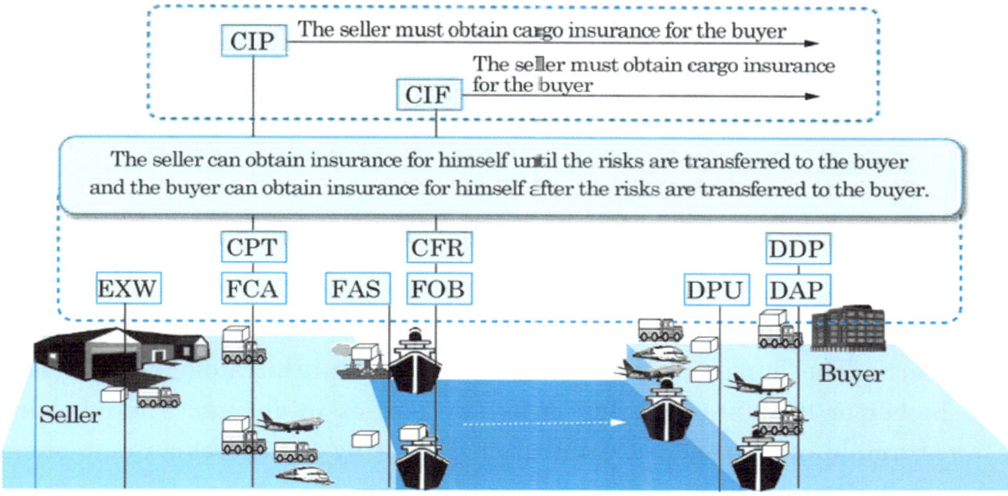

4.8 Terms of Dispute Settlement

1. Force Majeure

Force Majeure literally means 'greater force'. Force Majeure clause excuses the seller or the buyer not to meet the contract obligations if the failure is caused by conditions beyond seller's or the buyer's control.

The party experiencing the difficulty to meet the obligations under the present contract due to the causes beyond its control shall give the other party a prompt written notice, with full details following the occurrence of the cause relied upon. Dates by which performance obligations are scheduled to be met will be extended for a period of time equal to the time lost due to any delay so caused.

The force majeure clause should be provided in the contract in an explicit manner. The following is an example of the clause.

> "The seller shall not be liable for failure to perform its part of this contract when such failure is due to force majeure including, fire, flood, strikes, labor troubles or other industrial disturbances, in-

evitable accidents, war(declared or undeclared), embargoes, blockades, legal restrictions, riots, insurrections, or any causes beyond the control of the seller."

2. Arbitration

Arbitration is the resolution of dispute between two parties through a voluntary or contractually required hearing and determination by an impartial third party. The impartial third party is called the arbitrator and is chosen by a higher or disinterested body or by two parties in dispute. The following is an example of a standard arbitration clause by the Korean Commercial Arbitration Board.

"All disputes, controversies, or differences which may arise between the parties, out of or in relation to or in connection with this contract, or for the breach thereof, shall be finally settled by arbitration in Seoul, Korea in accordance with the Commercial Arbitration Rules of the Korean Commercial Arbitration Board and under the Laws of Korea. The award rendered by the arbitrator(s) shall be final and binding upon both parties concerned."

The ICC International Court of Arbitration recommends that all parties wishing to have recourse to ICC arbitration include the following standard clause in their contracts:

"All disputes arising out of or in connection with the present contract shall be finally settled under the Rules of Arbitration of the International Chamber of Commerce by one or more arbitrators appointed in accordance with the said Rules in the International Court of Arbitration in Paris."

When dealing with non-English speaking buyers, it is appropriate to specify the language of the arbitration in the arbitration clause.

Chapter **5**

Incoterms® 2020

Chapter

5

Incoterms® 2020

5.1 Introduction to Incoterms® 2020

1. What the Incoterms® rules do

The Incoterms rules explain a set of eleven of the most commonly-used three-letter trade terms, e.g. CIF, DAP, etc., reflecting business-to-business practice in contracts for the sale and purchase of goods.

The Incoterms rules describe

- ▶ Obligations: Who does what as between seller and buyer, e.g. who organises carriage or insurance of the goods of who obtains shipping documents and export or import licences;
- ▶ Risk: Where and when the seller 'delivers" the goods, in other words where risk transfers from seller to buyer; and
- ▶ Costs: Which party is responsible for which costs, for example transport, packaging, loading or unloading costs, and checking of security-related costs.

The Incoterms rules cover these areas in a set of ten articles, numbered A1/B1 etc., the A articles representing the seller's obligations and the B articles representing the buyer's obligations.

2. What the Incoterms® rules not to do

The Incoterms® rules are NOT in themselves-and are therefore no substitute for-a contract of sale. They are devised to reflect trade practice for no particular type of goods-and for any. They can be used as much for the trading of a bulk cargo of iron ore as for five containers of electronic equipment of ten pallets of airfreighted fresh flowers.

The Incoterms rules do NOT deal with the following matters:

- whether there is a contract of sale at all;
- the specifications of the goods sold;
- the time, place, method of currency of payment of the price;
- the remedies which can be sought for breach of the contract of sale;
- most consequences of delay and other breaches in the performance of contractual obligations;
- the effect of sanctions;
- the imposition of tariffs;
- export or import prohibitions;
- force majeure or hardship;
- intellectual property rights; or
- the method, venue, or law of dispute resolution in case of such breach.

Perhaps most importantly, it must be stressed that the Incoterms® rule do NOT deal with the transfer of property/title/ownership of the goods sold.

These are matters for which the parties need to make specific provision in their contract of sale. Failure to do so is likely to cause problems later if disputes arise about performance and breach. In essence, the Incoterms® 2020 rules are not themselves a contract of sale: they only become part of that contract when they are incorporated into a contract which already exists. Neither do the Incoterms® rules provide the law applicable to the contract. there may be legal regimes which apply to the contract, whether international, like the Convention on the International Sale of Goods (CISG); of domestic mandatory law relating, for example, to health and safety or the environment.

3. Classification of the 11 Incoterms® 2020 rules

RULES FOR ANY MODE OR MODES OF TRANSPORT

EXW	EX WORKS
FCA	FREE CARRIER
CPT	CARRIAGE PAID TO
CIP	CARRIAGE AND INSURANCE PAID TO
DAP	DELIVERED AT PLACE
DPU	DELIVERED AT PLACE UNLOADED
DDP	DELIVERED DUTY PAID

RULES FOR SEA AND INLAND WATERWAY TRANSPORT

FAS	FREE ALONGSIDE SHIP
FOB	FREE ON BOARD
CFR	COST AND FREIGHT
CIF	COST INSURANCE AND FREIGHT

4. Order within the Incoterms® 2020 rules

All the ten A/B articles in each of the Incoterms® rules are important-but some are more important than others.

There has, indeed, been a radical shake-up in the internal order in which the ten articles within each Incoterms® rule have been organised. In Incoterms® 2020, the internal order within each Incoterms® rule now follows this sequence:

A1/B1 General obligations
A2/B2 Delivery/Taking delivery
A3/B3 Transfer of risks
A4/B4 Carriage
A5/B5 Insurance
A6/B6 Delivery/transport document
A7/B7 Export/import clearance
A8/B8 Checking/packaging/marking
A9/B9 Allocation of costs
A10/B10 Notices

A : The Seller's Obligations	B : The Buyer's Obligations
A1. General Obligations	B1. General Obligations
A2. Delivery	B2. Taking delivery
A3. Transfer of risks	B3. Transfer of risks
A4. Carriage	B4. Carriage
A5. Insurance	B5. Insurance
A6. Delivery/transport document	B6. Proof of delivery
A7. Export/import clearance	B7. Export/import clearance
A8. Checking/packing/marking	B8. Checking/packing/marking
A9. Allocation of costs	B9. Allocation of costs
A10. Notices	B10. Notices

It will be noticed that concerning the Incoterms® 2020 rules, after recording in A1/B1 the basic goods/payment obligations of the parties, Delivery and the Transfer of risks are moved to a more prominent location, namely to A2 and A3 respectively.

The broad sequence thereafter goes:

- ancillary contracts (A4/B4 and A5/B5, carriage and insurance):
- transport documents (A6/B6):
- export/import clearance (A7/B7):
- packaging (A8/B8):
- costs (A9/B9); and
- notices (A10/B10).

5.2 Contents of Incoterms® 2020

1. Rules for any mode or modes of transport

1) EXW(Ex Works)

EXW(insert named place of delivery) Incoterms® 2020

1. Delivery and risk -"Ex works' means that the seller delivers the goods to the buyer

- when it places the goods at the disposal of the buyer at a named place (like a factory or warehouse), and
- that named place may or may not be the seller's premises.

For delivery to occur, the seller does not need to load the goods on any collecting vehicle, nor does it need to clear the goods for export, where such clearance is applicable.

2. Mode of transport - This rule may be used irrespective of the mode or modes of transport, if any, selected.

3. place or precise point of delivery - The parties need only name the place of delivery. However, the parties are well advised also to specify as clearly as possible the precise point within the named place of delivery. A named precise point of delivery makes it clear to both parties when the goods are delivered and when risk transfers to the buyer; such precision also marks the point at which costs are for the buyer's account. If the parties do not name the point of delivery, then they are taken to have left it to have left it to the seller to select the point "that best suits its purpose". This means that the buyer may incur the risk that the seller may choose a point just before the point at which goods are lost or damaged. Best for the buyer therefore to select the precise point within a place where delivery will occur.

4. A note of caution to buyers - EXW is the incoterms® rule which imposes the least set of obligations on the seller. From the buyer's perspective, therefore, the rule should be used with care for different reasons as set out below.

5. Loading risk - Delivery happens-and risk transfers - when the goods are placed, not loaded, at the buyer's disposal. However, risk of loss of or damage to the goods occurring while the loading operation is carried out by the seller, as it may well be, might arguably lie with the buyer, who has not physically participated in the loading. Given this possibility, it would be advisable, where the seller is to load the goods, for the parties to agree in advance who is to bear the risk of any loss of or damage to the goods during loading. This is a common situation simply because the seller is more likely to have the necessary loading equipment at its own premises or because applicable safety or security rules prevent access to the seller's premises by unauthorised personnel. Where the buyer is keen to avoid any risk during loading at the seller's premises, then the buyer ought to consider choosing the FCA rule (under which, if the goods are delivered at the seller's premises, the seller owes the buyer an obligation to load, with the risk of loss of or damage to the goods during that operation remaining with the seller).

6. Export clearance - With delivery happening when the goods are at the buyer's disposal either at the seller's premises or at another named point typically within the seller's jurisdiction or within the same Customs Union, there is no obligation on the seller to organise export clearance or clearance within third countries through which the goods pass in transit. Indeed, EXW may be suitable for domestic trades, where there is no intention at all to export the goods. The seller's participation in export clearance is limited to providing assistance in obtaining such documents and information as the buyer may require for the purpose of exporting the goods. Where the buyer intends to export the goods and where it anticipates difficulty in obtaining export clearance, the buyer would be better advised to choose the FCA rule, under which the obligation and cost of obtaining export clearance lies with the seller.

"Ex Works" means that the seller delivers the goods to the buyer by placing them at the disposal of the buyer at the agreed point, if any, at the named place of delivery. The seller does not need to load the goods on any collecting vehicle, nor does it need to clear the goods for export, where such clearance is applicable.

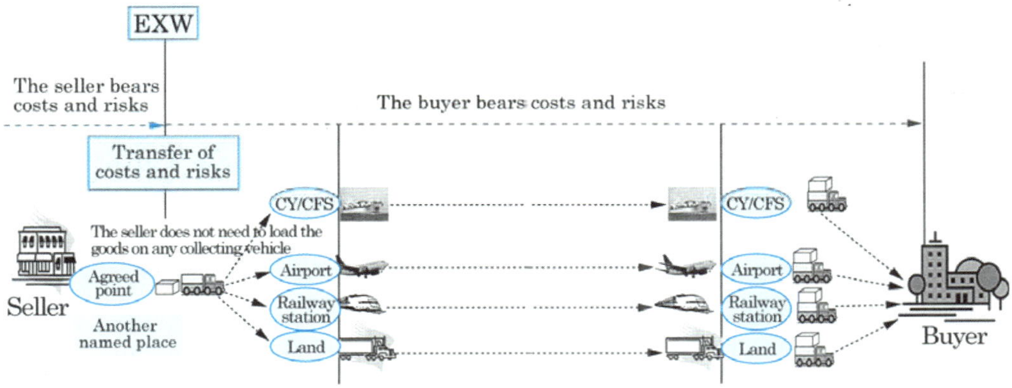

- The buyer has to clear the goods for export and import
- The seller has no obligation to the buyer to load the goods on any collecting vehicle nominated by the buyer
- Where the seller is in a better position to load the goods, FCA is usually more appropriate
- The seller delivers when it places the goods at the agreed point, if any at the named place of delivery
- US$10.00/pc EXW Abc Factory, 155-40 Baejae-ro, Seo-gu, Daejeon, Korea, Incoterms® 2020.

2) FCA(Free Carrier)

FCA(insert named place of delivery) Incoterms® 2020

1. Delivery and risk - "Free Carrier(named place)" means that the seller delivers the goods to the buyer in one or other of two ways.

▶ Frist, when the named place is the seller's premises, the goods are delivered.

  ▸ when they are loaded on the means of transport arranged by the buyer.

▶ Second, when the named place is another place, the goods are delivered

  ▸ when, having been loaded on the seller's means of transport,
  ▸ they reach the named other place and
  ▸ are ready for unloading from that seller's means of transport and

- at the disposal of the carrier or of another person nominated by the buyer

Whichever of the two is chosen as the place of delivery, that place identifies where risk transfers to the buyer and the time from which costs are for the buyer's account.

2. Mode of transport - This rule may be used irrespective of the mode of transport selected and may also be used where more than one mode of transport is employed.

3. Place or point of delivery-A sale under FCA can be concluded naming only the place of delivery, either at the seller's premises or elsewhere, without specifying the precise point of delivery within that named place. However, the parties are well advised also to specify as clearly as possible the precise point within the named place of delivery. A named precise point of delivery makes it clear to both parties when the goods are delivered and when risk transfers to the buyer; such precision also marks the point at which costs are for the buyer's account. Where the precise point is not identified, however, this may cause problems for the buyer. The seller in this case has the right to select the point "that best suits its purpose": that point becomes the point of delivery, from which risk and costs transfer to the buyer. If the precise point of delivery is not identified by naming it in the contract, then parties are taken to have left it to the seller to select the point "that best suits its purpose". This means that the buyer may incur the risk that the seller may choose a point just before the point at which goods are lost or damaged. Best for the buyer therefore to select the precise point within a place where delivery will occur.

4. 'or procure goods so delivered' - The reference to "procure" here caters for multiple sales down a chain (string sales), particularly, although not exclusively, common in the commodity trades.

5. Export/import clearance - FCA requires the seller to clear the goods for export, where applicable, However, the seller has no obligation to clear the goods for import or for transit through third countries, to pay any import duty or to carry out any import customs formalities.

6. Bills of lading with an on-board notation in FCA sales - We have already seen that FCA is intended for use irrespective of the mode or modes of transport used. Now if goods are being picked up by the buyer's road-haulier in Las Vegas, it would be rather uncommon to expect a bill of lading with an on-board notation to be issued by the carrier from Las Vegas, which is not a port and which a vessel cannot reach for goods to be placed on board. Nonetheless, sellers selling FCA Las Vegas do sometimes find themselves in a situation where they need a bill of lading with an on-board notation(typically because of a bank collection or a letter of credit requirement), albeit necessarily stating that the goods have been placed on board in Los Angeles as well as stating that they were received for carriage in Las Vegas. To cater for this possibility of an FCA seller needing a bill of lading with an on-board notation, FCA incoterms 2020® has, for the first time, provided the following optional mechanism. If the parties have so agreed in the contract, the buyer must instruct its carrier to issue a bill of lading with an on- board notation to the seller. The carrier may or may not, of course, accede to the buyer's request, given that the carrier is only bound and entitled to issue such a bill of lading once the goods are on board in Los Angeles. However, if and when the bill of lading is issued to the seller by the carrier at the buyer's cost and risk, the seller must provide that same document to the buyer, who will need the bill of leading in order to obtain discharge of the goods from the carrier. This optional mechanism becomes unnecessary, of course, if the parties have agreed that the seller will present to the buyer a bill of lading stating simply that the goods have been received for shipment rather than that have been shipped on board. Moreover, it should be emphasised that even where this optional mechanism is adopted, the seller is under no obligation to the buyer as to the terms of the contract of carriage. Finally, when this optional mechanism is adopted, the dates of delivery inland and loading on board will necessarily be different, which may well create difficulties for the seller under a letter of credit.

"Free Carrier" means that the seller delivers the goods to the carrier or another person nominated by the buyer at the named point, if any, at the named place, or procure goods so delivered. If the named place is the seller's premises, delivery is completed when the goods have been loaded on the means of transport porvided by the buyer and in any other case, delivery is completed when the goods are placed at the disposal of the carrier or another person nominated by the buyer on the seller's maens of transport ready for unloading.

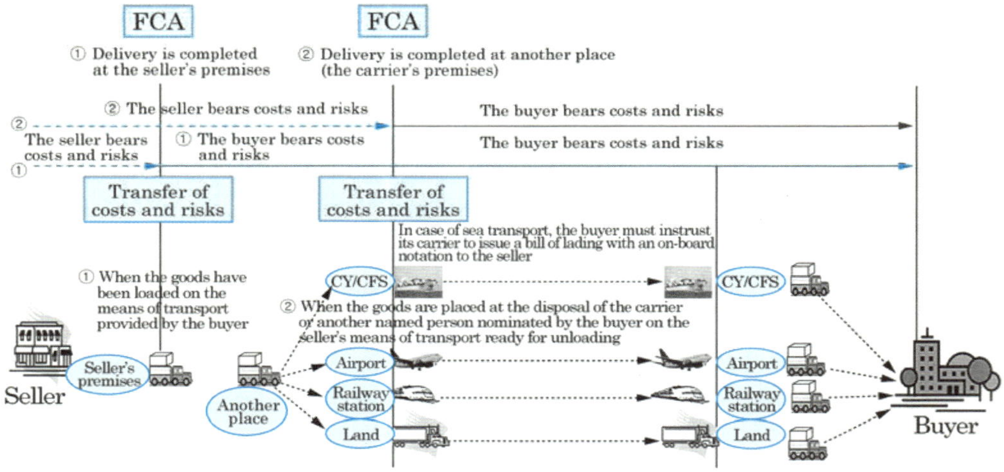

- The seller clears the goods for export and the buyer clears the goods for import
- The seller delivers the goods to the carrier or another person nominated by the buyer at the seller's premises or another named place
- US$12.00/pc FOB Busan Port, 330 Sinhangnam-ro, Gangseo-gu, Busan, Korea, Incoterms® 2020.

3) CPT(Carriage Paid To)

CPT(insert named place of destination) Incoterms® 2020

1. Delivery and risk - "Carriage Paid To" means that the seller delivers the goods-and transfers the risk - to the buyer

- ▶ by handing them over to the carrier
- ▶ contracted by the seller
- ▶ or by procuring the goods so delivered.
- ▶ The seller may do so by giving the carrier physical possession of the goods in the manner and at the place appropriate to the means of transport used.

Once the goods have been delivered to the buyer in this way, the seller does not guarantee that the goods will reach the place of destination in sound condition, in the stated quantity or indeed at all.

This is because risk transfers from seller to buyer when the goods are delivered to the buyer by handing them over to the carrier; the seller must nonetheless contract for the carriage of the goods from delivery to the agreed destination. Thus, for example, goods are handed over to a carrier in Las Vegas (which is not a port) for carriage to Southampton (a port) or to Winchester (which is not a port). In either case, delivery transferring risk to the buyer happens in Las Vegas, and the seller must make a contract of carriage to either Southampton or Winchester.

2. Mode of transport - This rule may be used irrespective of the mode of transport selected and may also be used where more than one mode of transport is employed.

3. Places (or points) of delivery and destination - In CPT, two locations are important: the place or point (if any) at which the goods are delivered (for the transfer of risk) and the place or point agreed as the destination of the goods (as the point to which the seller promises to contract for carriage).

4. Identifying the place or point of delivery with precision - The parties are well advised to identify both places, or indeed points within those places, as precisely as possible in the contract of sale. Identifying the place or point (if any) of delivery as precisely as possible is important to cater for the common situation where several carriers are engaged, each for different legs of the transit from delivery to destination. Where this happens and the parties do not agree on a specific place or point of delivery, the default position is that risk transfers when the goods have been delivered to the first carrier at a point entirely of the seller's choosing and over which the buyer has co control. Should the parties wish the risk to transfer at a later stage (e.g. at a sea or river port or at an airport), or indeed an earlier one (e.g. an inland point some way away from a sea or river port), they need to specify this in their contract of sale and to carefully think through the consequences of so doing in case the goods are lost or damaged.

5. Identifying the destination as precisely as possible - The parties are also well advised to identify as precisely as possible in the contract of sale the point within the agreed place of destination, as this is the point to which the seller must contract for carriage and this is the point to which the costs of carriage fall on the seller.

6. **'or procuring the goods so delivered'** - The reference to "procure" here caters for multiple sales down a chain (string sales), particularly common in the commodity trades.

7. **Costs of unloading at destination** - If the seller incurs costs under its contract of carriage related to unloading at the named place of destination, the seller is not entitled to recover such costs separately from the buyer unless otherwise agreed between the parties.

8. **Export/import clearance** - CPT requires the seller to clear the goods for export, where applicable. However, the seller has no obligation to clear the goods for import or for transit through third countries, or to pay any import duty or to carry out any import customs formalities.

"Carriage Paid To" means that the seller delivers the goods to the buyer by handing them over to the carrier comtracted by the seller or by procuring the goods so delivered and that the seller must contract or porcure a contract and pay for the carriage of the goods from the agreed point of delivery if any, at the place of delivery to the named place of destination or, if agreed, any point an that place.

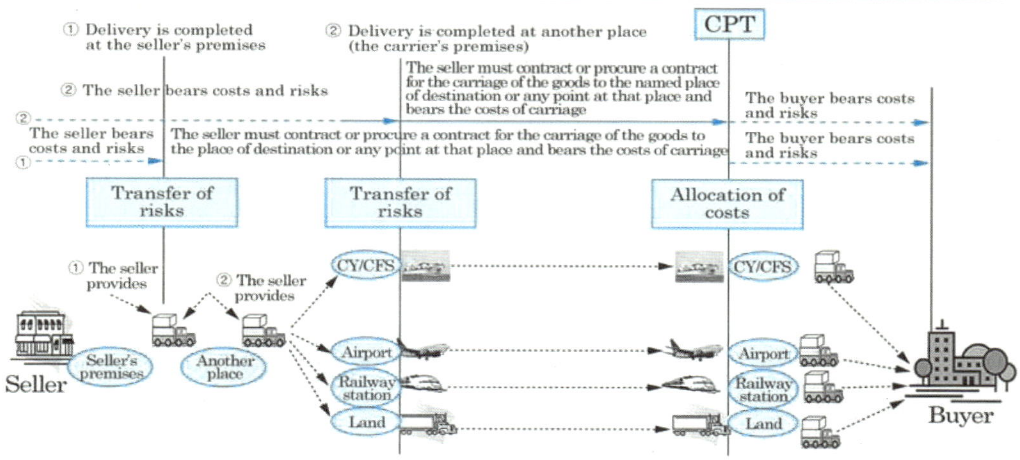

- The seller clears the goods for export and the buyer clears the goods for import
- The seller delivers the goods to the carrier or another person nominated by the seller at an agreed place
- The seller must contract or procure a contract for the carriage of the goods to the place of destination or any point at that place and bears the costs of carriage
- Risks passes and costs are transferred at different places
- US$14.00/pc CPT New York Station Terminal, 7th Ave & West 32nd St, New York City, NY 10001, Incoterms® 2020.

4) CIP(Carriage and Insurance Paid To
CIP(named place of destination) Incoterms® 2020

1. Delivery and risk - "Carriage and Insurance Paid To" means that the seller delivers the goods - and transfers the risk - to the buyer

- ▶ by handing them over to the carrier
- ▶ contracted by the seller
- ▶ or by procuring the goods so delivered.
- ▶ The seller may do so by giving the carrier physical possession of the goods in the manner and at the place appropriate to the means of transport used.

Once the goods have been delivered to the buyer in this way, the seller does not guarantee that the goods will reach the place of destination in sound condition, in the stated quantity or indeed at all. This is because risk transfers from seller to buyer when the goods are delivered to the buyer by handing them over to the carrier; the seller must nonetheless contract for th carriage of the goods from delivery to the agreed destination. Thus, for example, goods are handed over to a carrier in Las Vegas (which is not a port) for carriage to Southampton (a port) or to Winchester (which is not a port). In either case, delivery transferring risk to the buyer happens in Las Vegas, and the seller must make a contract of carriage to either Southampton or Winchester.

2. Mode fo transport - This rule may be used irrespective of the mode of transport selected and may also be used where more than one mode of transport is employed.

3. Places (or points) of delivery and destination - In CIP two locations are important: the place or point at which the goods are delivered (for the transfer of risk) and the place or point agreed as the destination of the goods (as the point to which the seller promises to contract for carriage).

4. Insurance - The seller must also contract for insurance cover against the buyer's risk of loss of or damage to the goods from the point of delivery to at least he point of destination. This may cause difficulty where the destination country requires insurance cover to be purchased locally: in this case the parties should consider selling and buying under CPT. The buyer should also note that under the CIP Incoterms® 2020 rule the seller is required to obtain extensive insurance cover complying with Institute Cargo Clauses (A) or similar clause, rather than with the more limited cover under Institute Cargo Clauses (C). It is, however, still open to the parties to agree on a lower level of cover.

5. Identifying the place or point of delivery with precision - The parties are well advised to identify both places, or indeed points within those places, as precisely as possible in the contract of sale. Identifying the place or point (if any) of delivery as precisely as possible is important to cater for the common situation where several carriers are engaged, each for different legs of the transit from delivery to destination. Where this happens and the parties do not agree on a specific place or point of delivery, the default position is that risk transfers when the goods have been delivered to the first carrier at a point entirely of the seller's choosing and over which the buyer has no control. Should the parties wish the risk to transfer at a later stage(e.g. at a sea or river port or at an airport), or indeed an early one (e.g. an inland point some way away from a sea or river port), they need to specify this in their contract of sale and to carefully think through the consequences of so doing in case the goods are lost or damaged.

6. Identifying the destination as precisely as possible - The parties are also well advised to identify as precisely as possible in the contract of sale the point within the agreed place of destination, as this is the point to which the seller must contract for carriage and insurance and this is the point to which the costs of carriage and insurance fall on the seller.

7. 'or procuring the goods so delivered' - The reference to "procure" here caters for multiple sales down a chain (string sales), particularly common in the commodity trades.

8. Costs of unloading at destination - If the seller incurs costs under its contract of carriage related to unloading at the named place of destination, the seller is not entitled to recover such costs separately from the buyer unless otherwise agreed between the parties.

"Carriage and Insurance Paid to" means that the seller delivers the goods to the buyer by handing them over to the carrier contracted by the seller or by procuring the goods so delivered and that the seller must contract or procure a contract and pay for the carriage of the goods from the agreed point of delivery if any, at the place of delivery to the named place of destination or, if agreed, any point at that place. The seller must obtain at its own cost insurance complying with the cover provided by ICC(A) against the buyer's risks of loss of or damage to the goods from the point of delivery to the point of destination.

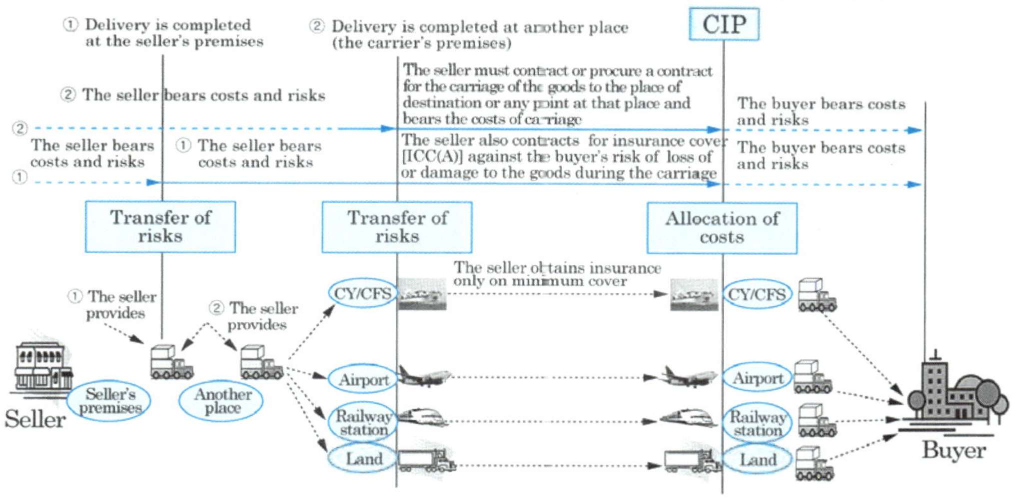

- The seller clears the goods for export and the buyer clears the goods for import
- The seller delivers the goods to the carrier or another person nominated by the seller at an agreed place
- The seller must contract or procure a contract for the carriage of the goods to the place of destination or any point at that place and bears the costs of carriage
- The seller contracts for insurance cover against the buyer's risk of loss or damage to the goods during the carriage
- Risk passes and costs are transferred at different places
- US$15.00/pc CIP New York Port, 70 Hamilton Ave. Brooklyn New York, USA, Incoterms® 2020

5) DAP(Delivered At Place)

DAP(insert named place of destination) Incoterms® 2020

1. Delivery and risk - "Delivery at Place" means that the seller delivers the goods- and transfers risk - to the buyer

- ▶ when the goods are placed at the disposal of the buyer
- ▶ on the arriving means of transport read for unloading
- ▶ at the named placed of destination or
- ▶ at the agreed point within that place, if any such point is agreed.

The seller bears all risks involved in bringing the goods to the named place of destination or to the agreed point within that place. In this Incoterms® rule, therefore, delivery and arrival at destination are the same.

2. Mode of transport - This rule may be used irrespective of the mode of transport selected and may also be used where more than one mode of transport is employed.

3. Identifying the place or point delivery/destination precisely-the parties are well advised to specify the destination place or point as cleary as possible and this for several reasons. First, risk of loss of or damage to the goods transfers to the buyer at that point of delivery/ destination - and it is best for the seller and the buyer to be clear about the point at which the critical transfer happens. Secondly, the costs before that place or point of delivery/destination are for the account of the seller and the costs after that place or point are for the account of the buyer. Thirdly, the seller must contract or arrange for the carriage of the goods to the agreed place or point delivery/destination. If it fails to do so, the seller is in breach of its obligations under the Incoterms DAP rule and will be liable to the buyer for any ensuing loss. Thus, for example, the seller would be responsible for any additional costs levied by the carrier to the buyer for any additional on-carriage.

4. 'or procuring the goods so delivered' - The reference to "procure" here caters for multiple sales down a chain (string sales), particularly common in the commodity trades.

5. Unloading costs - The seller is not required to unload the goods from the arriving means of transportation. However, if the seller incurs costs under its contract of carriage related to unloading at the place of delivery/destination, the seller is not entitled to recover such costs separately from the buyer unless otherwise agreed between the parties.

6. Export/import clearance - DAP requires the seller to clear the goods for export, where applicable. However, the seller has no obligation to clear the goods for import or for post-delivery transit through third countries, to pay any import duty or to carry out any import customs formalities. As a result, if the buyer fails to organise import clearance, the goods will be held up at a port or inland terminal in the destination country. Who bears the risk of any loss that might occur while the goods are thus held up at the port of entry in the destination country? The answer is the buyer: delivery will not have occurred yet, B3(a) ensuring that the risk of loss of or damage to the goods is with the buyer until transit to a named inland point can be resumed. If, in order to avoid this scenario, the parties intend the seller to clear the goods for import, pay any import duty or tax and carry out any import customs formalities, the parties might consider using DDP.

"Delivered at Place" means that the seller delivers when the goods are placed at the disposal of the buyer on the arriving means of transport ready for unloading at the named place of destination or at the agreed point whthin that place, if any such point is agreed or are procured so delivered. The seller must contract or arrange at its own cost for the carriage of the goods to the named place of destination or to the agreed point, if any, at the named place of destination.

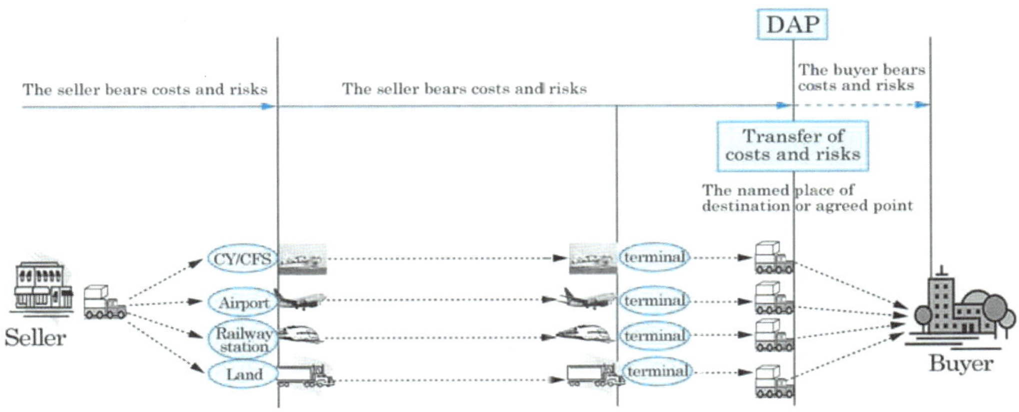

- The seller clears the goods for export and the buyer clears the goods for import
- The seller delivers when the goods are placed at the disposal of the buyer on the arriving means of transport ready for unloading at the named place or point of destination or procured so delivered.
- The seller must contract or arrange at its own cost for the carriage of the goods to the named place or point of destination
- US$19.00/pc DAP Abc Warehouse at 1322 Omaha, NE, USA, Incoterms® 2020

6) DPU(Delivered at Place Unloaded)

DPU(insert named place of destination) Incoterms® 2020

1. Delivery and risk - "Delivered at Place Unloaded" means that the seller delivers the goods – and transfers risk – to the buyer

- ▶ when the goods,
- ▶ once unloaded from the arriving means of transport,
- ▶ are placed at the disposal of the buyer
- ▶ at a named place of destination or
- ▶ at the agreed point within that place, if any such point is agreed.

The seller bears all risks involved in bringing the goods to and unloading them at the named place of destination. In this Incoterms® rule, therefore, the delivery and arrival at destination are the same. DPU is the only Incoterms® rule that requires the seller to unload goods at destination. The seller should therefore ensure that it is in a position to organise unloading at the named place. Should the parties intend the seller not to bear the risk and cost of unloading, the DPU rule should be avoided and DAP should be used instead.

2. Mode of transport - This rule may be used irrespective of the mode of transport selected and may also be used where more than one mode of transport is employed.

3. Identifying the place or point of delivery/destination precisely - The parties are well advised to specify the destination place or point as clearly as possible and this for several reasons. First, risk of loss of or damage to the goods transfers to the buyer at that point of delivery/destination - and it is best for the seller and the buyer to be clear about the point at which that critical transfer happens. Secondly, the costs before that place or point of delivery/destination are for the account of the seller and the costs after that place or point are for the account of the buyer. Thirdly, the seller must contract or arrange for the carriage of the goods to the agreed place or point of delivery/destination. If it fails to do so, the seller is in breach of its obligations under this rule and will be liable to the buyer for any ensuing loss. The seller would, for example, be responsible for any additional costs levied by the carrier to the buyer for any additional on-carriage.

4. 'or procuring the goods so delivered' - The reference to "procure" here caters for multiple sales down a chain (string sales), particularly common in the commodity trades.

5. Export/import clearance - DPU requires the seller to clear the goods for export, where applicable. However, the seller has no obligation to clear the goods for import or for post-delivery transit through third countries, to pay any import duty or to carry out any import customs formalities. As a result, if the buyer fails to organise import clearance, the goods will be held up at a port or inland terminal in the destination country. Who bears the risk of any loss that might occur while the goods are thus held up at the port of entry in the destination country? The answer is the buyer: delivery will not have occurred yet, B3(a) ensuring that the risk of loss of or damage to the goods is with the buyer until transit to a named inland point can be resumed. If, in order to avoid this scenario, the parties intend the seller to clear the goods for import, pay any import duty or tax and carry out any import customs formalities, the parties might consider using DDP.

"Delivered at Place Unloaded" means that the seller delivers when the goods, once unloaded form the arriving means of transport, are placed at the disposal of the buyer at the named place of destination or at the agreed point within that place, if any such point is agreed or are procured so delivered. The seller must contract or arrange at its own cost for the carriage of the goods to the named place of destination or to the agreed point, if any, at the named place of destination.

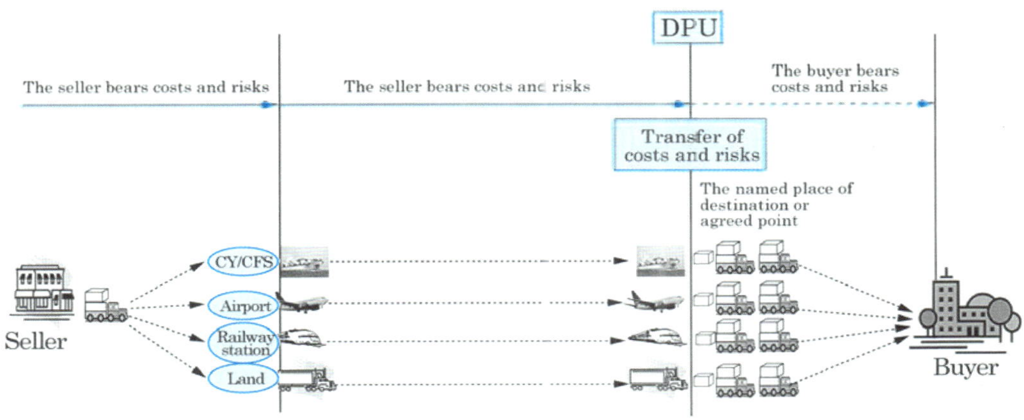

- The seller clears the goods for export and the buyer clears the goods for import
- The seller delivers when the goods, once unloaded from the arriving means of transport, are placed at the disposal of the buyer at the named place or point of destination or procured so delivered.
- The seller must contract at or arrange at its own cost for the carriage of the goods to the named place or point of destination
- US$19.00/pc DPU Chicago Airport, IL, USA, Incoterms® 2020.

7) DDP(Delivered Duty Paid)

DDP(insert named place of destination) Incoterms® 2020

1. Delivery and risk - "Delivered Duty Paid" means that the seller delivers the goods to the buyer

▶ when the goods are placed at the disposal of the buyer,

▶ cleared for import,

▶ on the arriving means of transport,

▶ ready for unloading,

▶ at the named place of destination or at the agreed point within that place, if any such point is agreed.

The seller bears all risks involved in bringing the goods to the named place of destination or to the agreed point within that place. In this Incoterms® rule, therefore, delivery and arrival at destination are the same.

2. Mode of transport - This rule may be used irrespective of the mode of transport selected and may also be used where more than one mode of transport is employed.

3. A note of caution to sellers: maximum responsibility - DDP, with delivery happening at destination and with the sellers being responsible for the payment of import duty and applicable taxes is the Incoterms® rule imposing on the seller the maximum level of obligation of all eleven Incoterms® rules. From the seller's perspective, therefore, the rule should be used with care for different reasons as set out in paragraph 7.

4. Identifying the place or point of delivery/destination precisely - The parties are well advised to specify the destination place or point as clearly as possible and this for several reasons. First, risk of loss of or damage to the goods transfers to the buyer at that point of delivery/destination - and it is best for the seller and the buyer to be clear about the point at which that critical transfer happens. Secondly, the costs before that place or point of delivery/destination are for the account of the seller, including the costs of import clearance, and the costs after that place or point, other than the costs of import, are for the account of the buyer. Thirdly, the seller must contract or arrange for the carriage of the goods to the agreed place or point of delivery/destination. If it fails to do so, the seller is in breach of its obligations under the Incoterms® rule DDP and will be liable to the buyer for any ensuing loss. Thus, for example, the seller would be responsible for any additional costs levied by the carrier to the buyer for any additional on-carriage.

5. 'or procuring the goods so delivered' - The reference to "procure" here caters for multiple sales down a chain (string sales), particularly common in the commodity trades.

6. Unloading costs - If the seller incurs costs under its contract of carriage related to unloading at the place of delivery/destination, the seller is not entitled to recover such costs separately from the buyer unless otherwise agreed between the parties.

7. Export/import clearance - As set out in paragraph 3, DDP requires the seller to clear the goods for export, where applicable, as well as for import and to pay any import duty or to carry out any customs formalities. Thus if the seller is unable to obtain import clearance and would rather leave that side of things in the buyer's hands in the country of import, then the seller should consider choosing DAP or DPU, under which rules delivery still happens at destination, but with import clearance being left to the buyer. There may be tax implications and this tax may not be recoverable from the buyer; see A9(d).

"Delivered Duty Paid" means that the seller delivers when the goods are placed at the disposal of the buyer on the arriving means of transport ready for unloading at the named place of destination or at the agreed point within that place, if any such point is agreed or are procured so delivered. The seller must contract or arrange at its own cost for the carriage of the goods to the named place of destination or to the agreed point, if any, at the named place of destination. The seller must carry out and pay for all export, transit, import clearance formalities.

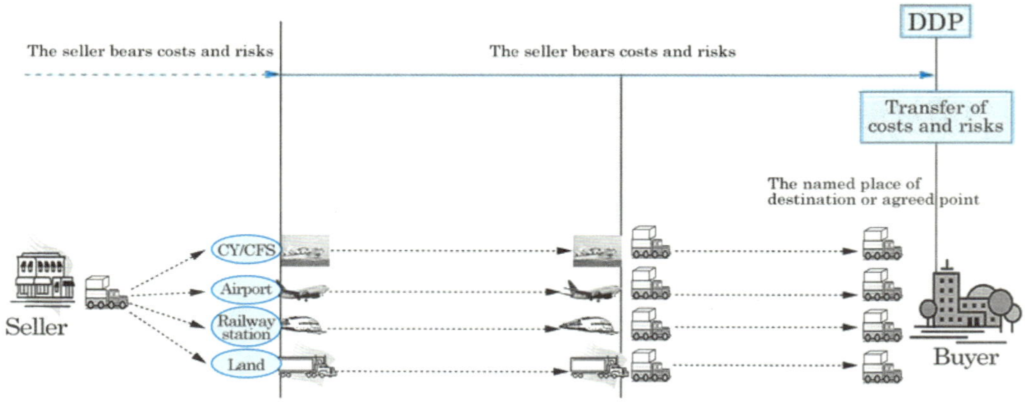

- The seller must carry out and pay for all export, transit, import clearance formalities
- The seller delivers when the goods cleared for import are placed at the disposal of the buyer on the arriving means of transport ready for unloading
- The seller must contract or arrange at its own cost for the carriage of the goods to the named place or point of destination
- DDP represents the maximum obligation for the seller
- US$20.00/pc DDP Chicago Airport, IL, USA, Incoterms® 2020

2. Rules for sea and inland waterway transport

1) FAS(Free Alongside Ship)

FAS(insert named port of shipment) Incoterms® 2020

1. Delivery and risk - "Free Alongside Ship" means that the seller delivers the goods to the buyer

- ▶ when the goods are placed alongside the ship (e.g. on a quay or a barge)
- ▶ nominated by the buyer
- ▶ at the named port of shipment
- ▶ or when the seller procures goods already so delivered.

The risk of loss of or damage to the goods transfers when the goods are alongside the ship, and the buyer bears all costs from that moment onwards.

2. **Mode of transport** - This rule is to be used only for sea or inland waterway transport where the parties intend to deliver the goods by placing the goods alongside a vessel. Thus, the FAS rule is not appropriate where goods are handed over to the carrier before they are alongside the vessel, for example where goods are handed over to a carrier at a container terminal. Where this is the case, parties should consider using the FCA rule rather than the FAS rule.

3. **Identifying the loading point precisely** - The parties are well advised to specify as clearly as possible the loading point at the named port of shipment where the goods are to be transferred from the quay or barge to the ship, as the costs and risks to that point are for the account of the seller and these costs and associated handling charges may vary according to the practice of the port.

4. **'or procuring the goods so delivered'** - The seller is required either to deliver the goods alongside the ship or to procure goods already so delivered for shipment. The reference to "procure" here caters for multiple sales down a chain (string sales), particularly common in the commodity trades.

5. **Export/import clearance** - FAS requires the seller to clear the goods for export, where applicable. However, the seller has no obligation to clear the goods for import or for transit through third counties, to pay any import duty or to carry out any import customs formalities.

"Free Alongside Ship" means that the seller delivers when the goods are placed alongside the ship(e. g., on a quay or a barge) nominated by the buyer at the named port of shipment or when the seller procures goods already so delivered. The risk of loss of or damage to the goods transfers when the goods are alongside the ship, and the buyer bears all costs from that moment onwards.

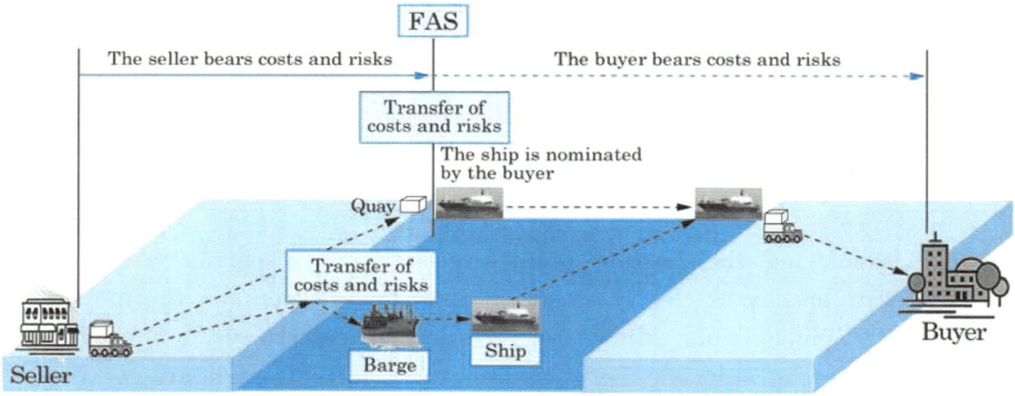

- The seller clears the goods for export and the buyer clears the goods for import
- The seller is required to deliver the goods alongside the ship or to procure goods already so delivered for shipment
- The buyer must contract at its own expense for the carriage of the goods from the named port of shipment
- Where the goods are in containers, the FCA rule should be used
- US$10.00/pc, FAS Busan Port, 330 Sinhangnam-ro, Gangseo-gu, Busan, Korea, Incoterms® 2020.

2) FOB(Free On Board)

FOB(insert named port of shipment) Incoterms® 2020

1. Delivery and risk - "Free On Board" means that the seller delivers the goods to the buyer

- ▶ on board the vessel
- ▶ nominated by the buyer
- ▶ at the named port of shipment
- ▶ or procures the goods already so delivered.

The risk of loss of or damage to the goods transfers when the goods are on board the vessel, and the buyer bears all costs from that moment onwards.

2. Mode of transport - This rule is to be used only for sea or inland waterway transport where the parties intend to deliver the goods by placing the goods on board a vessel. Thus, the FOB rule is not appropriate where goods are handed over to the carrier before they are on board the vessel, for example where goods are handed over to a carrier at a container terminal. Where this is the case, parties should consider using the FCA rule rather than the FOB rule.

3. 'or procuring the goods so delivered' - The seller is required either to deliver the goods on board the vessel or to procure goods already so delivered for shipment. The reference to 'procure' here caters for multiple sales down a chain (string sales), particularly common in the commodity trades.

4. Export/import clearance - FOB requires the seller to clear the goods for export, where applicable. However, the seller has no obligation to clear the goods for import or for transit through third countries, to pay any import duty or to carry out any import customs formalities.

"Free on Board" means that the seller delivers the goods on board the vessel nominated by the buyer at the named port of shipment or procures the goods already so delivered. The risk of loss of or damage to the goods passes when the goods are on board the vessel, and the buyer bears all costs from that moment onwards.

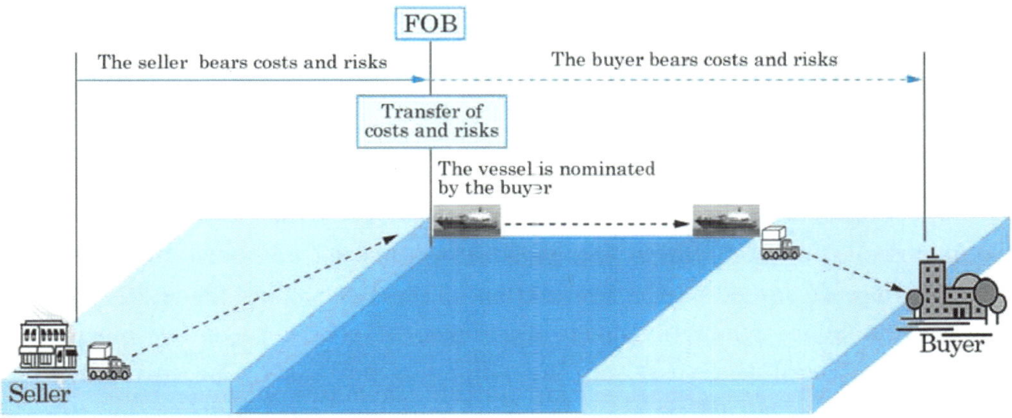

- The seller clears the goods for export and the buyer clears the goods for import
- The seller is required to deliver the goods on board the vessel or to procure goods already so delivered for shipment
- The buyer must contract at its own expense for the carriage of the goods from the named port of shipment
- Where the goods are in containers, the FCA rule should be used
- US$12.00/pc, FOB Busan Port, 330 Shinhangnam-ro, Gangseo-gu, Busan, Korea, Incoterms® 2020

3) CFR(Cost and Freight)

CFR(insert named port of destination) Incoterms® 2020

1. Delivery and risk - "Cost and Freight" means that the seller delivers the goods to the buyer.

▶ on board the vessel

▶ or procures the goods already so delivered.

The risk of loss of or damage to the goods transfers when the goods are on board the vessel, such that the seller is taken to have performed its obligation to deliver the goods whether or not the goods actually arrive at their destination in sound condition, in the stated quantity or, indeed, at all. In CFR, the seller owes no obligation to the buyer to purchase insurance cover: the buyer would be well-advised therefore to purchase some cover for itself.

2. Mode of transport - This rule is to be used only for sea or inland waterway transport. Where more than one mode of transport is to be used, which will commonly be the case where goods are handed over to a carrier at a container terminal, the appropriate rule to use is CPT rather than CFR.

3. 'or procuring the goods so delivered' - The reference to "procure" here caters for multiple sales down a chain (string sales), particularly common in the commodity trades.

4. Ports of delivery and destination - in CFR, two ports are important: the port where the goods are delivered on board the vessel and the port agreed as the destination of the goods. Risk transfers from seller to buyer when the goods are delivered to the buyer by placing them on board the vessel at the shipment port or by procuring the goods already so delivered. However, the seller must contract for the carriage of the goods from delivery to the agreed destination. Thus, for example, goods are placed on board a vessel in Shanghai (which is a port) for carriage to Southampton (also a port). Delivery here happens when the goods are on board in Shanghai, with risk transferring to the buyer at that time; and the seller must make a contract of carriage from Shanghai to Southampton.

5. Must the shipment port be named? - While the contract will always specify a destination port, it might not specify the port of shipment, which is where risk transfers to the buyer. If the shipment port is of particular interest to the buyer, as it may be, for example, where the buyer wishes to ascertain that the freight element of the price is reasonable, the parties are well advised to identify it as precisely as possible in the contract.

6. Identifying the destination point at the discharge port - The parties are well advised to identify as precisely as possible the point at the named port of destination, as the costs to that point are for the account of the seller. The seller must make a contract or contracts of carriage that cover(s) the transit of the goods from delivery to the named port or to the agreed point within that port where such a point has been agreed in the contract of sale.

7. Multiple carriers - It is possible that carriage is effected through several carriers for different legs of the sea transport, for example, first by a carrier operating a feeder vessel from Hong Kong to Shanghai, and then onto an ocean vessel from Shanghai to Southampton. The question which arises here is whether risk transfers from seller to buyer at Hong Kong or at Shanghai: where does delivery take place? The parties may well have agreed this in the sale contract itself. Where, however, there is no such agreement, the default position is that risk transfers when the goods have been delivered to the first carrier, i.e. Hong Kong, thus increasing the period during which the buyer incurs the risk of loss or damage. Should the parties wish the risk to transfer at later stage (here, Shanghai) they need to specify this in their contract of sale.

8. Unloading costs - If the seller incurs costs under its contract of carriage related to unloading at the specified point at the port of destination, the seller is not entitled to recover such costs separately from the buyer unless otherwise agreed between the parties.

9. Export/Import clearance - CFR requires the seller to clear the goods for export, where applicable. However, the seller has no obligation to clear the goods for import or for transit through third countries, to pay any import duty or to carry out any import customs formalities.

"Costs and Feight" means that the seller delivers the goods on board the vessel or procures the goods already so delivered. The risk of loss of or damage to the goods passes when the goods are on board the vessel. The seller must contract or procure a contract for the carriage of the goods from the agreed point of delivery to the named port of destination.

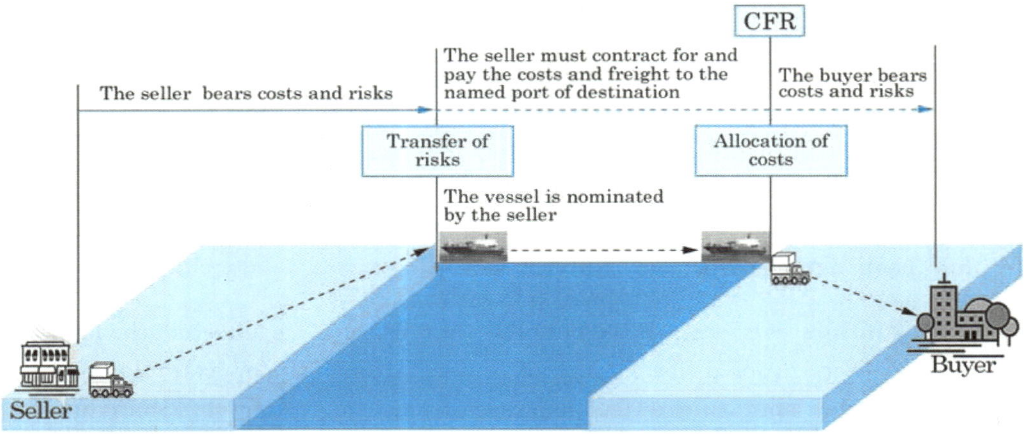

- The seller clears the goods for export and the buyer clears the goods for import
- The seller is required to deliver the goods on board the vessel or to procure goods already so delivered for shipment
- The seller must contract or procure a contract for the carriage of the goods from the agreed port of delivery to the named port of destination
- Risk passes and costs are transferred at different places
- US$15.00/pc, CFR Long Beach Port, 231 Windsor Way Long Beach, CA 90802 USA, Incoterms® 2020

4) CIF(Cost Insurance and Freight)
CIF(insert named port of destination) Incoterms® 2020

1. Delivery and risk -"Cost Insurance and Freight" means that the seller delivers the goods to the buyer

- ▶ on board the vessel
- ▶ or procures the goods already so delivered.

The risk of loss of or damage to the goods transfers when the goods are on board the vessel, such that the seller is taken to have performed its obligation to deliver the goods whether or not the goods actually arrive at their destination in sound condition, in the stated quantity or, indeed, at all.

2. Mode of transport - This rule is to be used only for sea or inland waterway transport. Where more than one mode of transport is to be used, which will commonly be the case where goods are handed over to a carrier at a container terminal, the appropriate rule to use is CIP rather than CIF.

3. 'or procuring the goods so delivered' - The reference to "procure" here caters for multiple sales down a chain (string sales), particularly common in the commodity trades.

4. Ports of delivery and destination - In CIF, two ports are important: the port where the goods are delivered on board the vessel and the port agreed as the destination of the goods. Risk transfers from seller to buyer when the goods are delivered to the buyer by placing them on board the vessel at the shipment port or by procuring the goods already so delivered. However, the seller must contract for the carriage of the goods from delivery to the agreed destination. Thus, for example, goods are placed on board a vessel in Shanghai (which is a port) for carriage to Southampton (also a port). Delivery here happens when the goods are on board in Shanghai, with risk transferring to the buyer at that time; and the seller must make a contract of carriage from Shanghai to Southampton.

5. Must the shipment port be named? - While the contract will always specify a destination port, it might not specify the port of shipment, which is where risk transfers to the buyer. If the shipment port is of particular interest to the buyer, as it may be, for example, where the buyer wishes to ascertain that the freight or the insurance element of the price is reasonable, the parties are well advised to identify it as precisely as possible in the contract.

6. Identifying the destination point at the discharge port - The parties are well advised to identify as precisely as possible the point at the named port of destination, as the costs to that point are for the account of the seller. The seller must make a contract or contracts of carriage that cover the transit of the goods from delivery to the named port or to the agreed point within that port where such a point has been agreed in the contract of sale.

7. Multiple carriers - It is possible that carriage is effected through several carriers for different legs of the sea transport, for example, first by a carrier operating a feeder vessel from Hong Kong to Shanghai, and then onto an ocean vessel from Shanghai to Southampton. The question which arises here is whether risk transfers from seller to buyer at Hong Kong or at Shanghai: where does delivery take place? The parties may well have agreed this in the sale contract itself. Where, however, there is no such agreement, the default position is that risk transfers when the goods have been delivered to the first carrier, i.e. Hong Kong, thus increasing the period during which the buyer incurs the risk of loss or damage. Should the parties wish the risk to transfer at a later stage (here, Shanghai) they need to specify this in their contract of sale.

8. Insurance - The seller must also contract for insurance cover against the buyer's risk of loss of or damage to the goods from the port of shipment to at least the port of destination. This may cause difficulty where the destination country requires insurance cover to be purchase locally: in this case the parties should consider selling and buying under CFR. The buyer should also note that under the CIF Incoterms® 2020 rule the seller is required to obtain limited insurance cover complying with Institute Cargo Clauses (C) or similar clause, rather than with the more extensive cover under Institute Cargo Clauses (A). It is, however, still open to the parties to agree on a higher level of cover.

9. Unloading costs - If the seller incurs costs under its contract of carriage related to unloading at the specified point at the port of destination, the seller is not entitled to recover such costs separately from the buyer unless otherwise agreed between the parties.

10. Export/Import clearance - CIF requires the seller to clear the goods for export, where applicable. However, the seller has no obligation to clear the goods for import or for transit through third countries, to pay any import duty or to carry out any import customs formalities.

"Costs, Insurance and Feight" means that the seller delivers the goods on board the vessel or procures the goods already so delivered. The risk of loss of or damage to the goods passes when the goods are on board the vessel. The seller must contract or procure for the carriage of the goods from the agreed point of delivery to the named port of destination. The seller must obtain, at its own cost, insurance complying with the cover provided by ICC(C) against the buyer's risks of loss of or damage to the goods from the port of shipment to the port ot destination.

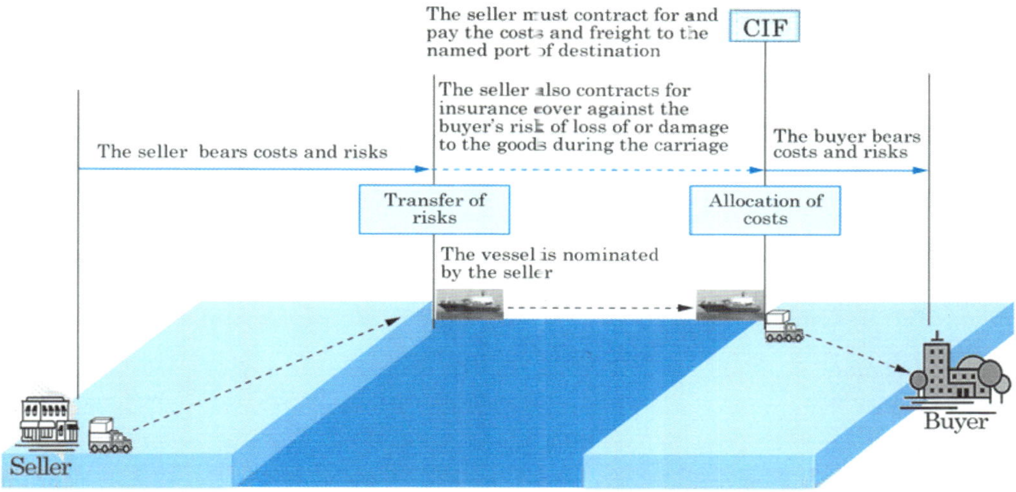

- The seller clears the goods for export and the buyer clears the goods for import
- The seller is required to deliver the goods on board the vessel or to procure goods already so delivered for shipment
- The seller must contract or procure a contract for the carriage of the goods from the agreed port of delivery to the named port of destination
- The seller must obtain, at its own cost, insurance complying with the cover provided by ICC(C) against the buyer's risks of loss of or damage to the goods during the carriage
- Risk passes and costs are transferred at different places
- When the goods are handed over to the carrier before they are on board the vessel, for example goods in containers, the CIP rule should be used
- US$10.00/pc, CIF New York Port, USA, Incoterms® 2020

Chapter 6

Trade Contract

Chapter

6

Trade Contract

6.1 Definition of Trade Contract

A trade contract is a single document in which the rights and obligations of the seller and the buyer are stipulated. A contract is a legally enforceable agreement between two or more parties that creates legal obligations between them.

International trade practice shows that the majority of transactions are carried out without signing a contract. However, it is strongly recommended to establish an international contract of sale for international transactions.

One can avoid doubts and misunderstandings concerning what has been agreed during the negotiation of terms if they are set down in writing. In certain cases, a verbal agreement is legally binding just like the seller makes a sale at an international trade fair sometimes.

International transactions are conducted according to the terms and conditions negotiated between the seller and the buyer. Usually terms of trade are stipulated in a trade contract and the trade contract indicates the seller's and the buyer's responsibilities. The contract should be signed by all parties directly involved.

6.2 Kinds of Trade Contract

1. Letter of Intent(LOI)

A letter of intent(LOI) is a document outlining an agreement between two or more parties before the agreement is finalized. A Letter of Intent resembles written contracts, but is usually not binding on the parties.

A LOI may also be referred to as a term sheet or discussion sheet. A contract, by contrast, is a legal document governed by contract law. Furthermore, there is also a specific difference between a letter of intent and a memorandum of understanding(MOU); LOI outlines the intent of one party toward another with regard to an agreement, and may only be signed by the party expressing that intent, whereas MOU must be signed by all parties to be a valid outline of an agreement. Nevertheless, LOIs are fairly often incorrectly referred to as MOUs and vice versa.

Letter of Intent

This letter of Intent(LOI) made and entered into this ×× day of, ×× 20××, by and between ABC Co., Ltd., a corporation duly organized and existing under the laws of Japan, having its principal office and place of business at 200, Ishida, Iseharashi, Kanagawa Prefecture, Japan(hereinafter referred to as ABC) and XYZ Co., Ltd., a corporation organized and existing under the laws of the Republic of Korea, having its principal office and place of business at, Seoul, Republic of Korea(hereinafter referred to as XYZ)

RECITALS :

WHEREAS, ABC has long been engaged in the manufacture and sale of certain laser system in Japan and other countries ; and

WHEREAS, ABC has acquired and possesses valuable technical information on the design, manufacture, installation and the use of such laser systems ; and

WHEREAS, ABC has the right to grant a license to manufacture, use and sell such laser system by the use of such technical information ; and

WHEREAS, XYX desires to obtain and ABC is willing to grant the right and license to manufacture, use and sell one of such laser system by utilizing such technical information to be furnished by ABC ;

NOW, THEREFORE, in consideration of the mutual premises tons covenants hereinafter, the parties agree as follows;

1. The parties shall cooperate to select one of such laser system which will be best fitted for local demand and marketability in the Republic of Korea. As of the date of this Letter of Intent, XYZ tentatively choose the system LCV II series.
2. XYZ's final selection of the system shall be made not later than end of June, 20××.
3. Upon XYZ's selection, both parties shall make best efforts to come to mutual consent on the terms and conditions for the technical incense agreement to be executed between parties, for XYZ's manufacture, use and sales of the selected laser system.

IN WITNESS WHEREOF, the parties herein have caused this Letter of Intent to be executed in duplicates by their respective duly authorized officer as of the date first above written.

For ABC Company Ltd.
Signature

For XYZ Company Ltd.
Signature.

2. Memorandum of Understanding(MOU)

A memorandum of understanding(MOU) is a written agreement between two or more parties. This document is not as binding as a contract, but it outlines a commitment between the parties to work together towards a common goal. The main purpose of MOU is to make sure that all parties know that they are in agreement with each other, and it can also serves as a binding contract.

MEMORANDUM OF UNDERSTANDING

On behalf of ABC, Mr.________ and Mr.________ visited XYZ, from June 15, 20×× to June 21, 20××, and had mutual discussion on the basis of the Proposal No.________ and finally agreed upon several factors to carry out the project.

Between ABC
And XYZ

Now therefore, it is hereby agreed and declared by and between the parties concerned hereto, as follows,

1. ABC is willing to set up a company to manufacture clothes in _______ under XYZ's cooperation such as machinery supplying, technical transfer assistance and marketing.
2. ABC shall get an industrial license within maximum thirty(30) days after applying it for the prompt progress of this project. The commercial production shall be started within the end of 20××.
3. ABC and XYZ agreed that the company will be named as_____.
4. ABC shall sell all their products except rejected clothes through XYZ for the minimum period of ten(10) years.
5. ABC shall issue a letter of credit for machineries and equipments regarding this clothes manufacturing project within four(4) months after signing MOU.
6. XYZ shall dispatch the drafts of marketing agreement, technical assistance agreement and machinery contract soon by D.H.L. The production capacity shall be considered as 2,000 pairs a day on the basis of eight(8) working hours a day.

In witness whereof, the parties concerned hereto have caused this MOU to be executed original in duplicates by their duly authorized representative on June 21, 20××.

Party ABC　　　　　　Party XYZ

WITNESS :

3. Agrement on General Terms and Conditions

Agreement on General Terms and Conditions of Business

This Agreement entered into between Daehan Trading Co., Ltd., Seoul, Korea,(hereinafter called the Seller) and M.C.P. Inc., New York, USA, (hereinafter called the Buyer), witnesses as follows;

1. **Business** : Both Seller and Buyer act as Principals and not as Agents.
2. **Goods** : Goods in business, their unit to be quoted, and their mode of packing shall be stated in the attached list.
3. **Quotations and Offers** : Unless otherwise specified in e-mails or letters, all quotations and offers submitted by either party to this Agreement shall be in U.S. Dollars on the basis of CIF New York.
4. **Firm Offers** : All offers shall be subject to a reply reached within the period stated in respective e-mails. When 'immediately reply' is used, it shall mean that a reply is to be received by the seller within three days from and including the date of the dispatch of a firm offer. In either case, however, sundays and all official holidays are excepted.
5. **Orders** : Any business closed by e-mail shall be confirmed in writing without delay, and orders thus confirmed shall not be cancelled unless by mutual consent.
6. **Credit** : Banker's irrevocable Letter of Credit shall be issued in favor of the seller within ten(10) days from the date of contract. Credit shall be made available twenty-one(21) days beyond the contracted time of shipment.
7. **Payment** : Drafts shall be drawn under irrevocable Letter of Credit at sight, documents attached, for full invoice value.
8. **Shipment** : All goods sold in accordance with this Agreement shall be shipped within the stipulated time. The date of Bill of Lading shall be taken as a conclusive proof of the date of shipment. Unless expressly agreed upon, the port of shipment shall be at the Seller's option.
9. **Marine Insurance** : All shipments shall be covered ICC(A) Clause for a sum equal to the amount of the invoice plus ten(10) percent, if no other conditions are particularly agreed upon. All policies shall be made out in U.S. Dollars and payable in New York.
10. **Quality** : The Seller shall guarantee all shipment to confirm to sam-

ples, types, or descriptions, with regard to quality and condition.

11. **Damage in Transit** : The seller shall ship all goods in good condition, and the buyer shall assume all risks of damage, deterioration or breakage during transportation.
12. **Claims** : Claims, if any, shall be submitted by e-mail within fourteen(14) days after arrival of goods at destination. Certificates recognized by surveyors shall be sent by mail without delay. All claims which can not be amicably settled between the Seller and the Buyer shall be submitted to Arbitration in Seoul. The arbitrators are consisted of three members. The decision of the arbitrators shall be final, and the losing party shall bear expenses thereof.
13. **Force Majeure** : The Seller shall not be responsible for the delay of shipment in all cases of force majeure, including mobilization, war, riots, civil commotion, hostilities, blockade, requisition of vessels, prohibition of export, fires, floods, earthquakes, tempest, and any other contingencies, which prevent shipment within the stipulated period. In the event of any of the aforesaid causes rising, documents proving its occurrence or existence shall be sent by the Seller to the Buyer without delay.
14. **Delayed Shipment** : In all cases of force majeure provided in Article 13, the period of shipment stipulated shall be extended for a period of twenty-one(21) days. In case shipment within the extended period should still be prevented by a continuance of the causes mentioned in Article 13 or the consequences of any of them, it shall be at the Buyer's option either to allow the late shipment of goods or to cancel the order by giving the Seller the notice of cancellation by e-mail.
15. **Shipping Notice** : Shipment effected against the contract of sale shall be immediately e-mailed.
16. **Shipment Samples** : In case shipment samples be required, the Seller shall forward them to the Buyer prior to shipment.
17. **Marking** : All shipments shall be marked as arranged otherwise.
18. **Expenses** : Both parties shall bear all their expenses relating to communication, traveling and other incidental expenses.
19. **Trade Terms** : Unless specially stated, the trade terms under this contract shall be governed and interpreted by the latest Incoterms (Incoterms 2010).
20. **Governing Law** : This agreement shall be governed as to matters including validity, construction and performance under and by the

United Nations Convention on Contract for the international Sae of Good 1980.

In witness whereof, Daehan Trading Co., Ltd., has hereunto set their hand on the 1st of March 20××, and M.C.P. Inc., has hereto set their hand on the 30th of March 20××. This Agreement shall be valid on and from the 1st of April 20××, and any of the Articles in the Agreement shall not be changed or modified unless by mutual consent.

(Buyer) M.C.P. Inc.	(Seller) Daehan Trading Co., Ltd.
(signed)	(signed)
President	President

4. Sales Contract

Sales Contract

Han Kook Co., Ltd., as Seller, hereby confirms having sold to Brown Co., Ltd., as Buyer, the following goods by this sales contract made on July 30, 20×× and on the terms and conditions hereinafter set forth.

ITEM NO.	COMMODITY & SPECIFICATION	QUANTITY	UNIT PRICE	AMOUNT
TOTAL AMOUNT				

□ Time of Shipment : July 30, 20××
□ Port of Shipment : Busan, Korea
□ Port of Destination : New York, U.S.A.
□ Payment

AT SIGHT	By an irrevocable letter of credit payable at sight
USANCE	By an irrevocable, confirmed and unconditional letter of credit
D/P	By documents against payment
D/A	By bill(s) of exchange drawn on Buyer due [60] days from B/L date
D/D	By a D/D(Demand Draft) within [10] days after the date of B/L
T/T	By a T/T(Telegraph Transfer) within [10] days after the date of B/L
M/T	By a M/T(Mail Transfer) within [10] days after the date of B/L

□ Insurance : Seller to cover the [CIF] price plus [ ]% against All Risks, War and SRCC Risks
□ Packing : Export standard packing
□ Marking : PCU
□ Special Terms & Conditions :
□ This Contract is subject to the general and conditions set forth on back hereof :

Seller	Buyer
Han Kook Co., Ltd. 159, Samsung-dong, Kangnam-gu, Seoul Korea Shinkyuo Lee Manager	Brown Co., Ltd. 140, West 51st Street, New York, Tom B. Baker Manager

General Terms and Conditions

Article 1. Quantity

Quantity set forth in this Contract is subject to a variation of ten [10] percent more or less at Seller's option.

Article 2. Shipment :

Date of bill of lading shall be accepted as a conclusive date of shipment. [ ] days grace in shipping shall be allowed. Partial shipment and/or transshipment shall be permitted unless otherwise stated in this

Contract. Seller shall not be responsible for any delay of shipment, should Buyer fail to provide timely letter of credit in conformity with this Contract or in case the sailing of the steamer designated by Buyer be deferred beyond the prearranged date of shipment.

Article 3. Packaging

Packing shall be at Seller's option In case special instructions are necessary, Buyer should notify Seller thereof in time to enable Seller to comply with the same and all additional cost thereby incurred shall be borne by Buyer. Shipping Mark shall be made as shown in the oblong of the front page of this Contract.

Article 4. Insurance

In case of CIF or CIP basis, [10] % of the invoice amount shall be insured, unless otherwise agreed; any additional insurance required by Buyer to be at his own expense; unless otherwise stated, insurance to be covered for marine insurance only FPA or ICC(C) Clause. Seller may, if he deems it necessary, insure against additional risks at Buyer's expense.

Article 5. Increased costs

If Seller's costs of performance are increased after the date of this Contract by reason of increased freight rates, taxes or other governmental charges or insurance rates, or if any variation in rates of exchange increases Seller's costs or reduces Seller's return, Buyer agrees to compensate Seller for such increased cost or loss of income. Further, if at any time Buyer requests shipment later than agreed and Seller agrees thereto, Seller may, upon completion of manufacture, store the Goods and charge all expenses thereby incurred to Buyer, plus reasonable storage charges when Seller stores the Goods in its own facilities.

Article 6. Payment

AT SIGHT L/C : An irrevocable letter of credit, without recourse, available against Seller's sight drafts shall be established through a prime bank satisfactory to Seller within [15] days after the date of this Contract and be kept valid at least [15] days after the date of last shipment. The amount of such letter of credit shall be sufficient to cover the Contract amount and additional charges and/or expenses to be borne by Buyer.

USANCE : For the payment of the Contract Price specified hereof the

Buyer shall provide the Seller with the irrevocable, confirmed and unconditional letter of credit(hereinafter called "L/C") in the amount of USD [ ] at [ ] months usance basis(after the date of draft issued by the Seller or bill of lading) in favor of the Seller to be issued within [ ] days from the signing date of the Contract under the agreed terms and conditions by the Seller and Buyer.

D/P : After shipment, the Seller shall deliver a sight bill(s) of exchange drawn on the Buyer together with the required documents to the Buyer through a bank. The Buyer shall effect the payment immediately upon the first presentation of the bill(s) of exchange and the required documents, i.e. D/P.

D/A : After shipment, the Seller shall deliver bill(s) of exchange drawn on the Buyer, payable [ ] days after [ ], together with the required documents to the Buyer through a bank for acceptance. The Buyer shall accept the bill(s) of exchange immediately upon the first presentation of the bill of exchange and the required documents and shall effect the payment on the maturity date of the bill(s) of exchange.

D/D : The Buyer shall pay the invoice value of the goods by means of D/D(Demand Draft) within [ ] days after the receipt of the required documents; within [ ] days after the date of the Bill of Lading.

T/T : The Buyer shall pay the invoice value of the goods to the Seller's account with the bank designated by the Seller by means of T/T (Telegraph Transfer) within [ ] days after the receipt of the required documents; within [ ] days after the date of the Bill of Lading.

M/T : The Buyer shall pay the invoice value of the goods by the Seller by means of M/T(Mail Transfer) within [ ] days after the receipt of the required documents; within [ ] days after the date of the Bill of Lading

Article 7. Inspection

The inspection of the Goods shall be done according to the export regulation of the Republic of Korea and/or by the manufacturer(s) which shall be considered as final. Should any specific inspector be designated by Buyer, all additional charges incurred thereby shall be at Buyer's account and shall be added to the invoice amount, for which the letter of credit shall be amended accordingly.

Article 8. Warranty

The Goods shall conform to the specification set forth in this

Contract and free from defects in material and workmanship for [ ] months from the date of shipment. The extent of Seller's liability under this warranty shall be limited to the repair or replacement as herein provided of any defective Goods or parts thereof. Provided, however, this warranty does not extend to any of the said Goods which have been : (a) subjected to misuse, neglect, accident or abuse, (b) improperly repaired, installed, transported, altered or modified in any way by any other party than Seller or (c) used in violation of instructions furnished by Seller. Except for the express limited warranties set forth in this article, seller makes no other warranty to buyer, express or implied, and herby expressly disclaims any warranty of merchantability or fitness for a particular purpose. In no event shall Seller be liable to Buyer under this Contract or otherwise for any lost profits or for indirect, incidental or consequential damages for any reason.

Article 9. Claims

Any claim by Buyer of whatever nature arising under this Contract shall be made by facsimile or cable within [ ] days after arrival of the Goods at the destination specified in the bills of lading. Full particulars of such claim shall be made in writing, and forwarded by registered mail to Seller within [ ] days after such fax or cabling. Buyer must submit with particulars the inspection report sworn by a reputable surveyor acceptable to the Seller when the quality or quantity of the Goods delivered is in dispute. Failure to make such claim within such period shall constitute acceptance of shipment and agreement of Buyer that such shipment fully complies with applicable terms and conditions.

Article 10. Remedy

Buyer shall, without limitation, be in default of this Contract, if Buyer shall become insolvent, bankrupt or fail to make any payment to Seller including the establishment of the letter of credit within the due period. In the event of Buyer's default, Seller may without prior notice thereof to Buyer exercise any of the following remedies among others :

(a) terminate this Contract;

(b) terminate this Contract as to the portion of the Goods in default only and resell them and recover from Buyer the difference between the price set forth in this Contract and the price obtained upon resale, plus any incidental loss or expense; or

(c) terminate the Contract as to any unshipped balance and recover from Buyer as liquidated damages, a sum of five(5) percent of the price of the unshipped balance. Further, it is agreed that the rights and remedies herein reserved to Seller shall be cumulative and in addition to any other or further rights and remedies available at law.

Article 11. Force Majeure

Neither party shall be liable for its failure to perform its obligations hereunder if such failure is the direct result of circumstances beyond that party's reasonable control, including but not limited to, prohibition of exportation, suspension of issuance of export license or other government restriction, act of God, war, blockade, revolution, insurrection, mobilization, strike, lockout or any labor dispute, civil commotion, riot, plague or other epidemic, fire, typhoon, flood.

Article 12. Patents

Trade Marks, Designs, etc. : Buyer is to hold Seller harmless from liability for any infringement with regard to patent, trade mark, copyright, design, pattern, etc., originated or chosen by Buyer.

Article 13. Governing Law

This Contract shall be governed under the laws of Korea.

Article 14. Arbitration

Any dispute arising out of or in connection with this contract shall be finally settled by arbitration in Seoul in accordance with the Arbitration Rules of the Korean Commercial Arbitration Board.

Article 15. Language

This Agreement may be executed in English and in other languages (including Korean). In the event of any difference or inconsistency among different versions of this Agreement, the English version shall prevail over in all respect.

Article 16. Trade Terms

All trade terms provided in the Contract shall be interpreted in accordance with the latest INCOTERMS 2000 of International Chamber of Commerce.

5. Distributorship Agreement

DISTRIBUTORSHIP AGREEMENT

This Agreement, made and entered into this January 1, 20×× by and between Korea Trading Co., Ltd. a corporation duly organized and existing under the laws of the Republic of Korea and having its principal office at ________ (hereinafter referred to as "Manufacturer") and America Trading Co., Ltd. a corporation duly organized and existing under the laws of the state of New York, U.S.A. having its principal office at ________ (hereinafter referred to as "Distributor").

WITNESSETH :

WHEREAS, Manufacturer wishes to appoint Distributor the exclusive distributor for the products(as hereinafter defined) in the territory of the United States of America,

WHEREAS, Distributor wishes to accept such appointment as an exclusive distributor.

IN CONSIDERATION OF the mutual covenants contained herein, the parties hereto agree as follows :

Article 1. Definitions

In this Agreement except where the context otherwise requires, the following terms and expressions shall have the meanings respectively defined as follows ;

1.1 "Products" means those products which are mentioned in the attached Annex.

1.2 "Territory" means the United States of America.

Article 2. Appointment and Acceptance

2.1 During the term and subject to the conditions hereinafter set forth, Manufacturer hereby appoints Distributor as an exclusive distributor for the products in the Territory, and Distributor accepts such appointment. During the term of this Agreement, Manufacturer shall not, either directly or indirectly, sell the products in the Territory without the prior consent of Distributor.

2.2 Distributor shall not purchase, import, export, sell, distribute, advertise or otherwise deal in products competitive with or similar to the products in the Territory.

Article 3. Orders and Shipment

3.1 In placing orders with Manufacturer, Distributor shall clearly describe the products and quantity required, and shall include precise instructions for packaging, invoicing and shipping.
The orders shall not be binding unless and until they are accepted by Manufacturer in its discretion. Manufacturer agrees to supply Distributor with products to enable fulfillment of the minimum purchases as set forth in Article 5 hereof. Manufacturer agrees to extend its best efforts to accept all orders as submitted by Distributor in excess of said minimum purchases.

3.2 Manufacturer shall be responsible for packaging the products in such manner to ensure except for perils of the sea safe and undamaged delivery.

Article 4. Price and Payment

4.1 The prices of the products shall be determined in accordance with the price lists attached hereto and made a part hereof, which price list may be changed from time to time by the Manufacturer with 30 days prior notice.

4.2 Within 30 days after receipt of Manufacturer's confirmation of order, Distributor shall issue an irrevocable Letter of Credit in favor of Manufacturer.

4.3 Currency of Payment shall be in United States Dollars.

Article 5. Minimum Purchase

5.1 Distributor guarantees minimum purchases of the products from Manufacturer in the following amount, on FOB Busan, Korea basis :

(1) First year : U$100,000
(2) Second year : U$250,000
(3) Third year : U$450,000

For the purpose of this Article, the products shall be considered purchased when shipped by manufacturer.

5.2 When Distributor has fulfilled the minimum purchase guarantee as stipulated in Article 5.1, this Agreement shall be automatically be extended by successive three years period subject to Article 13, provided, however, that each successive period shall require a 10% increase of the minimum purchase volume.

5.3 If Distributor fails to purchase the minimum amount as stipulated in Article 5.1 and 5.2, Manufacturer may terminate this Agreement by a written notice as hereinafter provided for in Article 14.1(2) within one month after the expiration of the three years period of this Agreement, but Distributor shall have no other liability in connection therewith.

Article 6. Technical Assistance

6.1 Manufacturer engages themselves to supply Distributor with necessary Technical Assistance by means of informative and illustrated materials and to send all advertising materials suitable for promotion and advertising of the products.

6.2 Manufacturer shall train a reasonable number of technical personnel either in Korea or on site in the Territory by consent of both sides if it becomes necessary due to introduction of any new Products or generally in order to achieve better installation and maintenance standards. Costs for round trips, meals, lodging, and other expenses of the dispatched personnel of Distributor or Manufacturer for training shall be borne by Distributor.

6.3 The above Technical Assistance shall be implemented in English Language.

Article 7. Spare Parts

7.1 Distributor shall keep a sufficient level of spare parts in order to provide an efficient After Sales Services. Manufacturer shall also advise Distributor of the required spare parts and any stocking will be discussed and mutually agreed before orders are placed.

7.2 Manufacturer shall supply to Distributor spare parts for the products so long as Distributor continues to purchase the products pursuant to the terms and conditions of this Agreement and for two years after the last shipment of the products to Distributor. The price of the Spare Parts shall be consented by both parties. And at Manufacturer's option, Distributor may purchase standard spare parts from Manufacturer's suppliers directly for two years after the last shipment.

Article 8. Inspection and Warranty

8.1 Promptly after the receipt of the products, Distributor shall inspect or shall cause its qualified agent to insure that the quality standards, as agreed to by the parties in writing, have been met. If any of the products or any part of a product is found not to be in compliance with the quality standards, Manufacturer shall supply Distributor free of charge replacement for the products or the part of a product not meeting the quality standards, and/or shall indemnify the Distributor against any loss and damage suffered by the Distributor.

8.2 Manufacturer warrants that the products at the time of shipment shall be free from defects in material and workmanship. This warranty does not extend to any of the said products which have been : (1) subject to misuse, neglect, accident or abuse, (2) improperly repaired, or altered or modified in any way, and (3) used in violation of instructions furnished by Manufacturer.

8.3 Claims by Distributor in regard to any defect in the products must be in writing and be dispatched by Distributor with full particulars within one(1) year after receipt of the products.

Article 9. Distributor's Responsibility

9.1 Distributor shall maintain adequate stocks of the products throughout the Territory to meet its customers' demand in time. Distributor shall maintain adequate stocks of replacement parts, facilities and qualified mechanics throughout the Territory and shall provide reasonable after sale services to its customers.

9.2 Distributor shall undertake for its own account, advertisement, and sales promotions of the products and devote its best efforts toward obtaining the largest sales volume of the products in the Territory.

9.3 Whenever Manufacturer shall render to Distributor any complaints as to products from any dealer or customer in the Territory, Distributor shall immediately make an investigation and take a proper action.

Article 10. Report

Distributor shall make quarterly reports to Manufacturer on the sales of the products, the inventory of the products and parts thereof, general market conditions and others as Manufacturer requires.

Article 11. Trademarks

11.1 Distributor recognizes that any of trademarks, tradenames, designs, copyrights and other proprietary rights, used on or embodied in the products("Proprietary Rights") shall remain the exclusive property of Manufacturer. Distributor shall not have or acquire any right, title or interest in proprietary rights : provided, however, that Distributor may with the consent of Manufacturer indicate that it is an authorized distributor of the products. Upon termination of this Agreement for anycause, Distributor shall cease holding itself out as a distributor of the products and cease using in any way Manufacturer's name or its proprietary rights or any material similar thereto.

11.2 Distributor shall not alter, deface, remove, cover or mutilate in any manner the trademark, serial or model numbers, brand or Manufacturer's name attached or affixed to any of the products, without the consent of Manufacturer.

Article 12. Status of Distributor

12.1 This Agreement does not in any way create the relationship of principal and agent between Manufacturer and Distributor : and under no circumstances shall Distributor be considered to be the agent of Manufacturer. Distributor shall not act or attempt to act, or represent itself, directly or by implication, as an agent of Manufacturer or in any manner assume or create, or attempt to assume or create, any obligation, liability, representation, warranty or guarantee on behalf of, or in the name of Manufacturer.

12.2 Distributor shall at all times comply with all applicable laws, regulations, and orders of any government of the Territory or political subdivisions thereof relating to or in any way affecting this Agreement and Distributor's performance hereunder, including the obtaining of any required licenses, permits or approvals.

12.3 Distributor shall not disclose to any third party, without the prior written consent of Manufacturer, or use for any purpose other than the performance of its obligations under this

Agreement, any confidential information concerning the products or business affairs of Manufacturer(including, but not limited to, prices, discounts or product specifications) which it receives directly or indirectly from Manufacturer, or which it acquires or develops in the course of its transactions with Manufacturer.

Article 13. Term

13.1 This Agreement shall become effective upon signing and shall continue in full force and effect for a period of three years from the date hereof, unless earlier terminated pursuant to Article 14, and shall thereafter be automatically extended for successive three year periods of time unless, three months prior to the expiration of the term or any extension thereof, a notice of intention to finally terminate is given in writing by one party to the other.

13.2 Upon the extension of this Agreement in accordance with Article 13.1, the minimum purchase amount for each period shall be renewed and a new minimum purchase amount shall be mutually agreed upon in writing by the parties within two(2) months after commencement of each new period.

Article 14. Termination

14.1 This Agreement may be terminated at the option of Manufacturer, effective upon thirty(30) days prior written notice of termination given to Distributor, in the event of the happening of the following events :

(1) Should Distributor becomes bankrupt or insolvent, or have its business placed in the hands of a receiver, assignee or trustee, whether by voluntary act or otherwise : or

(2) Should Distributor fail to meet the minimum annual purchase requirements or otherwise fail to meet promptly any of its obligations pursuant to this Agreement : or

(3) Should Distributor be acquired by, or should itself acquire, in whole or in part a manufacturer of the products which in the reasonable judgement of Manufacturer competes to material extent with the products ; or

(4) Should Distributor attempts to assign this Agreement or any

rights hereunder without Manufacturer's prior written consent ; or

(5) If Distributor ceases to function as a going concern or to conduct its operations in the normal course of business.

14.2 All monies owed to Manufacturer upon termination shall become immediately due and payable and no cancellation or termination of this Agreement shall serve to release Distributor or its successors or assignee from any obligations under this Agreement.

Article 15. Force Majeure

Neither party shall be liable to the other party for nonperformance or delay in performance of any of its obligations under the Agreement due to war, revolution, riot, strike or other labor dispute, fire, flood, acts of government or any other causes reasonably beyond its control. Upon the occurrence of such a force majeure condition, the affected party shall immediately notify the other party of any further developments with evidence proving its occurrence. Immediately after such condition is removed, the affected party shall perform such obligation with all due speed.

Article 16. Governing Law

This Agreement shall be interpreted and governed by the laws of the Republic of Korea.

Article 17. Arbitration

All disputes, controversies or differences which may arise between the parties out of or in relation to or in connection with this Agreement or for the breach thereof shall be finally settled by arbitration in Seoul, Korea in accordance with the Commercial Arbitration Rules of the Korean Commercial Arbitration Board and under the law of Korea. The award rendered by the arbitrator(s) shall be final and binding upon both parties concerned.

Article 18. Miscellaneous Provisions

18.1 Notices

Any notice required or permitted to be given hereunder shall be in writing, and may be given by personal service, registered airmail, or by cable, facsimile or telex if confirmed on the same day in writing by registered airmail.

18.2 Entire Agreement-Amendments

This Agreement constitutes the entire understanding of Manufacturer and Distributor with respect to the subject matter hereof. No amendment, modification or alteration of any term of this Agreement shall be binding on either party unless the same shall be made in writing and executed by or on behalf of the parties hereto.

18.3 Assignment and Succession

This Agreement shall inure to the benefit of and be binding upon the parties hereto and their respective successors. No assignment of this Agreement shall be valid without the prior written consent of the other party hereto.

18.4 Waiver

All waivers hereunder must be in writing, and the failure of any party at any time to require the other party's performance of any obligations under this Agreement shall not affect the right subsequently to require performance of the obligation. Any waiver of any breach of any provision of this Agreement shall not be construed as a waiver of any continuing or succeeding breach of such provision or a waiver or modification of the provision.

18.5 Severability

If any one or more of the provisions contained in this Agreement shall be declared invalid, illegal or unenforceable in any respect, under any applicable law, the validity, legality and enforceability of the remaining provisions contained herein shall not in any way be affected and in such case the parties hereto oblige themselves to reach the intended purpose of the invalid provision by a new, valid and legal stipulation.

18.6 Headings

The section headings herein are included for purposes of convenience only any shall not affect the construction or interpretation of any of the provision of this Agreement. IN WITNESS WHEREOF, the parties hereto have caused this Agreement to be executed by their respective duly authorized officers.

Manufacturer,	Distributor
Korea Trading Co., Ltd.	America Trading Co., Ltd.
(signed)	(signed)

Chapter **7**

Order and Acknowledgement

Chapter

7 Order and Acknowledgement

The buyer often makes an offer in the form of an order in which case the seller should upon its receipt examine it in detail, and if there are doubtful points about the items and conditions in the order, he should contract the buyer and solve the problems.

Needless to say, exact compliance with every items of an order and exact performance of all the items and conditions are indispensable to succeed in international trade. When the seller accepts an order, he must make out an acceptance or acknowledgement of order and send it to the buyer.

7.1 Placing an Order

1. Order by e-mail

The essential qualities of an order by e-mail are accuracy and clarity. Failure in either of these may lead to trouble that cannot later be put right. When sending an order by mail:

① include full details of description, quantities, prices and so on.

② confirm the terms of conditions agreed in preliminary negotiations.

2. Legal position of parties

The seller who has quoted is not legally bound to accept the buyer's order, unless the quotation was made as a firm offer. According to English law, the buyer's order is an offer to buy and the arrangement is not legally binding until the seller has accepted the offer. After that, both parties are legally bound to their agreement.

1) The buyer's obligations

When a binding agreement comes into force, the buyer is required by law

① to accept the goods supplied, provided they comply with the terms of order;

② to pay for them at the time of delivery, unless there is an agreement to the contrary;

③ to check the goods as soon as possible(failure to give a prompt notice of faults to the seller will be taken as acceptance of the goods)

2) The seller's obligations

The seller is required by law

① to deliver the goods exactly at the agreed time;

② to guarantee the goods to be free from faults of which the buyer could not be aware at the time of purchase.

If faulty goods are delivered, the buyer can demand either reduction in price, or replacement of the goods, or cancellation of the order. He may also be able to claim damages. Routine orders for standard goods are short and formal, but they must include essential details concerning the goods, delivery and terms of payment. Where the order covers two or more items, they should be tabulated. This lessens the chances of items being overlooked.

7.2 Acknowledging the Order

When the seller receives an order that cannot be met at once, he needs to acknowledge it straight away. For small, routine orders, a printed acknowledgement or postcard may be enough, but a short letter stating when delivery may be expected is better and helps to create a good will.

If the goods ordered cannot be supplied, the seller needs to explain why, and to let the buyer know if suitable substitutes are available. When delivery to regular customers can be made immediately, the seller sends an invoice, sometimes with the goods and sometimes separately. The addition of a printed note at the foot, thanking the customer and hoping that he will find the goods satisfactory, is a worthwhile courtesy. When the invoice is sent separately from the goods, it serves as an advice note.

Whether the order does not carry a number, refer by name to the goods ordered-in general terms if there are a number of items. "First" order should be acknowledged by e-mail. The e-mail should;

① express a pleasure of receiving the order
② add a favorable comment on the goods ordered
③ include an assurance of prompt and careful attention
④ draw an attention to other products
⑤ express a hope for further orders.

7.3 Declining the Order

There are times when the seller does not accept the buyer's order as for example:

① where he is not satisfied with the buyer's terms and conditions
② where the buyer's credit is suspect
③ where the goods are not available.

E-mails rejecting orders must be written with the utmost care and with an eye to good will and future business. When sending such e-mails;

① express a regret your inability to meet the buyer's needs
② propose an alternative product, if one is available
③ express a hope for the opportunity to serve him another time

7.4 Sample Letters of Order and Acceptance

1. Order and Acceptance of Cosmetics

1) An order

Dear Mr. Lee,

We are pleased to give you our order for a trial based on your quotation and samples.

H. S.	Item No.	Description	Content	Q'ty	U/PRC CIP Beirut	Amount
3304.991000	270090001	Cleansing Lotion	125ml	120	@U$3.00	U$360,00
	270090002	Cleansing Foam	125ml	120	@U$2.27	U$272.40
	270090004	Scrub Foam	125ml	120	@U$2.30	U$276.00
	270090011	Skin Softener	125ml	120	@U$2.90	U$348.00
	270090016	Massage Cream	100gr	120	@U$4.30	U$516.00
	270090026	Toning Lotion	126ml	120	@U$2.90	U$348.00
	270090031	Moisturizing Cream	50ml	120	@U$3.49	U$418.00
	270090032	Sapolan Cream	40ml	120	@U$6.33	U$759.60
	270090033	Enriched Night Cr.	50ml	120	@U$3.43	U$411.60
TOTAL :				1,080pcs		U$3,709.60

In order to cover this order, we will instruct The Banque de Liban Et D'outre Mer in Beirut, Lebanon to issue an irrevocable L/C at sight in your favor for the amount of U$3,709.60.

Very truly yours,

2) An acceptance

Dear Mr. Aziz,

We received your order of May 12 and we thank you for your cooperation and assistance rendered to us. As you know well, we always try to meet the reasonable wishes of our customers.

We would like to accept your order and the products can be arranged for shipment by air as soon as possible after receipt of your L/C. As the products are extremely selling well in many countries, we don't have any doubt that they will prove suitable in your market. We will advise you when your order is ready for shipment and shall be pleased to assist you to the best of our ability at all times.

We assure you of our best attention to its execution. Also, we hope that your trial order will lead to a fruitful business relationship and repeat orders in the near future.

Yours faithfully,

2. Order and Acceptance Subject to the Extension of Delivery

1) An order

Gentlemen :

Thank you for your accepting our counter offer asking you to reduce the prices of computers by 5% each and you will find every particulars in our order sheet attached to this e-mail. This order is based on the samples and quotation you sent us last month.

As indicated in the order sheet, you need to execute this order in strict compliance with the stipulations in our L/C later.

We place this order on the clear understanding that the consignment is dispatched in time to reach us by the end of September as our customers urgently want them by that time at least.

We really hope you will promptly accept our order and make your careful execution as usual.

Very truly yours,

2) An acceptance subject to the extension of delivery date

Gentlemen :

We thank you for your order of computers developed lately for export and we would like to mention that every models you requested are in stock except the model No. 121.

We ran out of stock for that model now and we are afraid we can not guarantee delivery for that item within the time suggested because the components needed for the products have been held up in Japan and may not arrive in time.

The minimum period necessary for shipment is two months and we are anxious to serve you meeting your delivery date. We shall, of course, do our best to complete the shipment by the date stipulated. However a delay of the shipment seems to be unavoidable.

Therefore, if you are kind enough to extend the time of delivery for one month up to the early of November, we can accept your offer.

Otherwise, we can not but to send the model No. 121 later, which will be unsatisfactory to you.

Your confirmation on this matter would be appreciated.

Very truly yours,

3) An acceptance of delivery date

Gentlemen :

Thank you for your e-mail dated August 24 and we are pleased to inform you that we accepted your request to extend the delivery date.

As we contracted with our local distributors according to your previous delivery schedule, we had a hard time persuading them to accept your revised delivery date. A further delay in delivery, therefore, will cause a serious problem as they will refuse to accept the products.

Please send us your Sales Contracts so that we can sign them before we instruct our bank to issue a letter of credit.

We want this initial order to be the first step for our pleasant business relationship and we hope you will arrange for an immediate shipment.

Sincerely yours,

3. Order and Recommendation for a Substitute

1) An order

Dear Sirs,

We have the pleasure of attaching our order sheet to this e-mail and we believe that you will find every particulars in our order correct.

We already instructed our bank, The British Bank of the Middle East, to issue an irrevocable L/C in your favor for the value of U$70,694 and it will reach you through their correspondent, The Hongkong and Shanghai Banking Corporation Limited in Seoul, within this week.

This order is based on our business negotiations with you and our customers here and the quality has to be the same as the samples you sent us.

Please inform us of the Expected Time of Departure at the port of shipment as well as Expected Time of Arrival at Duabi and we trust that you will execute this trial order in strict compliance with the instructions in the L/C.

If your shipment turns out satisfactory, we can expect repeat orders from our customers,

Very truly yours,

2) Recommendation for a new model

Dear Sirs,

Thank you very much for your order No. 2001 asking us to ship the products not later than July 20.

We looked into your order sheet and we are sorry to inform you that the item No.#11 is no longer in production as domestic demand for this item has been reduced to the extent that we can not meet our break even point.

We would like to recommend a new model No.#101 which gives an attractive appearance and adds a greater decorative value maintaining every functions of the old model. We have received many repeat orders from other distributors since they were put on the market three months ago and this is a clear evidence that they will get a widespread popularity in the near future.

We will send you some samples and let us know if you can take this new model instead of No.#11 so that we can ship them together with other products.

We look forward to hearing from you as soon as possible

Sincerely yours,

4. Recommendation for a Substitute

Dear Sirs,

Thank you for your order of November 11 for 5,000 pcs of silk blouse and we are very sorry to inform you that we can not fill your order for the products you asked for as we can no longer supply that item.

As they are rather outmoded, the new model No. 20 which has recently been designed by our laboratory is now winning a popularity among overseas customers. The latest new model is much superior in design and quality to the old one and the materials procured from both domestic and overseas suppliers have gone up in prices rapidly for the last few years.

Considering other factors, we believe this model will interest you and really hope you can take advantage of good opportunity. We want this will lead you to place a large order with us soon.

Yours sincerely,

5. Refusal of an Order

Gentlemen :

We thank you very much for your order of high quality semiconductors and we fully understand that this is a promising business considering your marketing ability.

After a careful consideration on your requirements, however, we have come to the conclusion that we are unable to accept the order.

To reach the standard of your specifications, we have to increase and improve our production facilities. Moreover, we need at least three months to complete the new production system, while the time of shipment expires before then.

We really sorry not to be able to accept your order this time and if we have any chance to do business with you sometime later, we will do our best to serve you.

Yours very truly.

Chapter 8

Letter of Credit

Chapter

8

Letter of Credit

While distrust does exist between a seller and a buyer as to whether the other party will carry out his obligations, the problem can nevertheless be resolved by the involvement of a third party that guarantees payment to the seller and goods to the buyer. Banks have been chosen as that party since banks are much better trusted in the business world.

With a bank's involvement, the seller looks to the bank for payment instead of relying upon the ability or willingness of the buyer to pay, but the seller cannot obtain payment unless he complies with all the terms in the document issued by the bank. At the same time, the bank pays on behalf of the buyer against documents which represent the goods. Therefore, banks assist in the settlement of international commercial transactions by providing a safeguard for the parties involved and ensuring payment to the seller if he complies with the terms in the document. These objectives are accomplished by the use of a document called documentary letter of credit.

8.1 Definition and Parties of Letter of Credit

1. Definition of Letter of Credit

Letter of Credit means any arrangement, however named or described, that is irrevocable and thereby constitutes a definite undertaking of the issuing bank to honour a complying presentation.[1)]

"Honour" means :

① to pay at sight if the credit is available by sight payment.

② to incur a deferred payment undertaking and pay at maturity if the credit is available by deferred payment.

③ to accept a bill of exchange(draft) drawn by the beneficiary and pay at maturity if the credit is available by acceptance.

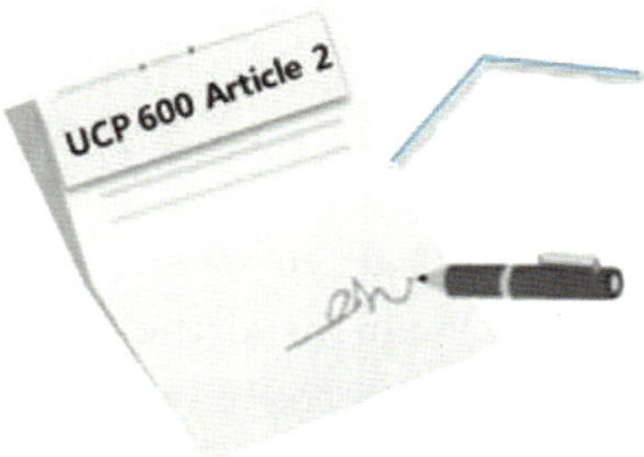

Credit means any arrangement, however named or described, that is irrevocable and thereby constitutes a definite undertaking of the issuing bank to honour a complying presentation.

"Letter of credit" or in strictly wording "Commercial Documentary Letter of Credit" may be defined as a letter or an instrument issued by a bank at the request of the buyer, authorizing the seller to draw drafts on a bank or the buyer for an amount not exceeding a stipulated sum, and guaranteeing the acceptance and payment of the drafts if drawn in compliance with the terms set forth in the letter of credit.

A commercial letter of credit is a contractual agreement between a bank, known as the issuing bank, on behalf of one of its customer, authorizing another bank, known as the advising or confirming bank, to make payment to the beneficiary. The issuing bank, on the request of its customer, issues the letter of credit. The issuing bank makes a commitment to honor the draft drawn under the credit. The beneficiary is normally the provider of goods and/or services.

---

1) UCP 600, Article 2.

2. Parties of Letter of Credit

1) Basic Parties

(1) Issuing Bank

Issuing bank means the bank that issues a credit at the request of an applicant or on its own behalf. The issuing banks' role is to provide a guarantee to the seller that the bank will pay the seller the amount due if the documents are complied with the terms and conditions in the letter of credit. The issuing bank located in the buyer's country issues letters of credit at the request of the buyer(applicant). The issuing bank will naturally be the 'drawee' in case the drafts are drawn on it.

(2) Beneficiary

Beneficiary means the party in whose favour a credit is issued. The letter of credit is a distinct and separate transaction from the contract on which it is based. The issuing bank is not liable for performance of the underlying contract between the customer and beneficiary. The issuing bank's obligation to the buyer is to examine all documents to insure that they meet all the terms and conditions of the credit.

(3) Confirming Bank

Confirming bank means the bank that adds its confirmation to a credit upon the issuing bank's authorization or request. The confirming bank adds its own undertaking to that of the issuing bank. The confirming bank is usually the advising bank.

A confirming bank is irrevocably bound to honour or negotiate as of the time it adds its confirmation to the credit.[2)]

A confirming bank undertakes to reimburse another nominated bank that has honoured or negotiated a complying presentation and forwarded the documents to the confirming bank. Reimbursement for the amount of a complying presentation under a credit available by acceptance or deferred payment is due at maturity, whether or not another nominated bank prepaid or purchased before maturity. A confirming bank's undertaking to reimburse another nominated bank is independent of the confirming bank's

2) UCP 600, Article 8. b.

undertaking to the beneficiary.[3)]

2) Other Parties

(1) Applicant

Applicant means the party on whose request the credit is issued. The applicant is the person who requests a bank to issue a letter of credit in favor of the beneficiary. Sometimes he is referred to as the "Opener" or "Accredited buyer" considering from his position in the sales contract. Consequently he also becomes the "Consignee" of the contracted goods, and eventually the "Accountee" of drafts.

(2) Advising Bank

Advising bank means the bank that advises the credit at the request of the issuing bank. An advising bank, usually a foreign correspondent bank of the issuing bank, will just advise the L/C to the beneficiary without any payment obligation. The advising bank would be responsible for sending the documents presented from the beneficiary to the issuing bank. If the issuing bank does not pay the beneficiary, the advising bank is not obligated to pay. Usually, the advising bank is located in the beneficiary's country and it is also called as notifying bank and it is generally the 'correspondent' of the issuing bank.

(3) Negotiating Bank

Negotiating bank means the bank with which the credit is available or any bank in the case of a credit available with any bank. The negotiating bank is in the beneficiary's country, which negotiates or discounts the drafts(bill of exchange) drawn under the credit by the beneficiary. The advising bank often becomes the negotiating bank.

(4) Paying Bank

Paying bank means the bank that makes payment to the beneficiary against presentation of stipulated documents.

---

3) UCP 600, Article 8. c.

(5) Accepting Bank

Accepting bank is the bank nominated in the credit to accept usance drafts drawn on it.

(6) Reimbursing Bank

Remitting bank is the bank which sends the documents to the issuing bank.

8.2 Characteristics of Letter of Credit

1. Principle of Independence

A credit by its nature is a separate transaction from the sale or other contract on which it may be based. Banks are in no way concerned with or bound by such contract, even if any reference whatsoever to it is included in the contract. Consequently, the undertaking of a bank to honour, to negotiate or to fulfil any other obligation under the contract is not subject to claims or defences by the applicant resulting from its relationship with the issuing bank or the beneficiary.

A beneficiary can in no case avail itself of the contractual relationships existing between the applicant and the issuing bank.[4)]

2. Principle of Abstraction

Banks deal with documents and not with goods, services or performance to which the documents may relate.[5)]

4) UCP 600, Article 4.
5) UCP 600, Article 5.

8.3 Flow of Documentary Credit

Payment credit, acceptance credit and negotiation credit can be used in international transaction. The following is an example of the flow of a negotiation credit at sight.

1. Contract of Sale

The seller and the buyer draw up a contract in which they agree to use a negotiation credit at sight.

2. Request for Issuing a L/C

The applicant(the buyer) requests its bank, the issuing bank, to issue a negotiation credit at sight in favor of the beneficiary(the seller). The issuing bank issues a credit at the request of the applicant.

3. Issue a L/C

The issuing bank issues a L/C at the request of the applicant and advises it to its correspondent bank(advising bank) in seller's country by means of SWIFT.

4. Advise the L/C to the Beneficiary

The advising bank establishes authenticity of the L/C using signature books or test codes, then advises the credit to the beneficiary. The confirming bank(if any) may confirm the L/C by adding its own payment undertaking.

5. Receive the L/C and start arranging the goods

The beneficiary examines if the terms and conditions of the L/C correspond to those in the contract of sale and the seller starts arranging the goods.

6. Contracts of Carriage and Insurance

Before shipment of the goods, the beneficiary effects an insurance on an insurance company, if necessary, and books ship's space on a shipping company. As for contract of carriage under the rules of CPT, CIP, DAT, DAP, DDP, CFR and CIF, the seller must contract or procure a contract for the carriage of the goods. As for contract of insurance under the rules of CIP, CIF, the beneficiary must obtain, at its own expense, cargo insurance.

7. Shipment of Goods

The beneficiary should clear the goods for export and place the goods at the place the carrier nominates, then the goods are shipped on board the vessel.

8. Issue Bill of Lading

After shipment, the carrier issues clean on board bill of lading. The vessel operating common carrier(VOCC) issues a master B/L(groupage B/L) for non-vessel operating common carrier(NVOCC) and the international freight forwarder issues house B/L for the beneficiary.

9. Ask for Negotiation

The beneficiary should arrange the documents required in the L/C such as commercial invoice, transport document, insurance document, etc. The seller presents the documents together with drafts to the negotiating bank. If the L/C is restricted to a bank for negotiation, the documents should be presented to that bank. The documents presented include ① commercial invoice, ② bill of lading, ③ insurance policy, ④ packing list, ⑤ country of origin, ⑥ inspection certificate and other documents stipulated in the credit.

10. Payment by the Negotiating Bank

The negotiating bank examines the documents presented by the beneficiary and pays the beneficiary against a complying presentation.

11. Send Drafts and Documents

The negotiating bank presents the documents together with drafts to the issuing bank. If the L/C grants the reimbursing bank to pay, the negotiating bank asks the reimbursing bank to pay while the negotiating bank presents the documents to the issuing bank.

12. Payment by the Issuing Bank

The issuing bank must honour if a presentation is complying. The issuing bank pays the negotiating bank or pays the reimbursing bank so that the reimbursing bank can pay back to the negotiating bank according to the requirements of the credit.

13. Present the Documents

The issuing bank presents the documents presented by the negotiating bank to the applicant(buyer).

14. Payment by the Applicant

The applicant(buyer) pays the issuing bank and receives the documents.

15. Arrival Notice of the Goods

The carrier gives an arrival notice of the goods to the applicant(buyer) and discharges the goods.

16. Clear the Goods for Import

The buyer clears the goods for import and pays import duty.

17. Present the B/L to the Carrier

The buyer presents the bill of lading to the carrier and asks for the delivery of the goods.

18. Receive the Goods from the Carrier

The applicant presents the bill of lading to the carrier and receives the goods.

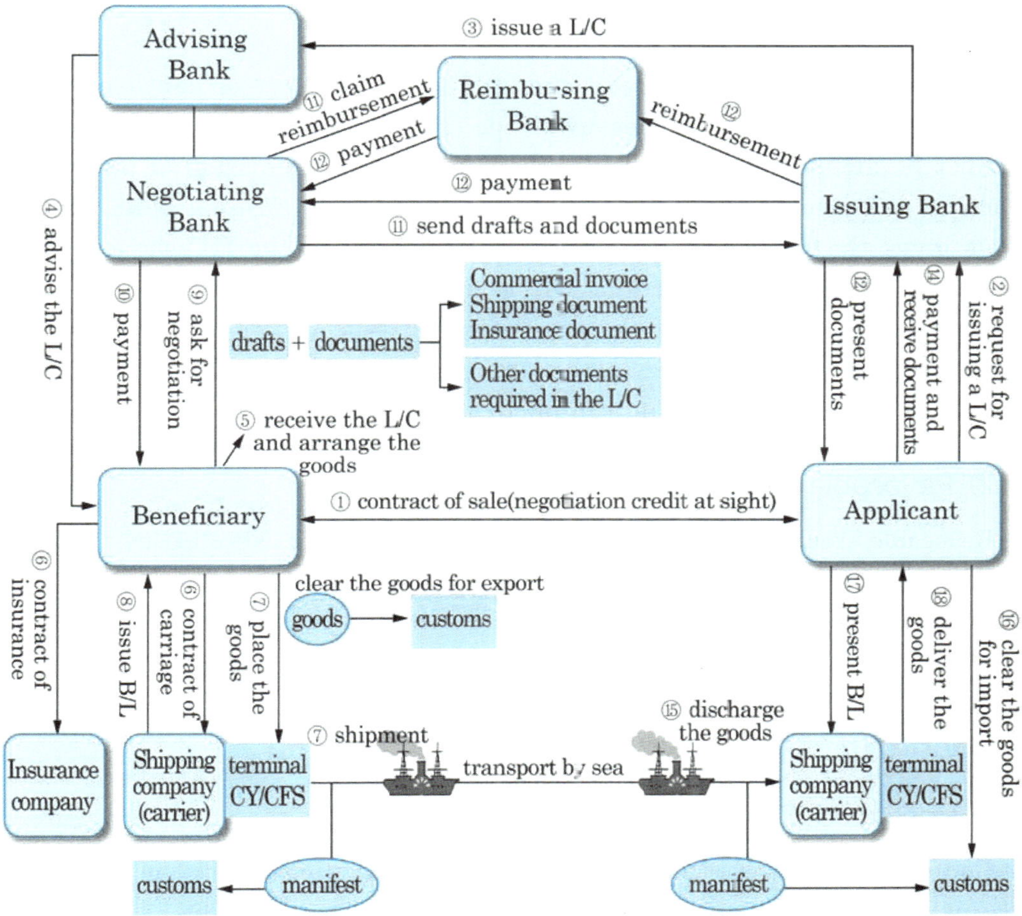

Figure 8.1 Workflow of documentary letter of credit

8.4 Types of Letter of Credit

1. Irrevocable Credit and Revocable Credit

1) Irrevocable Credit

Irrevocable credit is the credit that cannot be changed or cancelled without the consents of all parties involved. An irrevocable credit, once issued, cannot be amended or cancelled without expressed permission of all parties such as the issuing bank, the beneficiary and the confirming bank, if any. This gives the beneficiary a confidence to engage in the transaction when payment otherwise is uncertain. The letter of credit guarantees payment no matter what happens. It is the most common type of letter of credit in international trade. According to the Article 3 in UCP 600, a credit is irrevocable even if there is no indication to that effect.

2) Revocable Credit

Revocable credit is the credit that may be amended or cancelled by the issuing bank at any moment and without prior notice to the beneficiary before the documents have been paid, accepted or negotiated. Revocable credit is not used any more and all letters of credit are irrevocable however named or described.

2. Confirmed Credit and Unconfirmed Credit

1) Confirmed Credit

Confirmed credit is the credit in which the issuing bank's obligation to pay is backed(confirmed) by a second bank. A confirmed credit has the commitment of the confirming bank besides that of the issuing bank's commitment. The confirming bank is the bank that adds its confirmation to a credit upon the issuing bank's authorization or request. Confirmation means a definite undertaking of the confirming bank, in addition to that of the issuing bank, to honour or negotiate a complying presentation.

2) Unconfirmed Credit

Unconfirmed letter of credit is the credit which has not been guaranteed or confirmed by any bank other than the issuing bank. An unconfirmed credit contains the commitment of the issuing bank only. The advising bank merely informs the beneficiary of the letter of credit.

3. Types of Credit

1) Payment Credit

Payment credit is the credit that a paying bank makes payment to the nominated bank the issuing bank appoints against complying presentation. The payment credit does not require drafts usually and it is classified into sight payment credit and deferred payment credit.

(1) Sight payment credit

Sight payment credit is the credit that requires payment to be made upon presentation of documents. It is a credit in which an issuing bank authorizes a seller to present documents of title without bill of exchange (draft) to the issuing bank or its correspondent and undertakes to pay the seller against the documents presented. Therefore, the bank(advising bank or paying bank) nominated by the issuing bank pays a complying presentation. Drafts would not normally be called for.

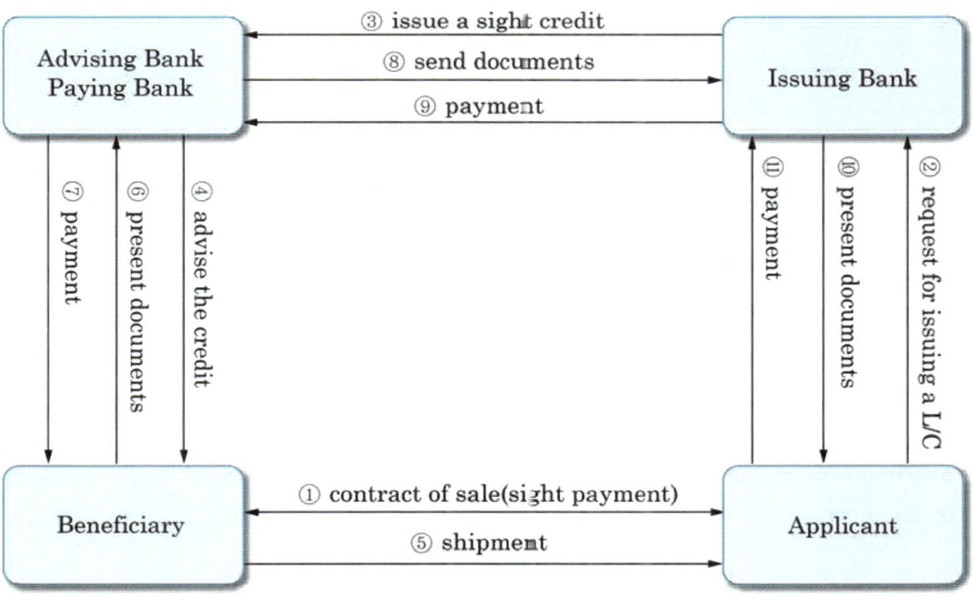

(2) Deferred payment credit

Deferred payment is the credit that requires payment to be made after a period of time specified in the letter of credit. The payment period is usually determined as specific number of days after the date of the transport document, the date of drafts or the date of complying presentation. Drafts are not required under deferred payment credit. The bank(advising bank or paying bank) nominated by the issuing bank incurs a deferred payment undertaking and pays at maturity.

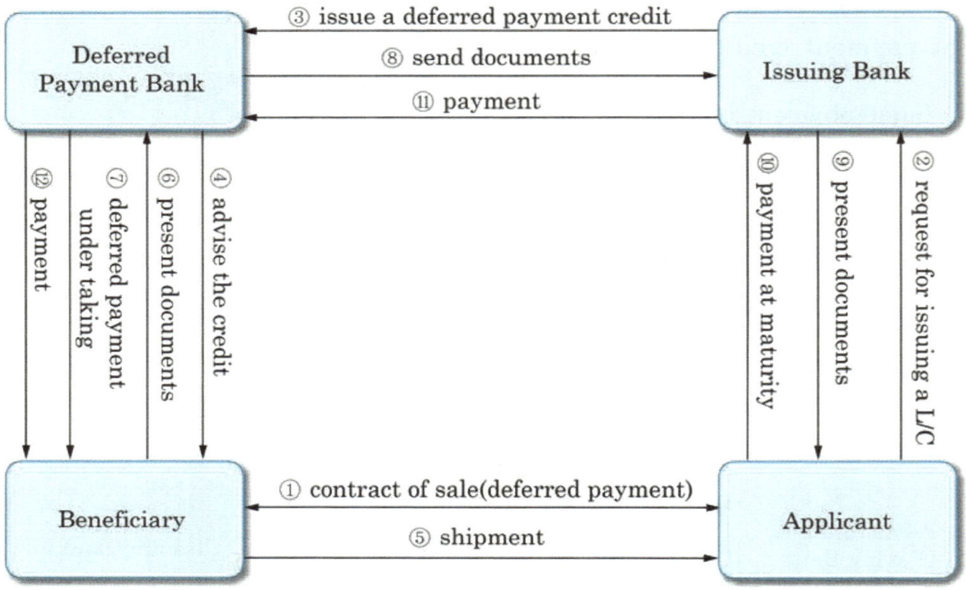

2) Acceptance Credit

Acceptance credit is the credit that is paid by a time draft authorizing payment after a specific date, if the documents are complied with the terms and conditions of the credit. An accepting bank nominated by the issuing bank accepts drafts drawn by the beneficiary and pays at maturity. It is a credit in which the issuing bank authorizes a seller to draw drafts on it or its correspondent in the country of the seller, and authorizes the nominated bank to accept the drafts drawn and pay at maturity.

(1) Shipper's usance credit

Shipper's usance credit is the credit that the seller bears the interest during the usance period on behalf of the buyer. The expression such as " Usance interest is for the account of beneficiary" is used in the credit and it is also called as seller's usance credit.

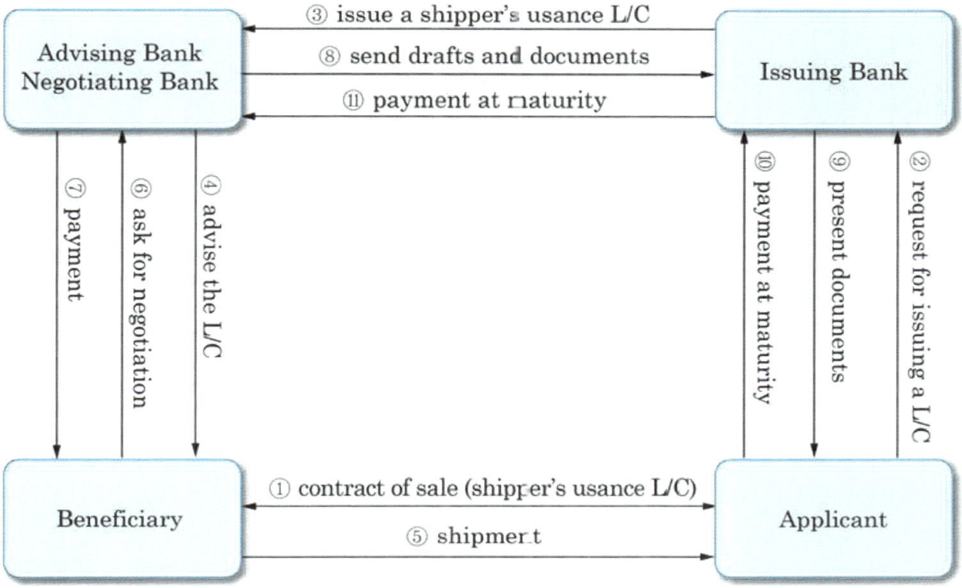

(2) Banker's usance credit

Banker's usance credit is the credit that the accepting bank pays interest during the usance period on behalf of the buyer. Usance drafts must be negotiated at sight basis and discount charges are for account of the buyer. The negotiating bank must negotiate the drafts at sight basis for the face amount and interest is for account of the buyer. Payment must be made on at sight basis with all discount charges for account of the buyer. The expression such as "Usance drafts must be negotiated on at sight basis and acceptance commission and discount charges are for the account of the buyer" is used.

① Overseas banker's usance credit

Overseas banker's usance credit is the credit that a bank in the seller's country(overseas bank) pays usance interest for account of the buyer.

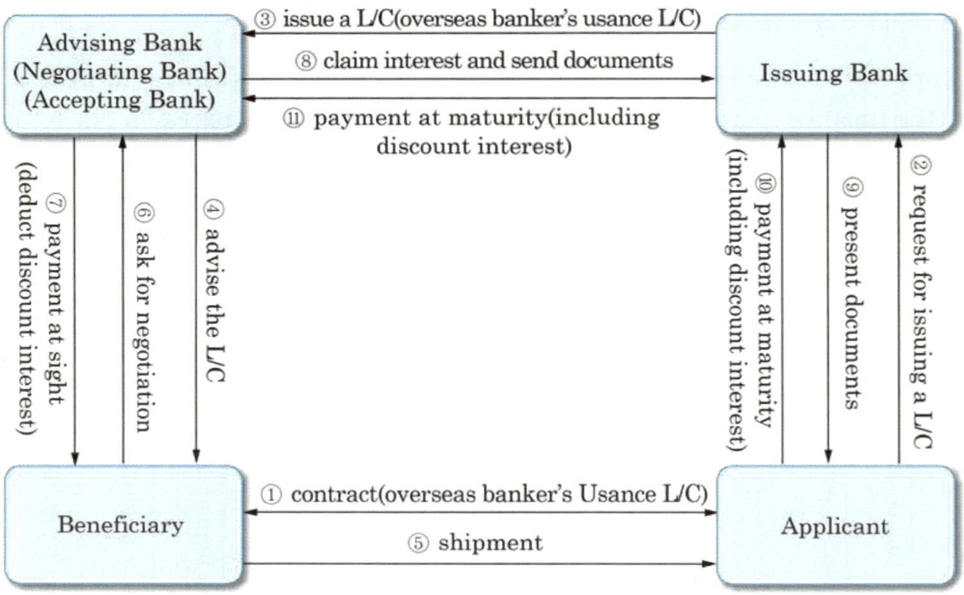

② Domestic banker's usance credit

Domestic banker's usance credit is the credit that a bank in the buyer's country(domestic bank) pays usance interest for account of the buyer.

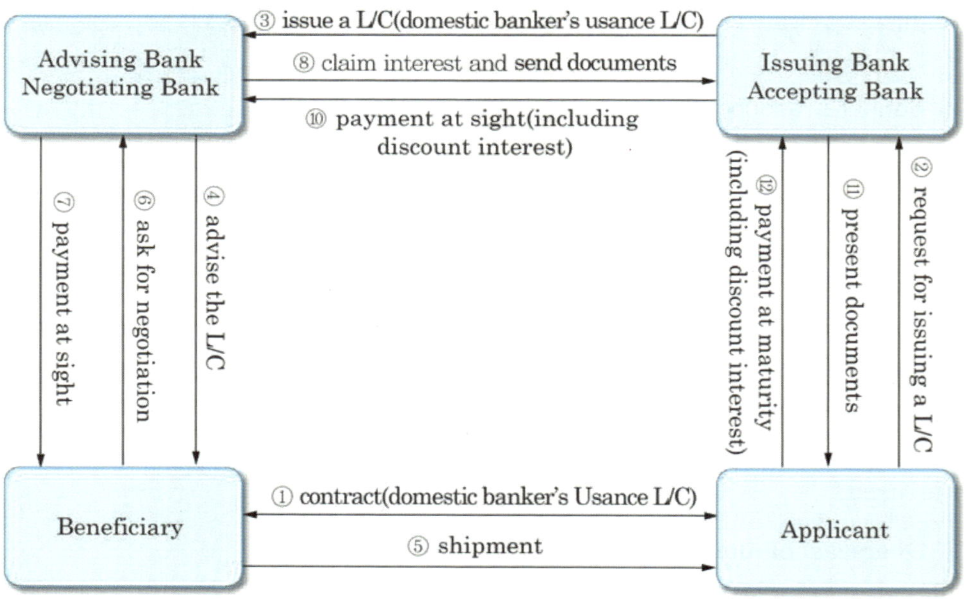

3) Negotiation Credit

Negotiation means the purchase by the nominated bank of drafts (drawn on a bank other than the nominated bank) and/or documents under a complying presentation, by advancing or agreeing to advance funds to the beneficiary on or before the banking day on which reimbursement is due to the nominated bank.[6]

Negotiation credit is the credit that authorizes the beneficiary to draw on the issuing bank and to negotiate the drafts with the nominated bank or with its own or any bank. The benefit of the negotiation credit is that the seller can discount the drafts prior to the date for payment under the credit and the bank discounting the drafts has the security of the issuing bank's undertaking to pay the drafts at maturity.

(1) Sight negotiation credit

Sight negotiation credit is the credit that the issuing bank guarantees drawers, endorsers and bona fide holders that drafts drawn under and negotiated in conformity with the terms of the credit will be duly honoured on presentation.

The negotiating bank nominated by the issuing bank effects negotiation under the credit, unless the credit is freely negotiable by any bank. Sight negotiation credit enables the beneficiary to obtain immediate funds from the bank authorized to negotiate by presenting that bank the documents called for under the credit including sight drafts.

(2) Usance negotiation credit

Usance negotiation credit is the credit that the issuing bank guarantees drawers, endorsers and bona fide holders that drafts drawn under and negotiated in conformity with the terms of the credit will be duly honoured at maturity.

The beneficiary will present the documents to this bank including usance drafts drawn on the party nominated in the credit. The negotiating bank will process the documents and forward them to the issuing bank for payment at maturity. The issuing bank will in due course inform the negotiating bank of the maturity date of the drafts.

---

6) UCP 600, Article 2.

Table 8-1 Comparison of negotiation credit, payment credit and acceptance credit

Types of Credit	Payment time	Contents	
Payment Credit	at sight	Sight payment credit	
	usance	Deferred payment credit	
Acceptance Credit	usance	Acceptance credit	
Negotiation Credit	at sight	Sight negotiation credit	Open credit Restricted credit
	usance	Usance negotiation credit	

4. Time of Payment

1) Sight Credit

Sight letter of credit is the credit that is payable on presentation of the necessary documents. It is the credit that is payable as soon as the required documents have been presented.

2) Usance Credit

Usance credit is the credit payable at a determined future date after presentation of conforming documents. It requires payment a certain number of days after the appropriate documents are presented. The due date is calculated based on the followings.

(1) at ××× days after B/L date

It means that payment is to be effected on a specified number of date after date of bill of lading.

(2) at ××× days after date

It means that payment is to be effected on a specified number of date after date of bill of exchange(or draft).

(3) At ××× days after sight

It means that payment is to be effected on a specified number of date after sight by the bank.

5. Transferable Credit and Non-transferable Credit

1) Transferable Credit

(1) Definition of transferable credit

A transferable credit means a credit that specifically states it is "transferable". A transferable credit may be made available in whole or in part to another second beneficiary at the request of the first beneficiary. A transferable credit is generally used when the first beneficiary is not the actual supplier of the goods, but an intermediary(middleman or agent). In a transferable letter of credit, the first beneficiary(the seller) may request the paying, accepting or negotiating bank to make the credit available in whole or in part to one or more second beneficiary(ies). The second beneficiary can be an export-manufacturer or an export-trader. The L/C is expressly designated "transferable" by the issuing bank at the request of the applicant.

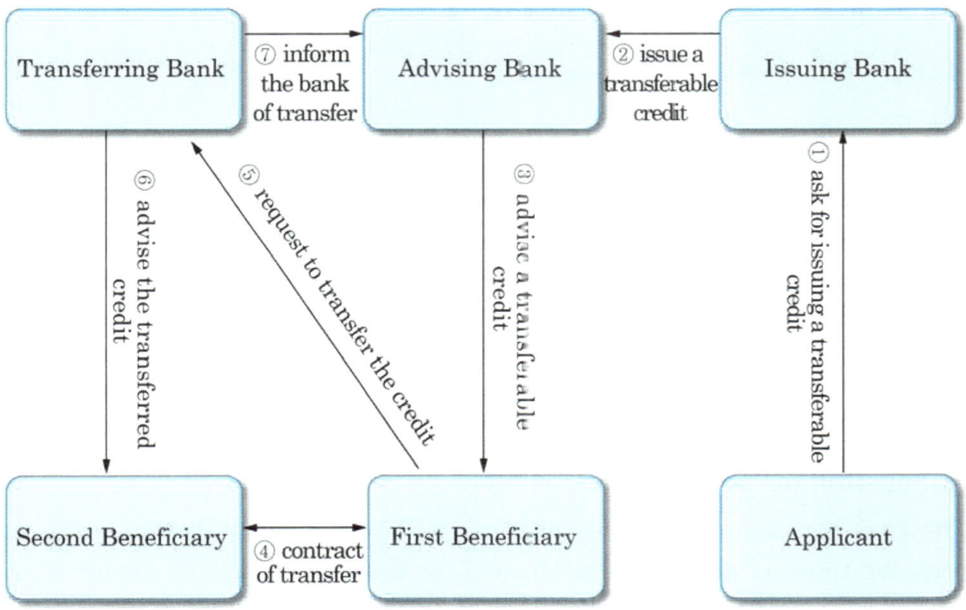

(2) Transfer of credit

A transferable credit can be transferred in part to more than one second beneficiary provided partial drawings or shipments are allowed. However, a transferred credit can not be transferred at the request of a second beneficiary to any subsequent beneficiary. The first beneficiary is not considered to be a subsequent beneficiary.[7)]

(3) conditions of the credit which can be reduced or curtailed

The transferred credit must accurately reflect the terms and conditions of the credit including confirmation. But, the followings may be reduced or curtailed when transferred.

① the amount of the credit
② any unit price stated therein
③ the expiry date
④ the period for presentation or
⑤ the latest shipment date or given period for shipment

(4) Increase of insurance cover

The percentage for which insurance cover must be effected may be increased to provide the amount of cover stipulated in the credit.

(5) Rights of transferer

① Substitution of the name of the applicant

The name of the first beneficiary may be substituted for that of the applicant in the credit. When transferring the credit, the first beneficiary may substitute its name for the applicant.

② Substitution of invoice and draft

The first beneficiary has the right to substitute its own invoice and draft, if any, for those of a second beneficiary for an amount not in excess of that stipulated in the credit, and upon such substitution the first beneficiary can draw under the credit for the difference, if any, between its invoice and the invoice of a second beneficiary.[8)]

---

7) UCP 600, Article 38, d.
8) UCP 600, Article 38, h.

③ **The place of honour or negotiation**

The first beneficiary, in its request for transfer, indicates that honour or negotiation is to be effected to a second beneficiary at the place to which the credit has been transferred, up to and including the expiry date of the credit.

Table 8-2 Conditions of the credit which can be reduced or curtailed

Division	Contents
Reduction, Curtailment	① the amount of the credit ② any unit price stated therein ③ the expiry date ④ the period for presentation or ⑤ the latest shipment date or given period for shipment
Increase of insurance cover	The percentage for which insurance cover must be effected may be increased to provide the amount of cover stipulated in the credit.

2) Non-transferable Credit

Non-transferable credit is the credit that can not be made available in whole or in part to another second beneficiary. The L/C usually indicates "transferable" in the case of a transferable credit. In the absence of such indication, the L/C is deemed to be non-transferable

6. With Recourse Credit and Without Recourse Credit

1) With Recourse Credit

"Recourse" means that the beneficiary doesn't consider the payment by the negotiating bank as final until the documents are accepted by the issuing bank. With recourse credit is the credit permitting the negotiating bank that negotiated the drafts drawn by the beneficiary, bona-fide holder and endorser to ask the beneficiary for reimbursement of the payment already made if they can not receive the payment from the issuing bank.

2) Without Recourse Credit

Without recourse credit is the credit not permitting the negotiating bank that negotiated the drafts drawn by the beneficiary, bona-fide holder and endorser to ask the beneficiary for reimbursement of the payment made even if they can not receive the payment from the issuing bank. Negotiation is normally effected on a with recourse basis in Korea.

7. Back-to-Back Credit

Back to Back credit is the term given to an ancillary credit, which arises where the beneficiary uses the credit granted to him by the issuing bank to support another credit granted by the beneficiary's bank to his supplier.

8. Revolving Credit

A revolving credit is the credit the amount of which remains constant for a given period and it becomes automatically available again for the full amount either immediately or perhaps as soon as an advice that earlier draft has been paid is received.

9. Standby L/C

A standby credit is a written instrument issued by a bank(Issuing Bank) at the request of its customer(Applicant) on behalf of a beneficiary, whereby the issuing bank agrees to provide financial remedy in the event that the applicant defaults on any terms and conditions specified under the Standby Letter of Credit.

This L/C is a kind of clean L/C and it is called commercial paper L/C, or guarantee L/C, or performance L/C. It is a document by which the issuing bank promises the beneficiary that it will bear some liabilities on behalf of the applicant if the later has not duly fulfilled his obligations as required by the contract. The standby credit is often used to guarantee performance or to strengthen the credit worthiness of a customer.

Table 8-3 Kinds of Letter of Credit

	Division	Kinds of Letter of Credit
Credits	Documents required	• Documentary credit • Clean credit
	Revocation	• Revocable credit • Irrevocable credit
	Confirmation	• Confirmed credit • Unconfirmed credit
	Forms	• Payment credit • Acceptance credit • Negotiation credit
	Payment Time	• Sight credit • Usance credit
	With Recourse Without Recourse	• With recourse credit • Without recourse credit
	Transfer	• Transferable credit • Non-transferable credit
	Use	• Local credit • Master credit
Special Credits	Purpose	• Stand-by credit • Red clause credit • Revolving credit • Back to Back credit

Form 8-1 A Sample of SWIFT L/C(1)

(MT 700) ISSUE OF A DOCUMENTARY CREDIT
From : BANK OF AMERICA, NEW YORK, U.S.A. ①
To : KOREA EXCHANGE BANK, 181, EULJIRO 2-GA, JUNG-GU, C.P.O Box 2924, SEOUL, KOREA ⑨
:27 Sequence of total : 1/1 ②
:40A form of documentary credit : IRREVOCABLE ③
:20 documentary credit number : MD1NY404NS00018 ④
:31C date of issue : 5/15/20×× ⑤
:31D date and place of expiry : 8/10/20×× KOREA ⑥
:50 applicant : BROWN CO., Ltd. 310 FIFTH AVE. NEW YORK, NY10118, U.S.A.⑦
:59 beneficiary : DAEHAN CO., LTD. CPO BOX 195, SEOUL, KOREA. ⑧
:32B currency code amount : USD500,000 ⑩
:39A percent credit amount tolerance : 10/10 ⑪
:41D available with by name, address : ANY BANK BY NEGOTIATION ⑫
:42C drafts at : SIGHT ⑬
:42A drawee : BANK OF AMERICA, 150 BROADWAY, NEW YORK, NY 10038, U.S.A ⑭
:43P partial shipments : ALLOWED ⑮
:43T transshipment : NOT ALLOWED ⑯
:44A loading on board/dispatch/taking in charge : BUSAN, KOREA ⑰
:44B for transportation to : NEW YORK, U.S.A. ⑱
:44C latest date of shipment : 7/25/20×× ⑲
:45A description of goods and/or services
2,000 PCS OF COMPUTERS AS PER SALES NOTE No. A01 DATED APRIL 10, 20×× CIF NEW YORK. INCOTERMS® 2010 ⑳
:46A documents required
+SIGNED COMMERCIAL INVOICE IN TRIPLICATE ㉑
+PACKING LIST IN TRIPLICATE ㉒
+FULL SET OF CLEAN ON BOARD OCEAN BILL OF LADING MADE OUT TO THE ORDER OF BANK OF AMERICA MARKED FREIGHT PREPAID AND NOTIFY ACCOUNTEE ㉓
+MARINE INSURANCE POLICY OR CERTIFICATE IN DUPLICATE, ENDORSED IN BLANK FOR 110PCT OF INVOICE VALUE, EXPRESSLY STIPULATING THAT CLAIMS ARE PAYABLE IN NEW YORK, USA AND IT MUST INCLUDE INSTITUTE CARGO CLAUSE(C) ㉔
+CERTIFICATE OF ORIGIN IN DUPLICATE ㉕
+INSPECTION CERTIFICATE IN DUPLICATE ㉖
+CERTIFICATE OF WEIGHT AND MEASUREMENT IN DUPLICATE ㉗
:47A additional conditions
SHIPMENT MUST BE EFFECTED BY SNCDV LINE ONLY ㉘
THIS CREDIT IS TRANSFERABLE ㉙
ALL DOCUMENTS MUST BEAR OUR CREDIT NUMBER ㉚
T/T REIMBURSEMENT NOT ALLOWED ㉛
:48 period for negotiation : DOCUMENTS MUST BE PRESENTED WITHIN 10 DAYS AFTER THE DATE OF BILL OF LADING BUT WITHIN THE CREDIT VALIDITY ㉜
:49 confirmation instructions : WITHOUT ㉝
:53A reimbursement bank : BANK OF AMERICA, NEW YORK, NY10015, U.S.A.㉞
:71B charges : ALL BANKING COMMISSIONS AND CHARGES OUTSIDE U.S.A. ARE FOR ACCOUNT OF BENEFICIARY ㉟
:78 instructions to the paying/accepting/negotiating bank: DRAFTS MUST BE SENT TO DRAWEE BANK FOR YOUR REIMBURSEMENT BY COURIER SERVICE IN ONE LOT.㊱ WE HEREBY ENGAGE WITH DRAWERS, ENDORSERS AND BONE FIDE HOLDERS THAT DRAFTS DRAWN UNDER AND NEGOTIATED IN CONFORMITY WITH THE TERMS OF THIS CREDIT WILL BE DULY HONORED ON PRESENTATION㊲ THE AMOUNT AND DATE OF NEGOTIATION OF EACH DRAFTS MUST BE ENDORSED ON THE REVERSE HEREOF BY THE NEGOTIATING BANK ㊳
:72 sender to receiver information : THIS CREDIT IS SUBJECT TO UCP(2007 REVISION) ICC PUBLICATION NO.600 ㊴

Form 8-2 A Sample of SWIFT L/C(AT SIGHT)

Application header block :	
: Input/Output Identifier	: I Outgoing Message
: Transaction Typer	: 700 issue of a documentary credit
: Transaction Priority	: n Normal
: From	: WOORI BANK, HUIHYUN-DONG, JUNG-GU, SEOUL, KOREA
: To	: BANK OF CHINA 20 NANJING EAST RD, HUANGPU, SHANGHAI, CHINA

Text Block :	
/27 : sequence of total	: 1/1
/40A : form of documentary credit	: IRREVOCABLE
/20 : documentary credit number	: M1234 606NS00018
/31C : date of issue	: 06/24/20××
/31D : date and place of expiry	: 08/20/20×× HONG KONG
/50 : applicant	: KOREA TOYS CO., LTD. 159-1 SAMSUNGDONG KANGNAMGU, SEOUL, KOREA
/59 : beneficiary	: CHINA TOYS CO., LTD. 25 NANJRM 1000 CHAI WAN IND. CITY PHAING WEST RD, HUANGPU, SHANGHAI, CHINA
/32B : currency code amount	: USD 150,000.00
/39A : pcrcent credit amount toterance	: 10/10
/41D : available with by name, address	: ANY BANK BY NEGOTIATION
/42C : drafts at	: AT SIGHT
/42A : drawee	: WOORI BANK HUIHYUN-DONG, JUNG-GU, SEOUL, KOREA
/43P : partial shipment	: ALLOWED
/43T : transshipment	: NOT ALLOWED
/44A : on board/Disp/taking charge	: SHANGHAI, CHINA
/44B : for transportation to	: BUSAN, KOREA
/44C : latest date of shipment	: 08/10/20××.
/45A : description of goods and/or services 700 PAIRS OF CHINESE GIANT BEAR TOYS FOB SHANHAI, CHINA	
/46A : documents required +SIGNED COMMERCIAL INVOICE IN QUINTUPLICATE +PACKING LIST IN TRIPLICATE +FULL SET OF CLEAN ON BOARD OCEAN BILL OF LANDING MADE OUT TO THE ORDER OF WOORI BANK MARKED FREIGHT COLLECT AND NOTIFY APPLICANT +CERTIFICATE OF ORIGIN +INSPECTION CERTIFICATE IN DUPLICATE	
/47A : additional conditions +ALL DOCUMENTS MUST BEAR OUR CREDIT NUMBER M1234 606NS00018 +T/T REIMBURSEMENT NOT ALLOWED +OUANTITY 10PCT MORE OR LESS ALLOWED +THIRD PARTY DOCUMENTS ACCEPTABLE	
/71B : charges	: ALL BANKING COMMISSIONS AND CHARGES INCLUDING REIMBURSEMENT CHARGES OUTSIDE KOREA ARE FOR ACCOUNT OF BENEFICIARY
/49 : confirmation instructions	: WITHOUT
/53A : reimbursement bank	: BANK OF CHINA 20 NANJING EAST RD, HUANGPU, SHANGHAI, CHINA
/78 : instructions to the pay/acc/neg bk DRAFTS MUST BE SENT TO DRAWEE BANK FOR YOUR REIMBURSEMENT AND ALL DOCUMENTS SHOULD BE SENT TO US BY COURIER SERVICE IN ONE LOT	
/72 : sender to receiver information	: THIS CREDIT IS SUBJECT TO UCP(2007 REVISION) ICC PUBLICATION NO. 600

Form 8-3 A Sample of SWIFT L/C(USANCE)

Adivice Br. : 충무로 *Adivice Date : 20××. 07. 24(FAX/A12)
Adivice of*Adivice No. : A-0663-902-03402
Issue of Documentary Credit*Credit No. : 128RN71218

* Beneficiary : TEL 3166-449
  SEOUL TRADING CO., LTD.
  25-5, CHUNGMURO 1-KA,
  SEOUL, KOREA
* Applicant :
  DUNHILL INC., LTD.
  440, FIFTH AVE. NEW YORK
  N.Y. 440014, U.S.A.
* Amount : USD21,700.00
* Issuing Bank : TEL 0222-1346-1234
  BANK OF AMERICA NEW YORK, U.S.A.
* Expiry Date : March 25, 20××.
* Senders bank : 123456

Gentlemen :
At the request of the issuing bank, and without any engagement or responsibility on our part, we are pleased to inform you that we have received the following AUTHENTICATED teletransmission dated October 21, 20××.

:700 Issue of Documentary Credit
:27 Sequence of Total: 1/1
:40A Form of Documentary Credit: IRREVOCABLE
:20 Documentary Credit Number : 128RN71218
:31C Date of Issue: October 20, 20××
:31D Date and Place of Expiry : December 20, 20××
:50 Applicant: DUNHILL INC., LTD. B.P. 6342312 N.Y.
:59 Beneficiary: SEOUL TRADING CO., LTD.
25-5 CHUNGMU-RO 1 GA CHUNG-GU SEOUL, KOREA
:32B Currency Code and Amount : USD 21,700.00
:39A Percentage Credit Amount tolerance: 10/10
:41A Available With·By·: KOEXKRSEXXX BY DEFERRED PAYMENT
:42P Deferred Payment Details: 90 DAYS AFTER ON BOARD DATE
:43P Partial Shipments : ALLOWED
:43T Transshipment : PROHIBITED
:44A Loading/Dispatch/Taking Charge at/from : BUSAN, KOREA
:44B For transportation to·: NEW YORK
:44C Latest Date of Shipment: December 05, 20××
:45A Description of Goods and/or Services:
RAYON/POLY(61/39 PERCENT)7000 M AT TOTAL AMOUNT USD 21,700 CIF NEW YORK AS PER PROFORMA INVOICE NUMBER A-1 DATED JULY 2, 20××.
:46A Documents Required
+COMMERCIAL INVOICE IN TRIPLICATE
+PACKING LIST IN TRIPLICATE
+FULL SET OF CLEAN OCEAN BILL OF LADING MADE OUT TO OUR ORDER MARKED FREIGHT PREPAID AND NOTIFY APPLICANT
+CERTIFICATE OF ORIGIN IN DUPLICATE
+INSURANCE POLICY OR CERTIFICATE IN DUPLICATE, ENDORSED IN BLANK FOR 110% OF THE INVOICE VALUE, EXPRESSLY STIPULATING THAT CLAIMS ARE PAYABLE IN NEW YORK, U.S.A.

Please note that we reserve the right to make such corrections to this advice as may be necessary upon receipt of the cable confirmation and assume no responsibility for any errors and / or omissions in the transmission and / or translation of the teletransmission, and for any forgery and/or alteration on the credit.
If the credit is available by negotiation, each presentation must be noted on the reverse of this advice by the bank where the credit is available.
THIS ADVICE IS SUBJECT TO THE UNIFORM CUSTOMS AND PRACTICE FOR DOCUMENTARY CREDITS(2007 REVISION, ICC PUBLICATION NO. 600)

8.5 Sample Letters of Letter of Credit

1. Advice of Issuing a L/C and Reply to it

1) An advice of issuing a L/C

Dear Sirs,

Thank you for your Sales Contract No. 2, and we found every particulars there correct.

We have arranged with the National Bank of Dubai for an irrevocable L/C in your favor for the amount of U$35,000, and it will reach you shortly through the advising bank, Korea Exchange Bank in Seoul, Korea.

As the products are urgently required, we would like to ask you to ship the products out by the earliest possible direct vessel.

Of course, we believe that you will execute our order in perfect condition according to the instructions specified in the L/C.

We are quite sure that there will be in rush of orders from our customers as long as your first shipment is satisfactory.

Very truly yours,

2) A reply

Dear Sirs,

We have received the L/C covering your order No. 2000/1 through the advising bank in Seoul.

The products which you have ordered are being prepared for shipment on time. We will expedite shipment to your satisfaction as usual and we also will pay our close consideration to the packaging of the products.

As soon as the shipment is executed, it will be advised to you by e-mail and we will send you the copies of shipping documents for your reference.

Please be assured that we will pay our most careful attention to the execution of your order this time.

Very truly yours,

2. Request of Issuing a L/C and Reply to It

1) A request of issuing a L/C

Gentlemen :

We thank you very much for your order of 2,000 units of our newly developed R-1100 robots.

We would like to invite your attention, however, that the Letter of Credit covering your order No. 10 has not reached us yet in spite of our repeated requests.

Our suppliers are urging us to give them a confirmation on arranging the products now, and it is not possible for us to receive the products on time from them unless we receive the L/C by the end of this week.

We shall appreciate your immediate action so that we may be able to make a shipment without further loss of time.

Your cooperation on this matter would be appreciated.

Yours truly,

2) An advice of issuing a L/C

Gentlemen :

Thank you for your e-mail informing that you haven't received the L/C.

We took up this matter with the issuing bank to check what has become of the L/C. According to them, the credit in question was issued on the 20th of this month and you will be notified by our bank's correspondent, the British Bank, soon.

We want you to inquire at that advising bank if they received the credit through our issuing bank and please let us know if there is any problem.

We are very sorry for not sending you an e-mail upon issuing the L/C and we really hope you will execute this important order to our complete satisfaction.

Very truly yours,

3. Request for Amending a L/C and Reply to It(I)

1) A request of extending shipment date and expiry date

Gentlemen :

Thank you for your L/C for 4,000 T.V sets issued by the National Bank of Dubai in U.A.E. We urged our producers to execute an early delivery of products to meet your requirements and it has been quite satisfactory so far.

There are nationwide labor strikes going on in major industrial sectors here, however, and a labor conflict has occurred in the factory where we placed your order and the production of the products has been stopped for the time being.

Under these circumstances, it will be difficult for us to dispatch the products by the date stipulated and we would like to ask you to extend the shipping date and expiry date in the L/C for ten days respectively.

We would appreciate it if you would accept our profound apologies for the inconvenience you have been put to.

Very truly yours,

2) A reply

Gentlemen :

We are surprised to learn that there are labor strikes going on in your country and never did we expect that the shipment would be delayed.

In fact, we received many offers for the same products at much lower prices from other competitors. But, as you assured us that shipment definitely wouldn't be delayed, we accepted your offer.

Our expansion program will be completed in about five months, or sooner if possible. It'll take about two months to set up this equipment and delay of your shipment will not allow us to set it up in time.

As the delay is beyond your control, nothing we can do about it but to accept your request. But, please take an action to advance the shipping date and inform us of the situation going on there.

Yours very truly,

4. Request for Amending a L/C and Reply to It(II)

1) A request for extending shipping date

Gentlemen :

Thank you for the irrevocable letter of credit No. Khl93648 covering 3,000 sets of computers and we have done our best to meet the delivery time stipulated in the L/C.

The parts delivered had some breakdown problems and we passed them on to our subcontractors again. We instructed them to examine the whole lot again and they said they surely will deliver them by the 20th of September.

As you know, our quality control standards are very strict. Nothing leaves our factory unless it's 100% pre-tested. This situation makes us not be able to ship the products by Choyang Sun V-353s sailing on the 18th., and we will try to ship them by the next earliest direct vessel, Arirang V-3 scheduled to sail on the 28th.

We are very sorry to trouble you, but shall be obliged if you can extend the shipping date and validity for 10 days respectively.

We believe that it is worth while to wait for perfect products and hope that you will agree with our proposal.

Sincerely yours,

2) A reply

Gentlemen :

We have just received your piece of advice that you cannot carry out the complete shipment within the shipping date due to the production problems and we instructed New York Bank to amend the L/C as follows;

Shipping date : September 30, 20××

Expiry date : October 15, 20××

As we know that we have had such good dealings with you and that it is worth waiting for better products, we are glad to accept your offer to extend the shipment date and expiry date this time.

We want you to make every effort to make shipment within the extended shipping date.

Please inform us of the shipping schedule as soon as possible.

Very truly yours,

5. Request for Amending the Port of Shipment and Reply to It

1) A request for amending the port of shipment

Gentlemen :

Thank you for your L/C covering household products.

We are afraid to inform you that the discrepancy on the final destination port stipulated in the L/C is putting us to trouble in executing your order. We mutually agreed on CFR Dammam in our last contract but the L/C says CPT Riyadh, Saudi Arabia.

As the shipment date is fast approaching, we request you to amend CPT Riyadh to CFR Dammam so that we can ship the products by the vessel nominated in the L/C within the time amended.

Your prompt attention to this matter would be appreciated.

Yours faithfully,

2) A reply(I)

Gentlemen :

Thank you for your e-mail dated October 21 and we are very sorry for having caused you much inconvenience.

We instructed the issuing bank to specify every instructions we agreed on and there must be a misunderstanding between us and the issuing bank.

According to your request, we have amended the destination port to CFR Dammam accordingly today and you will be advised of this amendment shortly through the Korea Exchange Bank in Seoul.

We will try to do our best not to make a mistake like this in the future and we hope that you execute this important order in strict accordance with the articles in the L/C.

Yours very truly,

3) A reply(III)

Gentlemen :

We received your e-mail informing that there is a discrepancy in the destination port between our contract and the L/C.

There must be a crucial mistake on our part and please accept our deep apologies for the inconvenience this time.

However, it takes a few days for you to receive the L/C amended by us and it may also be hard for you to ship the products within the shipping date. As the products are in urgent need, we want you to expedite shipment as scheduled.

Instead, we will bear the additional inland costs arising from Dammam to Riyadh and will put the difference down to your account directly if you let us know the amount and your account No.

Please give us your confirmation on it by e-mail immediately.

Yours very truly,

6. Amendment of Payment Terms in the L/C

Gentlemen :

The L/C we received said that the payment was to be made at 120 days after B/L date. However, we agreed to do business on at sight basis and it was expressly mentioned in your order sheet. Therefore, please amend the payment terms in the L/C as stated in your order sheet. Upon receipt of your L/C amended, we will make a complete shipment to give you a perfect satisfaction.

Yours truly,

7. Advice of Amendment by the Advising Bank

Gentlemen :

Please refer to the L/C No.17811 for U$30,000 issued by JV Grapro Koral International Co., Ltd., Kazakhstan on November 23, 20××.

The following contents reached us from the Alem Bank Kazakhstan, Alma-Ata ;

"AT THE REQUEST OF OUR CUSTOMER, WE AMEND THE L/C NO.17811 AS FOLLOWS ;"

SHIPPING DATE IS EXTENDED TO THE 30TH OF JUNE. 20××.

EXPIRY DATE IS EXTENDED TO THE 15TH OF JULY. 20××.

All other terms and conditions remain unchanged and please attach this letter to the original L/C dated June 1, 20×× as an amendment.

Very truly yours,
Kookmin Bank

8. Notice of Remittance

Gentlemen :

We have received your e-mail informing us that the products we placed an order with you are ready and we did not settle our payment yet.

Upon checking on our part, we have found that our accounting department made an oversight in making a remittance to you.

The sum of USD25,000 had been sent to you today by Telegraphic Transfer and we are very sorry to have kept you waiting, but we hope you will realize that we don't have any intention to delay our payment on purpose.

We trust you will sent us the shipping schedule as soon as possible

Very truly yours,

Form 8-4 D/A Sales Note

HANKUK TRADING CO., LTD.
C.P.O. BOX 118, SEOUL, KOREA

D/A SALES NOTE

Messrs : Parfums Beaute De Suh S.A. Date : September 11, 20××
Siege Et Usine No: PFS112
3, Rue Edmond Poillot
28000, Chartres, France

Dear Sirs,

We as Seller confirm having sold you as Buyer the following goods on the terms and conditions as stated below and on the back thereof.

Item #	Description	Quantity	Unit Price	Amount
	Empty bottles with cap for Soon Simple Care Set			
701090-1000	Skin Softener 35ml	130pcs	FRF5.67	FRF737.10
	Cleansing Lotion 35ml	130pcs	FRF5.67	FRF737.10
	Total Care Cream 20gr	130pcs	FRF5.42	FRF704.60
420212-1010	Bags	130pcs	FRF8.50	FRF1,105.00
	Total:	520pcs		FRF3,283.80

* Remarks : Korea Exchange Bank, 17-19 Ave Montaigne, 75008 Paris, France as buyer's bank and bank of Seoul, head office, Korea as seller's bank.

Payment : At 90 days from B/L date in France Franc(Usance interest to be covered by the seller)
Price : CIP Paris, France by Air
Insurance : To be covered by the seller
Inspection : Seller's inspection to be final
Shipment : Not later than September 20, 20××
Destination : Paris, France
Origin : Republic of Korea
Packing : Seller's export standard packing

Buyer
S. K. Lee
Manager

Seller
Y. S. Shin
Manager

Chapter 9

International Cargo Transport

Chapter

9 International Cargo Transport

International cargo transport is one of the component parts of the world economic processes. Transport is a very important means in international trade because goods sold by the seller have to be delivered to the buyer abroad, and the delivery of goods is made possible by transport services.

Transport can be divided into ocean transport(including inland waterway transport), air transport, inland transport(including road and rail transport) and multimodal transport.

9.1 Ocean Transport

Ocean transport has been the most important mode of transport in international trade. As most international trade is conveyed by sea transport, sellers and buyers are more concerned with transport by sea than other modes of transport. Ocean carriage, also called ocean shipping or marine transportation, is the most widely used mode of transport in international trade as well as the most efficient form in terms of energy. It still has the attraction of being a cheap mode of transport for delivering large quantities of goods over long distances. However, it is slow, vulnerable to bad weather and less punctual if compared with road or air transport. Before a shipment is made, the seller has to consider many different factors influencing his transport considerations such as cost, safety, speed and convenience.

Forms of ocean transport are divided into liner, tramper and specialized carrier.

1. Liner(Line Vessel)

1) Definition and Characteristics

Liner is the passenger or cargo vessel that operates over a regular route according to an advertised time table. Liner shipping is the service of transporting goods by means of high-capacity, ocean-going ships that transit regular routes on fixed schedules. It has the following characteristics.

- fixed routes, ports, schedules and fixed freight
- loading and unloading charges included in freight
- good service
- simple procedures
- ideal for cargo of small quantity

2) Structure of freight rates

Like prices of any other commodities and services, freight rate is also determined by supply and demand of ocean transport. The demand for a particular mode of international transport service is basically derived from the demand for the commodities carried and is affected by the elasticity of demand for the commodities.

For ocean or air transport, the demand is determined by the competition between carriers and the competition of substitutes or alternatives for the commodity carried.

On any particular route, the demand is determined by the competition from carriers of the same mode on the same route, the competition from other modes of transport on the same route, and the competition from carriers operating from alternative supply areas which may be competitive with similar commodities.

In normal times, an important factor affecting elasticity of demand for ocean or air transport is the cost of transport in relation to the market of the goods carried.

Generally speaking, the following factors are important in fixing freight rates.

- competition between various modes of transport
- nature of commodity in terms of quantity to be shipped, period of shipment, measurement and value of cargo
- origin and destination of cargo that represent distance, risk and convenience of transport
- overall transport cost including fuel, wages for the crew, port dues, etc.
- nature of packing and convenience of handling
- susceptibility of cargo to damage and pilferage
- general loadability of transport unit
- additional facilities such as heavy lifts or livestock facilities required to complete the transport
- Actual routing when two or more routes are available

(1) Basic rates

All liners establish their own basic rates according to products.

(2) Surcharges

Surcharge is the fee or other charges added to the basic rates according to goods or routes. The examples of surcharges are Bunker Adjustment Factor(BAF), Heavy Lift Surcharge, Bulky or Lengthy Cargo Surcharge, Congestion Surcharge, Canal Surcharge, War Risk Surcharge, Currency Adjustment Factor(CAF), etc.

3) Calculation of freight rates

For most types of cargo, freight is charged by measurement or weight.

(1) Measurement

International LCL(Less than a Container Load) ocean freight rates are primarily based on volume, not on the weight of cargo. Ocean freight rates for international ocean freight shipments will be based on ocean freight rates per cubic meter, not on the weight of cargo in kilograms or pounds.

One cubic meter(CBM) is a large volume for ocean freight shipment. One cubic meter is a measurement of volume ocean freight shipment takes and is equal to space of one meter wide, one meter long, and one meter high (1m×1m×1m).

(2) Weight

Weight freight rate is mostly calculated based on one metric ton(M/T) which equals to 1,000kgs. But, long ton(2,240lbs=1,016kgs) and shotr ton (2,000lbs=906kgs) are used sometimes.

(3) Ad valorem rate

Ad valorem rate is a method for charging freight according to the value of goods and services rather than by a fixed rate or by weight or quantity. For valuable cargoes such as jewelry, artworks, etc., ad valorem freight rate is charged in proportion to the estimated value of the cargo.

4) Freight Prepaid and Freight Collect

(1) Freight Prepaid

Freight Prepaid means freight charges that are paid at the place or port of shipment by the seller. The carrier is supposed to invoice to the shipper for the transportation charges. CPT, CIP, CFR, CIF, DAT, DAP and DDP rules require the seller to pay the main carriage or ocean freight.

(2) Freight Collect

Freight Collect means freight charges that are paid at the place or port of destination by the buyer. The carrier is supposed to invoice the consignee and the goods will be delivered at destination by the carrier against payment of transport costs. EXW, FCA, FOB, FAS rules require the buyer to pay the main carriage or ocean freight.

(3) Shipping Conference

Shipping conference means that shipping companies have formed an association to agree on and set freight rates over different shipping routes. The liner conference runs fixed schedules, follows fixed routes and charges standard rates called the conference rates, and often provides international services for the carriage of cargo.

5) Kinds of shipping conference

(1) Open Conference

All conferences operating to and from the United States are open conferences. An open conference practically has to accept any shipping lines that apply for membership in accordance.

(2) Closed Conference

Most European based shipping conferences are closed conferences. A closed conference admits new members at the discretion of existing members. A closed conference regulates the participation of each member in the trade via negotiations.

6) Conference Operations

(1) Contract Rate System or Dual Rate System

Contract Rate System or Dual Rate System is a contract that a shipper agreeing to move his goods exclusively in conference carriers receives a percentage reduction(about 10 to 15 percent) from the non-contract rate regardless of volume of goods shipped.

The contract discourages a shipper from using non-conference carriers, since a single defection normally means that he must make a substantial penalty payment and that he is deprived of the future benefits of the reduced rate.

(2) Deferred Rebate System

Deferred Rebate System is a system that the carrier returns a part of the original freight payment(about 10 percent) to a shipper if the shipper has been a "faithful" or "loyal" customer over the specified period(about six months) and has complied with all the terms of the rebate agreement or arrangement between the carrier and the shipper. In this system of deferred rebate, the shipper must use that carrier's services for a period of six months(account period) to earn the discount, but he receives the discount at the end of a second six month period(deferred period), only if he continues to use that carrier's service exclusively during this second period. The shipper can generally lose the rebate earned during the initial six-month period and any rebate earned during the second six-month period if he uses the services of any other carrier.

7) Fidelity Rebate System

Fidelity Rebate System is a system that the carrier returns a part of the original freight payment to a shipper if the shipper has been a "faithful" or "loyal" customer over the specified period(about 4 months) and has complied with all the terms of the rebate agreement or arrangement between the carrier and the shipper. Unlike Deferred Rebate System, the shipper receives the discount after the contract period is finished.

Table 9-1 Kinds of conference operations and their contents

Division	Contents
Dual Rate System	A contract that a shipper agreeing to move his goods exclusively in conference carriers receives a percentage reduction(about 10 to 15 percent) from the non-contract rate
Deferred Rebate System	A system that a carrier returns a part of the freight payment to the shipper using the conference carrier's services over the specified period(about 6 months ; account period) only if the shipper uses a second six-month period(deferred period)
Fidelity Rebate System	A system that the carrier returns a part of the original freight payment to a shipper if the shipper has been a "faithful" or "loyal" customer over the specified period(about 4 months) and has complied with all the terms of the rebate agreement after this period is finished

2. Tramper(Tramp Ships)

1) Definition of tramper

A tramper follows no firm schedule and does not have regular routes and sails off to where the goods are available. Tramper services refer to shipping services provided irregularly through specialized routes dictated by the shipping needs of various shippers. Their rates are not fixed but are determined by negotiations. Such cargo include coal, grain, timber, ores, fertilizers, etc., which are carried in complete shipload. Tramp vessels are engaged under chartering mainly on a voyage basis and occasionally are chartered to supplement existing liner services to meet peek cargo shipment demands.

2) Charter Party

A contract of sea carriage by charter party is a maritime contract which enables the owner of a tramp vessel either directly or through a ship broker to lease a vessel, or part thereof to a shipper(charterer) or steamship line or any vessel-operating enterprise.

The contract of sea carriage by charter party is divided into partial charter and whole charter. The whole charter is again divided into voyage(trip) charter, time charter and bareboat charter.

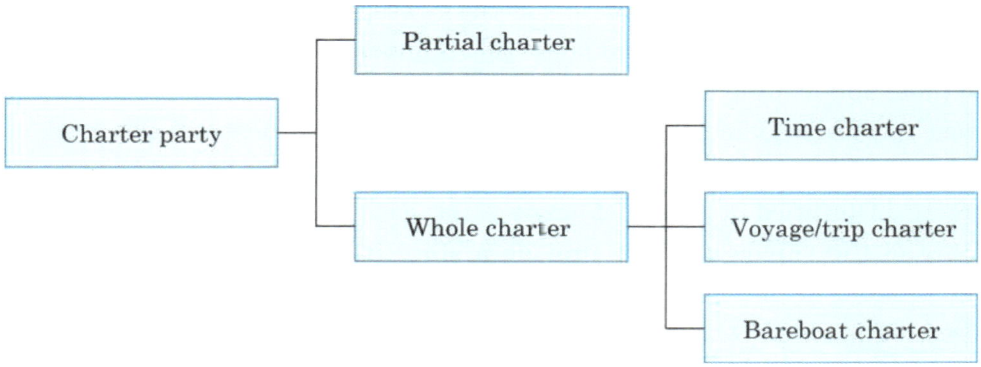

(1) Time Charter

Time charter is a charter that the charterer hires a vessel from the shipowner for a specific amount of time. The owner still manages the vessel but the charterer selects the ports of destination and controls the operation of the ship.

The owner provides the crew, but the crew takes orders from the charterer. The owner is also responsible for insuring the vessel, repairing the vessel and supplying food for ship's personnels. The charterer is responsible for everything else.

(2) Voyage Charter

Voyage charter(or trip charter) is a charter that a part or all of a vessel is leased to the charterer for a voyage to a port or a set of different ports.

Under the voyage charter, the owner of the tramp is obligated to provide a seaworthy ship while the charterer is obligated to provide a full load of cargo. The voyage charter is the most common charter in tramp shipping.

The charterer is only responsible for providing the cargo at a specified port and accepting it at the destination port. Time becomes an issue in the voyage charter if the tramp ship is late in her schedule or loading or discharging are delayed. If a tramp ship is delayed, the charterer pays demurrage, which is a penalty, to the shipowner. The number of days a tramp ship is chartered are called laydays.

Under a voyage charter, payment by the charterer is usually based on an agreed rate per ton for a full and complete cargo. Should the charterer fail to provide sufficient cargo to fill the ship, he is liable for what is termed dead freight, a prorata payment for the space not used.

A voyage charter also stipulates the number of days known as laydays (laytime) for loading and unloading. Laydays are total number of days allowed for loading and unloading the cargo. Should these be exceeded, the charterer is liable for a demurrage charge for each day in excess, and conversely is entitled to dispatch money for each day not taken up. The liability of the shipowner is to provide a ship that is seaworthy and to avoid unjustifiable deviation of route.

Demurrage is an extra charges a shipper pays for detaining a freight ship beyond time permitted for loading or unloading. On the other hand, if loading and unloading are completed in advance, the shipowner will pay dispatch money as a reward to the party who charters ship.

Dispatch is an amount paid by a vessel's operator to a charterer if loading or unloading is completed in less time than stipulated in the charter agreement. Demurrage and dispatch are considered as a way of encouraging timely shipment and are sometimes specified in the shipment clause.

Laydays can be defined as the days kept aside in a ship's voyage schedule for loading and unloading of the cargo. Laydays represent the time at which a ship must reach the charterer for cargo operations. Laydays begin to run when the vessel is berthed or when its arrival is recorded as arrived ship.

Laytime can be defined as the amount of time allowed to a ship in a voyage charter for loading and unloading of cargo at a port. If a ship fails to complete the work during this alotted time and the ship is required to stay at a port for a longer time, then demurrage(fine) is incurred to the shipowner.

(3) Laydays of voyage charter

① **Customary Quick Dispatch(C.Q.D)**

Customary Quick Dispatch means that the charterer must load and/or discharge the goods as fast as possible according to the circumstances prevailing in the ports of loading or discharging. There is no provision for demurrage or dispatch. From the standpoint of an owner, it gives very little assurance, if any, of a quick load and/or discharge.

② **Running Laydays**

Running Laydays includes consecutive days including weekends and holidays and consecutive days of 24 hours including weekends and holidays.

③ **Weather Working Days(WWD)**

Weather Working Days means the working days or pan of a working day during which it is possible(if the vessel is loading or discharging) or would be possible(if the vessel is not loading or discharging) to load or discharge the cargo without interference due to the bad weather.

- WWD Sundays and holidays excepted(WWW SHEX)
- WWD Sundays and holidays excepted unless used
- WWD Sundays and holidays excepted unless used, but only time actually used to count.

(4) Costs of loading and unloading

Under voyage charter contract, the parties concerned need to agree which party is going to pay stevedorage(fee levied for loading and unloading cargo).

① **Berth terms(Liner terms)**

Berth terms is the term that the shipowner pays the costs of loading and discharging.

② **Free In(FI)**

Free In is the term that the charterer pays the cost of loading while the shipowner pays the cost of discharging.

③ **Free Out(FO)**

Free Out is the term that the shipowner pays the cost of loading while the charterer pays the cost of discharging.

④ **Free In and Out(FIO)**

Free In and Out is the term that the shipowner excludes the cost of loading and discharging and if appropriate to the type of cargo, stowing, dunnaging, lashing and securing or trimming, all of which are paid by the charterer or shipper or receiver as the case may be. This type of rate is typically found in voyage charter-parties. Since the shipowner has no control over loading and discharging, these generally have suitable clauses for laytime and demurrage to allow for delays at the loading and discharging ports.

⑤ **Free In, Out and Stowage(FIOS)**

Free In and Out and Stowage is the term that charterer pays the cost of loading, discharging and stowage. It is normally payable by the charterer or the shipper. It is used in carriage of general cargo.

⑥ **Free In, Out, Stowage and Trimming(FIOST)**

Free In, Out, Stowage and Trimming is the term that charterer pays the cost of loading, discharging, stowage and trimming. It is normally payable by the charterer or the shipper. it is used in carriage of bulk cargo.

(5) Bareboat Charter

Bearboat charter is the hiring or leasing of a ship for a period of time during which the shipowner provides only the ship while the charterer provides the crew together with all stores and bunkers and pays all operating costs.

This type of charter is favored by persons or companies who wish to own a ship for investment purposes but who do not have the desire or expertise to operate the ship. Similarly, it is favored by persons or companies who have a particular requirement for a ship and the expertise with which to operate one but without the wish or ability to purchase.

3. Container Transport

Container transport is a method of transporting freight over long distances, often internationally. Containers can be transported via truck, rail, and ship, and the freight itself does not have to be handled during any mode changes. Container transport reduces cargo handling, and therefore improves security, reduces loss and damage, and allows for faster transport.

1) Characteristics of Containerization

(1) Offer different kinds of services

It offers ① door-to-door service under FCL/FCL(Full Container Load/Full Container Load), ② door to container freight station(CFS) service under FCL/LCL(Full Container Load/Less than a Container Load), ③ CFS to CFS service under LCL/LCL, or ④ CFS to door service under LCL/FCL conditions.

(2) Save labor and handling expense

It can be handled quickly and easily by standardized equipment and can thus save labors and loading and unloading charges.

(3) Low risk of cargo damage

The low risk of cargo damage and pilferage enables more favorable cargo premiums to be obtained, compared with break-bulk cargo shipments.

(4) Reduce packaging

Less packaging is required for containerized consignments. In some cases, particularly with specialized ISO(International Standards Organization) containers such as refrigerated ones or tanks, no packaging is required. This can produce substantial cost savings in the international transit and raises service quality.

(5) Provide better service

Faster transits, coupled with more reliable maritime schedules, and ultimately increased service frequency, produce savings in warehouse accommodation needs, lessen risks of obsolescent stock and speed up capital turnover.

2) Types of Containers

20 feet and 40 feet containers are widely used international transport.

Dry Container

Reefer Container

Tank Container

Open Top Container

Flat Rack Container

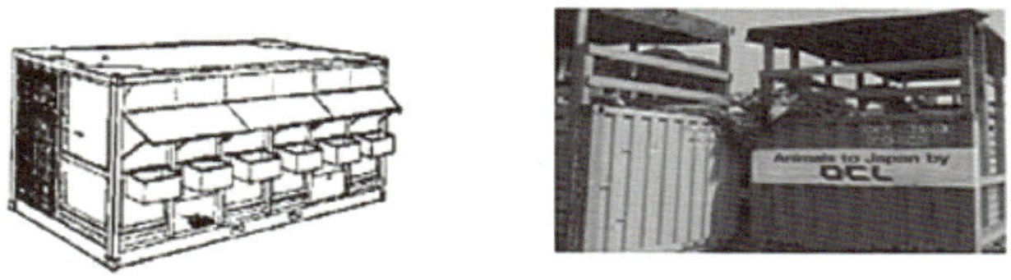

Livestock(Pen) Container

Platform Container

Garment Container

Fan Container

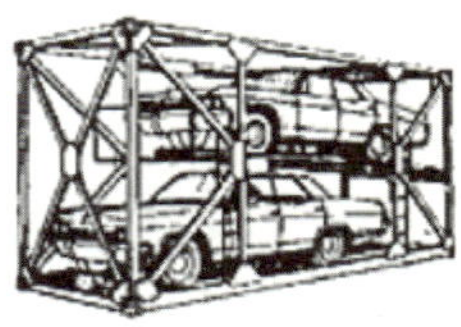

Vehicle Rack Container

3) Modes of Transport by Container

(1) CY/CY(FCL/FCL : Door to Door)

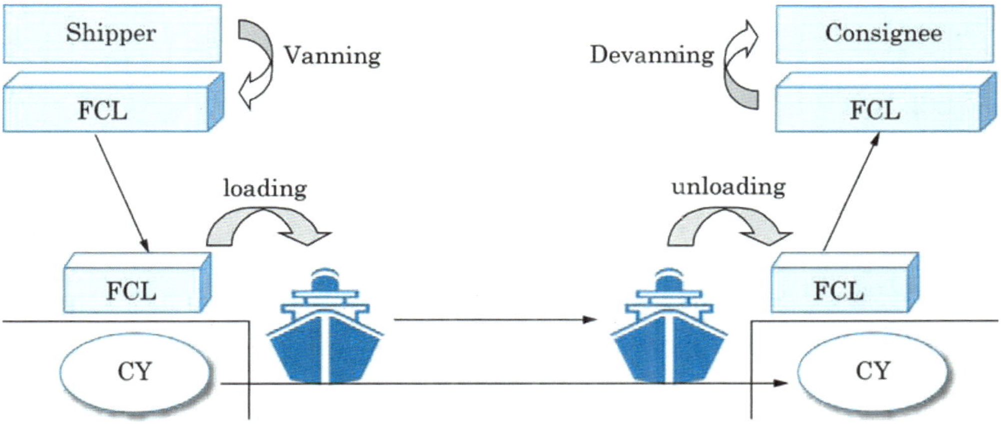

(2) CY/CFS(FCL/LCL : Door to Pier)

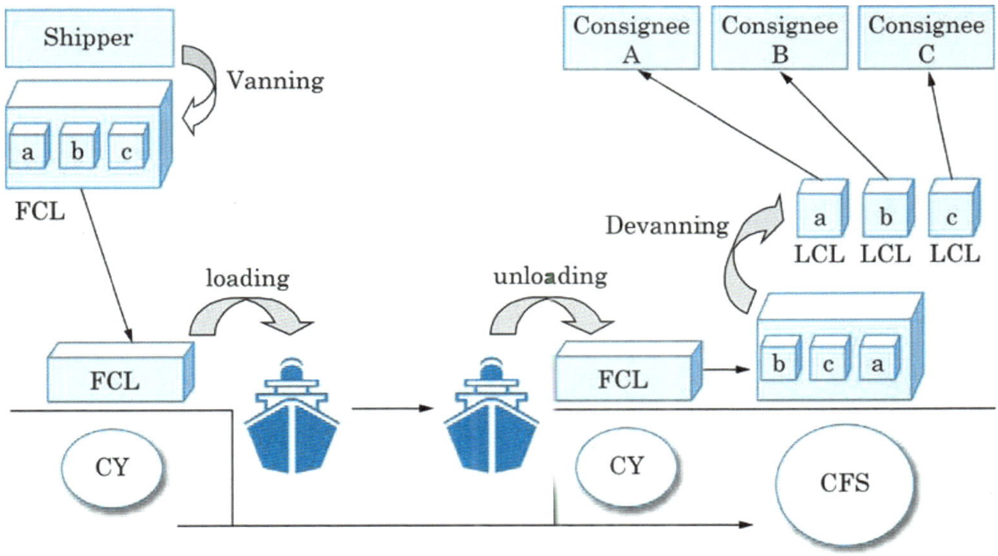

(3) CFS/CY(LCL/FCL : Pier to Door)

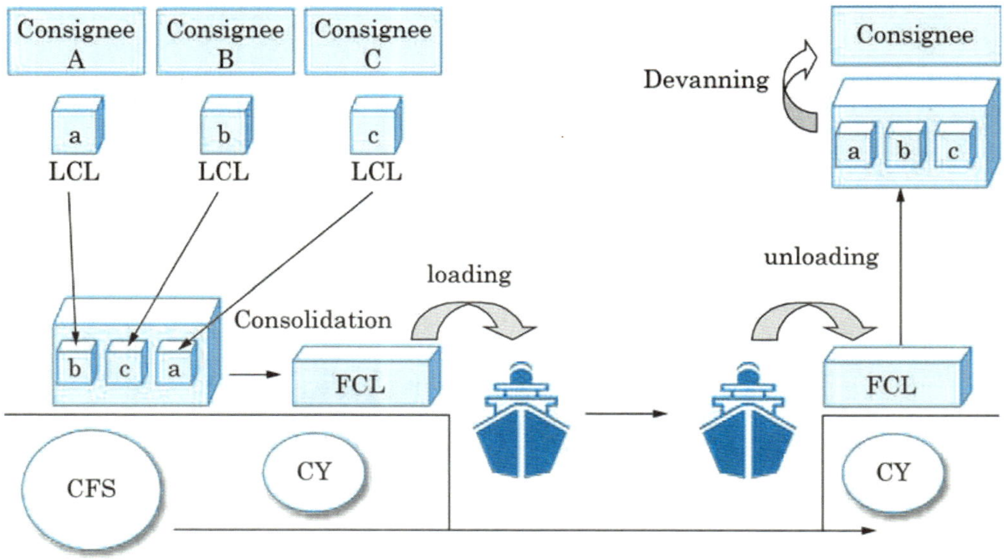

(4) CFS/CFS(LCL/LCL : Pier to Pier)

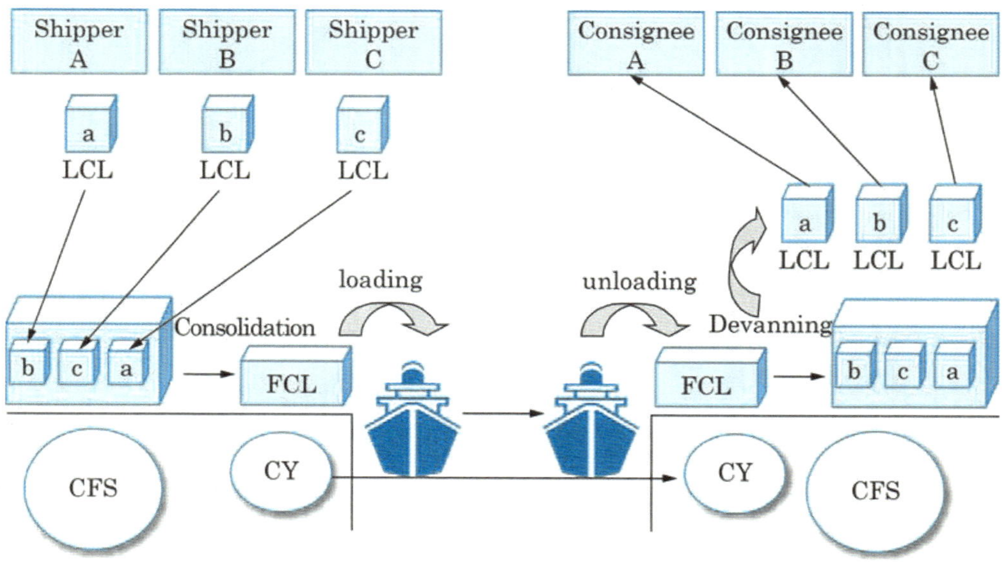

4. Bill of Lading

1) Definition of bill of lading

Bill of Lading means a document which evidences a contract of carriage by sea and the taking over or loading of the goods by the carrier, and by which the carrier undertakes to deliver the goods against surrender of the document. A provision in the document that the goods are to be delivered to the order of a named person, or to order, or to bearer, constitutes such an undertaking.[1)]

It is a document of title to the goods enabling the shipper or owner of the goods to endorse title to other parties, sell goods in transit, and present to banks with other documents for payment under documentary credits. Abbreviated generally as B/L, it is the most important document for sea transport.

2) Number of Bill of Lading

In practice, three(3) original bills of lading(full set) and a few non-negotiable copies may be issued. Three negotiable bills of lading issued, namely "full set" bills of lading, must be handed over to the negotiating bank with other relative documents for the negotiation of the drafts, then they are to be sent to the consignee through the banks. If one of the three(3) original bills of lading is used, the others are void. A bill of lading must appear to be the sole original bill of lading or, if issued in more than one original, be the full set as indicated on the bill of lading.[2)]

3) Functions of bill of lading

(1) Receipt of goods

Bill of Lading is a document issued by a carrier acknowledging that stated goods have been received. It is signed by the carrier, approving that the goods corresponding to the contract description have been received in good condition.

(2) Evidence of contract

Bill of lading is the evidence of contract and treated by the law as the ac-

---

1) United Nations Convention on the Carriage of Goods by Sea(Hamburg Rules, 1978), Article 1, 7.
2) UCP 600, Article 20, iv.

tual contract once it has been endorsed to a third party.

(3) Document of title

Bill of lading entitles the holder of the bill of lading who at the same time is the owner of the goods to sell the goods while they are still in transit to any third party simply by endorsing the bill of lading and delivering it to a third party. Moreover, the bill of lading can be used as a document of title only if it is negotiable and it can be transferred to any third party simply by delivery or endorsement.

4) Types of Bill of Lading

(1) On board bill of lading(Shipped bill of lading)

On board bill of lading is the bill of lading issued after the goods have been loaded on board the ship and it must state that the goods are on board a named ship and state the date of shipment. This is a bill of lading which is issued only after the loading of the goods on board the vessel mentioned in the bill of lading has been completed. Since shipped bill of lading provides better guarantee for the consignee to receive the cargo at the destination, the buyer will normally require the seller to issue the shipped B/L.

(2) Received bill of lading(Received for shipment bill of lading)

Received bill of lading is the bill of lading which acknowledges that the goods have only been received for shipment, and does not state that goods are shipped. This bill of lading begins with "Received for shipment in apparent good order and condition ……". And it will not meet the requirements of bank for the negotiation of the documentary drafts. It merely confirms that the goods have been handed over to, and are in the custody of the shipowner. The buyer under CIF contract will not accept such B/L because, in the absence of the date of shipment, he is in no position to anticipate the arrival of the consignment.

(3) Clean bill of lading

Clean bill of lading is the bill of lading bearing no clause or notation expressly declaring a defective condition of the goods or their packaging. The word "clean" needs not appear on the bill of lading, even if a credit has a requirement for that bill of lading to be "clean on board".[3)]

(4) Foul bill of lading(Dirty bill of lading)

Foul bill of lading is the bill of lading with adverse remarks or notations by the carrier that the goods received for shipment look wet, damaged, or otherwise in doubtful condition, or not of correct quantity. Foul bill of lading is incomplete one bearing such remarks or exceptions as "2 cases short in dispute", etc. Buyers and their banks normally do not accept foul B/L for payment under a letter of credit.

(5) Order bill of lading

Order bill of lading is the bill of lading in which the goods are consigned to the order of a named party. It is made out "to order", "to our order", "to order of shipper", "to order of xxx bank", etc. for delivery of the goods and it can be transferred by endorsement to third parties.

(6) Straight bill of lading

Straight bill of lading is the bill of lading which stipulates that the goods are to be delivered only to the named consignee. The consignee only identifies himself to claim the goods. It is often used when payment for the goods has been made in advance.

Non-negotiable bill of lading which states that the goods are consigned or destined to a specified person. It is marked "non-negotiable" or "not negotiable" on its face.

(7) Bearer bill of lading(blank bill of lading)

Bearer bill of lading(blank bill of lading) is the bill of lading that there is no definite consignee of the goods. Anyone who holds the B/L is entitled to the goods the B/L represents. No endorsement is needed for the transfer of the blank bill. Due to the high risk involved, this bill is rarely used.

(8) Negotiable bill of lading

Negotiable bill of lading is the bill of lading that can be transferred to a third party by endorsement. These types of bills of lading are usually endorsed on the reverse. The opposite of negotiable bill of lading is the straight bill of lading or non-negotiable bill of lading.

---

3) UCP 600, Article 27.

(9) Non-negotiable bill of lading

Non-negotiable bill of lading is the bill of lading that cannot be transferred to a third party. It is not capable of being used to transfer title in the goods described in it. A straight or uniform bill of lading may not be transferred and is only deliverable to the named consignee.

(10) Short form bill of lading

Short form bill of lading is the bill of lading without the terms and conditions of carriage(the rights, responsibilities and liabilities of the carrier and the shipper) printed on its back. It is a bill of lading on which the detailed conditions of transport are not listed in full. It is not different from the long form B/L. The shipper and the carrier are bound by the conditions of carriage whether the terms and conditions of carriage are printed on the B/L or not.

(11) Long form bill of lading

Long form bill of lading is the bill of lading with the terms and conditions of carriage(the rights, responsibilities and liabilities of the carrier and the shipper) printed on its back.

(12) Direct bill of lading

Direct bill of lading is the bill of lading which covers direct shipment from the port of shipment to the port of destination.

(13) Transhipment bill of lading

Transhipment bill of lading is a bill of lading permitting cargo to be transhipped from one vessel to another to reach the final destination.

(14) Charter party bill of lading

Charter party bill of lading is the bill of lading containing an indication that it is subject to a charter party. It is not acceptable by banks under letters of credit unless so authorized in the credit.

(15) Groupage bill of lading(Master bill of lading)

Groupage bill of lading is the bill of lading issued by a carrier to an international freight forwarder who collects and/or delivers individual cargoes and it is covered under one bill of lading.

(16) House bill of lading(Forwarder's B/L)

House bill of lading is the bill of lading issued by an international freight forwarder to a shipper after the forwarder received the groupage B/L from the carrier.

(17) FIATA combined transport bill of lading

FIATA Multimodal Transport Bill of Lading(FBL) is a carrier-type transport document set up by FIATA for the use by freight forwarders acting as multimodal transport operators(MTO). The FBL can also be issued as a marine bill of lading. A freight forwarder acting as MTO or marine carrier issuing a FBL is responsible for the performance of transport. The freight forwarder does not only assume responsibility for delivery of the goods at destination, but also for all carriers and third parties engaged by him for the performance of whole transport.

(18) Through bill of lading

Through bill of lading is the bill of lading invoking a series of contracts to carry goods to a final destination by more than two different modes of transport including ocean transport. The first carrier takes responsibility for the goods only up to a specified point(still called the "place of delivery") and then passes responsibility to a second carrier for "on-carriage" to the final destination

(19) Multimodal Transport Bill of Lading(Combined Transport Bill of Lading)

Multimodal transport bill of lading(combined transport bill of lading) is issued by combined transport operator that covers the multi-modal transport on a door to door basis in one contract of carriage. It is a bill of lading covering shipment of goods by more than two different modes of transport. The carrier signing the bill of lading(the "contractual carrier") frequently subcontracts with other carriers, but still takes responsibility for delivery of the goods to the place of delivery.

(20) Surrender Bill of Lading

Surrender bill of lading is a document issued by the seller that allows the buyer to legally own the items the seller shipped. When the buyer pays for a shipment, the seller surrenders its ownership rights to the items so he cannot claim title or power over them. This tends to be a cleaner method of transferring ownership than some other bill of lading documents provide.

If a shipment is not under the terms 'Document against Payment' or under Letter of Credit, the shipper does not send original bill of lading to the buyer but surrenders original bills of lading and gives them to the carrier. Surrendering procedure of bills of lading simplify the mechanism of transport procedures.

Once after completion of export customs formalities, the seller hands over cargo to carrier to move final destination.

If the seller wants to surrender original bills of lading, he can submit all originals with a request letter to the carrier of goods with necessary original bill of lading surrender charges if any. Once after receiving original bills of lading, the carrier arranges to send a message to his counterpart at destination port stating that original bills of lading are surrendered at shipment port and the consignee may not present original bills of lading at the time of delivery.

The carrier at the shipment port advises his agent at the destination port to release goods to consignee without original bill of lading. A copy of such message is sent to the seller also as a proof of surrendering original bills of lading.

The seller, in turn, sends across the said release message copy to his buyer for smooth delivery of goods without insisting original bill of lading. The consignee at the destination port takes delivery of goods by obtaining delivery order from carrier after verifying the identity of consignee.

(21) Switch bill of lading

Switch bill of lading is the second set of bill of lading that may be issued by the carrier(or agent) in exchange for the first set of bill of lading originally issued when the shipment was effected. It is a B/L substituted by a carrier for an original B/L in accordance with the terms of a letter of credit (L/C). The original B/L(which shows the actual supplier as the shipper) is switched with another B/L that shows the middleman as the shipper and protects the identity of the actual supplier.

A switch bill of lading is requested generally when there has been a change in the original trading conditions. Some of the reasons could be :

- Goods could have been resold and the discharge port has now been changed to another port.
- The seller(who could be an intending agent) does not wish the name of the actual seller to be known to the consignee in case the consignee strikes a deal with the seller directly.
- The seller does not want the buyer to know the actual country of origin of the cargo.

(22) Third party bill of lading

Third party Bill of Lading is the bill of lading issued by a third party who sends the goods to the buyer instead of the actual seller in the L/C.

(23) Stale bill of lading

Stale bill of lading is the bill of lading which has passed the deadline time of the L/C. The B/L may be rejected if presented more than 21 days after the date of shipment.

Bill of Lading

② Shipper/Exporter DAEHAN CO.,, LTD CPO BOX 195 SEOUL, KOREA		⑫ B/L No. ; PCS-96010
③ Consignee TO ORDER OF BANK OF AMERICA		World Trans Corporation C.P.O. Box. 1234 Seoul, Korea TEL :(02)624-1212 FAX :(02)624-1234
④ Notify Party BROWN CO., LTD. 310 FIFTH AVE, NEW YORK, NY 10118, USA		
Pre-Carriage by	⑥ Place of Receipt BUSAN CY, KOREA	
⑤ Ocean Vessel WONIS JIN	⑦ Voyage No. V-234E	

⑧ Port of Loading	⑨ Port of Discharge	⑩ Place of Delivery	⑪ Final Destination
BUSAN, KOREA	NEW YORK, U.S.A	NEW YORK CY, U.S.A	(for the merchant's reference only)

⑬ Container No.	⑭ Seal No. Marks & No	⑮ No. & Kinds of Containers or Packages	⑯ Description of Goods	⑱ Gross Weight	Measurement
ISCU1104	0559 929 PCU NEW YORK, U.S.A C/NO. 1-50 MADE IN KOREA	1 CNTR (20'CNTR)	"SAID TO CONTAIN" 2,000SETS OF COMPUTERS ⑰ ㉓ "Freight Prepaid" L/C No. MD1NY404NS0 0018	4,631 KGS	58,000 CBM
Total No. of Containers or Packages(in words)			SAY : ONE CONTAINER ONLY		

⑲ Freight and Charges	⑳ Revenue tons	㉑ Rate	㉒ Per	㉓ Prepaid	㉔ Collect
FREIGHT PREPAID CFS CHARGE+THC WHARFAGE CNTR TAX DOCK'S FEE				W100,000 W 2,500 W 10,000 W 5,000	

㉕ Freight prepaid at BUSAN, KOREA	㉖ Freight payable at	㉙ Place and Date of Issue BUSAN, KOREA, JULY 20, 20××
㉗ Total prepaid in	㉘ No.of original B/L THREE(3)	
㉚ Laden on Board the Vessel JULY 20, 20××		Signature ㉛ World Trans Corporation as an agent for Hyundai Shipping Co., Ltd., Carrier

5) Endorsement of a bill of lading

The title to the goods is transferable to another party by endorsement, usually on the reverse(back) of the bill of lading(B/L) by the title holder of the B/L. If the endorsement of B/L is required in the letter of credit(L/C), all the originals must be endorsed.

(1) Full endorsement

Full endorsement is a qualifying comment or signature that specifies the person who is supposed to receive the payment documents. It is always followed by the signature of the person who is endorsing the document, which makes it complete and legal.

(2) Order endorsement

If the consignee is not known at the time the shipper instructs shipment on a particular vessel, then the bill of lading may also be made out to order. In this case, only the party to whom they are endorsed with the words 'deliver to …' or 'deliver to the order of …' can take delivery.

(3) Blank endorsement

Blank endorsement is an endorsement consisting of nothing but a signature and allowing any party in possession of the endorsed item to execute a claim.

Deliver to ( )	( )
ABC Trading Co., Ltd	ABC Trading Co., Ltd
Signed	Signed
S.K.Lee, President	S.K.Lee, President

5. Seaway Bill(SWB)

Seaway Bill is a shipping document that is only a receipt of cargo taken on board a vessel and which, unlike a bill of lading, is not a document of title.

Seaway bill serves as an evidence of contract and receipt of goods. This document is more relevant for non-commercial transactions, sales between the headquarter and subsidiaries or where there is no involvement of any documentary credits.

Seaway bill cannot be endorsed to order of someone else. It has to be consigned to a direct customer only. Delivery of cargo covered under a Seaway Bill of Lading can be made only to the consignee on the bill of lading or his authorized representative

6. Inland Waterway Transport

Inland waterway system is usually linked to the seaport and thereby acts as a distributor and feeder to the shipping services. In some countries, especially underdeveloped ones, inland waterways are a major form of distribution as the road and rail systems are unable to cope or are nonexistent in many areas. Inland waterway transport can relieve port congestion through overside loading and discharge. This eliminates the cargoes through the port warehouse which can prove costly in tariffs and time-consuming through customs proceeding. It also has the advantage of low rate and it is suitable for a range of commodities extending from general cargoes to bulk shipment of timber, coal, oil, chemicals and so on. However, the transits are slow compared with road or rail.

7. International Freight Forwarder

International freight forwarder, forwarder, or forwarding agent, also known as a Non-Vessel Operating Common Carrier(NVOCC), is a person or company that organizes shipments for individuals or corporations to get goods from the manufacturer or producer to a market, customer or final point of distribution. Forwarders contract with a carrier to move the goods. A forwarder does not move the goods but acts as an expert in supply chain management.

Ocean freight forwarders prepare and process documentation and perform related activities pertaining to shipments. NVOCC is a common carrier that holds itself out to the public to provide ocean transport and issues its own bills of lading or equivalent documents, but does not operate the vessels that transport cargoes.

International freight forwarders have additional expertise in preparing and processing customs and other documentation and performing activities pertaining to international shipments.

- book ship's space
- arrange documentation
- collect cargoes
- deal with customs entries and other legal formalities
- group a number of consignments
- give pieces of advice on markets

9.2 Air Transport

1. Advantages of Air Transport

Advantages of air transport are as follows;

- **High speed and quick transit**

  This is particularly important for perishable and seasonal goods.

- **Low risk of damage and pilferage**

  Air transport offers tighter security than other modes of transport for the goods carried. Insurance underwriters consequently offer favorable insurance rates.

- **Low packing cost**

  Air transport makes the goods less subject to damage and pilferage. Because of this, packing cost can be reduced. The savings on packing cost can offset the higher freight compared with surface transport.

- **Smaller amount of capital tied up in transit and interest savings**

  Sometimes the buyer is allowed to pay after the goods arrive at destination. Then, if the transportation of goods is completed faster and in better condition, financial settlement is usually faster. This improves the cash flow situation of the seller.

- **Reduce need for extensive warehouse accommodation and less risk of stock piling**

  The high speed of air transport enables buyers to get quick supplies. So, buyers do not need a big stock and extensive warehousing facilities. On one hand, it reduces costs; on the other hand, it reduces the risk of stockpiling.

- **Ideal for palletized and a wide variety of high value and small volume consumer cargoes.**

  Air transport is most suitable for high value and small volume cargoes. Computers, electronic goods and medicine are usually shipped by air.

- **Expand trade and new markets**

  Because of high speed, goods like flowers and some food can be sold to new markets that would not have existed without air transport. For goods that need regular maintenance, the development of market depends heavily on the quality of after sale services. Buyer will be willing to purchase some goods only when they are certain that air transport can provide timely support to the services.

2. Disadvantages of Air Transport

Disadvantages of air transport are as follows;

- Limited capacity, dimension and weight restrictions
- High operating expenses and high transport cost
- Vulnerable to disruption when weather is bad
- Expensive handling cost because of consignments tend not to be consolidated
- Sparsely located facilities

3. Air Waybill(AWB)

1) Definition of Air Waybill

Air Waybill(AWB) is a document of proof of receipt issued by air carrier of goods to shipper on receipt of goods for on carriage. Air Waybill(AWB) or air consignment note is a straightforward legal document contracting a named airline company to fly a specified package of goods from the airport of one named sender to the airport of another named recipient. It refers to a receipt issued by an international airline for goods and an evidence of the contract of carriage, but it is not a document of title to the goods.

2) Functions of Air Waybill

There are several purposes that an air waybill serves, but its main functions are as follows ;

(1) Contract of Carriage.

Air Waybill is the evidence of the contract of carriage.

(2) Evidence of Receipt of Goods

Air Waybill is the document issued by the carrier acknowledging that stated goods have been received in good condition.

(3) Freight Bill

Air Waybill may be used as a bill or invoice together with supporting documents since it may indicate charges to be paid by the consignee. An original copy of the air waybill is used for the carrier's accounting

(4) Certificate of Insurance

Air Waybill may also serve as an evidence if the carrier is in a position to insure the shipment and is requested to do so by the shipper.

(5) Customs Declaration

Although customs authorities require various documents like commercial invoice, packing list, etc. Air Waybill is proof of the freight amount billed for the goods carried and may be presented for customs clearance.

Air Waybill

Shipper's Name and Address | Shipper's Account Number

Not negotiable
Air Waybill
issued by
KOREAN AIR

Copies 1, 2 and 3 of this Air Waybil are originals and have the same validity.

Consignee's Name and Address | Consignee's Account Number

Telephone :

It is agreed that the goods described herein are accepted in apparent good order and condition (except as noted) for carriage SUBJECT TO THE CONDITIONS OF CONTRACT ON THE REVERSE HEREOF. THE SHIPPER'S ATTENTION IS DRAWN TO THE NOTICE CONCERNING CARRIER'S LIMITATION OF LIABILITY. Shipper may increase such limitation of liability by declaring a higher value for carriage and paying a supplemental charge if required.

Issuing Carrier's Agent Name and City

Accounting Information

Agent's IATA Code | Account No.

Airport of Departure(Addr. of First Carrier) and Requested Routing

TO	By First Carrier / Routing and Destination	to	by	to	by	Currency	CHGS Code	WT/VAL PPD	WT/VAL COLL	Other PPD	Other COLL	Declared Value for Carriage	Declared Value for Customs

Airport of Destination	Flight/Date	For Carrier Use Only	Flight/Date	Amount of Insurance	INSURANCE-If Carrier offers Insurance, and such insurance is requested in accordance with conditions on reverse hereof, indicate amount to be insured in figures in box marked 'amount of Insurance'.

Handling Information

No. of Pieces RCP	Gross Weight	kg lb	Rate Class / Commodity item No.	Chargeable Weight	Rate / Charge	Total	Nature and Quantity of Goods (incl. Dimensions or Volume)

Prepaid	Weight Charge	Collect	Other Charges
	Valuation Charge		
	Tax		
	Total Other Charges Due Agent		Shipper certifies that the particulars on the face hereof are correct and that insofar as any part of the consignment contains dangerous goods, such part is properly described by name and is in proper condition for carriage by air according to the applicable Dangerous Goods Regulations.
	Total Other Charges Due Carrier		Signature of Shipper or his Agent
Total Prepaid		Total Collect	
Currency Conversion Rates		CC Charges In Dest. Currency	Executed on(date)at(place)Signature of Issuing Carrier or its Agent
For Carrier's Use Only at Destination		Charges at Destination	Total Collect Charges

ORIGINAL 3(FOR SHIPPER)

9.3 International Multimodal Transport

1. Definition of International Multimodal Transport

Multimodal transport(also known as combined transport) is the transport of goods under a single contract, but performed with at least two different means of transport. The carrier is liable for the entire carriage, even though it is performed by several different modes of transport such as rail, sea and road, for example. The carrier does not have to possess all the means of transport, and in practice usually does not, and the carriage is often performed by sub-carriers called as actual carriers. The carrier responsible for the entire carriage is referred to as a multimodal transport operator(MTO).

Following the containerization of international multimodal transport, a brand new mode of transport "international multimodal transport" had been introduced in the transport industry. International multimodal transport means the carriage of cargo by at least two modes of transport on the basis of a multimodal transport contract from a place at which the cargoes are collected in one country to a place designated for delivery in another country. The operation of pick up and delivery of goods carried out in the performance of a unimodal transport, for example, sending goods from warehouse to an airport, is not considered as international multimodal transport.

Although different modes of transport such as sea, air, rail, etc. are combined, only one multimodal transport operator is responsible for taking the cargo from the consignor and delivering them to the consignee. This adds simplicity to the transport. The use of containers in multimodal transport means high efficiency, better quality of transport, lower cost and so on. Multimodal transport document is the only one document used, which also adds to the economy and simplicity of the documentation process.

2. Multimodal Transport Document

Multimodal transport document is a document that evidences a multimodal transport contract, the taking in charge of the goods by the multimodal transport operator and an undertaking by him to deliver the goods in accordance with the terms of that contract. It is a shipping document, similar to a bill of lading, which evidences cargo being shipped via multiple modes of transport.

When the goods are taken in charge by the multimodal transport operator, he shall issue multimodal transport document which, at the option of the consignor, shall be in either negotiable or non-negotiable form. A negotiable multimodal transport document is made out to order or to bearer. A non-negotiable multimodal transport document shall indicate a named consignee.

3. Land Bridge

Intermodal environments created several new transport routes. One of the striking changes made was the concept of "Land Bridges." A land bridge is the concept that cargo traveling on ocean liners can cross a land obstacle by being unloaded in one port and reloaded onto another means of transport such as train, truck, another ship or airplane to bring the cargo to the final destination.

1) Siberia Land Bride(SLB)

Siberia land bridge is a multimodal transport system that goods shipped at the ports in Far East are transported to the destinations by sea, land and air.

(1) Trans-Rail

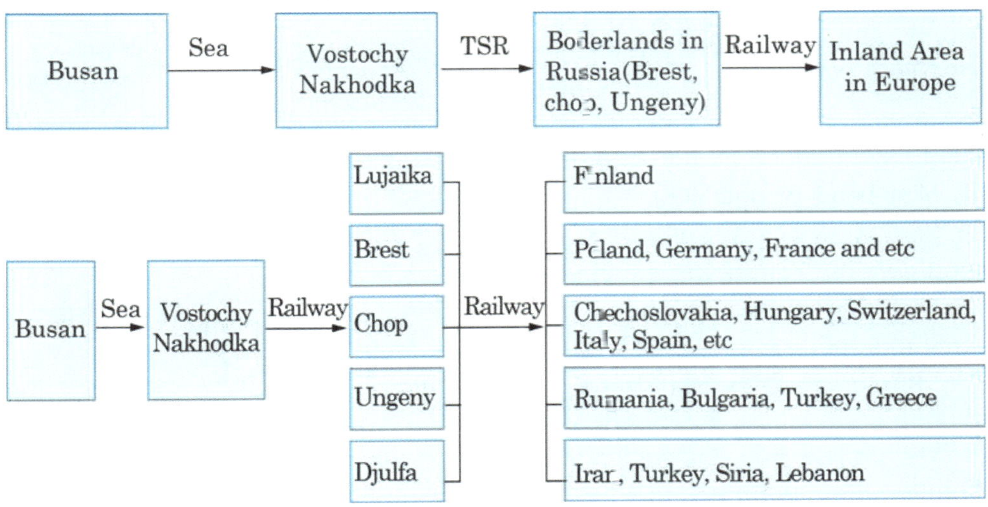

(2) Trans-Sea

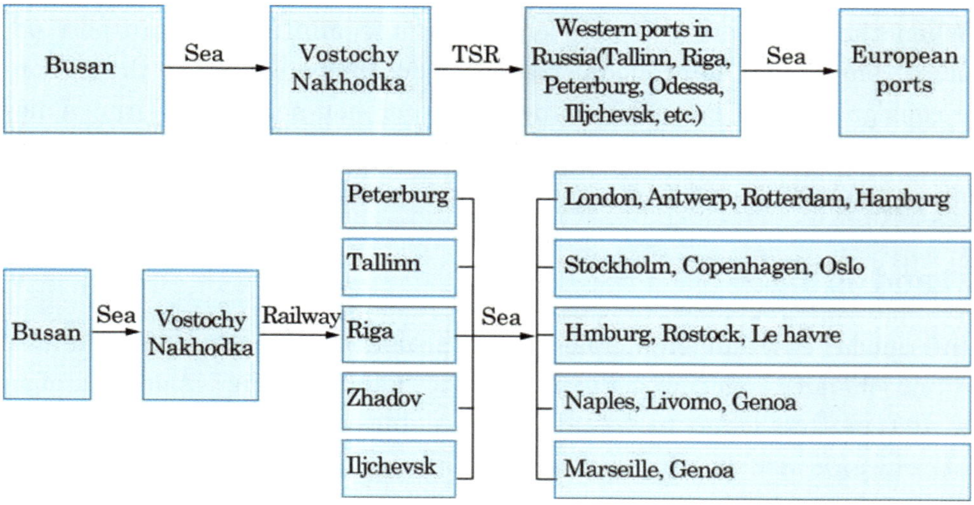

(3) Tracons

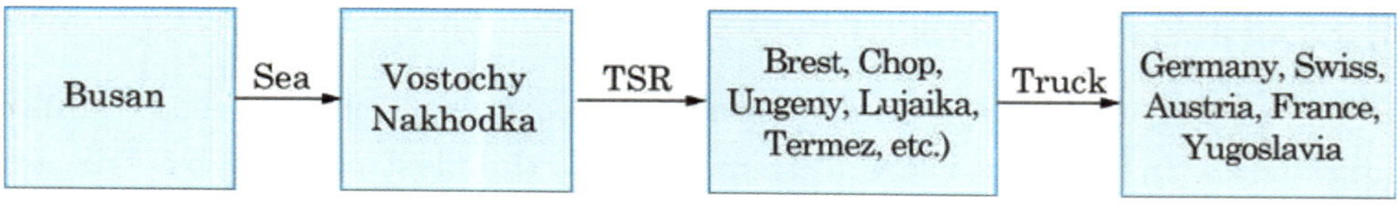

2) America Land Bride(ALB)

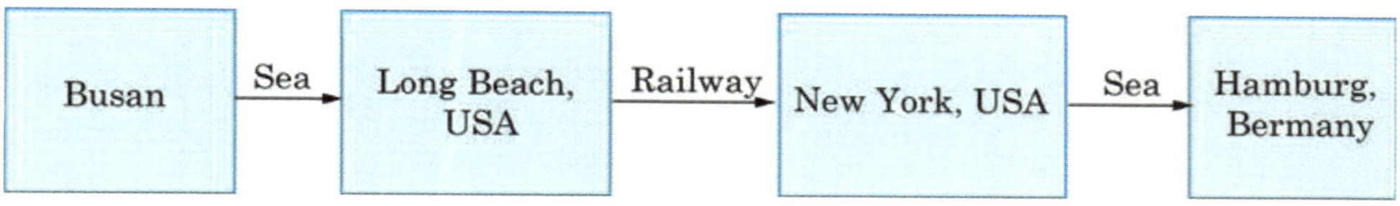

(1) Mini Land Bridge(MLB)

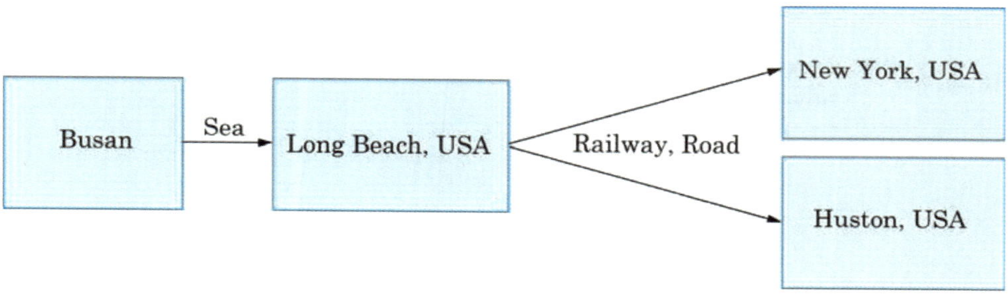

(2) Micro Land Bridge(MLB)

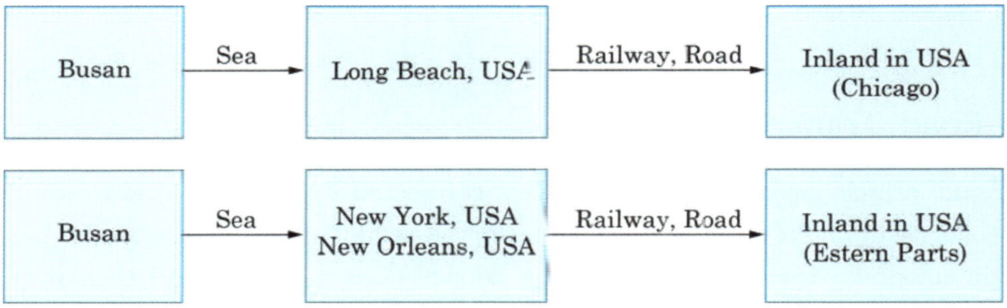

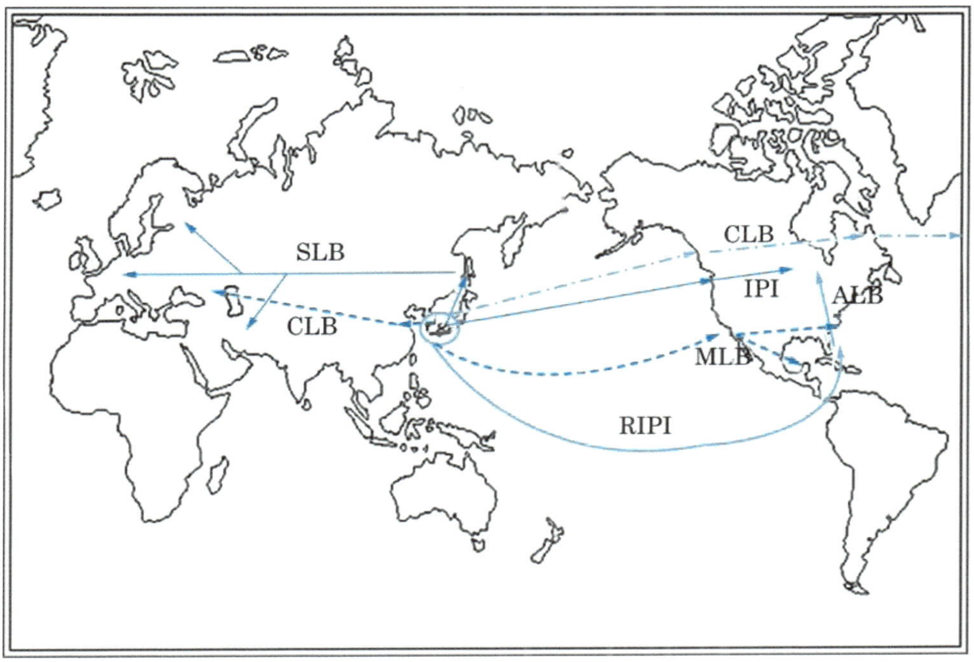

Source : Soonhwan Jeon, Trade Practice, Hanol Publishing Co., Ltd., 2013, p.476.

- IPI : Interior Point Intermodal
- RIPI : Reverse Interior Point Intermodal

9.4 Land Transport

1. Road Transport

Road vehicle used between countries connected by roads is a low capacity but very versatile unit of transport, very flexible in its operation. It has a high distributive ability of offering a door-to-door service. Road transport is ideal for general merchandise and selective bulk cargoes in small quantities. But besides limited capacity, road transport has relatively high operating cost. There is also a high risk of pilferage and damage although the driver accompanies the vehicle throughout the transit. One of the problems facing road transport is the complication in relation to customs examination and duty payments when a vehicle is involved in crossing several frontiers.

2. Rail Transport

Rail transport is a major mode of transport in terms of capacity, only second to ocean transport. It is capable of achieving relatively high speed and is most economical especially if it provides the complete trainload for a shipper on a regular basis. Besides, it is less prone to interruption by poor weather. But it is confined to railroad and therefore less flexible.

Rail transport can be divided into international combined rail transport and domestic rail transport. The most important document for rail transport is consignment note. Once the forwarding railway station has accepted the goods for carriage together with the consignment note, the contract of carriage comes into existence.

3. Pipeline

Pipeline networks are mainly used for the distribution of oil and gas. One advantage of the network is the low cost of distribution as very little labor is needed in the network, although the cost of installing such as a system may be moderately high. Another advantage is the 24-hour availability of the network. Besides, the network needs little maintenance during operation. From an environment point of view, pipeline networks cause little disruption to the environment during installation and create no noise or fumes during distribution of cargo. The disadvantage of pipeline network is limited capacity. Until a new pipeline is installed, the market growth is somewhat inhibited.

9.5 Sample Letters of Transport

1. Ask for Freight Rate to a Shipping Company

1) An offer

Dear Sirs,

Your name and address have been recommended to us as a reliable shipping company for European countries.

As we have many business connections in Western Europe, we may be able to do business with your shipping company if the rates of freight are satisfactory to us.

Please quote us the lowest rate of freight for 19,480pcs of "Soon" brand cosmetic sets weighing 760kgs and measuring 6.183 cubic meters from Busan to Le Havre in France

The goods will be ready for shipment by next week and please let us know the earliest vessel available at the early of next month by e-mail.

Very truly yours,

2) A reply

Dear Mr. Lee,

In reply to your thankful inquiry of September 12, we attach the shipping schedule to this e-mail in which you will find every details of our vessel schedules for coming two months from Busan to Le Havre.

As you may realize, we can quote you the rate of freight for cosmetic sets at U$200.00 per one cubic meter. We are sure that nobody can quote at this low rate.

The first vessel available at the early of next month is Cgm Korrigan V-2343 sailing on the 3rd in Busan.

Also, we will be glad to quote the rates of freight for other destination ports in Western Europe for other consignments.

We hope to be favored with your instruction.

Yours faithfully,

2. Ask for Freight Rate to an International Freight Forwarder

1) An offer

Dear Sirs,

We have a consignment of accessories and clothes now waiting to be shipped from Busan to Long Beach, U.S.A.

The products packed in 100 cartons of accessories and 200 cartons of clothes are weighing 325kgs and measuring 12 cubic meters.

As our customers want the products urgently, we would be appreciated it if you would let us know the possible earliest direct vessel together with your competitive rate of freight by return e-mail as soon as possible.

Very truly yours,

2) A reply

Dear Mr. Kim,

Thank you for your e-mail offer of yesterday inquiring us about the rate of freight and vessel schedule.

The first vessel you asked for will be 'Trade Luck 043W' which is due to sail on the 29th, and the second one will sail on the 2nd of next month. However, the products have to reach us by the 27th for shipment by the first vessel.

Considering our mutual business relations in the future, we will quote you at US$250 per cubic meter to Long Beach Port, which bears no margin on our side this time.

We will send you our shipping request form and return it to us right away by e-mail after you fill it out.

Yours faithfully,

3. Acceptance for Ship's Space

Gentlemen :

We are very pleased to hear from you that you secured the flight No. KE902 scheduled to depart from Paris to Incheon on January 5 for our consignment of 980kgs of material "Ceramide H03" packed in an iron-hooped wooden case.

The products are placed at our warehouse and they are ready to be picked up anytime.

We fully understand your freight rate increased by 10% than before due to the seasonal demand rushed in now and we are glad to accept your rate even though we really wanted more of a discount.

Instead, we want you to execute this business to our complete satisfaction as we do not want to have any problem with our partner in Korea.

Very truly yours,

4. Shipping Advice for Electronic Products

Gentlemen :

We are glad to inform you that the consignment covering your order No. CS311806 for 43,200pcs of WF(M) and 15,720pcs of WF(R) has been shipped by Zim Canada V-10E on August 31 and it will be arrived at long beach port on September 14.

As specified in your L/C, we attach the following shipping documents.

1. Two copies of commercial invoice
2. Two copies of packing list
3. Two copies of clean on board bill of lading
4. A copy of marine cargo insurance policy

We really hope that the products will reach you in perfect condition as usual and will give you a complete satisfaction.

Yours very truly,

5. Shipping Advice for Clothes

Gentlemen :

We have shipped the consignment covering our contract No. 41 by Trade Luck 043W which left here on August 19.

GEOSYSTEM 2,375 pairs of ladies' clothes

Alma Ata, Kazakhstan
C/No. 1-235
Made in Korea

In compliance with the terms of payment, we have drawn drafts at sight and negotiated them through The Uri Bank in Seoul together with other documents required in the L/C No. 17812/IMP issued by Lem Bank, Kazakhstan. We trust that you will honor the drafts upon presentation.

We believe this consignment will reach you in good order and hope we will serve you again in the near future.

Yours very truly,

6. Shipping Advice for Health Food

Gentlemen :

We are pleased to inform you that we have airfreighted your order No. 213 dated July 17 for 72 cartons of health food by KE901 at 10:00 PM today, and the cargo will arrive at Charles de Gaulle Airport at 21:00 today. The relevant documents are as follows;

1. Commercial invoice in two copies
2. Packing list in two copies
3. An airway bill
4. A certificate of origin
5. Insurance policy in two copies
6. A weight and an inspection certificate

We thank you for this business and trust that this cargo will reach you in good condition and we look forward to receiving your further orders soon.

Yours very truly,

7. Shipment Notice

Gentlemen :

We inform you that your order No. 342 dated September 30 covering 2,000 bottles of Koreawang Drink(120ml) has been shipped by Adam Abraham which left here in Busan on November 17 and she is scheduled to arrive at Dubai on or about December 10.

Sharjah Warehousing Co., Ltd. will take care of this consignment on arrival at Dubai and they will take every steps required to hand them over to you to your complete satisfaction.

We are sure that you will be quite satisfied with the goods reached in good order and that you may place further orders with us in the near future.

Yours faithfully,

8. Payment Notice

Dear Sirs,

With reference to your order No. 132 dated July 12 for computers, we have shipped the products by CGM Korrigan 2343 sailed on September 23 from Busan. This vessel is scheduled to arrive at Le Havre port on October 25.

We enclose two non-negotiable clean on board bills of lading made out to the order of the issuing bank, a copy of marine insurance policy covering the invoice amount plus 10 percent, two copies of commercial invoice and one copy of inspection certificate as you requested.

To cover this shipment, we have drawn drafts on the issuing bank at 120 days after sight for full invoice value under the L/C and the drafts were presented to Korea Exchange Bank together with original shipping documents. We, therefore, ask you to honor the drafts at maturity.

We hope that the products will be in your hands in good condition and we look forward to your additional orders.

Yours faithfully,

9. Notice of Shipment Delay(1)

Dear Sirs,

We are very sorry to inform you that it seems impossible for us to execute your order No. 23 dated March 13 within the stipulated time due to a strike of our local supplier.

We received your requests several times for a punctual shipment as contracted and there was no doubt that we could ship the products by Trade Luck 023W sailing on May 2.

Our supplier informed that the work at the factory has been suspending for two weeks because of a temporal strike and it is impossible for them to meet the delivery date mutually agreed on.

They estimate, however, that the strike will be over within this week and assure us that they will give us a special priority to deliver the goods.

As we have been doing everything possible to carry out our business, we can promise you a definite shipment by the next earliest direct vessel.

We want you to accept our deep apologies for the inconvenience the delay has caused you.

Very truly yours,

10. A Notice of Shipment Delay(2)

Gentlemen :

In order to execute your order No. 142, we went through legal formalities on our side and booked the freight space on the Adam Abraham due to sail on November 19

Owing to a traffic strike in the southern part of this country, however, the supplies of raw & sub-materials have been held up and we can not manufacture the products by the end of this week as scheduled.

Under these circumstances, we may not be able to ship the products by the vessel referred to, and we want you to extend the date of shipment and expiry date for one month respectively.

Of course, we are well aware that the shipment of your products are much overdue the shipment time contracted, but we will make every possible effort to re-book on the first ship available after the strike, which at present seems to be the Golden Gate sailing around December 5.

We apologize for the inconvenience you have been put to and assure you that nothing like this accident will happen in the future.

Yours faithfully,

Chapter 10

Marine Insurance

Chapter

10 Marine Insurance

10.1 Concept of Marine Insurance

1. Definition of Marine Insurance

A contract of marine insurance is a contract whereby the insurer undertakes to indemnify the assured, in manner and to the extent thereby agreed, against marine losses, that is to say, the losses incident to marine adventure.[1)]

Marine insurance is defined as a contract of insurance whereby the insurance company in return for premium collected undertakes to indemnify the insured in a manner and to the extent thereby agreed against marine losses, that is to say, the losses incidental to marine adventure. Indemnity implies that the purpose of an insurance contract is to enable a party to cover the loss that it has suffered.

Sellers and buyers face all the time uncertainties of loss of their goods. Insurance is used to protect their financial interests against such risks and actual losses. Trade and insurance can and do exist independently, but in proper context, insurance is an indispensable adjunct. Without adequate insurance and protection of the interests of those with goods in transit, international trade would be negatively affected.

1) Marine Insurance Act, 1906, Article 1.

2. Parties of Marine Insurance

1) Insurer(Assurer, Underwriter)

Insurer is the insurance company which agrees to pay someone who pays them for insurance for loss suffered pursuant to the terms of an insurance policy. An insurer is frequently an insurance company and is also known as an underwriter.

2) Policyholder

Policyholder is the person that owns an insurance policy and has the right to exercise all privileges under the contract of insurance. A policyholder may or may not be the insured, or the sole or one of the beneficiaries of the policy.

3) Insured(Assured)

Insured is one who is covered by an insurance policy. An insured also refers to the one who buys insurance from the insurer or the insurance company. The insured may be the buyer under FOB contract, or the seller under CIF contract or the shipping company.

3. Subject-matter Insured

Subject-matter of insured is anything that insurance can be effected against the risk of loss from maritime perils. Subject matters of insurance that an insured covers are hull, cargo and so on.

4. Insurable Value and Insured Amount

1) Insurable Value

Insurable Value is the value of subject-matter insured(property) stated in an insurance contract indicating the limit of indemnity that will be paid at the time of loss.

2) Insured Amount

Insured Amount is the maximum amount that an insurer has to pay the insured according to the insurance contract.

5. Insurable Interest

Insurable means that the person insuring must have the absolute ownership of the subject-matter insured. Interest means that the person insuring must be the one who stands to bear some financial loss if the risk materializes.

Insurable Interest is the economic relationship between a person and the subject-matter insured. Insurable interest exists when an insured person derives a financial or other kind of benefit from the continuous existence of the insured object. A person has an insurable interest in something when loss-of or damage-to that thing would cause the person to suffer a financial loss or other kind of loss.

If a person does not posses the ownership or he will not suffer from any financial loss, he will not have insurable interest in the subject matter and will not be given the coverage.

Every contract of marine insurance by way of gaming or wagering is void. A contract of marine insurance is deemed to be gaming or wagering contract where the assured has not an insurable interest and the contract is entered into with no expectation of acquiring such an interest.2)

The assured must be interested in the subject-matter insured at the time of the loss though he needs not be interested when the insurance is effected.3)

6. Risks

Two types of risks are covered by marine insurance.

The first type is the perils of the sea that include both natural calamities and fortuitous accidents. Natural calamities refer to earthquake, heavy weather such as hurricane and thunderstorm, etc. These events should be exceptional to some extent and the ordinary action of the wind and waves are not considered natural calamities. Fortuitous accidents include fire, smoking, stranding, sinking, collision, etc. However, fire caused by inherence vice or nature of the cargo is excluded. All the perils must occur at sea, otherwise, the insurance will not cover them.

The second type of risks covered is extraneous risks. These risks include

2) Marine Insurance Act, 1906, Article 4(1~2)
3) Marine Insurance Act, 1906, Article 6(1)

ordinary risks such as theft, pilferage, rain damage, shortage, breakage, etc. and special risks such as strike, war, failure to deliver, etc.

10.2 Marine Loss

1. Physical Loss

1) Total Loss

Total loss can be classified into actual total loss and constructive total loss.

(1) Actual Total Loss(ATL)

There is an actual total loss where the subject-matter insured is destroyed, or so damaged as to cease to be a thing of the kind insured, or where the assured is irretrievably deprived thereof.[4]

Actual total loss means a loss that occurs when the insured property is totally destroyed or is damaged in such a way that it can be neither recovered nor repaired for further use, or the insured is irretrievably deprived of it.

Actual Total Loss occurs when the insured property

① is totally destroyed

② is so damaged that it is no longer the thing that was insured

③ is deprived irretrievably

④ is disappeared.

On the occurrence of an actual total loss, no notice of abandonment need be given to the insurer.

(2) Constructive Total Loss(CTL)

Constructive total loss may occur if the cargo is not actually lost, but is so seriously damaged as to make the goods no longer any use for the purpose for which they were originally intended. A constructive total loss may

4) Marine Insurance Act, 1906, Article 57(1)

also occur when the cost of salvaging the shipment would be more than the salvaged value of the merchandise. When a ship or a cargo is so badly damaged that the cost of repair would be greater than the market value, they are treated as totally lost. In the case of constructive total loss, most insurance policies provide for the payment of a total loss up to the insured amount.

There is a constructive total loss[5)]

- Where the assured is deprived of the possession of his ship or goods by a peril insured against
  - ① it is unlikely that he can recover the ship or goods
  - ② the cost of recovering the ship or goods would exceed their value when recovered.
- In the case of damage to a ship, where she is so damaged by a peril insured against that the cost of repairing the damage would exceed the value of the ship when repaired.

① Abandonment

Abandonment is a right of the owner of an insured property to abandon it where the cost of repairing the damage exceeds its value(called constructive total loss). The insured party can still claim full settlement from the insurer(who becomes the owner of the abandoned property), after serving the notice of abandonment to the insurer subject to the conditions of the insurance policy.

Abandonment is a clause in a property insurance contract that, under the case of constructive total loss, permits the property owner to abandon damaged property and still claim a full settlement amount.

If the insured party's property cannot be recovered, or the cost to recover or repair it is more than its total value, it can be abandoned and the insured party is entitled to a full settlement amount.

② Subrogation

Subrogation means that when an underwriter has paid a loss under his policy, he is entitled to place himself in the position of the assured to take over all rights of the assured in respect of the loss he has paid such as the title to the subject matter insured and the right in a law suit in case of an accident like a ship collision.

---

5) Marine Insurance Act, 1906, Article 60(2)

The Assurer shall be subrogated to all the rights which the Assured may have against any other person or entity, in respect of any payment made under this policy, to the extent of such payment.

Subrogation is the act of the insurer(insurance company) claiming the legal rights of subject-matter insured that the insurer reimbursed the insured for losses. Subrogation occurs in marine insurance when the insurer pays for the damage of the insured and then makes its own claim against others who may have caused the loss, insured the loss or contributed to it.

2) Partial Loss

Partial loss means a partial damage to or the total loss of part of the insured cargo. Partial loss can be divided into general average loss and particular average loss.

(1) Particular Average Loss

Particular average loss means a loss that is born solely by the owner of the lost property such as ship or cargo. It occurs when a storm or fire damages part of the shipper's cargo and no one else's cargo had to be sacrificed to save the voyage. The owner of cargo whose goods were damaged or lost should refer to his insurance company provided his policy covers the specific type of loss suffered.

Particular average loss is a partial loss of the subject-matter insured caused by a peril insured against and which is not general average loss.[6]

(2) General Average Loss

General average loss is a loss caused by or directly consequential on a general average act. It includes a general average expenditure as well as a general average sacrifice.[7]

There is a general average act where any extraordinary sacrifice or expenditure is voluntarily and reasonably made or incurred in time of peril for the purpose of preserving the property imperilled in the common adventure.[8]

General average loss means a sacrifice made for the common safety of

6) Marine Insurance Act, 1906, Article 64(1)
7) Marine Insurance Act, 1906, Article 66(1)
8) Marine Insurance Act, 1906, Article 66(2)

both the cargo and the ship. All parties in a sea venture proportionally share any losses resulting from a voluntary sacrifice of part of the ship or cargo to save the whole in an emergency. Sometimes, when the whole ship is threatened by a peril of the sea or some other hazard, part of the cargo or vessel have to be sacrificed in order to save the ship and some of the cargo. Then the act of general average would be declared. According to maritime law, those interests whose property was saved must contribute proportionally to cover the losses of the one whose property was voluntarily sacrificed.

In order for General Average to be properly declared,

① there must be an event which is beyond the shipowner's control, which imperils the entire adventure
② there must be a voluntary sacrifice
③ there must be something saved

2. Expenses

Marine insurance also covers some expenses incurred in reducing the loss of the subject matter insured either by the issured himself or a party other than the insurer and/or the issured. Expenses such as salvage charges, particular charge, sue & labour expenses and survey fees encourage efforts to save the subject matter insured.

1) Salvage Charges

Salvage charges means the charges recoverable under a maritime law by a salvor independently of contract.[9)]

2) Sue and Labour Charges

Sue and labour charges are costs incurred by an insured in averting or diminishing a loss, and recoverable from the insurer, generally in addition to the insured sum. The sue and labour clause requires the shipowner to make every attempt to reduce or save the exposed interests from loss.

3) Particular Charges

Particular charges are expenses incurred by or on behalf of the assured

9) Marine Insurance Act, 1906, Article 65(2)

for the safety or preservation of the subject-matter insured, other than general average and salvage charges.

3. Liability Loss

Liability loss means that the insurer pays the loss arising from the collision between the insured vessel and another vessel on behalf of the insured vessel.

Both to blame clause forms part of some bills of lading and refers to who was at fault and responsible for payments if two vessels collided while one was carrying cargo pursuant to a bill of lading. Generally, when two vessels collide, they become liable to each other proportionately for the total damage.

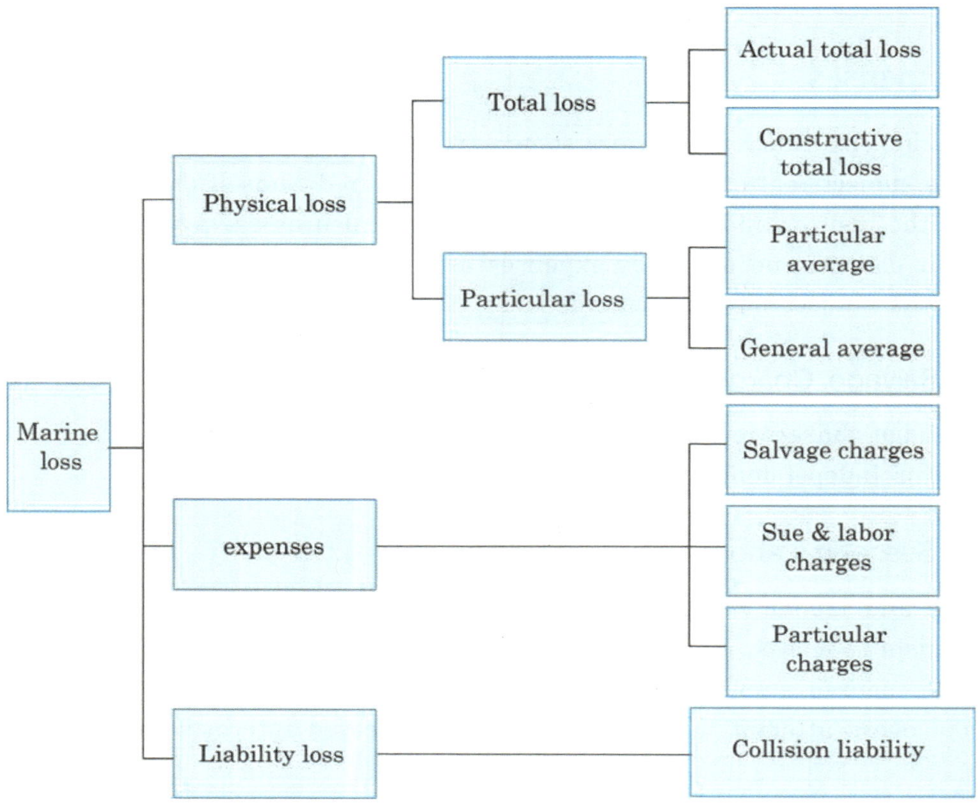

10.3 Scope of Insurance Coverage

1. Institute Cargo Clause

Institute Cargo Clause(ICC) is a set of terms for cargo insurance policies voluntarily adopted as standard terms by many international marine insurance organizations, including the Institute of London Underwriters and the International Underwriting Association of London.

Table 10-1 Classification of Institute Cargo Clause(2009)

Division	Article	Contents
Risks Covered	1 2 3	Risks Clause General Average Clause Both to Blame Collision Clause
Exclusions	4 5 6 7	
Duration	8 9 10	Transit Clause Termination of Contract of Carriage Clause Change of Voyage Clause
Claims	11 12 13 14	Insurable Interest Clause Forwarding Charges Clause Constructive Total Loss Clause Increased Value Clause
Benefit of Insurance	15	
Minimizing Losses	16 17	Duty of Assured Clause Waiver Clause
Avoidance of Delay	18	
Law and Practice	19	

Institute cargo clauses are attached to a type of marine insurance that covers cargo in transit. These clauses are to specify what items in the cargo are covered should there be damage or loss to the shipment. Institute cargo clauses can cover everything from the cargo itself to the container that holds it to the mode of transport used to ship it. These clauses were developed by the International Chamber of Commerce as a means of insurance for cargo while it is being shipped from the original location to its final destination.

Widest insurance cover is provided under 'Institute Cargo Clause A', a more restrictive cover under 'Institute Cargo Clause B', and the most restrictive cover under 'Institute Cargo Clause C.' These clauses have replaced the older 'All Risks,' 'With Average,' and 'Free from Particular Average' clauses.

2. Risks Covered

1) Institute Cargo Clause[ICC(A)]

Institute Cargo Clause(A) is considered the widest insurance coverage and the insured should expect to pay the highest premium because the insured is asking for total coverage.

(1) Risks Covered

Institute Cargo Clause[ICC(A)] covers all risks of loss of or damage to the subject-matter insured except as excluded by the provisions of Clauses 4, 5, 6 and 7 below. This insurance covers every risks other than the risks mentioned in ①~⑪ in [Table 10-2].

(2) General Average

Institute Cargo Clause[ICC(A)] covers general average and salvage charges, adjusted or determined according to the contract of carriage and/or the governing law and practice, incurred to avoid or in connection with the avoidance of loss from any cause except those excluded in Clauses 4, 5, 6 and 7.

(3) Blame to Blame Collision Clause

Institute Cargo Clause[ICC(A)] indemnifies the Assured, in respect of any risk insured herein, against liability incurred under any Both to Blame Collision Clause in the contract of carriage. In the event of any claim by carriers under the said Clause, the Assured agree to notify the Insurers who shall have the right, at their own cost and expense, to defend the Assured against such claim.

2) Institute Cargo Clause[ICC(B)]

Institute Cargo Clause(B) is considered a more restrictive coverage and the insured should expect to pay a moderate premium because perhaps the insured is only requesting the more valuable items in your cargo to be covered or only partial cargo coverage.

(1) Risks Covered

Institute Cargo Clause[ICC(B)] covers all risks of loss of or damage to the subject-matter insured except as excluded by the provisions of Clauses 4, 5, 6 and 7 below. This insurance covers the risks in ①~⑪ in [Table 10-2] and does not cover other risks.

(2) General Average

The risks covered under Institute Cargo Clause[ICC(B)] clause are the same as the risks in Clause[ICC(A)] clause.

(3) Blame to Blame Collision Clause

Institute Cargo Clause[ICC(B)] indemnifies the Assured, in respect of any risk insured herein, against liability incurred under any Both to Blame Collision Clause in the contract of carriage just as the Clause [ICC(A)] does.

3) Institute Cargo Clause[ICC(C)]

Institute Cargo Clause(C) is considered the most restrictive coverage and the insured will probably pay the lowest premium but his cargo coverage will be much less.

(1) Risks Covered

Institute Cargo Clause[ICC(C)] covers all risks of loss of or damage to the subject-matter insured except the risks in ⑥ and ⑨~⑫ in [Table 10-2] and exclusions in 4, 5, 6 and 7.

(2) General Average

The risks covered under Institute Cargo Clause[ICC(C)] clause are the same as the risks in Clause[ICC(A)] clause.

(3) Blame to Blame Collision Clause

Institute Cargo Clause[ICC(C)] indemnifies the Assured, in respect of any risk insured herein, against liability incurred under any Both to Blame Collision Clause in the contract of carriage just as the Clause[ICC(A)] does.

Table 10-2 Risks covered in ICC(A), ICC(B) and ICC(C) Clauses

Article	Contents			
1	Loss of damage to the subject-matter insured reasonably attributable to	A	B	C
	① fire or explosion	O	O	O
	② vessel or craft being stranded, grounded, sunk or capsized	O	O	O
	③ overturning or derailment of land conveyance	O	O	O
	④ collision or contract of vessel craft or conveyance with any external object other than water	O	O	O
	⑤ discharge of cargo at a port of distress	O	O	O
	⑥ earthquake volcanic eruption or lightning	O	O	×
	Loss of or damage to the subject-matter insured caused by			
	⑦ general average sacrifice	O	O	O
	⑧ jettison	O	O	O
	⑨ washing overboard	O	O	×
	⑩ entry of sea lake or river water into vessel, craft hold, conveyance, container or place of storage	O	O	×
	⑪ total loss of any package lost overboard or dropped whilst loading on to, or unloading from, vessel or craft	O	O	×
	⑫ every risks except the above	O	×	×
2	⑬ General Average(except exclusions)	O	O	O
3	⑭ Both to Blame Collision Clause	O	O	O

3. Exclusions

1) General Exclusions

In no case shall this insurance cover

1. loss damage or expense attributable to wilful misconduct of the Assured.
2. ordinary leakage, ordinary loss in weight or volume, or ordinary wear and tear of the subject-matter insured.

3. loss damage or expense caused by insufficiency or unsuitability of packing or preparation of the subject-matter insured.
4. loss damage or expense caused by inherent vice or nature of the subject-matter insured.
5. loss damage or expense caused by delay, even though the delay be caused by a risk insured against.
6. loss damage or expense caused by insolvency or financial default of the owners, managers, charterers or operators of the vessel.
7. deliberate damage to or deliberate destruction of the subject-matter insured or any part thereof by the wrongful act of any person or persons.
8. loss damage or expense directly or indirectly caused by or arising from the use of any weapon or device employing atomic or nuclear fission and/or fusion or other like reaction or radioactive force or matter.

2) Unseaworthiness of Vessel

In no case shall this insurance cover loss damage or expense arising from

1. unseaworthiness of vessel or craft or unfitness of vessel or craft for the safe carriage of the subject-matter insured, where the Assured are privy to such unseaworthiness or unfitness, at the time the subject-matter insured is loaded therein
2. unfitness of container or conveyance for the safe carriage of the subject-matter insured, where loading therein or thereon is carried out prior to attachment of this insurance or by the Assured or their employees and they are privy to such unfitness at the time of loading.
3. The Insurers waive any breach of the implied warranties of seaworthiness of the ship and fitness of the ship to carry the subject-matter insured to destination.

3) War

In no case shall this insurance cover loss damage or expense caused by

1. war civil war revolution rebellion insurrection, or civil strife arising therefrom, or any hostile act by or against a belligerent power
2. capture seizure arrest restraint or detainment, and the consequences thereof or any attempt thereat
3. derelict mines torpedoes bombs or other derelict weapons of war.

4) Strikes

In no case shall this insurance cover loss damage or expense

1. caused by strikers, locked-out workmen, or persons taking part in labour disturbances, riots or civil commotions
2. resulting from strikes, lock-outs, labour disturbances, riots or civil commotions
3. caused by any act of terrorism being an act of any person acting on behalf of, or in connection with, any organization which carries out activities directed towards the overthrowing or influencing, by force or violence, of any government whether or not legally constituted
4. caused by any person acting from a political, ideological or religious motive.

Table 10-3 Exclusions

Article	Contents	A	B	C
4	① loss damage or expense attributable to wilful misconduct of the Assured	x	x	x
	② ordinary leakage, ordinary loss in weight or volume, or ordinary wear and tear of the subject-matter insured	x	x	x
	③ loss damage or expense caused by insufficiency or unsuitability of packing or preparation of the subject-matter insured	x	x	x
	④ loss damage or expense caused by inherent vice or nature of the subject-matter insured	x	x	x
	⑤ loss damage or expense caused by delay	x	x	x
	⑥ loss damage or expense caused by insolvency or financial default of the owners, managers, charterers or operators of the vessel	x	x	x
	⑦ deliberate damage to or deliberate destruction of the subject-matter insured or any part thereof by the wrongful act of any person	o	x	x
	⑧ loss damage or expense directly or indirectly caused by or arising from the use of any weapon or device employing atomic or nuclear fission	x	x	x
5	⑨ unseaworthiness of vessel or craft or unfitness of vessel or craft for the safe carriage of the subject-matter insured	x	x	x
6	⑩ war civil war revolution rebellion insurrection, or civil strife arising therefrom	x	x	x
7	⑪ loss damage or expense caused by strikers, locked-out workmen, or persons taking part in labour disturbances, riots or civil commotions	x	x	x

4. Duration

1) Commencement of Insurance

The insurance attaches from the time the subject-matter insured is first moved in the warehouse or at the place of storage(at the place named in the contract of insurance) for the purpose of the immediate loading into or onto the carrying vehicle or other conveyance for the commencement of transit and continues during the ordinary course of transit.

2) Termination of Insurance

The insurance terminates either

1. on completion of unloading from the carrying vehicle or other conveyance in or at the final warehouse or place of storage at the destination named in the contract of insurance,
2. on completion of unloading from the carrying vehicle or other conveyance in or at any other warehouse or place of storage, whether prior to or at the destination named in the contract of insurance, which the Assured or their employees elect to use either for storage other than in the ordinary course of transit or for allocation or distribution, or
3. when the Assured or their employees elect to use any carrying vehicle or other conveyance or any container for storage other than in the ordinary course of transit or
4. on the expiry of 60 days after completion of discharge overside of the subject-matter insured from the oversea vessel at the final port of discharge, whichever shall first occur.

10.4 Sample Letters of Marine Insurance

1. Request for an Insurance Rate to a Insurance Company

1) A request

Gentlemen :

We will ship 500sets of computers by Dong-jin V-103 which is due to sail from Busan on April 12 to Long beach port in U.S.A.

We, therefore, ask you to quote us your lowest rate for marine insurance ICC(C) for 110% of the invoice amount of U$600,000.

Your prompt reply to this e-mail would be highly appreciated.

Very truly yours,

2) A reply

Dear Mr. Whang,

In response to your e-mail dated April 4, we are glad to quote you the rate of Marine insurance at 0.243 percent for a total cover of U$600,000 for computers.

Considering the rates quoted by our competitors, you will find that the rate we are offering is exceptionally low.

We attach a declaration form and look forward to receiving it filled out by you if this rate is satisfactory to you.

Yours truly,

2. Request for Effecting a Marine Insurance

1) A request

Gentlemen,

As for the shipment of used furniture by s/s Arirang due to leave for Darkar in Senegal on the 21st of May, our partner, Socida Ltd, has a right to effect an insurance on the goods as the contract is based on FOB.

They instructed us to effect a marine insurance with you on ICC(B) including War Risks at the rate which was mutually agreed upon by both of you.

One copy of commercial invoice and packing list are attached for your information. Please effect an insurance for US$150,000 and send us marine insurance cargo policy in duplicate and some copies together with your invoice for the insurance premium.

Very truly yours,

2) A reply from an insurance company

Gentlemen,

As you requested in your e-mail of October 22, we have effected an insurance for U$250,000 on 20pcs of furniture at the rate of 0.21 percent quoted from Busan to Dakar ICC(B) including war risks.

We will send you have the marine insurance policy with the statement of premium in a few days and please remit the amount to our accounting department as soon as possible.

Yours faithfully,

3) A request for effecting an insurance with ICC(A)

Gentlemen,

We would like to draw your attention that we made up our mind to make an insurance contract with you at the rate you quoted us by telephone yesterday on the shipment of products for the sum of USD85,000.00

The products will be loaded on Choyang Sun V-353S waiting at the dock No.3 for sailing on December 3.

We want you to cover us on ICC(A) and deliver the marine insurance policy to us as soon as it is ready.

Please send us your draft of the policy by fax so that we can check if everything is perfect.

Very truly yours,

4) A notice from the seller

Gentlemen,

According to your instruction, we duly have made an insurance contract with First Fire & Marine Insurance Co., Ltd. at 0.352 percent for U$9,490, ICC(B) including T.P.N.D. on 4 sets of Press for Woven Fabric shipped by Golden Gate on last Friday from Busan to Osaka, Japan.

The rate at which we covered is the best rate of premium at present here and we want you to send us the amount in the receipt for which we already paid on behalf of you.

Yours faithfully,

5) A claim for a Claim Settlement to an Insurance Company

Gentlemen,

We would like to inform you that the consignment covering skin care cosmetics were delivered in bad condition as you see in the survey report attached to this e-mail.

Of course, we filed our claim with the shipping company concerned, but they rejected our claim by notifying us that they were not liable for this matter.

In accordance with the policy instructions, we don't have any choice but to ask you to indemnify for the sum of U$30,000 to compensate for the loss we have.

We will send you the following relative documents for your reference.

1. Marine Insurance Policy No. : 02-3-A-1004209
2. Ocean Bill of Lading No. : SEO/D14451
3. Loading Port : Busan, Korea
4. Discharging Port : Hamburg, Germany
5. Discharging Date : Oct. 21, 19xx
6. Commercial Invoice No. : K5225F(01)
7. E-mails with the shipping company
8. A survey Report

Chapter 11

Bill of Exchange and Documents

Chapter

11

Bill of Exchange and Documents

11.1 Bill of Exchange

1. Definition of Bill of Exchange

A bill of exchange(draft) is an unconditional order in writing, addressed by one person to another, signed by one the person giving it, requiring the person to whom it is addressed to pay on demand or at a fixed or determinable future time a sum certain in money to or to the order of a specified person, or to bearer.[1]

A bill of exchange is a written, unconditional order by one party(the drawer) to another(the drawee) to pay a certain sum either immediately(a sight bill) or on a fixed date(a term bill), for payment of goods and/or services received.

In the collection method of payment for goods a bill of exchange is always drawn on the buyer by the seller to get paid. The seller gets payment against the delivery just by a bill of exchange for the sum agreed as settlement in the contract. By using a draft with other shipping documents through the banking system, the seller can ensure greater control of the goods as the goods cannot be released until the bill of lading is paid or accepted by the buyer.

1) Bills of Exchange Act, 1882, Article 3(1)

2. Types of Bill of Exchange

A bill of exchange may be made payable, for example, at sight or after sight, which(respectively) means it is either payable upon presentation or demand or within a particular period after the demand is made.

1) Sight Bill of Exchange

A sight bill of exchange(a sight bill) is a bill of exchange payable on demand. On delivery of a sight bill to the drawee, the drawee pays immediately. It is a type of bill of exchange, in which the seller holds the title to the transported goods until the buyer receives and pays for it.

The sight bill is to be presented to the drawee as soon as it is received by a bank, and the payment is to be made immediately upon presentation.

2) Usance Bill of Exchange

An usance bill of exchange(a usance draft, a time draft) is a bill of exchange payable at a fixed future date or a determinable future time such as 30 days after presentation(after sight) or date. The purpose of a time draft is to allow the buyer to pay for the goods bought at maturity. As regards usance bill, payment is made at a certain number of days or months after date or after sight.

A bill drawn at thirty days after sight(at 30 d/s) means that the drawee must pay the bill at thirty days after the date on which the bill has been presented. A bill drawn at thirty days after date(at 30 d/d) means that the drawee must pay the bill at thirty days after the date on which the bill has been drawn regardless of the time elapsed in presenting it.

The payment is on the due date determinable in accordance with the stipulations of the Letter of Credit(L/C). The maturity date(the due date) can be at a stated period after sight or after date.

(1) After B/L date

It is a notation used on financial instruments(such as draft or bill of exchange) to fix the maturity date as a fixed number of days past the date of bill of lading or the date of shipment.

When the credit requires the tenor to be 30 days after the bill of lading date, the draft can show the tenor different ways as follows;

- "30 days after B/L date, October 15, 20××.
- "30 days after the date of shipment, October 15, 20××"

The on board date in the bill of lading is always considered the date of the bill of lading. The maturity date is 30 days after B/L date.

(2) After Date

It is a notation used on financial instruments(such as draft or bill of exchange) to fix the maturity date as a fixed number of days after the draft is drawn. For example, if a draft stipulates "30 days after date", it means that the draft is due(payable) 30 days after the date it is drawn. This has the effect of fixing the date of the maturity of the draft, independent of the date of acceptance of the draft. The maturity date is 30 days after the date of the draft.

(3) After sight

It is a notation on a draft that indicates that payment is due a fixed number of days after the draft has been presented to the drawee. For example, if a draft stipulates "30 days after sight", it means that the draft is due(payable) 30 days after the draft is presented.

BILL OF EXCHANGE

(title of draft)

No. *No of draft* Date. *Date of issue*

For *amount(number)* Place *Place of issue*

At *(tenor)* sight of this First Bill of Exchange (Second of the same tenor and date being unpaid) pay to ABC Bank or order the sums of *(payee)* *amount(character)*

Value received and charge the same to account of *(valuation clause)* *(accountee)*

Drawn under *(issuing bank)* L/C No. *(L/C No.)* dated *(date of issue)*

To *drawee)*

(drawer)

Authorized signature

BILL OF EXCHANGE

(title of draft)

No. *No of draft* Date. *Date of issue*

For *amount(number)* Place *Place of issue*

At *(tenor)* sight of this Second Bill of Exchange (First of the same tenor and date being unpaid) pay to ABC Bank or order *(payee)* the sums of *amount(character)*

Value received and charge the same to account of *(valuation clause)* *(accountee)*

Drawn under *(issuing bank)* L/C No. *(L/C No.)* dated *(date of issue)*

To *drawee)*

(drawer)

Authorized signature

11.2 Sample Letters of Bill of Exchange

1. Advice of Issuing Sight Drafts

1) An advice of issuing sight drafts

Gentlemen :

We are pleased to inform you that we have shipped 3,000kgs of "Seagull" Vegetable Wax you placed an order with us by HJ, Cheju V-070W which left Busan on April 6.

We have drawn our drafts at sight for U$33,000 on the Bank of New York under the L/C No. 089923 and forwarded the relative shipping documents to our negotiating bank, Korea Exchange Bank, Seoul.

Therefore, we want you to protect the drafts on presentation and we really hope the products will reach you to your satisfaction.

Very truly yours,

2) An advice of accepting the drafts by the seller

Dear Mr. Ham,

We duly have received your e-mail of April 13 asking us to honor the drafts you have drawn on the issuing bank for the products we need urgently.

Thank you for your prompt shipment of the products. The drafts were presented by New York Bank and duly paid by us and we have received the shipping documents.

We are waiting for the vessel which will reach here soon and we will keep in touch with you as soon as we receive them in good condition.

Yours very truly,

2. Advice of Issuing Usance Drafts(1)

1) An advice of issuing an usnace draft

Dear Mr. Thomas,

This is to inform you that we have shipped 10 cases of Imitation Pearls by Pacific Bear which left Busan on December 12.

To cover the shipment, we have drawn our drafts at 90days after sight on Chemical Bank in Houston for U$23,500.00 under the credit No. 81932.

The drafts with other documents will be forwarded to the issuing bank through Korea Exchange Bank in Seoul and we ask you kindly to protect the drafts at maturity.

We hope that the products will reach you safely in due course and that we will receive your further orders for which we will pay our best attention at all times.

Yours very truly,

2) An advice of accepting an usance draft

Dear Mr. Kim,

Thank you for your e-mail dated December 12 informing us that you have negotiated your drafts drawn at 90 days after sight under the credit No.81932.

As for the drafts presented by Chemical Bank, we are glad to inform you that we accepted the drafts accordingly, and we will pay discount charge at maturity.

Pacific Bear will reach here safely soon and we wish to be able to write you as to the safe arrival of the products before long.

Very truly yours,
Busy Bee Co., Ltd.

3. Advice of Issuing Usance Drafts(2)

Gentlemen :

We have completed the shipment of the laundry detergents covering your order No. 121 by vessel 'C. Jupiter' sailed from Busan on November 23 heading for Long Beach, U.S.A.

As you requested, one non-negotiable bill of lading and one copy of commercial invoice will be transmitted by fax for your reference.

Full set of clean on board B/L, Commercial Invoice in duplicate, Packing List in duplicate, Insurance Policy in duplicate have been negotiated through the Wester Minister Bank, Seoul together with the drafts drawn on the issuing bank at 30 days after sight under the L/C No.79091.

We shall be pleased to hear that the products have arrived safely and in good order.

Very truly yours,

4. Request for Payment to the Draft Dishonoured

Dear Sirs,

We were very surprised to hear that the bill of exchange No. 211 dated March 12 was not met when presented.

As you have never failed to meet your obligations on the bills we have drawn so far, we are surprised to know that the payment has not been made. Also we did not receive any reply from you on this matter and we would be appreciated it if you could explain the reason why the draft was not honored.

We instructed our bank today to present the draft again and we believe you will protect it immediately.

Should payment not been made by you without any special reason, we can not help starting legal proceedings for dishonor.

Yours truly,

5. Advice of Payment for a Collection Draft

Dear Sirs,

This is to notify you that the products invoiced by you on December 12 have arrived here safely and they were found satisfactory. In settlement of the amount of invoice, Korea Exchange Bank has presented your bill of exchange, D/A for U$35,800 at 120 days after sight together with shipping documents under our contract No. 11.

We have accepted the bill upon presentation and duly received the documents. Of course, the bill will be paid by us in due course.

We are sure that our customers will be satisfied with your prompt execution to our order and we are ready to place a further order with you.

Yours faithfully,

6. Request for Accepting the Draft Overdue

Dear Sirs,

We have completed the shipment for your order No. 132 on November 25 and drawn our drafts on you for the full invoice amount of U$100,000 at 60 days after sight under L/C No.076643.

We know that you have cleared your accounts punctually on the due date. We draw your attention, however, that your account this time is now three weeks overdue.

We are of an opinion that you must have overlooked for some reasons and we want you to honor the drafts immediately after you receive this e-mail.

Yours faithfully,

7. Request for Payment(1)

Dear Sirs,

For your order No. 324 dated April 2 for Men's Sweaters, amounting to U$8,500, we have sent you a statement of your account. We regret to inform you, however, that we still didn't receive your remittance in settlement of the above.

As we have some heavy bills to meet in a few days, we ask you to clear your account as soon as possible.

8. Request for Payment(2)

Gentlemen :

We are sorry to trouble you again by reminding you of our repeated e-mails asking the payment of your account which is two months overdue.

Having waited for two weeks since we sent you our third e-mail on April 23, we couldn't help concluding that you were facing to meet your obligation in a correct manner.

We want you to ask lastly to settle your full account by the end of May. If we don't receive your remittance by that time, there is no choice but to take legal proceedings against you to protect ourselves even though we are reluctant to do so.

Yours faithfully,

9. Apology for the Delay of Payment(1)

Dear Sirs,

We received your e-mail informing us that our payment was not settled due on September 3.

Upon checking, we have found that the person in charge in our accounting department made an oversight in making a remittance to you.

To settle this problem, we immediately have sent you the sum of U$15,000 by Telegraphic Transfer.

We apologize for this regrettable mistake and we will take every measures to prevent the recurrence of similar error in the future.

Yours faithfully,

10. Apology for the Delay of Payment(2)

Gentlemen :

Your inquiry regarding an outstanding balance for the sum of U$10,000 for the products shipped on February 16 was immediately checked against our contract No. 23 on which we had mutually agreed.

Our contract indicated that U$10,000 had, in fact, not been paid due to an oversight on our part. The amount concerned was forwarded to your account in Uri Bank by telegraphic transfer today.

Please accept our sincere apology for the inconvenience this matter has caused you.

We hope we can continue our business relations as usual.

Yours sincerely,

11. Apology for the Delay of Payment(3)

Dear Sirs,

Please allow us to apologize for our delay in payment of the U$8,000 for soaps you placed an order with us. A mail transfer for this amount was sent today.

Enclosed for your convenience is a copy of the transfer form as well as a copy of your statement. If you didn't receive payment yet, please notify us so that we can have the transaction traced.

We think that we may be able to place other orders with you soon.

Yours faithfully,

11.3 Documents

1. Definition of Documents

Documents mean every documents required for presentation including commercial invoice, transport documents, insurance documents and other supplementary documents stipulated in the contract except a draft.

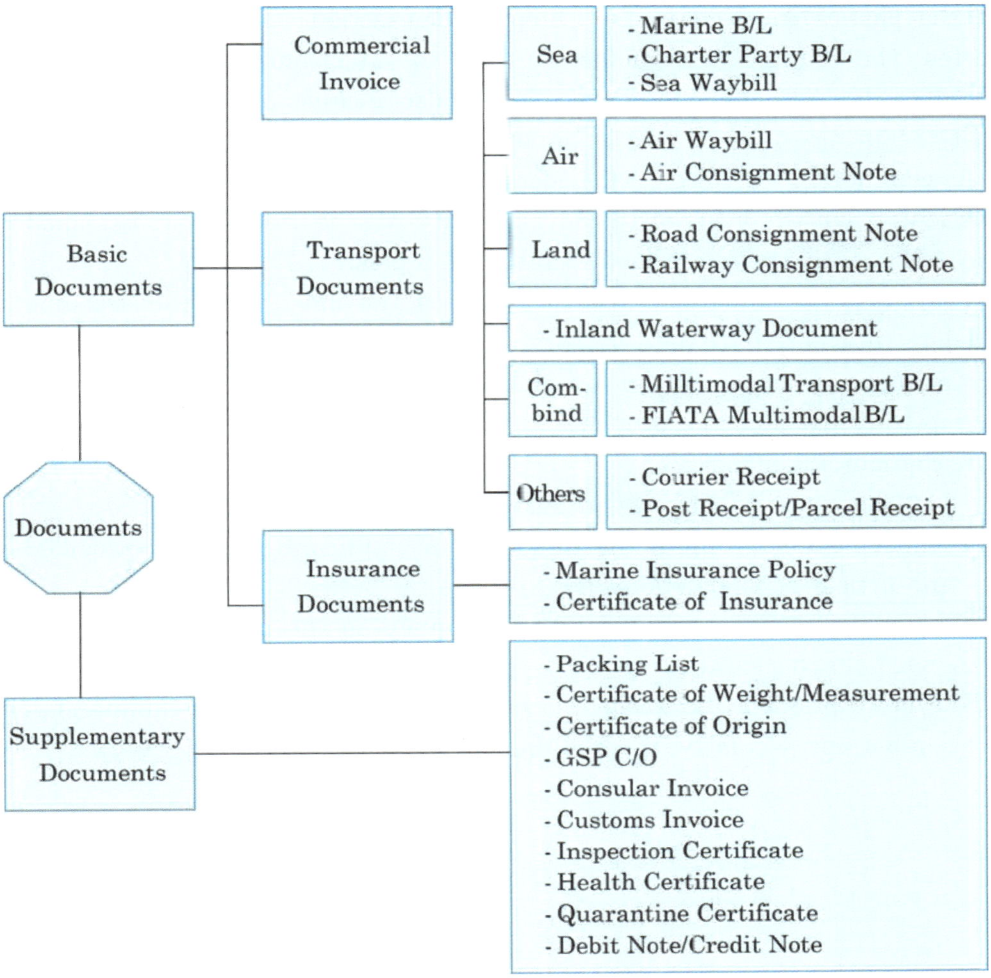

2. Kinds of Documents

1) Commercial Invoice

A commercial invoice is a document identifying the seller and the buyer of the goods and services, invoice number, date, shipping date, mode of transport, delivery and payment terms and a complete list and description of the goods and services being sold including prices and quantities.

It is used as a customs declaration provided by the person or corporation that exports goods across international borders. Although there is no standard format, the document must include a few specific pieces of information such as the parties involved in the shipping transaction, the goods being transported, the country of manufacture, and the Harmonized System codes for those goods. A commercial invoice must also include a statement certifying that the invoice is true, and a signature.

A commercial invoice gives details of the goods and the value in particular. On the basis of the invoice, duty will be assessed. It is issued by the seller with the prescribed number of copies.

Therefore, a commercial invoice is one of the most important documents used in international trade. It serves as a record of the essential details of a transaction. A great attention should be given to the fact that the commercial invoice must be accurate in all respects.

A commercial invoice;[2)]

- must appear to have been issued by the beneficiary
- must be made out in the name of the applicant(except as provided in sub-article of UCP 600 38(g))
- must be made out in the same currency as the credit
- need not be signed

The description of the goods, services or performance in a commercial invoice must correspond with that appearing in the credit.[3)]

---

2) UCP 600 Article 19, a.
3) UCP 600 Article 18, c.

COMMERCIAL INVOICE

①Shipper/Seller DAEHAN CO., LTD CPO BOX 195 SEOUL, KOREA	⑦Invoice No. and date 8905 BK 1007 JULY 25. 20×× ⑧L/C No. and date MD1NY404NS00018, MAY 15. 20××
② Consignee TO THE ORDER OF BANK OF AMERICA	⑨Buyer(if other than consignee) BROWN CO., LTD. 310 FIFTH AVE. NEW YORK NY, USA
③Departure date JULY. 20, 20××	⑩Other references COUNTRY OF ORIGIN : REPUBLIC OF KOREA
④Vessel/flight ⑤From WONIS JIN BUSAN, KOREA ⑥To NEW YORK, U.S.A	⑪Terms of delivery and payment CIF NEW YORK L/C AT SIGHT

⑫Shipping Marks	⑬No.&kind of packages	⑭Goods description	⑮Quantity	⑯Unit price	⑰Amount
PCU NEW YORK, U.S.A C/NO.1-50 MADE IN KOREA		COMPUTER	2,000PCS	US$250	US$500,000

Signed by
⑱

2) Transport Documents

(1) Bill of Lading[4]

a. A bill of lading, however named, must appear to :

i. indicate the name of the carrier and be signed by:

- the carrier or a named agent for or on behalf of the carrier, or
- the master or a named agent for or on behalf of the master.

Any signature by the carrier, master or agent must be identified as that of the carrier, master or agent.

Any signature by an agent must indicate whether the agent has signed for or on behalf of the carrier or for or on behalf of the master.

ii. indicate that the goods have been shipped on board a named vessel at the port of loading stated in the credit by :

- pre-printed wording, or
- an on board notation indicating the date on which the goods have been shipped on board.

The date of issuance of bill of lading will be deemed to be the date of shipment unless the bill of lading contains an on board notation indicating the date of shipment, in which case the date stated in the on board notation will be deemed to be the date of shipment. If the bill of lading contains the indication "intended vessel" or similar qualification in relation to the name of the vessel, an on board notation indicating the date of shipment and the name of the actual vessel is required.

iii. indicate shipment from the port of loading to the port of discharge stated in the credit.

If the bill of lading does not indicate the port of loading stated in the credit as the port of loading, or if it contains the indication "intended" or similar qualification in relation to the port of loading, an on board notation indicating the port of loading as stated in the credit, the date of shipment and the name of the vessel is required. This provision applies even when loading on board or shipment on a named vessel is indicated by pre-printed wording on the bill of lading.

---

4) UCP 600 Article 20.

iv. be the sole original bill of lading or, if issued in more than one original, be the full set as indicated on the bill of lading.

v. contain terms and conditions of carriage or make reference to another source containing the terms and conditions of carriage (short form or blank back bill of lading). Contents of terms and conditions of carriage will not be examined.

vi. contain no indication that it is subject to a charter party.

b. For the purpose of this article, transhipment means unloading from one vessel and reloading to another vessel during the carriage from the port of loading to the port of discharge stated in the credit.

c. i. A bill of lading may indicate that the goods will or may be transhiped provided that the entire carriage is covered by one and the same bill of lading.

ii. A bill of lading indicating that transhipment will or may take place is acceptable, even if the credit prohibits transhipment, if the goods have been shipped in a container, trailer or LASH barge as evidenced by the bill of lading.

d. Clauses in a bill of lading stating that the carrier reserves the right to tranship will be disregarded.

(2) Air Transport Document[5)]

The Air Waybill(AWB) is the consignment note used for the carriage of goods by air. It is often called an air consignment note and is not a document of title or transferable/negotiable instrument. It is basically a receipt for the goods for dispatch and is an evidence of the conditions of carriage.

There are usually 12 copies of each air waybill for distribution to the shipper, sales agent, issuing carrier(airline operator), consignee, delivery receipt, airport of destination, third carrier(if applicable), second carrier and airport of departure.

Copies 1, 2 and 3 are the originals. Each copy is not always used but merely as circumstances demand. For example, the second carrier's copy would be used only if the consignment was conveyed on another airline to complete the transit.

---

5) UCP 600 Article 23.

a. An air transport document, however named, must appear to :

i. indicate the name of the carrier and be signed by:

- the carrier or
- a named agent for or on behalf of the carrier

  Any signature by the carrier or agent must be identified as that of the carrier or agent.

  Any signature by an agent must indicate that the agent has signed for or on behalf of the carrier.

ii. indicate that the goods have been accepted for carriage.

iii. indicate the date of issuance. This date will be deemed to be the date of shipment unless the air transport document contains a specific notation of the actual date of shipment, in which case the date stated in the notation will be deemed to be the date of shipment. Any other information appearing on the air transport document relative to the flight number and date will not be considered in determining the date of shipment.

iv. indicate the airport of departure and the airport of destination stated in the credit.

v. be the original for consignor or shipper, even if the credit stipulates a full set of originals.

vi. contain terms and conditions of the carriage or make reference to another source containing the terms and conditions of carriage. Contents of terms and conditions of carriage will not be examined.

b. For the purpose of this article, transhipment means unloading from one aircraft and reloading to another aircraft during the carriage from the airport of departure to the airport of destination stated in the credit.

c. i. An air transport document may indicate that the goods will or may be transhiped provided that the entire carriage is covered by one and the same air transport document.

ii. An air transport document indicating that transhipment will or may take place is acceptable, even if the credit prohibits transhipment.

(3) Transport Document Covering at Least Two Different Modes of Transport.[6)]

Multimodal transport documents(combined transport documents) evidences the contract of carriage of goods by at least two modes of transport, issued by a combined transport operator under a combined transport contract. It is quite similar to through B/L and combined transport B/L used for ocean transport, but is broader than them.

Through B/L and multimodal transport B/L are always connected with sea, and used for any transport combined with sea, while combined transport document can be applied to any kind of multimodal transport.

Several carriers are involved in through B/L while combined transport document is issued by only one carrier, that is, multimodal transport operator.

a. A transport document covering at least two different modes of transport(multimodal or combined transport document), however named, must appear to :

i. indicate the name of the carrier and be signed by:

- the carrier or a named agent for or on behalf of the carrier, or
- the master or a named agent for or on behalf of the master.

  Any signature by the carrier, master or agent must be identified as that of the carrier, master or agent.

  Any signature by an agent must indicate whether the agent has signed for or on behalf of the carrier or for or on behalf of the master.

ii. indicate that the goods have been dispatched, taken in charge or shipped on board at the place stated in the credit by :

- pre-printed wording, or
- an on board notation indicating the date on which the goods have been dispatched, taken in charge or shipped on board.

  The date of issuance of the transport document will be deemed to be the date of dispatch, taking in charge or shipped on board, and the date of shipment. However, if the transport document indicates, by stamp or notation, a date of dispatch, taking in charge or shipped on board, this date will be deemed to be the

6) UCP600 Article 19.

date of shipment.

iii. indicate the place of dispatch, taking in charge or shipment and the place of final destination stated in the credit, even if;
   a. the transport document states, in addition, a different place of dispatch, taking in charge or shipment or place of final destination.
   b. the transport document contains the indication "intended" or similar qualification in relation to the vessel, port of loading or port of discharge.

iv. be the sole original transport document or, if issued in more than one original, be the full set as indicated on the transport document.

v. contain terms and conditions of carriage and make reference to another source containing the terms and conditions of carriage (short form or blank back transport document). Contents of terms and conditions of carriage will not be examined.

vi. contain no indication that it is subject to a charter party.

b. For the purpose of this article, transhipment means unloading from one means of conveyance and reloading to another means of conveyance(whether or not in different modes of transport) during the carriage from the place of dispatch, taking in charge or shipment to the place of final destination stated in the credit.

c. i. A transport document may indicate that the goods will or may be transhiped provided that the entire carriage is covered by one and the same transport document.

ii. A transport document indicating that transhipment will or may take place is acceptable, even if the credit prohibits transhipment.

3) Insurance Policy

Insurance policy is the most commonly used document that contains all the details concerning the goods, coverage, premium and the insured value. All this information must be sufficient enough for the insured party to asses the risk and make insurance decision. It is always filled out by the insured.

When all is fixed, the insurer will normally return the duplicate to the insured with their rubber seal. The signed insurance policy will become the legal document that serves as the shipping document evidencing insurance cover.

Certificate of Insurance is the simplified version of the insurance policy serving the same functions in the transaction.

4) Packing List

A packing list itemizes the material in each individual package and indicates the type of package such as box, crate, drum, carton and so on. It shows the individual net, legal, tare and gross weights and measurements for each package. Packing list is used by the shipper or forwarding agent to determine the total shipment weight and volume and whether the correct cargo is being shipped. In addition, customs officials may use the list to check the cargo.

A packing list gives details of the contents of all the packages making up the consignments and is required by Customs authorities if the packing information is not shown on the invoice.

5) Certificate of Origin

A certificate of origin(C/O) is an important international trade document attesting that the goods in a particular export shipment are wholly obtained, produced, manufactured or processed in a particular country.

Certificate of origin can be issued by a government agency, chamber of commerce or relevant associations. An importing country often asks for such a certificate in order to extend preferential duties to the goods from acceptable countries, to apply import controls such as sanction, quota, or anti-dumping duty and to collect statistics.

6) Certificate of Quality

A certificate of quality is a document attesting that an individual or a company has achieved the requirements necessary to be certified in a particular field. It shows that the individual or company has met all of the requirements that were given to them and that they did it in a quality fashion. It means that they have met or exceeded expectations in the way of business ethics, customer satisfaction, tax payment history, and of adapting to changes as needed.

A certificate of quality confirms that the quality or specification of the goods is in accordance with the sales contract at the time of shipment. It may be issued by the seller or a relevant government department as required under L/C or sales contract. It is essential that cargo description in the quality certificate conforms to its terms found in other relevant documents such as commercial invoice, L/C and insurance policy.

7) Certificate of Weight

A certificate of weight is a document issued commonly by customs authorities of the exporting country certifying the correct gross weight of the goods being shipped. A certificate of weight is usually requested by the buyer to confirm that the weight of the goods is in accordance with the sales contract at the time of shipment. It may be issued by the seller or a relevant government department as required under L/C or sales contract.

8) Certificate of Inspection

A certificate of inspection is a document certifying that the item meets the required specifications and was in good condition and correct quantity when it left the port of shipment. This certificate is issued to ensure that the goods meet a certain standard. The seller must arrange beforehand with the buyer who is to carry out such an inspection and who is to pay for the inspection.

Bill of Lading

② Shipper/Exporter DAEHAN CO., LTD. CPO BOX 195 SEOUL, KOREA	⑫ B/L No. ; PCS-96010
③ Consignee TO ORDER OF BANK OF AMERICA	**World Trans Corporation** C.P.O. Box. 1234 Seoul, Korea TEL : (02)624-1212 FAX : (02)624-1234
④ Notify Party BROWN CO., LTD. 310 FIFTH AVE, NEW YORK, NY 10118, USA	

Pre-Carriage by	⑥ Place of Receipt BUSAN CY, KOREA
⑤ Ocean Vessel WONIS JIN	⑦ Voyage No. V-234E

⑧ Port of Loading	⑨ Port of Discharge	⑩ Place of Delivery	⑪ Final Destination
BUSAN, KOREA	NEW YORK, U.S.A	NEW YORK CY, U.S.A	(for the merchant's reference only)

⑬ Container No. ⑭ Seal No. Marks & No	⑮ No. & Kinds of Containers or Packages	⑯ Description of Goods	⑱ Gross Weight	Measurement
ISCU1104 0559 929 PCU NEW YORK, U.S.A C/NO. 1-50 MADE IN KOREA	1 CNTR (20'CNTR)	"SAID TO CONTAIN" 2,000SETS OF COMPUTERS ⑰ ㉕ "Freight Prepaid" L/C No. MD1NY404NS0 0018	4,631 KGS	58,000 CBM
Total No. of Containers or Packages(in words)	SAY : ONE CONTAINER ONLY			

⑲ Freight and Charges	⑳ Revenue tons	㉑ Rate	㉒ Per	㉓ Prepaid	㉔ Collect
FREIGHT PREPAID					
CFS CHARGE+THC				W100,000	
WHARFAGE				W 2,500	
CNTR TAX				W 10,000	
DOCK'S FEE				W 5,000	

㉕ Freight prepaid at BUSAN, KOREA	㉖ Freight payable at	㉙ Place and Date of Issue BUSAN, KOREA, JULY 20, 20××
㉗ Total prepaid in	㉘ No. of original B/L THREE(3)	
㉚ Laden on Board the Vessel JULY 20, 20××		Signature ㉛ World Trans Corporation as an agent of Hyundae Shipping Co., Ltd., Carrier

AIR WAYBILL

Shipper's Name and Address

Shipper's Account Number

Not negotiable

Air Waybill **KOREAN AIR**

issued by

Copies 1, 2 and 3 of this Air Waybil are originals and have the same validity.

Consignee's Name and Address

Consignee's Account Number

Telephone :

It is agreed that the goods described herein are accepted in apparent good order and condition (except as noted) for carriage SUBJECT TO THE CONDITIONS OF CONTRACT ON THE REVERSE HEREOF. THE SHIPPER'S ATTENTION IS DRAWN TO THE NOTICE CONCERNING CARRIER'S LIMITATION OF LIABILITY. Shipper may increase such limitation of liability by declaring a higher value for carriage and paying a supplemental charge if required.

Issuing Carrier's Agent Name and City

Accounting Information

Agent's IATA Code

Account No.

Airport of Departure(Addr. of First Carrier) and Requested Routing

TO	By First Carrier	Routing and Destination	to	by	to	by	Currency	CHGS Code	WT/VAL		Other		Declared Value for Carriage	Declared Value for Customs
									PPD	COLL	PPD	COLL		

Airport of Destination	Flight/Date	For Carrier Use Only	Flight/Date	Amount of Insurance	INSURANCE–If Carrier offers Insurance, and such insurance is requested in accordance with conditions on reverse hereof, indicate amount to be insured in figures in box marked 'amount of Insurance'.

Handling Information

No. of Pieces RCP	Gross Weight	kg lb	Rate Class / Commodity item No.	Chargeable Weight	Rate / Charge	Total	Nature and Quantity of Goods (incl. Dimensions or Volume)

Prepaid	Weight Charge	Collect	Other Charges
	Valuation Charge		
	Tax		
	Total Other Charges Due Agent		Shipper certifies that the particulars on the face hereof are correct and that insofar as any part of the consignment contains dangerous goods, such part is properly described by name and is in proper condition for carriage by air according to the applicable Dangerous Goods Regulations.
	Total Other Charges Due Carrier		Signature of Shipper or his Agent
Total Prepaid		Total Collect	
Currency Conversion Rates		CC Charges In Dest. Currency	Executed on(date)at(place)Signature of Issuing Carrier or its Agent
For Carrier's Use Only at Destination		Charges at Destination	Total Collect Charges

ORIGINAL 3(FOR SHIPPER)

INSURANCE POLICY

LIG Insurance

LIG Tower, 649-11, Yeoksam-dong, Gangnam-gu, Seoul, 135-550 Korea

TELEPHONE : 1544-0114
FACSIMILE : 0505-136-0500

MARINE CARGO INSURANCE POLICY

Assured(s), etc

Policy No.

Claim, if any, payable at:

Ref. No.

Amount insured

Survey should be approved by:

Conditions

Local Vessel or Conveyance	From(interior port or place of loading)
Ship or Vessel called the	Sailing on or about
at and from	transhipped at
arrived at	thence to

Goods and Merchandises

Subject to the following Clauses as per back hereof
Institute Classification Clause, On-Deck Clause (A)(B)
Institute Extended Radioactive Contamination Exclusion Clause
Institute Chemical, Biological, Bio-chemical, Electromagnetic
Weapon and Cyber Attack Exclusion Clause
Termination of Transit Clause (Terrorism)
Computer Millennium Clause (Cargo)
With Named Peril Extension
Co-insurance Clause

Marks and Numbers as per Invoice No. specified above.

Place and Date signed in

No. of Policies Issued.

☐ For the use only with the New Marine Policy Form

Notwithstanding anything contained herein or attached hereto to the contrary, this insurance is understood and agreed to be subject to English law and practice only as to liability for and settlement of any and all claims.

This insurance does not cover any loss or damage to the property which at the time of the happening of such loss or damage is insured by or would but for existence of this Policy be insured by any fire or other insurance policy or policies except in respect of any excess beyond the amount which would have been payable under the fire or other insurance policy or policies had this insurance not been effected.

We, LIG INSURANCE CO., LTD. Hereby agree, in consideration of the payment to us by or on behalf of the Assured of the premium as arranged, to insure against loss damage liability or expense to the extent and in the manner herein provided.

In Witness whereof, I the Undersigned of LIG INSURANCE CO., LTD. on behalf of the said Company have subscribed My Name in the place specified as above to the policies, the issued numbers thereof being specified as above, of the same tenor and date, one of which being accomplished, the others to be void, as of the specified as above.

☐ For the use only with the Old Marine Policy Form

1. Warranted free of capture, seizure, arrest restraint or detainment, and the consequences thereof or of any attempt thereat, also from the consequences of hostilities or warlike operations, whether there be a declaration of war or not; but this warranty shall not exclude collision, contact with any fixed of floating object(other than a mine or torpedo), stranding, heavy weather or fire unless caused directly (and independently of the nature of the voyage or service which the vessel concerned or, in the case of a collision, any other vessel involved therein, is performing) by a hostile act by or against a belligerent power ; and for the purpose of this warranty "power" includes any authority maintaining naval, military or air forces in association with a power.

Further warranted free from the consequences of civil war, revolution, rebellion, insurrection, or civil strife arising therefrom, or piracy.

2. Warranted free of loss or damage

(a) Caused by strikers, locked-out workmen, or persons taking part in labour disturbances, riots or civil commotions;

(b) Resulting from strikes, lock-outs, labour disturbances, riots or civil commotions.

3. (a) Should the risks excluded by Clauses 1(F.C. & S. Clause) be reinstated in this Policy by deletion of the said Clause, or should the risks or any of them mentioned in that clause or the risks of mines, torpedoes, bombs or other engines of war be insured under this Policy, Clauses (b) below shall become operative and anything contained in this contract which is inconsistent with Clause(b) or which affords more extensive protection against the aforesaid risks than that afforded by the Institute War Clauses relevant to the particular form of transit covered by this insurance is null and void.

(b) This policy is warranted free of any claim based upon loss of, or frustration of, the insured voyage or adventure caused by arrests restraints or detainments of kings Princes Usurpers or persons attempting to usurp power.

The descriptions to be inserted in the following clauses are shown as above. *Be it Known that* as well in his or their own Name, as for and in the Name and Names of all and every other Person or Persons to whom the same doth, may, or shall appertain, in part or in all, doth make Assurance, and cause himself or themselves and them and every or them, to be Assured, lost or not lost, at and from ______ upon any kind of Goods and Merchandises, in the good ship or vessel called the ______ whereof is Master, for this present Voyage, ______ or whosoever else shall go for Master in the said Ship, or by whatsoever other Name or Names the said Ship, or the Master thereof, is or shall be named or called, beginning the Adventure upon the said Goods and merchandises from the loading thereof aboard the said Ship as above, and shall so continue and endure during her abode there, upon the said the Ship, &c ; and further, until the said Ship, with all her Goods and Merchandises whatsoever, shall be arrived at ______ and upon the Goods and Merchandises until the same be there discharged and safely landed; and it shall be lawful for the said Ship, &c., in this Voyage to proceed and sail to and touch and stay at any Ports or Places whatsoever without Prejudice to this Assurance. The said Goods and Merchandises &c., for so much as concerns the Assured by agreement between the Assured and Assurers in this Policy, are and shall be valued at ______ TOUCHING the Adventures and Perils which the said Company are contented to bear and do take upon themselves in this Voyage, they are, of the Seas, Men-of-War, Fire, Enemies, Pirates, Rovers, Thieves, Jettisons, Letters of Mart and Countermart, Surprisals, Takings at Sea, Arrests, Restraints and Detainments of all Kings, Princes and People of what Nation, Condition, or Quality soever, Barratry of the Master and Mariners, and of all other Perils, Losses and Misfortunes that have or shall come to the Hurt, Detriment or Damage of the said Goods and Merchandises, or any Part thereof ; and in case of any Loss or Misfortune, it shall be lawful to the Assured, his or their Factors, Servants and Assigns, to sue, labour and travel for, in and about the Defence, Safeguard and Recovery of the said Goods and Merchandises, or any part thereof, without Prejudice to this Assurance; to the Charges whereof the said Company will contribute. And it is especially declared and agreed that no acts of the Assurer or Assured in recovering, saving, or preserving the property assured, shall be considered as a waiver or acceptance of abandonment. And it is agreed that this writing or Policy of Assurance shall be of as much Force and Effect as the surest Writing or Policy of Assurance made in London. And so the Said Company are contented, and do hereby promise and bind Themselves to the Assured, his or their Executors, Administrators, or Assigns, for the true Performance of the Premises ; confessing themselves paid the Consideration due unto them for this Assurance, at and after the rate of ______ as arranged ______ Per Cent.

N.B-Corn, Fish, Salt, Fruit, Flour and Seed are warranted free from Average, unless general, or the Ship be stranded; Sugar, Tobacco, Hemp, Flax, Hides and Skins are warranted free from Average, under Five Pounds per cent ; and all other Goods, also the Ship and Freight, are warranted free from Average, under three Pounds per cent, unless general, or the Ship be stranded, sunk or burnt.

All questions of liability arising under this policy are to be governed by the laws and customs of England.

IN WITNESS whereof, I the Undersigned of the LIG INSURANCE CO., LTD. on behalf of the said Companies have subscribed My Name in the place specified as above to the policies, the issued numbers thereof being specified as above, of the same tenor and date, one of which being accomplished, the others to be void, as of the date specified as above.

- In the event of loss or damage arising under this Policy, no claims will be admitted unless a survey has been held with the approval of this Company's Office or Agents specified in this Policy.

In case of loss or damage, please follow the "IMPORTANT" clause printed on the back hereof.

For **LIG INSURANCE CO.,LTD.**

AUTHORIZED SIGNATORY

PACKING LIST

①Shipper/Seller DAEHAN CO., LTD. CPO BOX 195 SEOUL, KOREA	⑧No. & date of invoice 8905 BK 1007 JULY 25. 20××
	⑨No. & date of L/C MD1NY404NS00018, MAY 15. 20××
②For account & risk of Messers. BROWN CO., LTD. 310 FIFTH AVE. NEW YORK NY, USA	⑩Consignee CHASE LINCOLN FIRST BANK N.A.
③Notify party Same as above	⑪Remarks : Details are as per P/O No.DIC-07-03-10 Dated March 10, 2007 to be issued by Wilson & Company, Limited. Origin : Republic of Korea

④Port of loading Busan, Korea	⑤Final destination New York, U.S.A	⑫Payment Terms L/C, At sight
⑥Carrier WONIS JIN	⑦Sailing on or about JULY 20, 20××	⑬Price Term : CIF NEW YORK, USA

⑭Marks & numbers of Pkg	⑮Description of Goods	⑯Quantity/Net wt	⑰Gross wt	⑱Measure
PCU NEW YORK, U.S.A C/NO.1-50 MADE IN KOREA	COMPUTER	2,000PCS	12,810KGS	17CBM

//

P.O.Box :
E-mail :
Telefax No. :
Telephone No. :

⑲ Signed by ____________________
Manager

CERTIFICATE OF ORIGIN

1. Exporter(Name, address, country) DAEHAN CO., LTD. CPO BOX 195 SEOUL, KOREA	ORIGINAL CERTIFICATE OF ORIGIN issued by THE KOREA CHAMBER OF COMMERCE & INDUSTRY Seoul, Republic of Korea
2. Consignee(Name, address, country) TO ORDER OF BANK OF AMERICA	3. Country of Origin REPUBLIC OF KOREA
4. Transport details FROM : BUSAN, KOREA TO : NEW YORK, USA ON BOARD DATE : JULY 21, 20××	5. Remarks COUNTRY OF ORIGIN REPUBLIC OF KORA

6. Marks & numbers ; number and kind of packages ; description of goods		7. Quantity
PCU NEW YORK, U.S.A C/NO.1-50 MADE IN KOREA	COMPUTER L/C NO. : MD1NY404NS00018	2,000PCS
///////////////	///	/////////////////

8. Declaration by the Exporter (Signature) (Name)	9. Certification Authorized Signatory
	Certificate No.

THE KOREA CHAMBER OF COMMERCE & INDUSTRY

CERTIFICATE OF INSPECTION

Date : October 12, 20××

To whom it may concern

Buyer	:	JV 'Grapro Koral Int., Co., Ltd.
Order No.	:	DA-001
Credit No.	:	17811/IMP
Item	:	Accessories
Quantity	:	4,130pcs
Amount	:	U$30,000
Shipment Date	:	December 29, 20××
B/L No.	:	B110920
Vessel No	:	Donam V-314

We, the undersigned, have duly inspected the goods specified in the above at the time of shipment and certify that the quality of the goods produced in accordance with buyer's requirements are permitted to be sold in overseas markets as well as in domestic market by Korean government.

Yours faithfully,

Dae Young Woolen Textile Co., Ltd.
Yung-sik, Kim
President

Chapter 12

Claim and Arbitration

Chapter

12

Claim and Arbitration

12.1 Claim

A claim is a demand or assertion by a claimant for compensation, payment, or reimbursement for a loss under a contract, or an injury due to negligence. In international trade, claims regarding quality and quantity or weight are common, even though proper inspection of the goods has been conducted by designated surveyors or public inspection bureaus. The goods may have been damaged or lost during transit. Therefore, it is necessary to include a discrepancy and claim clause in a contract. In case the goods delivered are inconsistent with the contract stipulations, the buyer should make a claim against the seller within the time limit of reinspection under the support of an inspection certificate or survey report issued by a nominated surveyor.

To file or to settle a claim, the following points should be first considered:

- whether the claim is justified by the contract
- whether the claim is made in time
- whether the claim is well supported by good documentation

Failing to have positive answers to all the above considerations would mean difficulties in settling the claim. If it is justified, timely and well-supported, a claim can be settled in the one of the following ways:

- making refund with compensation for other direct losses and expenses such as banking charges, storage and inspection charges, etc.

- devaluating the goods according to the degree of inferiority, extent of damage and amount of losses
- replacing the defective goods with ones that conform to the specifications, quality and performance as stipulated in the contract.

Whatever complaints or claims may be, we must try to handle them quickly, amicably to satisfy all parties concerned without referring them to arbitration.

12.2 Force Majeure

Force majeure, also called as Act of God, is an event that can be neither anticipated nor reduced to control such as an industrial strike that leads to loss of profits, or a war destroying a whole cargo or some others of the kind.

Force majeure clause usually excuses a party who breaches the contract because the party's performance is prevented by the occurrence of an event that is beyond the party's reasonable control. A force majeure clause may excuse performance on the occurrence of such events as natural disasters, labor strikes, bankruptcy, or failure of subcontractors to perform. A force majeure clause in the contract should specify the scope of force majeure events, consequences, time limit of notice to the other contractor, certificates and the agencies who issue them.

In practice, we usually specify a force majeure clause as follows:

> "Force Majeure : The seller shall not be responsible for the delay of shipment due to force majeure including fire, flood, strikes, labor troubles or other industrial disturbances, inevitable accidents, war(declared or undeclared), embargoes, blockades, legal restrictions, riots, insurrections, or any causes beyond the control of the seller."

12.3 Arbitration

1. Definition of Arbitration

Arbitration is the solution of a dispute between the two parties through a voluntary or contractually required hearing and determination by an impartial third party. The impartial third party is called the arbitrator and is chosen by a higher or disinterested body, or by the two parties in dispute. Internationally, the main arbitration body is the International Chamber of Commerce(ICC).

In international trade, when disputes arise between the seller and the buyer, it can be settled through friendly consultation, litigation or arbitration. Negotiation or mediation is the best method of all and beneficial to both parties. The majority of the disputes are settled by this way and friendly business relations are thus maintained between sellers and buyers. If the dispute cannot be settled through amicable negotiation or mediation, arbitration will be the next best alternative as litigation is usually costly and time-consuming.

2. Function of the Clause

An arbitration agreement can be made before or after a dispute arises. Such an agreement has the following functions.

- It embodies the agreement of both parties that, if any dispute arises with regard to the obligations which one party has undertaken to the other, such a dispute shall be settled by a tribunal of their own constitution.
- It excludes the court from having jurisdiction over the dispute
- It gives jurisdiction to the arbitrator

It should be noted that, in some countries, an arbitration agreement cannot exclude the court from having jurisdiction over the dispute.

An arbitration clause in an international contract may state, for example, as follows:

Any controversy or claim arising out of or relating to this contract, or the breach thereof, shall be settled by arbitration in accordance with the International Chamber of Commerce(ICC), and judgement upon the award rendered by the arbitrator may be entered in any court having jurisdiction thereof.

"All disputes, controversies, or differences which may arise between the parties, out of or in relation to or in connection with this contract, or for the breach thereof, shall be finally settled by arbitration in Seoul, Korea in accordance with the Commercial Arbitration Rules of the Korean Commercial Arbitration Board and under the Laws of Korea. The award rendered by the arbitrator(s) shall be final and binding upon both parties concerned."

3. Contents of the Clause

1) Location

Location is not only a matter of convenience. It is also related to the application of the law system under which the dispute is settled. The location can be anywhere in the seller's country, the buyer's country or a third country. No matter where the arbitration takes place, the location must be politically and professionally acceptable.

2) Agency

An arbitration clause should specify an arbitration agency, which is of primary importance and a matter of great concern to either contracting party. There are usually two types of arbitration agency :

- permanent organization of arbitration that provides facilities and personnel
- temporary arbitration tribunal set up for a particular dispute

3) Procedures

(1) Submit dispute to arbitration

If a dispute is to be submitted to a permanent organization, the application is sent directly to the tribunal and the defendant(also called respondent). If the dispute is to be submitted to a temporary organization, the application is sent directly to the defendant.

(2) Appoint arbitrators

Two points must be considered in appointing arbitrators : number of arbitrators and qualifications of arbitrators. Usually, one or three arbitrators are appointed. The arbitration organization can appoint one arbitrator. Or both the plaintiff(also called claimant) and the defendant appoint one arbitrator each and a third arbitrator is appointed by the arbitration organization. Another possibility is that a chief arbitrator is appointed by the arbitration organization and the chief arbitrator appoints two other arbitrators.

It is also important to consider the qualifications of the arbitrators, particularly the nationality and the professional background to ensure an impartial quality award.

In case that one party refuses to appoint an arbitrator, the other can either ask the organization to appoint one for the former when there is an arbitration organization or ask a law court to appoint one for the former if no organization has been agreed upon.

(3) Hear a case

Case hearing can be carried out by face-to-face reply or correspondence. In some countries, the tribunal can give the order of interim measures of protection while the arbitration is going on. For example, the goods can be placed under a third party's control or perishable goods can be sold.

(4) Issue an award

An award is the decision made by the arbitration tribunal. It must be in written form with or without explanations or reasons.

4) Effects

The award is “final and binding” in most countries provided that there are no illegal actions by any party involved in the arbitration process. If one party refuses to obey the award, the other can ask a court to enforce the implementation of the award. According to the laws of some countries, a law suit against the award is allowed. Then, there must be a time limit to file the suit.

5) Fees

Fees can be borne by the losing party of the dispute and can be divided between the two parties or can be paid according to the award.

12.4 Sample Letters of Claims and Arbitration

1. Claim for Short in Quantity

1) A claim

Dear Mr. Kim,

Subject : A shortage in toys

We received your consignment covering our order No.10 for toys for children. Upon checking the products against your commercial invoice delivered to us, we discovered a shortage in numbers for item No.11 and No.13. 30pcs and 25pcs for No. 10 and No. 13 were found short in numbers respectively. There was not any sign we can judge that they were tampered in transit as the boxes packed arrived in good condition.

We are of an opinion that the shortage is due to the mistake in packing and we want you to have this matter settled amicably as soon as possible as we don't want to lodge a claim with you.

We ask you, therefore, to investigate this matter and send us the products immediately on receipt of this e-mail.

Yours truly,

2) A reply

Dear Mr. Foster,

Thank you for your e-mail of August 12 in which you complained about the goods dropped in the boxes even though those were listed in the invoice.

After we have paid our prompt and careful attention to your e-mail, we found that our manufacturer couldn't meet the numbers of the goods you placed an order as they recorded more than 10% of production loss which was much more than before.

As those items were produced only for your market, we don't have enough materials to make the replacements for the shortage right away. Instead, as a settlement, we would like to send the goods in your next order. And, of course, the amount you paid for the shortage this time will be deducted in our next invoice.

We apologize for the errors we made and we will assure you that nothing like this case will occur in the future.

Yours truly,

2. Claim for Non-delivery

1) A claim

Dear Mr. Min,

We received today the shipping advice for the shipment covering our order No. 120 for a 20 feet container of garments and we have prepared everything required for selling those products here in the market.

With the shipping documents presented from the issuing bank, we asked a local forwarding agent to pick up the products from the shipping company referred to in your e-mail.

However, your consignment was found not to be shipped by "Arirang" sailed on the 15th of April while the bill of lading issued by Dongyang Shipping Co., Ltd. says it was shipped by that vessel as scheduled.

We want you to give a prompt attention to this e-mail and give a complete explanation in return.

Yours truly,

2) A reply

Dear Mr. Lamos,

Thank you for your e-mail dated May 11 and we regret to learn that our consignment covering your order No. 120 has not reached.

All the records we have indicate that the products were loaded on the vessel. We handed the goods over to the CY according to the shipping company's instructions.

We can not find any error on our part as evidenced by the clean on board B/L issued by that company.

Therefore, please lodge a claim with the agent of the shipping company and the insurance company concerned to settle this matter. We are sure that this will be settled by the shipping company, otherwise, the insurance company will handle this matter accordingly.

Meanwhile, we will take every steps possible here to assist you and you will be rest assured that every orders from now on will be executed to your satisfaction.

Yours very truly,

3. Claim for the Goods Dented in

1) A claim

Dear Mr. Son,

The shipment by "SNCDV" Line has been delivered to a warehouse, but we would like to invite your attention that one role of electric wire weighing about 3,000kg was found dented in and they are exposed beyond repair.

Judging by its badly damaged condition, we guess that an accident was made on account of bad handling. There is no doubt in our opinion that this mistake is very unfortunate because the products are urgently required by our customers who have been impatient to receive your products.

We want you to have this matter settled as soon as possible and please let us know what you can do for this item unsuited for our purpose.

We hope that you will investigate this matter and give us a prompt solution in return.

Yours truly,

2) A reply

Dear Mr. Lincoln,

Thank you for your e-mail of March 13 and we are sorry to hear that the products we shipped were damaged.

We have paid our prompt attention to the matter and found that the damage in the products has been caused by a rough handling by our local forwarding agent.

Since the fault is with us though the mistake was not made by our company actually, we would like to offer you to accept the products at a reduction of 25% which is a great loss to us.

We have no excuse how much we have caused you inconvenience and we assure you that we will execute your orders from now on with our maximum care.

Very truly yours,

4. Claim for the Goods Broken

1) A claim

Dear Mr. Jeon,

We received your consignment for the raw materials of cosmetics shipped by Canteville, but we regret to inform you that some of them were leaked and the glasses containing materials were broken.

We have to ask you, therefore, to arrange the materials listed in the attached file and send them to us immediately so that we can put them into production immediately.

Otherwise, there is no choice but to file a claim for compensation, which is not good to both of us.

We believe you will pay your prompt attention to this matter.

Very truly yours,

2) A reply(1)

Dear Mr. Bush,

We received your e-mail informing us that some of the materials were found leaked and some glasses were broken.

You may realize that this kind of problem is unusual through our previous transactions for the last 5 years and we are very sorry to put you into inconvenience.

Specialists in charge of packing informed us that the products were first packed in safe containers individually and then packed in wooden boxes. According to them, the products should have been delivered in good condition as they were packed with the utmost care.

We think that they must have been carelessly handled in transit and we will check this matter up with the shipping company.

Also, I will let you know the result by tomorrow.

Very truly yours,

3) A reply(2)

Dear Sirs,

We are very sorry to learn from your e-mail that some of the raw-materials of cosmetics supplied by us were badly leaked and broken when delivered.

Our production department informed us that the materials were first packed in plastic containers and then in wooden boxes.

What we would like to point out is that inland transport calls for special packing precautions. By reinforcing rail end-packings for the consignments, we will prevent the possible damages.

Therefore, we would like to allow you a special discount of 10% on those materials to compensate for your problems.

We believe you will accept our solution for this matter and we will do our best not to occur this kind of incident again.

We want you to accept our apologies for the trouble caused to you by our mistake and to accept our solution on this matter.

Yours faithfully,

5. Claim for the Shipment Delayed

1) A claim

Dear Mr. Shim,

We placed an order with you on understanding that delivery could be made by May 2. We have not yet received the products and would appreciate your immediate advice as to when we may expect them.

We are in serious problems and are receiving numerous complaints from our domestic customers as we could not meet our delivery date.

Please let us know the reason for this delay and also we want to know if you can effect a shipment by the next direct vessel before May 10.

We believe, therefore, that you will do your utmost to ensure that the consignment arrives soon.

Otherwise, we shall have to cancel the order as we can not wait any longer.

Yours very truly,

2) A reply

Dear Mr. Drugman,

We are very sorry to learn in your e-mail dated May 4 that the products were not shipped by Arirang, a direct vessel departed on May 2.

All of our automatic manufacturing lines have been fully operated day and night to meet your order. Orders rushed in since you placed an order with us have made it impossible to produce the products as scheduled.

In fact, we have been enjoying our reputation for being punctual in meeting the delivery time stipulated and never did we fail to deliver our customers' orders in time.

However, we surely may be able to send the products you need by the very next vessel sailing on May 11 and we rely upon your leniency for the matter of recent delay.

We will do our best not to cause any inconvenience in the future.

Yours faithfully,

6. Claim for Different Color

1) A claim

Dear. Mr. Kim,

Thank you for your prompt dispatch of the clothes covering our order No. 132-IM dated September 15.

Upon examining the products carefully, we were surprised to find that the quality delivered was quite different from that of your samples.

This mistake is very unfortunate because the products are urgently required by our customers who have been impatient to receive the products. Almost all of them are so poor that we can not but to imagine there must have been some big mistakes on your side when producing them.

As the products will not be accepted by our agents, we would like to ask you to take them back and dispatch the same quality clothes ordered.

We would request you, therefore, to take the matter up with the relative parties to ascertain if this is the above case. We may be able to extend the date of shipment if you want on the condition that you can guarantee to send the right products as contracted.

Very truly yours,

2) A reply

Dear Mr. Linder,

In reference to your e-mail of November 3 reporting different quality in our consignment, we sincerely regret the inconvenience caused you by our mistake.

We are of an opinion that some mistakes have been made in selecting the materials suited for you and we already asked our branch office in your country today to visit your company within this week to compare the quality of the products dispatched with the samples.

In case we are responsible for the wrong selection of the materials, we will arrange right products immediately and send them by air.

Yours faithfully,

7. Claim for a Delayed Shipment

Gentlemen :

Late shipment was beyond our ability due to the production problems popped up unexpectedly. However, we are very sorry to hear that you may lose the market opportunity for the products as they will be too late for the season.

We negotiated with our supplier seriously to meet your offer of 35% reduction in prices, but they are ready to settle this matter if you accept 25% allowance.

Considering every factors affecting price increases in the products now, 25% is quite a concession for them and we guess it is a good proposition.

We believe that you will gladly accept their suggestion.

Very truly yours,

8. Claim for Compensation to a Shipping Company

8-8

Gentlemen :

In connection with the consignment covering 3,000 pcs of leather jackets shipped by Golden Gate S-3 arrived at Long Beach port on January 21, 20××, many were found severely damaged and torn off.

We drew a conclusion through an investigation done on our side that they must be handled badly in transit.

As the products we referred to are of no use to us, we would like to ask you to take this matter up immediately and compensate for us for the amount of U$55,000 which is net amount invoiced for the products in question only.

Also, we already filed a claim with the insurance company to take every steps available to settle this matter and they said they would survey this matter with their utmost care.

For your reference, we will send a copy of ocean bill of lading you issued together with a survey report done by an authorized surveyor.

We trust that you will pay your prompt attention to this e-mail.

Yours very truly,

Appendix

1. ICC Rules for the Use of Domestic and International Trade Terms(Incoterms® 2020)
2. Uniform Customs and Practice for Documentary Credits, 2007 Revision, ICC Publication No.600("UCP")
3. UCP Supplement for Electronic Presentation(eUCP)
4. Uniform Rules for Collections, 1995 Revision, ICC Publication No. 522(URC)

Incoterms® 2020

ICC Rules for the Use of Domestic and International Trade Terms

Entry into force: January 1, 2020

ICC

EXW | Ex Works

EXW(insert named place of delivery) incoterms® 2020

EXPLANATORY NOTES FOR USERS

1. **Delivery and risk** - "Ex works' means that the seller delivers the goods to the buyer
   - when it places the goods at the disposal of the buyer at a named place (like a factory or warehouse), and
   - that named place may or may not be the seller's premises.

   For delivery to occur, the seller does not need to load the goods on any collecting vehicle, nor does it need to clear the goods for export, where such clearance is applicable.

2. **Mode of transport** - This rule may be used irrespective of the mode or modes of transport, if any, selected.

3. **place or precise point of delivery** - The parties need only name the place of delivery. However, the parties are well advised also to specify as clearly as possible the precise point within the named place of delivery. A named precise point of delivery makes it clear to both parties when the goods are delivered and when risk transfers to the buyer; such precision also marks the point at which costs are for the buyer's account. If the parties do not name the point of delivery, then they are taken to have left it to have left it to the seller to select the point "that best suits its purpose". This means that the buyer may incur the risk that the seller may choose a point just before the point at which goods are lost or damaged. Best for the buyer therefore to select the precise point within a place where delivery will occur.

4. **A note of caution to buyers** - EXW is the incoterms® rule which imposes the least set of obligations on the seller. From the buyer's perspective, therefore, the rule should be used with care for different reasons as set out below.

5. **Loading risk** - Delivery happens - and risk transfers - when the goods are placed, not loaded, at the buyer's disposal. However, risk of loss of or damage to the goods occurring while the loading operation is carried out by the seller, as it may well be, might arguably lie with the buyer, who has not physically participated in the loading. Given this possibility, it would be advisable, where the seller is to load the goods, for the parties to agree in advance who is to bear the risk of any loss of or damage to the goods during loading. This is a common situation simply because the seller is more likely to have the necessary loading equipment at its own premises or because applicable safety or security rules prevent access to the seller's premises by unauthorised personnel. Where the buyer is keen to avoid any risk during loading at the seller's premises, then the buyer ought to consider choosing the FCA rule (under which, if the goods are delivered at the seller's premises, the seller owes the buyer an obligation to load, with the risk of loss of or damage to the goods during that operation remaining with the seller).

6. **Export clearance** - With delivery happening when the goods are at the buyer's disposal either at the seller's premises or at another named point typically within the seller's jurisdiction or within the same Customs Union, there is no obligation on the seller to organise export clearance or clearance within third countries through which the goods pass in transit. Indeed, EXW may be suitable for domestic trades, where there is no intention at all to export the goods. The seller's participation in export clearance is limited to providing assistance in obtaining such documents and information as the buyer may require for the purpose of exporting the goods. Where the buyer intends to export the goods and where it anticipates difficulty in obtaining export clearance, the buyer would be better advised to choose the FCA rule, under which the obligation and cost of obtaining export clearance lies with the seller.

A THE SELLER'S OBLIGATIONS

B THE BUYER'S OBLIGATIONS

A1 General obligations

The seller must provide the goods and the commercial invoice in conformity with the contract of sale and any other evidence of conformity that may be required by the contract.

Any document to be provided by the seller may be in paper or electronic form as agreed or, where there is no agreement, as is customary.

B1 General obligations

The buyer must pay the price of the goods as provided in the contract of sale. Any document to be provided by the buyer may be in paper or electronic form as agreed or, where there is no agreement, as is customary.

A2 Delivery

The seller must deliver the goods by placing them at the disposal of the buyer at the agreed point, if any, at the named place of delivery, not loaded on any collecting vehicle. if no specific point has been agreed within the named place of delivery, and if there are several points available, the seller may select the point that best suits its purpose. The seller must deliver the goods on the agreed date or within the agreed period

B2 Taking delivery

The buyer must take delivery of the goods when they have been delivered under A2 and notice given A10

A3 Transfer of risks

The seller bears all risks of or damage to the goods until they have been delivered in accordance with A2, with the exception of loss or damage in the circumstance described in B3.

B3 Transfer of risks

The buyer bears all risks of loss of or damage to the goods from the time they have been delivered under A2

If the buyer fails to give notice in accordance with B10, then the buyer bears all risks of loss of or damage to the goods from the agreed date or the end of the agreed period for delivery, provided that the goods have been clearly identified as the contract goods.

A4 Carriage

The seller has no obligation to the buyer to make a contract of carriage.

However, the seller must provide the buyer, at the buyer's request, risk and cost, with any information in the possession of the seller, including transport-related security requirements, that the buyer needs for arranging carriage

B4 Carriage

It is up to the buyer to contract or arrange at its own cost for the carriage of the goods from the named place of delivery.

A5 Insurance

The seller has no obligation to the buyer to make a contract of insurance.

However, the seller must provide the buyer, at the buyer's request, risk and cost with information in the possession of the seller that the buyer needs obtaining insurance.

B5 Insurance

The buyer has no obligation to the seller to make a contract of insurance.

A6 Delivery/transport document

The seller has no obligation to the buyer.

B6 Proof of delivery

The buyer must provide the seller with appropriate evidence of having taken delivery.

A7 Export/import clearance

Where applicable, the seller must assist the buyer, at the buyer's request, risk and cost, in obtaining any documents and/or information related to all export/transit/import clearance formalities required by the countries of export/transit/import, such as:

- ▶ export/transit/import licence ;
- ▶ security clearance for export/transit/import;
- ▶ pre-shipment inspection; and
- ▶ any other official authorisation

B7 Export/import clearance

Where applicable, it is up to the buyer to carry out and pay for all export/transit/import clearance formalities required by the countries of export/transit/import, such as;

- ▶ all export/transit/import licence;
- ▶ security clearance for all export/transit/import;
- ▶ pre-shipment inspection; and
- ▶ any other official authorisation.

A8 Checking/ packaging/marking

The seller must pay the costs of those checking operations(such as checking quality, measuring, weighing, counting) that are necessary for the purpose of delivering the goods in accordance with A2.

The seller must, at its own cost, package the goods, unless it is usual foe the particular trade to transport the type of goods sold unpackaged. The seller must package and mark the goods in the manner appropriate for their transport, unless the parties have agreed on specific packaging or marking requirements.

B8 Checking/packing/marking

The buyer has no obligation to the seller.

A9 Allocation of costs

The seller must pay all costs relating to the goods until they have been delivered in accordance with A2, other than those payable by the buyer under B9.

B9 Allocation of costs

The buyer must:

a) pay all costs relating to the goods from the time they have been delivered under A2;

b) reimburse all costs and charges incurred by the seller in providing assistance or information under A4, A5 orA7;

c) pay, where applicable, all duties, taxes and other charges, as well as the cost of costs of carrying out customs formalities payable upon export; and

d) pay any additional costs incurred by failing either to take delivery of the goods when they have been placed at its disposal or to give appropriate notice in accordance with B10, provided that the goods have been clearly identified as the contract goods.

A10 Notices

The seller must give the buyer any notice needed to enable the buyer to take delivery of the goods.

B10 Notices

The buyer must, whenever it is agreed that the buyer is entitled to determine the time within an agreed period and/or the point of taking delivery within the named place, give the seller sufficient notice.

FCA | Free Carrier

FCA(insert named place of delivery) Incoterms® 2020

EXPLANATORY NOTES FOR USERS

1. **Delivery and risk** - "Free Carrier(named place)" means that the seller delivers the goods to the buyer in one or other of two ways.
   - ▶ Frist, when the named place is the seller's premises, the goods are delivered.
     - ▸ when they are loaded on the means of transport arranged by the buyer.
   - ▶ Second, when the named place is another place, the goods are delivered
     - ▸ when, having been loaded on the seller's means of transport,
     - ▸ they reach the named other place and

- are ready for unloading from that seller's means of transport and
- at the disposal of the carrier or of another person nominated by the buyer

Whichever of the two is chosen as the place of delivery, that place identifies where risk transfers to the buyer and the time from which costs are for the buyer's account.

2. **Mode of transport** - This rule may be used irrespective of the mode of transport selected and may also be used where more than one mode of transport is employed.

3. **Place or point of delivery** - A sale under FCA can be concluded naming only the place of delivery, either at the seller's premises or elsewhere, without specifying the precise point of delivery within that named place. However, the parties are well advised also to specify as clearly as possible the precise point within the named place of delivery. A named precise point of delivery makes it clear to both parties when the goods are delivered and when risk transfers to the buyer; such precision also marks the point at which costs are for the buyer's account. Where the precise point is not identified, however, this may cause problems for the buyer. The seller in this case has the right to select the point "that best suits its purpose": that point becomes the point of delivery, from which risk and costs transfer to the buyer. If the precise point of delivery is not identified by naming it in the contract, then parties are taken to have left it to the seller to select the point "that best suits its purpose". This means that the buyer may incur the risk that the seller may choose a point just before the point at which goods are lost or damaged. Best for the buyer therefore to select the precise point within a place where delivery will occur.

4. **'or procure goods so delivered'** - The reference to "procure" here caters for multiple sales down a chain (string sales), particularly, particularly, although not exclusively, common in the commodity trades.

5. **Export/import clearance** - FCA requires the seller to clear the goods for export, where applicable, However, the seller has no obligation to clear the goods for import or for transit through third countries, to pay any import duty or to carry out any import customs formalities.

6. **Bills of lading with an on-board notation in FCA sales** - We have already seen that FCA is intended for use irrespective of the mode or modes of transport used. Now if goods are being picked up by the buyer's road-haulier in Las Vegas, it would be rather uncommon to expect a bill of lading with an on-board notation to be issued by the carrier from Las Vegas, which is not a port and which a vessel cannot reach for goods to be placed on board. Nonetheless, sellers selling FCA Las Vegas do sometimes find themselves in a situation where they need a bill of

lading with an on-board notation(typically because of a bank collection or a letter of credit requirement), albeit necessarily stating that the goods have been placed on board in Los Angeles as well as stating that they were received for carriage in Las Vegas. To cater for this possibility of an FCA seller needing a bill of lading with an on-board notation, FCA incoterms 2020® has, for the first time, provided the following optional mechanism. If the parties have so agreed in the contract, the buyer must instruct its carrier to issue a bill of lading with an on-board notation to the seller. The carrier may or may not, of course, accede to the buyer's request, given that the carrier is only bound and entitled to issue such a bill of lading once the goods are on board in Los Angeles. However, if and when the bill of lading is issued to the seller by the carrier at the buyer's cost and risk, the seller must provide that same document to the buyer, who will need the bill of leading in order to obtain discharge of the goods from the carrier. This optional mechanism becomes unnecessary, of course, if the parties have agreed that the seller will present to the buyer a bill of lading stating simply that the goods have been received for shipment rather than that have been shipped on board. Moreover, it should be emphasised that even where this optional mechanism is adopted, the seller is under no obligation to the buyer as to the terms of the contract of carriage. Finally, when this optional mechanism is adopted, the dates of delivery inland and loading on board will necessarily be different, which may well create difficulties for the seller under a letter of credit.

A THE SELLER'S OBLIGATIONS

B THE BUYER'S OBLIGATIONS

A1 General obligations

The seller must provide the goods and the commercial invoice in conformity with the contract of sale and any other evidence of conformity that may be required by contract.

Any document to be provided by the seller may be in paper or electronic form as agreed or, where there is no agreement, as is customary.

B1 General obligations

The buyer must pay the price of the goods as provided in the contract of sale.

Any document to be provided by the buyer may be in paper or electronic form as agreed or, where there is no agreement, as is customary.

A2 Delivery

The seller must deliver the goods to the carrier or another person nominated by the buyer at the named point, if any, at the named place, or procure goods so delivered.

The seller must deliver the goods

1. on the agreed date or,
2. at the time within the agreed period notified by the buyer under B10(b) or,
3. if no such time is notified, then at the end of the agreed period .

Delivery is completed either:

a) If the named place is the seller's premises, when the goods have been loaded on the means of transport provided by the buyer; or,

b) In any other case, when the goods are placed at the disposal of the carrier or another person nominated by the buyer on the seller's means of transport ready for unloading.

If no specific point has been notified by the buyer under B10(d) within the named place of delivery, and if there are several points available, the seller may select the point that best suits its purpose.

B2 Taking delivery

The buyer must take delivery of the goods when they have been delivered under A2

A3 Transfer of risks

The seller bears all risks of loss of or damage to the goods until they have been delivered in accordance with A2, with the exception of loss or damage in the circumstance described in B3.

B3 Transfer of risks

The buyer bears all risks of loss of or damage to the goods from the time they have been delivered under A2.

If:

a) the buyer fails to nominate a carrier or another person under A2 or to give notice in accordance with B10; or

b) the carrier or person nominated by the buyer under B10(a) fails to take the goods into its charge, then, the buyer bears all risks of loss of or damage to the goods:

(i) from the agreed date, or in the absence of an agreed date,

(ii) from the time selected by the buyer under B10(b); or, if no such time has been notified,

(iii) from the end of any agreed period for delivery,

provided that the goods have been clearly identified as the contract goods.

A4 Carriage

The seller has no obligation to the buyer to make a contract of carriage.

However, the seller must provide the buyer, at the buyer's request, risk and cost, with any information in the possession of the seller, including transport-related security requirements, that the buyer needs for arranging carriage.

If agreed, the seller must contract for carriage on the usual teams at the buyer's risk and cost.
The seller must comply with any transport-related security requirements up to delivery

B4 Carriage

The buyer must contract or arrange at its own cost for the carriage of the goods from the named place of delivery, except when the contract of carriage is made by the seller as provided for in A4.

A5 Insurance

The seller has no obligation to the buyer to make a contract of Insurance.
However, the seller must provide the buyer, at the buyer's request, risk and cost, with information in the possession of the seller that the buyer needs for obtaining insurance.

B5 Insurance

The buyer has no obligation to the seller to make a contract of insurance.

A6 Delivery/transport document

The seller must provide the buyer at the seller's cost with the usual proof that the goods have been delivered in accordance with A2.
The seller must provide assistance to the buyer, at the buyer's request, risk and cost, in obtaining a transport document.
Where the buyer has instructed the carrier to issue to the seller a transport document under B6, the seller must provide any such document to the buyer.

B6 Delivery/transport document

The buyer must accept the proof that the goods have been delivered in accordance with A2.
If the parties have so agreed, the buyer must instruct the carrier to issue to the seller, at the buyer's cost and risk, a transport document stating that the goods have been loaded(such as a bill of leading with an on board notation).

A7 Export/import clearance

a) Export clearance

Where applicable, the seller must carry out and pay for all export clearance formalities by the country of export, such as;

- ▶ export licence;
- ▶ security clearance for export;
- ▶ pre-shipment inspection; and
- ▶ any other official authorisation

b) Assistance with import clearance

Where applicable, the seller must assist the buyer, at the buyer's request, risk and cost, in obtaining any documents and/or information related to all transit/import clearance formalities, including security requirements and pre-shipment inspection, needed by any country of transit or the country of import.

B7 Export/import clearance

a) Assistance with export clearance

Where applicable, the buyer must assist the seller at the seller's request, risk and cost in obtaining any documents and/or information related to all export clearance formalities, including security requirements and pre-shipment inspection, needed by the country of export.

b) Import clearance

Where applicable, the buyer must carry out and pay for all formalities required by any country of transit and the country of import, such as:

- import licence and any licence required for transit;
- security clearance for import and transit;
- pre-shipment inspection; and
- any other official authorisation.

A8 Checking/packaging/marking

The seller must pay the costs of those checking operations(such as checking quality, measuring, weighing, counting) that are necessary for the purpose of delivering the goods in accordance with A2.

The seller must, at its own cost, package the goods, unless it is usual for the particular trade to transport the type of goods sold unpackaged. The seller must package and mark the goods in the manner appropriate for their transport, unless the parties have agreed on specific packaging or marking requirements.

B8 Checking/packing/marking

The buyer has no obligation to the seller.

A9 Allocation of costs

The seller must pay:

All costs relating to the goods until they have been delivered in accordance with A2, other than those payable by the buyer under B9;

The costs of providing the usual proof to the buyer under A6 that the goods have been delivered;

Where applicable, duties, taxes and any other costs related to export clearance under A7(a); and

The buyer for all costs and charges related to providing assistance in obtaining documents and information in accordance with B7(a)

B9 Allocation of costs

The buyer must pay:

a) all costs relating to the goods from the time they have been delivered under A2, other than those payable by the seller under A9;

b) the seller for all costs and charges related to providing assistance in obtaining documents and information in accordance with A4, A5, A6 and A7(b);

c) where applicable, duties, taxes and any other costs related to transit or import clearance under B7(b); and

d) any additional costs incurred, either because:

(i) the buyer fails to nominate a carrier or another person under B10, or

(ii) the carrier or person nominate by the buyer under B10 fails to take the goods into its charge.

provided that the goods have been clearly identified as the contract goods.

A10 Notices

The seller must give the buyer sufficient notice either that the goods have been delivered in accordance with A2 or that the carrier or another person nominated by the buyer has failed to take the goods within the time agreed.

B10 Notices

The buyer must notify the seller of

a) the name of the carrier or another person nominated within sufficient time as to enable the seller to deliver the goods in accordance with A2;

b) the selected time, if any, within the period agreed for delivery when the carrier or person nominated will receive the goods;

c) the mode of transport to be used by the carrier or the person nominated including any transport-related security requirements; and

d) the point where the goods will be received within the named place of delivery.

CPT | Carriage Paid To

CPT (insert named place of destination) Incoterms® 2020

EXPLANATORY NOTES FOR USERS

1. **Delivery and risk** - "Carriage Paid To" means that the seller delivers the goods - and transfers the risk - to the buyer
   - by handing them over to the carrier
   - contracted by the seller
   - or by procuring the goods so delivered.
   - The seller may do so by giving the carrier physical possession of the goods in the manner and at the place appropriate to the means of transport used.

   Once the goods have been delivered to the buyer in this way, the seller does not guarantee that the goods will reach the place of destination in sound condition, in the stated quantity or indeed at all. This is because risk transfers from seller to buyer when the goods are delivered to the buyer by handing them over to the carrier; the seller must nonetheless contract for the carriage of the goods from delivery to the agreed destination. Thus, for example, goods are handed over to a carrier in Las Vegas (which is not a port) for carriage to Southampton (a port) or to Winchester (which is not a port). In either case, delivery transferring risk to the buyer happens in Las Vegas, and the seller must make a contract of carriage to either Southampton or Winchester.

2. **Mode of transport** - This rule may be used irrespective of the mode of transport selected and may also be used where more than one mode of transport is employed.

3. **Places (or points) of delivery and destination** - In CPT, two locations are important: the place or point (if any) at which the goods are delivered (for the transfer of risk) and the place or point agreed as the destination of the goods (as the point to which the seller promises to contract for carriage).

4. **Identifying the place or point of delivery with precision** - The parties are well advised to identify both places, or indeed points within those places, as precisely as possible in the contract of sale. Identifying the place or point (if any) of delivery as precisely as possible is important to cater for the common situation where several carriers are engaged, each for different legs of the transit from delivery to destination. Where this happens and the parties do not agree on a specific place or point of delivery, the default position is that risk transfers when the

goods have been delivered to the first carrier at a point entirely of the seller's choosing and over which the buyer has co control. Should the parties wish the risk to transfer at a later stage (e.g. at a sea or river port or at an airport), or indeed an earlier one (e.g. an inland point some way away from a sea or river port), they need to specify this in their contract of sale and to carefully think through the consequences of so doing in case the goods are lost or damaged.

5. **Identifying the destination as precisely as possible** - The parties are also well advised to identify as precisely as possible in the contract of sale the point within the agreed place of destination, as this is the point to which the seller must contract for carriage and this is the point to which the costs of carriage fall on the seller.

6. **'or procuring the goods so delivered'** - The reference to "procure" here caters for multiple sales down a chain (string sales), particularly common in the commodity trades.

7. **Costs of unloading at destination** - If the seller incurs costs under its contract of carriage related to unloading at the named place of destination, the seller is not entitled to recover such costs separately from the buyer unless otherwise agreed between the parties.

8. **Export/import clearance** - CPT requires the seller to clear the goods for export, where applicable. However, the seller has no obligation to clear the goods for import or for transit through third countries, or to pay any import duty or to carry out any import customs formalities.

A THE SELLER'S OBLIGATIONS

B THE BUYER'S OBLIGATIONS

A1 General obligations

The seller must provide the goods and the commercial invoice in conformity with the contract of sale and any other evidence of conformity that may be required by the contract.

Any document to be provided by the seller may be in paper or electronic form as agreed or, where there is no agreement, as is customary.

B1 General obligations

The buyer must pay the price of the goods as provided in the contract of sale.

Any document to be provided by the buyer may be in paper or electronic form as agreed or, where there is no agreement, as is customary

A2 Delivery

The seller must deliver the goods by handing them over to the carrier contracted in accordance with A4 or by procuring the goods so delivered. In either case the seller must deliver the goods on the agreed date or within the agreed period.

B2 Taking delivery

The buyer must take delivery of the goods when they have been delivered under A2 and receive them from the carrier at the named place of destination or if agreed, at the point within that place.

A3 Transfer of risks

The seller bears all risks of loss of or damage to the goods until they have been delivered in accordance with A2, with the exception of loss or damage in the circumstance described in B3.

B3 Transfer of risks

The buyer bears all risks of loss of or damage to the goods from the time they have been delivered under A2.
If the buyer fails to give notice in accordance with B10, then the buyer bears all risks of loss of or damage to the goods from the agreed date or the end of the agreed period for delivery, provided that the goods have been clearly identified as the contract goods.

A4 Carriage

The seller must contract or procure a contract for the carriage of the goods from the agreed point of delivery, if any, at the place of delivery to the named place of destination or, if agreed, any point at that place. The contract of carriage must be made on usual terms at the seller's cost and provide for carriage by the usual route in a customary manner of the type normally used for carriage of the type of goods sold. If a specific point is not agreed or is not determined by practice, the seller may select the point of delivery and the point at the named place of destination that best suit its purpose.
The seller must comply with any transport-related security requirements for transport to the destination.

B4 Carriage

The buyer has no obligation to the seller to make a contract of carriage.

A5 Insurance

The seller has no obligation to the buyer to make a contract of insurance. However, the seller must provide the buyer, at the buyer's request, risk and cost, with information in the possession of the seller that the buyer needs for obtaining insurance.

B5 Insurance

The buyer has no obligation to the seller to make a contract of insurance.

A6 Delivery-transport document

If customary or at the buyer's request, the seller must provide the buyer, at the seller's cost, with the usual transport document[s] for the transport contracted in accordance with A4.

This transport document must cover the contract goods and be dated within the period agreed for shipment. If agreed or customary, the document must also enable the buyer to claim the goods from the carrier at the named place of destination and enable the buyer to sell the goods in transit by the transfer of the document to a subsequent buyer or by notification to the carrier.

When such a transport document is issued in negotiable form and in several originals, a full set of originals must be presented to the buyer.

B6 Delivery/transport document

The buyer must accept the transport document provided under A6 if it is in conformity with the contract.

A7 Export/import clearance

a) Export clearance

Where applicable, the seller must carry out and pay for all export clearance formalities required by the country of export of export, such as:

- export licence;
- security clearance for export;
- pre-shipment inspection; and
- any other official authorisation.

b) Assistance with import clearance

Where applicable, the seller must assist the buyer, at the buyer's request, risk and cost, in obtaining any documents and/or information related to all transit/import clearance formalities, including security requirements and pre-shipment inspection, needed by and country of transit or the country of import.

B7 Export/import clearance

a) Assistance with export clearance

Where applicable, the buyer must assist the seller at the seller's request, risk and cost in obtaining any documents and/or information related to all export clearance formalities, including security requirements and pre-shipment inspection, needed by the country of export.

b) Import clearance

Where applicable, the buyer must carry out and pay for all formalities required by any country of transit and the country of import, such as:

- import licence and any licence required for transit;
- security clearance for import and any transit;
- pre-shipment inspection; and
- any other official authorisation.

A8 Checking/packing/marking

The seller must pay the costs of those checking operations (such as checking quality, measuring, weighing, counting) that are necessary for the purpose of delivering the goods in accordance with A2.

The seller must, at its own cost, package the goods, unless it is usual for he particular trade to transport the type of goods sold unpackaged. The seller must package and mark the goods in the manner appropriate for their transport, unless the parties have agreed on specific packaging or marking requirements.

B8 Checking/packaging/marking

The buyer has no obligation to the seller.

A9 Allocation of costs

The seller must pay:

a) all costs relating to the goods until they have been delivered in accordance with A2, other than those payable by the buyer under B9;

b) transport and all other costs resulting from A4, including the costs of loading the goods and transport-related security costs;

c) any charges for unloading at the agreed place of destination but only if those charges were for the seller's account under the contract of carriage;

d) the costs of transit that were for the seller's account under the contract of carriage;

e) the costs of providing the usual proof to the buyer under A6 that the goods have been delivered;

f) where applicable, duties, taxes and any other costs related to export clearance under A7(a); and

g) the buyer for all costs and charges related to providing assistance in obtaining documents and information in accordance with B7(a).

B9 Allocation of costs

The buyer must pay:

a) all costs relating to the goods from the time they have been delivered under A2, other than those payable by the seller under A9;

b) the costs of transit, unless such costs were for the seller's account under the contract of carriage;

c) unloading costs, unless such costs were for the seller's account under the contract of carriage;
d) the seller for all costs and charges related to providing assistance in obtaining documents and information in accordance with A5 and A7(b);
e) where applicable, duties, taxes and any other costs related to transit or import clearance under B7(b); and
f) any additional costs incurred if it fails to give notice in accordance with B10, from the agreed date or the end of the agreed period for shipment, provided that the goods have been clearly identified as the contract goods.

A10 Notices

The seller must notify the buyer that the goods have been delivered in accordance with A2.
The seller must give the buyer any notice required to enable the buyer to receive the goods.

B10 Notices

The buyer must, whenever it is agreed that the buyer is entitled to determine the time for dispatching the goods and/or the point of receiving the goods within the named place of destination, give the seller sufficient notice.

CIP | Carriage and Insurance Paid To

CIP (insert named place of destination) Incoterms® 2020

EXPLANATORY NOTES FOR USERS

1. **Delivery and risk** - "Carriage and Insurance Paid To" means that the seller delivers the goods - and transfers the risk - to the buyer
   - ▶ by handing them over to the carrier
   - ▶ contracted by the seller
   - ▶ or by procuring the goods so delivered
   - ▶ The seller may do so by giving the carrier physical possession of the goods in the manner and at the place appropriate to the means of transport used.

   Once the goods have been delivered to the buyer in this way, the seller does not guarantee that the goods will reach the place of destination in sound condition, in the stated quantity or indeed at all. This is because risk transfers from seller to buyer when the goods are delivered to the buyer by handing them over to the carrier; the seller must nonetheless contract for th carriage of the goods from delivery to the agreed destination. Thus, for example, goods are handed over to a carrier in Las Vegas (which is not a port) for carriage to Southampton (a port) or to Winchester (which is not a port). In either case, delivery transferring risk to the buyer happens in Las Vegas, and the seller must make a contract of carriage to either Southampton or Winchester.

2. **Mode fo transport** - This rule may be used irrespective of the mode of transport selected and may also be used where more than one mode of transport is employed.

3. **Places (or points) of delivery and destination** - In CIP two locations are important: the place or point at which the goods are delivered (for the transfer of risk) and the place or point agreed as the destination of the goods (as the point to which the seller promises to contract for carriage).

4. **Insurance** - The seller must also contract for insurance cover against the buyer's risk of loss of or damage to the goods from the point of delivery to at least he point of destination. This may cause difficulty where the destination country requires insurance cover to be purchased locally: in this case the parties should consider selling and buying under CPT. The buyer should also note that under the CIP Incoterms® 2020 rule the seller is required to obtain extensive insurance cover complying with Institute Cargo Clauses (A) or similar clause, rather than with the more limited cover under Institute Cargo Clauses (C). It is, however, still open to the parties to agree on a lower level of cover.

5. **Identifying the place or point of delivery with precision** - The parties are well advised to identify both places, or indeed points within those places, as precisely as possible in the contract of sale. Identifying the place or point (if any) of delivery as precisely as possible is important to cater for the common situation where several carriers are engaged, each for different legs of the transit from delivery to destination. Where this happens and the parties do not agree on a specific place or point of delivery, the default position is that risk transfers when the goods have been delivered to the first carrier at a point entirely of the seller's choosing and over which the buyer has no control. Should the parties wish the risk to transfer at a later stage(e.g. at a sea or river port or at an airport), or indeed an early one (e.g. an inland point some way away from a sea or river port), they need to specify this in their contract of sale and to carefully think through the consequences of so doing in case the goods are lost or damaged.

6. **Identifying the destination as precisely as possible** - The parties are also well advised to identify as precisely as possible in the contract of sale the point within the agreed place of destination, as this is the point to which the seller must contract for carriage and insurance and this is the point to which the costs of car-

riage and insurance fall on the seller.

7. **'or procuring the goods so delivered'** - The reference to "procure" here caters for multiple sales down a chain (string sales), particularly common in the commodity trades.

8. **Costs of unloading at destination** – If the seller incurs costs under its contract of carriage related to unloading at the named place of destination, the seller is not entitled to recover such costs separately from the buyer unless otherwise agreed between the parties.

9. **Export/import clearance** - CIP requires the seller to clear the goods for export, where applicable. However, the seller has no obligation to clear the goods for import or for transit through third countries, or to pay any import duty or to carry out any import customs formalities.

A THE SELLER'S OBLIGATIONS

B THE BUYER'S OBLIGATIONS

A1 General obligations

The seller must provide the goods and the commercial invoice in conformity with the contract of sale and any other evidence of conformity that may be required by the contract.

Any document to be provided by the seller may be in paper or electronic form as agreed or, where there is no agreement, as is customary.

B1 General obligations

The buyer must pay the price of the goods as provided in the contract of sale.

Any document to be provided by the buyer may be in paper may be in paper or electronic form as agreed or, where there is no agreement, as is customary.

A2 Delivery

The seller must deliver the goods by handing them over to the carrier contracted in accordance with A4 or by procuring the goods so delivered. In either case the seller must deliver the goods on the agreed date or within he agreed period.

B2 Taking delivery

The buyer must take delivery of the goods when they have been delivered under A2 and receive them from the carrier at the maned place of destination of if agreed, at the point within that place.

A3 Transfer of risks

The seller bears all risks of loss of or damage to the goods until they have been delivered in accordance with A2, with the exception of loss or damage in the circumstance described in B3

B3 Transfer of risks

The buyer bears all risks of loss of or damage to the goods from the time they have been delivered under A2.

If the buyer fails to give notice in accordance with B10, then the buyer bears all risks of loss of or damage to the goods from the agreed date or the end of the agreed period for delivery, provided that the goods have been clearly identified as the contract goods.

A4 Carriage

The seller must contract or procure a contract for the carriage of the goods from the agreed point of delivery, if any, at the place of delivery to the named place of destination or, if agreed, any point at that place, The contract of carriage must be made on usual terms at the seller's cost and provide for carriage by the usual route in a customary manner of the type normally used for carriage of the type of goods sold. If a specific point is not agreed or is not determined by practice, the seller may select the point of delivery and the point at the named place of destination that best suit its purpose.

The seller must comply with any transport-related security requirements for transport to the destination.

B4 Carriage

The buyer has no obligation to the seller to make a contract of carriage.

A5 Insurance

Unless otherwise agreed or customary in the particular trade, the seller must obtain at its own cost cargo insurance complying with the cover provided by Clauses (A) of the Institute Cargo Clauses (LMA/IUA) or any similar clauses as appropriate to the means of transport used. The insurance shall be contracted with underwriters or an insurance company of good repute and entitle the buyer, or any other person having an insurable interest in the goods, to claim directly from the insurer.

When required by the buyer, the seller must, subject to the buyer providing any necessary information requested by the seller, provide at the buyer's cost any additional cover, if procurable, such as cover complying with the Institute War Clauses and/or Institute Strikes Clauses (LMA/IUA) or any similar clauses (unless such cover is already included with the cargo insurance described in

the preceding paragraph).
The insurance shall cover at a minimum, the price provided in the contract plus 10% (i.e. 110%) and shall be in the currency of the contract.
The insurance shall cover the goods from the point of delivery set out in A2 to at least the named place of destination.
The seller must provide the buyer with the insurance policy or certificate or any other evidence of insurance cover.
Moreover, the seller must provide the buyer, at the buyer's request, risk and cost, with information that the buyer needs to procure any additional insurance.

B5 Insurance

The buyer has no obligation to the seller to make a contract of insurance.
However, the buyer must provide the seller, upon request, with any information necessary for the seller to procure any additional insurance requested by the buyer under A5.

A6 Delivery/transport document

If customary or at the buyer's request, the seller must provide the buyer, at the seller's cost, with the usual transport document[s] for the transport contracted in accordance with A4.
This transport document must cover the contract goods and be dated within the period agreed for shipment, If agreed or customary, the document must also enable the buyer to claim the goods from the carrier at the maned place of destination and enable the buyer to sell the goods in transit by the transfer of the document to a subsequent buyer or by notification to the carrier.
When such a transport document is issued in negotiable form and in several originals, a full set of originals must be presented to the buyer.

B6 Delivery/transport document

The buyer must accept the transport document provided under A6 if it is in conformity with the contract.

A7 Export/Import clearance

a) Export clearance

Where applicable, the seller must carry out and pay for all export clearance formalities required by the country of export, such as;

▶ export licence;
▶ security clearance for export;
▶ pre-shipment inspection; and
▶ any other official authorisation.

b) Assistance with import clearance

Where applicable, the seller must assist the buyer, at the buyer's request, risk and cost, in obtaining any documents and/or information related to all transit/import clearance formalities, including security requirements and pre-shipment inspection, needed by any country of transit or the country of import.

B7 Export/import clearance

a) Assistance with export clearance

Where applicable, the buyer must assist the seller at the seller's request, risk and cost in obtaining any documents and/or information related to all export clearance formalities, including security requirements and pre-shipment inspection, needed by the country of export.

b) Import clearance

Where applicable, the buyer must carry out and pay for all formalities required by any country of transit and the country of import, such as:

- import licence and any licence required for transit;
- security clearance for import and any transit;
- pre-shipment inspection; and
- any other official authorisation.

A8 Checking/packaging/marking

The seller must pay the costs of those checking operations (such as checking quality, measuring, weighing, counting) that are necessary for the purpose of delivering the goods in accordance with A2.

The seller must, at its own cost, package the goods, unless it is usual for the particular trade to transport the type of goods sold unpackaged. The seller must package and mark the goods in the manner appropriate for their transport, unless the parties have agreed on specific packaging or marking requirements.

B8 Checking/packaging/marking

The buyer has no obligation to the seller.

A9 Allocation of costs

The seller must pay:

a) all costs relating to the goods until they have been delivered in accordance with A2, other than those payable by the buyer under B9;

b) transport and all other costs resulting from A4, including the costs of loading the goods and transport-related security costs;

c) any charges for unloading at the agreed place of destination but only if those chages were for the seller's account under the contract of carriage;

d) the costs of transit that were for the seller's account under the contract of carriage;

e) the costs of providing the usual proof to the buyer under A6 that the goods have been delivered;
f) the costs of insurance resulting from A5;
g) where applicable, duties, taxes and any other costs related to export clearance under A7(a); and
h) the buyer of all costs and charges related to providing assistance in obtaining documents and information in accordance with B7(a).

B9 Allocation of costs

The buyer must pay:

a) all costs relating to the goods from the time they have been delivered under A2, other than those payable by the seller under A9;
b) the costs of transit, unless such costs were for the seller's account under the contract of carriage;
c) unloading costs. unless such costs were for the seller's account under the contract of carriage;
d) the costs of any additional insurance procured at the buyer's request under A5 and B5;
e) the seller for all costs and charges related to providing assistance in obtaining document and information in accordance with A5 and A7(b);
f) where applicable, duties, taxes and any other costs related to transit or import clearance under B7(b); and
g) any additional costs incurred if it fails to give notice in accordance with B10, from the agreed date or the end of the agreed period for shipment, provided that the goods have been clearly identified as the contract goods.

A10 Notices

The seller must notify the buyer that the goods have been delivered in accordance with A2.

The seller must give the buyer any notice required to enable the buyer to receive the goods.

B10 Notices

The buyer must, whenever it is agreed that the buyer is entitled to determine the time for dispatching the goods and/or the point of receiving the goods within the named place of destination, give the seller sufficient notice.

DAP | Delivery at Place

DAP (insert named place of destination) Incoterms® 2020

EXPLANATORY NOTES FOR USERS

1. **Delivery and risk** - "Delivery at Place" means that the seller delivers the goods- and transfers risk - to the buyer
   - when the goods are placed at the disposal of the buyer
   - on the arriving means of transport read for unloading
   - at the named placed of destination or
   - at the agreed point within that place, if any such point is agreed.

   The seller bears all risks involved in bringing the goods to the named place of destination or to the agreed point within that place. In this Incoterms® rule, therefore, delivery and arrival at destination are the same.

2. **Mode of transport** - This rule may be used irrespective of the mode of transport selected and may also be used where more than one mode of transport is employed.

3. **Identifying the place or point delivery/destination precisely** - the parties are well advised to specify the destination place or point as cleary as possible and this for several reasons. First, risk of loss of or damage to the goods transfers to the buyer at that point of delivery/destination - and it is best for the seller and the buyer to be clear about the point at which the critical transfer happens. Secondly, the costs before that place or point of delivery/destination are for the account of the seller and the costs after that place or point are for the account of the buyer. Thirdly, the seller must contract or arrange for the carriage of the goods to the agreed place or point delivery /destination. If it fails to do so, the seller is in breach of its obligations under the Incoterms DAP® rule and will be liable to the buyer for any ensuing loss. Thus, for example, the seller would be responsible for any additional costs levied by the carrier to the buyer for any additional on-carriage

4. **'or procuring the goods so delivered'** - The reference to "procure" here caters for multiple sales down a chain (string sales), particularly common in the commodity trades.

5. **Unloading costs** - The seller is not required to unload the goods from the arriving means of transportation. However, if the seller incurs costs under its contract

of carriage related to unloading at the place of delivery/destination, the seller is not entitled to recover such costs separately from the buyer unless otherwise agreed between the parties.

6. **Export/import clearance** - DAP requires the seller to clear the goods for export, where applicable. However, the seller has no obligation to clear the goods for import or for post-delivery transit through third countries, to pay any import duty or to carry out any import customs formalities. As a result, if the buyer fails to organise import clearance, the goods will be held up at a port or inland terminal in the destination country. Who bears the risk of any loss that might occur while the goods are thus held up at the port of entry in the destination country? The answer is the buyer: delivery will not have occurred yet, B3(a) ensuring that the risk of loss of or damage to the goods is with the buyer until transit to a named inland point can be resumed. If, in order to avoid this scenario, the parties intend the seller to clear the goods for import, pay any import duty or tax and carry out any import customs formalities, the parties might consider using DDP.

A THE SELLER'S OBLIGATIONS

B THE BUYER'S OBLIGATIONS

A1 General obligations

The seller must provide the goods and the commercial invoice in conformity with the contract of sale and any other evidence of conformity that may be required by the contract.

Any document to be provided by the seller may be in paper or electronic form as agreed or, where there is no agreement, as is customary.

B1 General obligations

The buyer must pay the price of the goods as provided in the contract of sale.

Any document to be provided by the buyer may be in paper or electronic form as agreed or, where there is no agreement, as is customary

A2 Delivery

The seller must deliver the goods by placing at the disposal of the buyer on the arriving means of transport ready for unloading at the agreed point, if any, at the named place of destination or by procuring the goods so delivered. In either case the seller must deliver the goods on the agreed date or within agreed period.

B2 Taking delivery

The buyer must take delivery of the goods when they have been delivered under A2.

A3 Transfer of risks

The seller bears all risks of loss of or damage to the goods until they have been delivered in accordance with A2, with the exception of loss or damage in the circumstances described in B3.

B3 Transfer of risks

The buyer bears all risks of loss of or damage to the goods from the time they have been delivered under A2.

If:

a) the buyer fails to fulfil its obligations in accordance with B7, then it bears all resulting risks of loss of or damage to the goods; or

b) the buyer fails to give notice in accordance with B10, then it bears all risks of loss of or damage to the goods from the agreed date or the end of the agreed period for delivery, provided that goods have been cleary identified as the contract goods.

A4 Carriage

The seller must contract or arrange at its own cost for the carriage of the goods to the named place of destination or to the agreed point, if any, at the named place of destination. If a specific point is not agreed or is not determined by practice, the seller may select the point at the named place of destination that best suits its purpose.

The seller must comply with any transport-related security requirements for transport to the destination.

B4 Carriage

The buyer has no obligation to the seller to make a contract of carriage.

A5 Insurance

The seller has no obligation to the buyer to make a contract of insurance.

B5 Insurance

The buyer has no obligation to the seller to make a contract of insurance.

However, the buyer must provide the seller, at the seller's request, risk and cost, with information that the seller needs for obtaining insurance.

A6 Delivery/transport document

The seller must provide the buyer, at the seller's cost. with any document required to enable the buyer to take over the goods.

B6 Delivery/transport document

The buyer must accept the document provided under A6.

A7 Export/import clearance

a) Export and transit clearance

Where applicable, the seller must carry out and pay for all export and transit clearance formalities required by the country of export any country of transit (other than country of import), such as:

- export/transit licence;
- security clearance for expert/transit;
- pre-shipment inspection; and
- any other official authorisation.

b) Assistance with import clearance

Where applicable, the seller must assist the buyer, at the buyer's request, risk and cost, in obtaining any documents and/or information related to all import clearance formalities, including security requirements and pre-shipment inspection, needed by the country of import.

B7 Export/import clearance

a) Assistance with export and transit clearance

Where applicable, the buyer must assist seller at the seller's request, risk and cost in obtaining any documents and/or information related to all export/transit clearance formalities, including security requirements and pre-shipment inspection, needed by the contry of export and any country of transit (other than the contry of import).

b) Import clearance

Where applicable the buyer must carry out and pay for all formalities required by the country of import, such as:

- import licence;
- security clearance for import;
- pre-shipment inspection; and
- any other official authorisation.

A8 Checking/packaging/marking

The seller must pay the costs of those checking operations (such as checking quality, measuring, weighing, counting) that are necessary for the purpose of delivering the goods in accordance with A2.

The seller must, at its own costs, package the goods, unless it is usual for the particular trade to transport the type of goods sold unpackaged. The seller must package and mark the goods in the manner appropriate for their transport, unless the parties have agreed on specific packaging or marking requirements.

B8 Checking/packaging/marking

The buyer has no obligation to the seller.

A9 Allocation of costs

The seller must pay:

a) all costs relating to the goods and their transport until they have been delivered in accordance with A2, other than those payable by the buyer under B9;
b) any charges for unloading at the place of destination but only if those charges were for the seller's account under contract of carriage;
c) the costs of providing the delivery/transport document under A6;
d) where applicable, duties, taxes and any other costs related to export and any transit clearance under A7(a); and
e) the buyer for all costs and charges related to providing assistance in obtaining documents and information in accordance with B5 and B7(a).

B9 Allocation of costs

The buyer must pay:

a) all costs relating to the goods from the time they have been delivered under A2;
b) all costs of unloading necessary to take delivery of the goods from the arriving means of transport at the named place of destination, unless such costs were for the seller's account under the contract of carriage;
c) the seller for all costs and charges related to providing assistance in obtaining documents and information in accordance with A7(b);
d) where applicable duties, taxes and any other costs related to import clearance under B7(b); and
e) any additional costs incurred by the seller if the buyer fails to fulfil its obligations in accordance with B7 or to give notice in accordance with B10, provided that the goods have been cleary identified ad the contract goods.

A10 Notices

The seller must give the buyer any notice required to enable the buyer to receive the goods.

B10 Notice

The buyer must, whenever it is agreed that buyer is entitled to determine the time within an agreed period and/or the point of taking delivery within the named place of destination, give the seller sufficient notice.

DPU | Delivered at Place Unloaded

DPU (insert named place of destination) Incoterms® 2020

EXPLANATORY NOTES FOR USERS

1. **Delivery and risk** - "Delivered at Place Unloaded" means that the seller delivers the goods – and transfers risk – to the buyer
   - when the goods,
   - once unloaded from the arriving means of transport,
   - are placed at the disposal of the buyer
   - at a named place of destination or
   - at the agreed point within that place, if any such point is agreed.

   The seller bears all risks involved in bringing the goods to and unloading them at the named place of destination. In this Incoterms® rule, therefore, the delivery and arrival at destination are the same. DPU is the only Incoterms® rule that requires the seller to unload goods at destination. The seller should therefore ensure that it is in a position to organise unloading at the named place. Should the parties intend the seller not to bear the risk and cost of unloading, the DPU rule should be avoided and DAP should be used instead.

2. **Mode of transport** - This rule may be used irrespective of the mode of transport selected and may also be used where more than one mode of transport is employed.

3. **Identifying the place or point of delivery/destination precisely** - The parties are well advised to specify the destination place or point as clearly as possible and this for several reasons. First, risk of loss of or damage to the goods transfers to the buyer at that point of delivery/destination - and it is best for the seller and the buyer to be clear about the point at which that critical transfer happens. Secondly, the costs before that place or point of delivery/destination are for the account of the seller and the costs after that place or point are for the account of the buyer. Thirdly, the seller must contract or arrange for the carriage of the goods to the agreed place or point of delivery/destination. If it fails to do so, the seller is in breach of its obligations under this rule and will be liable to the buyer for any ensuing loss. The seller would, for example, be responsible for any additional costs levied by the carrier to the buyer for any additional on-carriage.

4. **'or procuring the goods so delivered'** - The reference to "procure" here caters for multiple sales down a chain (string sales), particularly common in the commodity trades.

5. **Export/import clearance** - DPU requires the seller to clear the goods for export, where applicable. However, the seller has no obligation to clear the goods for import or for post-delivery transit through third countries, to pay any import duty or to carry out any import customs formalities. As a result, if the buyer fails to organise import clearance, the goods will be held up at a port or inland terminal in the destination country. Who bears the risk of any loss that might occur while the goods are thus held up at the port of entry in the destination country? The answer is the buyer: delivery will not have occurred yet, B3(a) ensuring that the risk of loss of or damage to the goods is with the buyer until transit to a named inland point can be resumed. If, in order to avoid this scenario, the parties intend the seller to clear the goods for import, pay any import duty or tax and carry out any import customs formalities, the parties might consider using DDP.

A THE SELLER'S OBLIGATIONS

B THE BUYER'S OBLIGATIONS

A1 General obligations

The seller must provide the goods and the commercial invoice in conformity with the contract of sale and any other evidence of conformity that may be required by the contract.
Any document to be provided by the seller may be in paper or electronic form as agreed or, where there is no agreement, as is customary.

B1 General obligations

The buyer must pay the price of the goods as provided in the contract of sale.
Any document to be provided by the buyer may be in paper or electronic form as agreed or, where there is no agreement, as is customary.

A2 Delivery

The seller must unload the goods from the arriving means of transport and must then deliver them by placing them at the disposal of the buyer at the agreed point, if any, at the named place of destination or by procuring the goods so delivered. In either case the seller must deliver the goods on the agreed date or within the agreed period.

B2 Taking delivery

The buyer must take delivery of the goods when they have been delivered under A2.

A3 Transfer of risks

The seller bears all risks of loss of or damage to the goods until they have been delivered in accordance with A2, with the exception of loss or damage in the circumstances described in B3.

B3 Transfer of risks

The buyer bears all risks of loss of or damage to the goods from the time they have been delivered under A2.

If:

a) the buyer fails to fulfil its obligations in accordance with B7, then it bears all resulting risks of loss of or damage to the goods; or

b) the buyer fails to fulfil its obligations in accordance with B10, then it bears all risks of loss of or damage to the goods from the agreed date or the end of the agreed period for delivery.

provided that the goods have been clearly indentified as the contract goods.

A4 Carriage

The seller must contract or arrange at its own cost for the carriage of the goods to the named place of destination or to the agreed point, if any, at the named place of destination. If a specific point is not agreed or is not determined by practice, the seller may select the point at the named place of destination that best suits its purpose.

The seller must comply with any transport-related security requirements for transport to the destination.

B4 Carriage

The buyer has no obligation to the seller to make a contract of carriage.

A5 Insurance

The seller has no obligation to the buyer to make a contract of insurance.

B5 Insurance

The buyer has no obligation to the seller to make a contract of insurance. However, the buyer must provide the seller, at the seller's request, risk and cost, with information that the seller needs for obtaning insurance.

A6 Delivery/transport document

The seller must provide the buyer, at the seller's cost, with any document required to enable the buyer to take over the goods.

B6 Delivery/transport document

The buyer must accept the document provided under A6.

A7 Export/import clearnace

a) Export and transit clearance

Where applicable, the seller must carry out and pay for all export and transit clearace formalities required by the country of export and any country of transit (other than the country of import), such as;

- ▶ export/transit licence;
- ▶ security clearance for export/transit;
- ▶ pre-shipment inspection; and
- ▶ any other official authorisation.

b) Assistance with import clearance

Where applicable, the seller must assist the buyer, at the buyer's request, risk and cost, in obtaining any documents and/or information related to all import clearance formalities, including security requirements and pre-shipment inspection, needed by the country of import.

B7 Export/import clearance

a) Assistance with export and transit clearance

Where applicable, the buyer must assist the seller at the seller's request, risk and cost in obtaining any documents and/or information related to all export/transit clearance formalities, including security requirements and pre-shipment inspection, needed by the country of export and any country of transit (other than the country of import).

b) Import clearance

Where applicable, the buyer must carry out and pay for all formalities required by the country of import, such as;

- ▶ import licence;
- ▶ security clearance for import;
- ▶ pre-shipment inspection; and
- ▶ any other official authorisation.

A8 Checking/packaging/marking

The seller must pay the costs of those checking operations (such as checking quality, measuring, weighing, counting) that are necessary for the purpose of delivering the goods in accordance with A2.

The seller must, at its own cost, package the goods, unless it is usual for the particular trade to transport the type of goods sold unpackaged.

The seller must package and mark the goods in the manner appropriate for their transport, unless the parities have agreed on specific packaging or marking requirements.

B8 Checking/packaging/marking

The buyer has no obligation to the seller.

A9 Allocation of costs

The seller must pay:

a) all costs relating to the goods and their transport until they have been unloaded and delivered in accordance with A2, other than those payable by the buyer under B9;

b) the cost of providing the delivery/transport document under A6;

c) where applicable, duties, taxes and any other costs related to export and any transit clearance under A7(a); and

d) the buyer for all costs and charges related to providing assistance in obtaining documents and information in accordance with B5 and B7(a)

B9 Allocation of costs

The buyer must pay:

a) all costs relating to the goods from the time they have been delivered under A2;

b) the seller for all costs and charges related to providing assistance in obtaining documents and information in accordance with A7(b);

c) where applicable. duties, taxes and any other costs related to import clearance under B7(b): and

d) any additional costs incurred by the seller if the buyer fails to fulfil its obligations in accordance with B7 or to give notice in accordance with B10, provided that the goods have been clearly identified as the contract goods.

A10 Notices

The seller must give the buyer any notice required to enable the buyer to receive the goods.

B10 Notices

The buyer must, whenever it is agreed that the buyer is entitled to determine the time within an agreed period and/or the point of taking delivery within the named place of destination, give the seller sufficient notice.

DDP | Delivered Duty Paid

DDP(insert named place of destination) Incoterms® 2020

EXPLANATORY NOTES FOR USERS

1. **Delivery and risk** - "Delivered Duty Paid" means that the seller delivers the goods to the buyer
   - when the goods are placed at the disposal of the buyer,
   - cleared for import,
   - on the arriving means of transport,

- ready for unloading,
- at the named place of destination or at the agreed point within that place, if any such point is agreed.

The seller bears all risks involved in bringing the goods to the named place of destination or to the agreed point within that place. In this Incoterms® rule, therefore, delivery and arrival at destination are the same.

2. **Mode of transport** - This rule may be used irrespective of the mode of transport selected and may also be used where more than one mode of transport is employed.

3. **A note of caution to sellers: maximum responsibility** - DDP, with delivery happening at destination and with the sellers being responsible for the payment of import duty and applicable taxes is the Incoterms® rule imposing on the seller the maximum level of obligation of all eleven Incoterms® rules. From the seller's perspective, therefore, the rule should be used with care for different reasons as set out in paragraph 7.

4. **Identifying the place or point of delivery/destination precisely** - The parties are well advised to specify the destination place or point as clearly as possible and this for several reasons. First, risk of loss of or damage to the goods transfers to the buyer at that point of delivery/destination - and it is best for the seller and the buyer to be clear about the point at which that critical transfer happens. Secondly, the costs before that place or point of delivery/destination are for the account of the seller, including the costs of import clearance, and the costs after that place or point, other than the costs of import, are for the account of the buyer. Thirdly, the seller must contract or arrange for the carriage of the goods to the agreed place or point of delivery/destination. If it fails to do so, the seller is in breach of its obligations under the Incoterms® rule DDP and will be liable to the buyer for any ensuing loss. Thus, for example, the seller would be responsible for any additional costs levied by the carrier to the buyer for any additional on-carriage.

5. **'or procuring the goods so delivered'** - The reference to "procure" here caters for multiple sales down a chain (string sales), particularly common in the commodity trades.

6. **Unloading costs** - If the seller incurs costs under its contract of carriage related to unloading at the place of delivery/destination, the seller is not entitled to recover such costs separately from the buyer unless otherwise agreed between the parties.

7. **Export/import clearance** - As set out in paragraph 3, DDP requires the seller to clear the goods for export, where applicable, as well as for import and to pay any import duty or to carry out any customs formalities. Thus if the seller is unable to obtain import clearance and would rather leave that side of things in the buyer's hands in the country of import, then the seller should consider choosing DAP or DPU, under which rules delivery still happens at destination, but with import clearance being left to the buyer. There may be tax implications and this tax may not be recoverable from the buyer; see A9(d).

A THE SELLER'S OBLIGATIONS

B THE BUYER'S OBLIGATIONS

A1 General obligations

The seller must provide the goods and the commercial invoice in conformity with the contract of sale and any other evidence of conformity that may be required by the contract.
Any document to be provided by the seller may be in paper or electronic form as agreed or, where is no agreement, as is customary.

B1 General obligations

The buyer must pay the price of the goods as provided in the contract of sale.
Any documents to be provided by the buyer may be in paper or electronic form as agreed or, where there is no agreement, as is customary.

A2 Delivery

The seller must deliver the goods by placing them at the disposal of the buyer on the arriving means of transport ready for unloading at the agreed point, if any, at the named place of destination or by procuring the goods so delivered. In either case the seller must deliver the goods on the agreed date or within the agreed period.

B2 Taking delivery

The buyer must take delivery of the goods when they have been delivered under A2.

A3 Transfer of risks

The seller bears all risks of loss of or damage to the goods until they have been delivered in accordance with A2, with the exception of loss or damage in the circumstances described in B3.

B3 Transfer of risks

The buyer bears all risks of loss of or damage to the goods from the time they have been delivered under A2.

If:

a) the buyer fails to fulfil its obligations in accordance with B7, then it bears all resulting risks of loss of or damage to the goods; or

b) the buyer fails to give notice in accordance with B10, then it bears all risks of loss of or damage to the goods from the agreed date or the end of the agreed period for delivery,

provided that the goods have been clearly identified as the contract goods.

A4 Carriage

The seller must contract or arrange at its own cost for the caariage of the goods to the named place of destination or to the agreed point, if any, at the named place of destination. If a specific point is not agreed or is not determined by practice, the seller may select the point at the named place of destination that best suits its purpose.

The seller must comply with any transport-related security requirements for transport to the destination.

B4 Carriage

The buyer has no obligation to the seller to make a contract of carriage.

A5 Insurance

The seller has no obligation to the buyer to make a contract of insurance.

B5 Insurance

The buyer has no obligation to the seller to make a contract of insurance.

However, the buyer must provide the seller, at the seller's request, risk and cost, with information that the seller needs for obtaining insurance.

A6 Delivery/transport document

The seller must provide the buyer, at the seller's cost, with any document required to enable the buyer to take over the goods.

B6 Delivery/ transport document

The buyer must accept the document provided under A6.

A7 Export/import clearance

Where applicable, the seller must carry out and pay for all export/transit/import clearance formalities required by the countries of export, transit and import, such as:

- export/transit/import licence;
- security clearance for export/transit/import;

▶ pre-shipment inspection; and
▶ any other official authorisation.

B7 Export/ import clearance

Where applicable, the buyer must assist the seller, at the seller's request, risk and cost in obtaining any documents and/or information related to all export/transit/import clearance formalities required by the countries of export/transit/import, such as:

▶ export/transit/import licence;
▶ security clearance for export, transit and import;
▶ pre-shipment inspection; and
▶ any other official authorisation.

A8 Checking/packaging/marking

The seller must pay the costs of those checking operations (such as checking quality, measuring, weighing, counting) that are necessary for the purpose of delivering the goods in accordance with A2.

The seller must, at its own cost, package the goods, unless it is usual for the particular trade to transport the type of goods sold unpackaged. The seller must package and mark the goods in the manner appropriate for their transport, unless the parties have agreed on specific packaging or marking requirements.

B8 Checking/packaging/marking

The buyer has no obligation to the seller.

A9 Allocation of costs

The seller must pay:

a) all costs relating to the goods and their transport until the have been delivered in accordance with A2, other than those payable by the buyer under B9;
b) any charges for unloading at the place of destination but only if those charges were for the seller's account under the contract of carriage;
c) the cost of providing the delivery/transport document under A6;
d) where applicable, duties, taxes and any other costs related to export, transit and import clearance under A7; and
e) the buyer for all costs and charged related to providing assistance in obtaining documents and information in accordance with B5 and B7.

B9 Allocation og costs

The buyer must pay:

a) all costs relating to the goods from the time they have been delivered under

A2;

b) all costs of unloading necessary to take delivery of the goods from the arriving means of transport at the named place of destination, unless such costs were for the seller's account under the contract of carriage, and

c) any additional costs incurred by the seller if the buyer fails to fulfil its obligations in accordance with B7 or to give notice in accordance with B10, provided that the goods have been clearly identified as the contract goods.

A10 Notices

The seller must give the buyer any notice required to enable the buyer to receive the goods.

B10 Notices

The buyer must, whenever it is agreed that the buyer is entitled to determine the time within an agreed period and/or the point of taking delivery within the named place of destination, give the seller sufficient notice.

FAS(Free Alongsid Ship) Incoterms® 2020

EXPLANATORY NOTES FOR USERS

1. **Delivery and risk** - "Free Alongside Ship" means that the seller delivers the goods to the buyer
   - ▶ when the goods are placed alongside the ship (e.g. on a quay or a barge)
   - ▶ nominated by the buyer
   - ▶ at the named port of shipment
   - ▶ or when the seller procures goods already so delivered.

   The risk of loss of or damage to the goods transfers when the goods are alongside the ship, and the buyer bears all costs from that moment onwards.

2. **Mode of transport** - This rule is to be used only for sea or inland waterway transport where the parties intend to deliver the goods by placing the goods alongside a vessel. Thus, the FAS rule is not appropriate where goods are handed over to the carrier before they are alongside the vessel, for example where goods are handed over to a carrier at a container terminal. Where this is the case, parties should consider using the FCA rule rather than the FAS rule.

3. **Identifying the loading point precisely** - The parties are well advised to specify as clearly as possible the loading point at the named port of shipment where the

goods are to be transferred from the quay or barge to the ship, as the costs and risks to that point are for the account of the seller and these costs and associated handling charges may vary according to the practice of the port.

4. **'or procuring the goods so delivered'** - The seller is required either to deliver the goods alongside the ship or to procure goods already so delivered for shipment. The reference to "procure" here caters for multiple sales down a chain (string sales), particularly common in the commodity trades.

5. **Export/import clearance** - FAS requires the seller to clear the goods for export, where applicable. However, the seller has no obligation to clear the goods for import or for transit through third counties, to pay any import duty or to carry out any import customs formalities.

A THE SELLER/S OBLIGATIONS

B THE BUYER'S OBLIGATIONS

A1 General obligations

The seller must provide the goods and the commercial invoice in conformity with the contract of sale and any other evidence of conformity that may be required by the contract.

Any document to be provided by the seller may be in paper or electronic form as agreed or, where there is no agreement, as is customary.

B1 General obligations

The buyer must pay the price of the goods as provided in the contract of sale.

Any document to be provided by the buyer may be in paper or electronic form as agrees or, where there is no agreement, as is customary.

A2 Delivery

The seller must deliver the goods either by placing them alongside the vessel nominated by the buyer at the loading point, if any, indicated by the buyer at the named port of shipment or by procuring the goods so delivered.

The seller must deliver the goods

1. on the agreed date

or

2. at the time within the agreed period notified by the buyer under B10

or

3. if no such time is notified, then at the end of the agreed period

and

4. in the manner customary at the port.

If no specific loading point has been indicated by the buyer, the seller may select the point within the named port of shipment that best suits its purpose.

B2 Taking delivery

The buyer must take delivery of the goods when they have been delivered under A2.

A3 Transfer of risks

The seller bears all risk of loss of or damage to the goods until they have been delivered in accordance with A2, with the exception of loss or damage in the circumstances described in B3.

B3 Transfer of risks

The buyer bears all risks of loss of or damage to the goods from the time they have been delivered under A2.

If.

a) the buyer fails to give notice in accordance with B10; or

b) the vessel nominated by the buyer fails to arrive on time to enable the seller to comply with A2, fails to take the goods, or closes for cargo earlier than the time notified in accordance with B10:

then the buyer bears all risks of loss of or damage to the goods:

(i) from the agreed date, or in the absence of an agreed date,

(ii) from the date selected by the buyer under B10, or, if no such date has been notified,

(iii) from the end of any agreed period for delivery,

provided that the goods have been clearly identified as the contract goods.

A4 carriage

The seller has no obligation to the buyer to make a contract of carriage. However, the seller must provide the buyer, at the buyer's request, risk and cost, with any information in the possession of the seller, including transport-related security requirements, that the buyer needs for arranging carriage. If agreed, the seller must contract for carriage on the usual terms at the buyer's risk and cost.

The seller must comply with any transport-related security requirements up to delivery.

B4 carriage

The buyer must contract at its own cost for the carriage of the goods from the named port of shipment, except when the contract of carriage is made by the seller as provided for in A4.

A5 Insurance

The seller has no obligation to the buyer to make a contract of insurance. However, the seller must provide the buyer, at the buyer's request, risk and cost, with information in the possession of the seller that the buyer needs for obtaining insurance.

B5 Insurance

The buyer has no obligation to the seller to make a contract of insurance.

A6 Delivery/transport document

The seller must provide the buyer, at the seller's cost, with the usual proof that the goods have been delivered in accordance with A2.

Unless such proof is a transport document, the seller must provide assistance to the buyer, at the buyer's request, risk and cost, in obtaining a transport document.

B6 Delivery/transport document

The buyer must accept the proof of delivery provided under A6.

A7 Export/import clearance

a) Export clearance

Where applicable, the seller must carry out and pay for all export clearance formalities required by the country of export, such as:

- ▶ export licence;
- ▶ security clearance for export;
- ▶ pre-shipment inspection; and
- ▶ any other official authorisation.

b) Assistance with import clearance

Where applicable, the seller must assist the buyer, at the buyer's request, risk and cost, in obtaining any documents and/or information related to all transit/import clearance formalities, including security requirements and pre-shipment inspection, needed by any country of transit or the country of import.

B7 Export/import clearance

a) Assistance with export clearance

Where applicable, the buyer must assist the seller at the seller's request, risk and cost in obtaining any documents and/or information related to all export clearance formalities, including security requirements and pre-shipment inspection, needed by the country of export.

b) Import clearance

Where applicable, the buyer must carry out and pay for all formalities required by any country of transit and the country of import, such as:

- ▶ import licence and any licence required for transit;
- ▶ security clearance for import and any transit;
- ▶ pre-shipment inspection; and
- ▶ any other official authorisation.

A8 Checking/packaging/marking

The seller must pay the costs of those checking operations (such as checking quality, measuring, weighing, counting) that are necessary for the purpose of delivering the goods in accordance with A2.

The seller must, at its own cost, package the goods, unless it is usual for the particular trade to transport the type of goods sold unpackaged. The seller must package and mark the goods in the manner appropriate for their transport, unless the parties have agreed on specific packaging or marking requirements.

B8 Checking/packaging/marking

The buyer has no obligation to the seller.

A9 Allocation of costs

The seller must pay:

a) all cost relating to the goods until they have been delivered in accordance with A2, other than those payable by the buyer under B9;

b) the costs of providing the usual proof to the buyer under A6 that the goods have been delivered;

c) where applicable, duties, taxes and any other costs related to export clearance under A7(a); and

d) the buyer for all costs and charges related to providing assistance in obtaining documents and information in accordance with B7(a).

B9 Allocation of costs

The buyer must pay:

a) all costs relating to the goods from the time they have been delivered under A2, other than those payable by the seller under A9;

b) the seller for all costs and charges related to providing assistance in obtaining documents and information in accordance with A4, A5, A6 and A7(b);

c) where applicable, duties, taxes and any other costs related to transit or import clearance under B7(b); and

d) any additional costs incurred, either because:

(i) the buyer has failed to give notice under B10, or

(ii) the vessel nominated by the buyer under B10 fails to arrive on time, fails to take the goods, or closes for cargo earlier than the time notified in accordance with B10,

provided that the goods have been clearly identified as the contract goods.

A10 Notices

The seller must give the buyer sufficient notice either that the goods have been delivered in accordance with A2 or that the vessel has failed to take delivery of the goods within the time agreed.

B10 Notices

The buyer must give the seller sufficient notice of any transport-related security requirements, the vessel name, loading point and, if any, the selected delivery date within the agreed period.

FOB(insert named port of shipment) Incoterms® 2020

EXPLANATORY NOTES FOR USERS

1. **Delivery and risk** - "Free On Board" means that the seller delivers the goods to the buyer
   - ▶ on board the vessel
   - ▶ nominated by the buyer
   - ▶ at the named port of shipment
   - ▶ or procures the goods already so delivered.

   The risk of loss of or damage to the goods transfers when the goods are on board the vessel, and the buyer bears all costs from that moment onwards.

2. **Mode of transport** - This rule is to be used only for sea or inland waterway transport where the parties intend to deliver the goods by placing the goods on board a vessel. Thus, the FOB rule is not appropriate where goods are handed over to the carrier before they are on board the vessel, for example where goods are handed over to a carrier at a container terminal. Where this is the case, parties should consider using the FCA rule rather than the FOB rule.

3. **'or procuring the goods so delivered'** - The seller is required either to deliver the goods on board the vessel or to procure goods already so delivered for shipment. The reference to 'procure' here caters for multiple sales down a chain (string sales), particularly common in the commodity trades.

4. **Export/import clearance** – FOB requires the seller to clear the goods for export, where applicable. However, the seller has no obligation to clear the goods for import or for transit through third countries, to pay any import duty or to carry out any import customs formalities.

A THE SELLER'S OBLIGATIONS

B THE BUYER'S S OBLIGATIONS

A1 General obligations

The seller must provide the goods and the commercial invoice in conformity with the contract of sale and any other evidence of conformity that may be required by the contract.

Any document to be provided by the seller may be in paper or electronic form as agreed or, where there is no agreement, as is customary.

B1 General obligations

The buyer must pay the price of the goods as provided in the contract of sale.

Any document to be provided by the buyer may be in paper or electronic from as agreed or, where there is no agreement, as is customary.

A2 Delivery

The seller must deliver the goods either by placing them on board the vessel nominated by the buyer at the loading point, if any, indicated by the buyer at the named port of shipment or by procuring the goods so delivered.

The seller must deliver the goods

1. on the agreed date
   or
2. at the time within the agreed period notified by the buyer under B10
   or
3. if no such time is notified, then at the end of the agreed period
   and
4. in the manner customary at the port

If no specific loading point has been indicated by the buyer, the seller may select the point within the named port of shipment that best suits its purpose.

B2 Taking delivery

The buyer must take delivery of the goods when they have been delivered under A2.

A3 Transfer of risks

The seller bears all risk of loss of or damage to the goods until they have been delivered in accordance with A2, with the exception of loss or damage in the circumstances described in B3.

B3 Transfer of risks

The buyer bears all risk of loss of or damage to the goods from the time they have been delivered under A2.

If.

a) the buyer fails to give notice in accordance with B10; or

b) the vessel nominated by the buyer fails to arrive on time to enable the seller to comply with A2, fails to take the goods, or closes for cargo earlier than the time notified in accordance with B10:

then the buyer bears all risks of loss of or damage to the goods:

(i) from the agreed date, or in the absence of an agreed date,

(ii) from the date selected by the buyer under B10, or, if no such date has been notified,

(iii) from the end of any agreed period for delivery,

A4 carriage

The seller has no obligation to the buyer to make a contract of carriage. However, the seller must provide the buyer, at the buyer's request, risk and cost, with any information in the possession of the seller, including transport-related security requirements, that the buyer needs for arranging carriage. If agreed, the seller must contract for carriage on the usual terms at the buyer's risk and cost.

The seller must comply with any transport-related security requirements up to delivery.

B4 carriage

The buyer must contract at its own cost for the carriage of the goods from the named port of shipment, except when the contract of carriage is made by the seller as provided for in A4.

A5 Insurance

The seller has no obligation to the buyer to make a contract of insurance. However, the seller must provide the buyer, at the buyer's request, risk and cost, with information in the possession of the seller that the buyer needs for obtaining insurance.

B5 Insurance

The buyer has no obligation to the seller to make a contract of insurance.

A6 Delivery/transport document

The seller must provide the buyer, at the seller's cost, with the usual proof that the goods have been delivered in accordance with A2.

Unless such proof is a transport document, the seller must provide assistance to the buyer, at the buyer's request, risk and cost, in obtaining a transport document.

B6 Delivery/transport document

The buyer must accept the proof of delivery provided under A6.

A7 Export/import clearance

a) Export clearance

Where applicable, the seller must carry out and pay for all export clearance formalities required by the country of export, such as:

- export license;
- security clearance for export;
- pre-shipment inspection; and
- any other official authorisation.

b) Assistance with import clearance

Where applicable, the seller must assist the buyer, at the buyer's request, risk and cost, in obtaining any documents and/or information related to all transit/import clearance formalities, including security requirements and pre-shipment inspection, needed by any country of transit or the country of import.

B7 Export/import clearance

a) Assistance with export clearance

Where applicable, the buyer must assist the seller at the seller's request, risk and cost in obtaining any documents and/ or information related to all export clearance formalities, including security requirements and pre-shipmen inspection, needs by the country of export.

b) Import clearance

Where applicable, the buyer must carry out and pay for all formalities required by any country of transit and the country of import, such as:

- import license and any license required for transit;
- security clearance for import and any transit;
- pre-shipment inspection; and
- any other official authorisation.

A8 Checking/packaging/ marking

The seller must pay the costs of those checking operations (such as checking quality, measuring, weighing, counting) that are necessary for the purpose of delivering the goods in accordance with A2. The seller must, at its own cost, package the goods, unless it is usual for the particular trade to transport the type of goods sold unpackaged. The seller must package and mark the goods in the manner appropriate for their transport, unless the parties have agreed on specific packaging or marking requirements.

B8 Checking/packaging/ marking

The buyer has no obligation to the seller.

A9 allocation of costs

The seller must pay:

a) all costs relating to the goods until they have been delivered in accordance with A2, other than those payable by the buyer under B9;

b) the costs of providing the usual proof to the buyer under A6 that the goods have been delivered;

c) where applicable, duties, taxes and any other costs related to export clearance under A7(a); and

d) the buyer for all costs and charges related to providing assistance in obtaining documents and information accordance with B7(a).

B9 Allocation of costs

The buyer must pay:

a) all costs relating to the goods from the time they have been delivered under A2, other than those payable by the seller under A9;

b) the seller for all costs and charges related to providing assistance in obtaining documents and information in accordance with A4, A5, A6 and A7(b); and

d) any additional costs incurred, either because:

(i) the buyer has failed to give notice under B10, or

(ii) the vessel nominated by the buyer under B10 fails to arrive on time, fails to take the goods, or closes for cargo earlier than the time notified in accordance with B10,

Provided that the goods have been clearly identified as the contract goods.

A10 Notice

The seller must give the buyer sufficient notice either that the goods have been delivered in accordance with A2 or that the vessel has failed to take the goods within the time agreed.

B10 Notice

The buyer must give the seller sufficient notice of any transport-related security requirements, the vessel name, loading point and, if any, the selected delivery date within the agreed period.

CFR | Cost and Freight

CFR(insert named port of destination) Incoterms® 2020

Explanatory notes for users

1. **Delivery and risk** - "Cost and Freight" means that the seller delivers the goods to the buyer.
   - on board the vessel
   - or procures the goods already so delivered.

   The risk of loss of or damage to the goods transfers when the goods are on board the vessel, such that the seller is taken to have performed its obligation to deliver the goods whether or not the goods actually arrive at their destination in sound condition, in the stated quantity or, indeed, at all. In CFR, the seller owes no obligation to the buyer to purchase insurance cover: the buyer would be well-advised therefore to purchase some cover for itself.

2. **Mode of transport** - This rule is to be used only for sea or inland waterway transport. Where more than one mode of transport is to be used, which will commonly be the case where goods are handed over to a carrier at a container terminal, the appropriate rule to use is CPT rather than CFR.

3. **'or procuring the goods so delivered'** - The reference to "procure" here caters for multiple sales down a chain (string sales), particularly common in the commodity trades.

4. **Ports of delivery and destination** - in CFR, two ports are important: the port where the goods are delivered on board the vessel and the port agreed as the destination of the goods. Risk transfers from seller to buyer when the goods are delivered to the buyer by placing them on board the vessel at the shipment port or by procuring the goods already so delivered. However, the seller must contract for the carriage of the goods from delivery to the agreed destination. Thus, for example, goods are placed on board a vessel in Shanghai (which is a port) for carriage to Southampton (also a port). Delivery here happens when the goods are on board in Shanghai, with risk transferring to the buyer at that time; and the seller must make a contract of carriage from Shanghai to Southampton.

5. **Must the shipment port be named?** - While the contract will always specify a destination port, it might not specify the port of shipment, which is where risk transfers to the buyer. If the shipment port is of particular interest to the buyer, as it may be, for example, where the buyer wishes to ascertain that the freight

element of the price is reasonable, the parties are well advised to identify it as precisely as possible in the contract.

6. **Identifying the destination point at the discharge port** - The parties are well advised to identify as precisely as possible the point at the named port of destination, as the costs to that point are for the account of the seller. The seller must make a contract or contracts of carriage that cover(s) the transit of the goods from delivery to the named port or to the agreed point within that port where such a point has been agreed in the contract of sale..

7. **Multiple carriers** - It is possible that carriage is effected through several carriers for different legs of the sea transport, for example, first by a carrier operating a feeder vessel from Hong Kong to Shanghai, and then onto an ocean vessel from Shanghai to Southampton. The question which arises here is whether risk transfers from seller to buyer at Hong Kong or at Shanghai: where does delivery take place? The parties may well have agreed this in the sale contract itself. Where, however, there is no such agreement, the default position is that risk transfers when the goods have been delivered to the first carrier, i.e. Hong Kong, thus increasing the period during which the buyer incurs the risk of loss or damage. Should the parties wish the risk to transfer at later stage (here, Shanghai) they need to specify this in their contract of sale.

8. **Unloading costs** - If the seller incurs costs under its contract of carriage related to unloading at the specified point at the port of destination, the seller is not entitled to recover such costs separately from the buyer unless otherwise agreed between the parties.

9. **Export/Import clearance** - CFR requires the seller to clear the goods for export, where applicable. However, the seller has no obligation to clear the goods for import or for transit through third countries, to pay any import duty or to carry out any import customs formalities.

A THE SELLER'S OBLIGATIONS

B THE BUYER'S OBLIGATIONS

A1 General obligations

The seller must provide the goods and the commercial invoice in conformity with the contract of sale and any evidence of conformity that may be required by the contract.

Any document to be provided by the seller may be in paper or electronic form as agreed or, where there is no agreement, as is customary.

B1 General obligations

The buyer must pay the price of the goods as provided in the contract of sale. Any document to be provided by the buyer may be in paper or electronic form as agrees or, where there is no agreement, as is customary.

A2 Delivery

The seller must deliver the goods either by placing them on board the vessel or by procuring the goods so delivered. In either case, the seller must deliver the goods on the agreed date or within the agreed period and in the manner customary at the port.

B2 Taking delivery

The buyer must take delivery of the goods when they have been delivered under A2 and receive them from carrier at the named port of destination.

A3 Transfer of risks

The seller bears all risks of loss of or damage to the goods until they have been delivered in accordance with A2, with the exception of loss or damage in the circumstance described in B3.

B3 Transfer of risks

The buyer bears all risks of loss of or damage to the goods from the time they have been delivered under A2. If the buyer fails to give notice in accordance with B10, then it bears all risks of loss of or damage to the goods from the agreed date or the end of the agreed period for shipment, provided that the goods have been clearly identified as the contract goods.

A4 Carriage

The seller must contract or procure a contract for the carriage of the goods from the agreed point of delivery. if any, at the place of delivery to the named port of destination or, if agreed, any point any that port. The contract of carriage must be made on usual terms at the seller's cost and provide for carriage by the usual route in a vessel of the type normally used for the transport of the type of goods sold.

The seller must comply with any transport-related security requirements for transport to the destination.

B4 Carriage

The buyer has no obligation to the seller make a contract of carriage.

A5 Insurance

The seller has no obligation to the buyer to make a contract of insurance. However, the seller must provide the buyer, at the buyer's request, risk and cost, with information in the possession of the seller that the buyer needs for obtaining insurance.

B5 Insurance

The buyer has no obligation to the seller to make a contract of insurance.

A6 Delivery/transport document

The seller must, as its own cost, provide the buyer with the usual transport document for the agreed port of destination.

This transport document must cover the contract goods, be dated within the period agreed for shipment, enable the buyer to claim the goods from the carrier at the port of destination and, unless otherwise agreed, enable the buyer to sell the goods in transit by the transfer of the document to a subsequent buyer or by notification to the carrier.

When such a transport document is issued in negotiable form and in several originals, a full set of originals must be presented to the buyer.

B6 Delivery/transport document

The buyer must accept the transport document document provided under A6 if it is in conformity with the contract.

A7 Export/import clearance

a) Export clearance

Where applicable, the seller must catty cut and pay for all export clearance formalities requtred by the country of expert, such as:

- ▶ export licence;
- ▶ security clearance for export;
- ▶ pre-shipment inspection; and
- ▶ any other official authorisation.

b) Assistance with import clearance

Where applicable, the seller must assist the buyer, at the buyer's request, risk and cost, in obtaining any documents and/or information related to all transit/import clearance formalities, including security requrements and pre-shipment inspection, needed by any county of transit or the country of import.

B7 Export/import clearance

a) Assistance with export clearance

Where applicable, the buyer must assist the seller at the seller's request, risk and cost in obtaining any documents and/or information related to all export clearance formalities, including security requirements and pre-shipment inspection, needed by the county of expcrt.

b) Import clearance

Where applicable, the buyer must carry out and pay for all formalities required by any country of transit and the county of transit and any licence required for transit;

- ▶ import licence and any licence required for transit;
- ▶ security clearance for import and any transit;
- ▶ pre-shipment inspection; and
- ▶ any other offical authorisation.

A8 Checking/packaging/marking

The seller must pay the costs of those checking operations (such as checking quality, measuring, weighing, counting) that are necessary for the purpose of delivering the goods in accordance with A2.

The seller must, at its own cost, package the goods, unless it is usual for the particular trade to transport the type of goods sold unpackaged. The seller must package and mark the goods in the manner appropriate for their transport, unless the parties have agreed on specific packaging or marking requirements.

B8 Checking/packaging/marking

The buyer has no obligation to the seller.

A9 Allocation of costs

The seller must pay:

a) all costs relating to the goods until they have been delivered in accordance with A2, other than those payable by the buyer under B9;

b) the fright and all other costs resulting from A4, including the costs of loading the goods on board and transport-related security costs;

c) any charges for unloading at the agreed port of discharge that were for the seller's account under the contract of carriage;

d) the costs of transit that were for the seller's account under the contract of carriage;

e) the costs of providing the usual proof to the buyer under A6 that the goods have been delivered;

f) where applicable, duties, taxes and any other costs related to export clearance under A7(a); and

g) the buyer for all costs and charges related to providing assistance in obtaining documents and information in accordance with B7(a).

B9 Allocation of costs

The buyer must pay:

a) all costs relating to the goods from the time they have been delivered under

A2, other than those payable by the seller under A9;

b) the costs of transit, unless such costs were for the seller's account under the contract of carriage;

c) unloading costs including lighterage and wharfage charges, unless such costs and charges were for the seller's account under the contract of carriage.

d) the seller for all costs and charges related to providing assistance in obtaining documents and information in accordance with A5 and A7(b).

e) where applicable, duties, taxes and any other costs related to transit or import clearance under B7(b); and

f) any additional costs incurred if it fails to give notice in accordance with B10, from the agreed date or the end of the agreed period for shipment, provided that the goods have been clearly identified as the contract goods.

A10 Notices

The seller must notify the buyer that the goods have been delivered in accordance with A2.

The seller must give the buyer any notice required to enable the buyer to receive the goods.

B10 Notice

The buyer must, whenever it is agreed that the buyer is entitled to determine the time for shipping the goods and/or the point of receiving the goods within the named port of destination, give the seller sufficient notice.

CIF | Cost Insurance and Freight

CIF (insert named port of destination) Incoterms® 2020

EXPLANATORY NOTE FOR USERS

1. **Delivery and risk** - "Cost Insurance and Freight" means that the seller delivers the goods to the buyer
   - ▶ on board the vessel
   - ▶ or procures the goods already so delivered.

   The risk of loss of or damage to the goods transfers when the goods are on board the vessel, such that the seller is taken to have performed its obligation to deliver the goods whether or not the goods actually arrive at their destination in sound condition, in the stated quantity or, indeed, at all.

2. **Mode of transport** - This rule is to be used only for sea or inland waterway transport. Where more than one mode of transport is to be used, which will commonly be the case where goods are handed over to a carrier at a container terminal, the appropriate rule to use is CIP rather than CIF.

3. **'or procuring the goods so delivered'** - The reference to "procure" here caters for multiple sales down a chain (string sales), particularly common in the commodity trades.

4. **Ports of delivery and destination** - In CIF, two ports are important: the port where the goods are delivered on board the vessel and the port agreed as the destination of the goods. Risk transfers from seller to buyer when the goods are delivered to the buyer by placing them on board the vessel at the shipment port or by procuring the goods already so delivered. However, the seller must contract for the carriage of the goods from delivery to the agreed destination. Thus, for example, goods are placed on board a vessel in Shanghai (which is a port) for carriage to Southampton (also a port). Delivery here happens when the goods are on board in Shanghai, with risk transferring to the buyer at that time; and the seller must make a contract of carriage from Shanghai to Southampton.

5. **Must the shipment port be named?** - While the contract will always specify a destination port, it might not specify the port of shipment, which is where risk transfers to the buyer. If the shipment port is of particular interest to the buyer, as it may be, for example, where the buyer wishes to ascertain that the freight or the insurance element of the price is reasonable, the parties are well advised to identify it as precisely as possible in the contract.

6. **Identifying the destination point at the discharge port** - The parties are well advised to identify as precisely as possible the point at the named port of destination, as the costs to that point are for the account of the seller. The seller must make a contract or contracts of carriage that cover the transit of the goods from delivery to the named port or to the agreed point within that port where such a point has been agreed in the contract of sale.

7. **Multiple carriers** - It is possible that carriage is effected through several carriers for different legs of the sea transport, for example, first by a carrier operating a feeder vessel from Hong Kong to Shanghai, and then onto an ocean vessel from Shanghai to Southampton. The question which arises here is whether risk transfers from seller to buyer at Hong Kong or at Shanghai: where does delivery take place? The parties may well have agreed this in the sale contract itself. Where, however, there is no such agreement, the default position is that risk transfers when the goods have been delivered to the first carrier, i.e. Hong Kong, thus increasing the period during which the buyer incurs the risk of loss or damage.

Should the parties wish the risk to transfer at a later stage (here, Shanghai) they need to specify this in their contract of sale.

8. **Insurance** - The seller must also contract for insurance cover against the buyer's risk of loss of or damage to the goods from the port of shipment to at least the port of destination. This may cause difficulty where the destination country requires insurance cover to be purchase locally: in this case the parties should consider selling and buying under CFR. The buyer should also note that under the CIF Incoterms® 2020 rule the seller is required to obtain limited insurance cover complying with Institute Cargo Clauses (C) or similar clause, rather than with the more extensive cover under Institute Cargo Clauses (A). It is, however, still open to the parties to agree on a higher level of cover.

9. **Unloading costs** - If the seller incurs costs under its contract of carriage related to unloading at the specified point at the port of destination, the seller is not entitled to recover such costs separately from the buyer unless otherwise agreed between the parties.

10. **Export/Import clearance** - CIF requires the seller to clear the goods for export, where applicable. However, the seller has no obligation to clear the goods for import or for transit through third countries, to pay any import duty or to carry out any import customs formalities.

A THE SELLER'S OBLIGATIONS

B THE BUYER'S OBLIGATIONS

A1 General obligations

The seller must provide the goods and the commercial invoice in conformity with the contract of sale and any other evidence of conformity that may be required by the contract.

Any document to be provided by the seller may be in paper or electronic form as agreed or, where there is no agreement as is customary.

B1 General obligations

The buyer must pay the price of the goods as provided in the contract of sale.

Any document to be provided by the buyer may be in paper or electronic form as agreed or, where there is no agreement, as is customary.

A2 Delivery

The seller must deliver the goods either by placing them on board the vessel or by procuring the goods so delivered. In either case, the seller must deliver the goods on the agreed date or within the agreed period and in the manner customary at the port.

B2 Taking delivery

The buyer must take delivery of the goods when they have beer delivered under A2 and receive them from the carrier at the named port of destination.

A3 Transfer of risks

The seller bears all risks of loss of or damage to the goods until they have been delivered in accordance with A2, with the exception of loss or damage in the circumstance described in B3.

B3 Transfer of risks

The buyer bears all risks of loss of or damage to the goods from the time they have been delivered under A2.

If the buyer fails to give notice in accordance with B10, then it bears all risks of loss of or damage to the goods from the agreed date or the end of the agreed period for shipment, provided that the goods have been clearly identified as the contract goods.

A4 Carriage

The seller must contract or procure a contract for the carriage of the goods from the agreed point of delivery, if any, at the place of delivery to the named port of destination or, if agreed, any point at that port. The contract of carriage must be made on usual terms at the seller's cost and provide for carriage by the usual route in a vessel of the type normally used for the transport of the type of goods sold.

The seller must comply with any transport-related security requirements for transport to the destination.

B4 Carriage

The buyer has no obligation to the seller to make a contract of carriage.

A5 Insurance

Unless otherwise agreed or customary in the particular trade, the seller must obtain, at its own cost, cargo insurance complying with the cover provided by Clauses (C) of the Institute Cargo Clauses (LMA/IUA) or any similar clauses. The insurance shall be contracted with underwriters or an insurance company of good repute and entitle the buyer, or any other person having an insurable interest in the goods, to claim directly from the insurer.

When required by the buyer, the seller must, subject to the buyer providing any necessary information requested by the seller, provide at the buyer's cost any additional cover, if procurable, such as cover complying with the Institute

War Clauses and/or Institute Strikes Clauses (LMA/IUA) or any similar clauses (unless such cover is already included with the cargo insurance described in the preceding paragraph).

The insurance shall cover, at a minimum, the price provided in the contract plus 10% (i.e. 110%) and shall be in the currency of the contract.

The insurance shall cover the goods from the point of delivery set out in A2 to at least the named port of destination.

The seller must provide the buyer with the insurance policy or certificate or any other evidence of insurance cover

Moreover, the seller must provide the buyer, at the buyer's request, risk and cost, with information that the buyer needs to procure any additional insurance.

B5 Insurance

The buyer has no obligation to the seller to make a contract of insurance.

However, the buyer must provide the seller, upon request, with any information necessary for the seller to procure any additional insurance requested by the buyer under A5.

A6 Delivery/transport document

The seller must, at its own cost, provide the buyer with the usual transport document for the agreed port of destination.

This transport document must cover the contract goods, be dated within the period agreed for shipment, enable the buyer to claim the goods from the carrier at the port of destination and, unless otherwise agreed, enable the buyer to sell the goods in transit by the transfer of the document to a subsequent buyer or by notification to the carrier.

When such a transport document is issued in negotiable form and in several originals, a full set of originals must be presented to the buyer.

B6 Delivery/transport document

The buyer must accept the transport document provided under A6 if it is in conformity with the contract.

A7 Export/import clearance

a) Export clearance

Where applicable, the seller must carry out and pay for all export clearance formalities required by the country of export, such as:

- export licence;
- security clearance for export;
- pre-shipment inspection; and
- any other official authorisation.

b) Assistance with import clearance

Where applicable, the seller must assist the buyer, at the buyer's request, risk and cost, in obtaining any documents and/or information related to all transit/import clearance formalities, including security requirements and pre-shipment inspection, needed by any country of transit or the country of import.

B7 Export/import clearance

a) Assistance with export clearance

Where applicable, the buyer must assist the seller at the seller's request, risk and cost in obtaining any documents and/or information related to all export clearance formalities, including security requirements and pre-shipment inspection, needed by the country of export.

b) Import clearance

Where applicable, the buyer must carry out and pay for all formalities required by any country of transit and the country of import, such as:

- import licence and any licence required for transit;
- security clearance for import and any transit;
- pre-shipment inspection; and
- any other official authorisation.

A8 Checking/packaging/marking

The seller must pay the costs of those checking operations (such as checking quality, measuring, weighing, counting) that are necessary for the purpose of delivering the goods in accordance with A2.

The seller must, at its own cost, package the goods, unless it is usual for the particular trade to transport the type of goods sold unpackaged. The seller must package and mark the goods in the manner appropriate for their transport, unless the parties have agreed on specific packaging or marking requirements.

B8 Checking/packaging/marking

The buyer has no obligation to the seller.

A9 Allocation of costs

The seller must pay:

a) all costs relating to the goods until they have been delivered in accordance with A2, other than those payable by the buyer under B9:

b) the freight and all other costs resulting from A4, including the costs of loading the goods on board and transport-related security costs;

c) any charges for unloading at the agreed port of discharge that were for the seller's account under the contract of carriage;

d) the costs of transit that were for the seller's account under the contract of carriage;
e) the costs of providing the usual proof to the buyer under A6 that the goods have been delivered;
f) the costs of insurance resulting from A5;
g) where applicable, duties, taxes and any other costs related to export clearance under A7(a); and
h) the buyer for all costs and charges related to providing assistance in obtaining documents and information in accordance with B7(a).

B9 Allocation of costs

The buyer must pay:
a) all costs relating to the goods from the time they have been delivered under A2, other than those payable by the seller under A9;
b) the costs of transit, unless such costs were for the seller's account under the contract of carriage;
c) unloading costs including lighterage and wharfage charges, unless such costs and charges were for the seller's account under the contract of carriage;
d) the costs of any additional insurance procured at the buyer's request under A5 and B5;
e) the seller for all costs and charges related to providing assistance in obtaining documents and information in accordance with A5 and A7(b);
f) where applicable, duties, taxes and any other costs related to transit or import clearance under B7(b); and
g) any additional costs incurred if it fails to give notice in accordance with B10, from the agreed date or the end of the agreed period for shipment, provided that the goods have been clearly identified as the contract goods.

A10 Notices

The seller must notify the buyer that the goods have been delivered in accordance with A2.

The seller must give the buyer any notice required to enable the buyer to receive the goods.

B10 Notices

The buyer must, whenever it is agreed that the buyer is entitled to determine the time for shipping the goods and/or the point of receiving the goods within the named port of destination, give the seller sufficient notice.

The Uniform Customs and Practice for Documentary Credits, 2007 Revision ICC Publication No. 600("UCP")

Article 1 Application of UCP

The Uniform Customs and Practice for Documentary Credits, 2007 Revision, ICC Publication no. 600("UCP") are rules that apply to any documentary credit("credit") (including, to the extent to which they may be applicable, any standby letter of credit) when the text of the credit expressly indicates that it is subject to these rules. They are binding on all parties thereto unless expressly modified or excluded by the credit.

Article 2 Definitions

For the purpose of these rules:

Advising bank means the bank that advises the credit at the request of the issuing bank.

Applicant means the party on whose request the credit is issued.

Banking day means a day on which a bank is regularly open at the place at which an act subject to these rules is to be performed.

Beneficiary means the party in whose favour a credit is issued.

Complying presentation means a presentation that is in accordance with the terms and conditions of the credit, the applicable provisions of these rules and international standard banking practice.

Confirmation means a definite undertaking of the confirming bank, in addition to that of the issuing bank, to honour or negotiate a complying presentation.

Confirming bank means the bank that adds its confirmation to a credit upon the issuing bank's authorization or request.

Credit means any arrangement, however named or described, that is irrevocable and thereby constitutes a definite undertaking of the issuing bank to honour a complying presentation.

Honour means:

a. to pay at sight if the credit is available by sight payment.
b. to incur a deferred payment undertaking and pay at maturity if the credit is available by deferred payment.
c. to accept a bill of exchange("draft") drawn by the beneficiary and pay at maturity if the credit is available by acceptance

Issuing bank means the bank that issues a credit at the request of an applicant or on its own behalf.

Negotiation means the purchase by the nominated bank of drafts(drawn on a bank other than the nominated bank) and/or documents under a complying presentation, by advancing or agreeing to advance funds to the beneficiary on or before the banking day on which reimbursement is due to the nominated bank.

Nominated Bank means the bank with which the credit is available or any bank in the case of a credit available with any bank.
Presentation means either the delivery of documents under a credit to the issuing bank or nominated bank or the documents so delivered.

Presenter means a beneficiary, bank or other party that makes a presentation.

Article 3 Interpretations

For the purpose of these rules:

Where applicable, words in the singular include the plural and in the plural include the singular.

A credit is irrevocable even if there is no indication to that effect.

A document may be signed by handwriting, facsimile signature, perforated signature, stamp, symbol or any other mechanical or electronic method of authentication.

A requirement for a document to be legalized, visaed, certified or similar will be satisfied by any signature, mark, stamp or label on the document which appears to satisfy that requirement.

Branches of a bank in different countries are considered to be separate banks.

Terms such as "first class", "well known", 'qualified", "independent", "official", "competent" or "local" used to describe the issuer of a document allow any issuer except the beneficiary to issue that document.

Unless required to be used in a document, words such as "prompt", "immediately" or "as soon as possible" will be disregarded.

The expression "on or about" or similar will be interpreted as a stipulation that an event is to occur during a period of five calendar days before until five calendar days after the specified date, both start and end dates included.

The words "to", "until", "till", "from" and "between" when used to determine a period of shipment include the date or dates mentioned, and the words "before" and "after" exclude the date mentioned.

The words "from" and "after" when used to determine a maturity date exclude the date mentioned.

The terms "first half" and "second half" of a month shall be construed respectively as the 1st to the 15th and the 16th to the last day of the month, all dates inclusive.

The terms "beginning", "middle" and "end" of a month shall be construed respectively as the 1st to the 10th, the 11th to the 20th and the 21st to the last day of the month, all dates inclusive.

Article 4 Credits v. Contracts

a. A credit by its nature is a separate transaction from the sale or other contract on which it may be based. Banks are in no way concerned with or bound by such contract, even if any reference whatsoever to it is included in the credit. Consequently, the undertaking of a bank to honour, to negotiate or to fulfil any other obligation under the credit is not subject to claims or defences by the applicant resulting from its relationships with the issuing bank or the beneficiary. A beneficiary can in no case avail itself of the contractual relationships existing between banks or between the applicant and the issuing bank.
b. An issuing bank should discourage any attempt by the applicant to include, as an integral part of the credit, copies of the underlying contract, proforma invoice and the like.

Article 5 Documents v. Goods, Services or Performance

Banks deal with documents and not with goods, services or performance to which the documents may relate.

Article 6 Availability, Expiry Date and Place for Presentation

a. A credit must state the bank with which it is available or whether it is available with any bank. A credit available with a nominated bank is also available with the issuing bank.
b. A credit must state whether it is available by sight payment, deferred payment, acceptance or negotiation.
c. A credit must not be issued available by a draft drawn on the applicant.
d. i. A credit must state an expiry date for presentation. An expiry date stated for honour or negotiation will be deemed to be an expiry date for presentation.
   ii. The place of the bank with which the credit is available is the place for

presentation. The place for presentation under a credit available with any bank is that of any bank. A place for presentation other than that of the issuing bank is in addition to the place of the issuing bank.

e. Except as provided in sub-article 29(a), a presentation by or on behalf of the beneficiary must be made on or before the expiry date.

Article 7 Issuing Bank Undertaking

a. Provided that the stipulated documents are presented to the nominated bank or to the issuing bank and that they constitute a complying presentation, the issuing bank must honour if the credit is available by:
   i. sight payment, deferred payment or acceptance with the issuing bank;
   ii. sight payment with a nominated bank and that nominated bank does not pay;
   iii. deferred payment with a nominated bank and that nominated bank does not incur its deferred payment undertaking or, having incurred its deferred payment undertaking, does not pay at maturity;
   iv. acceptance with a nominated bank and that nominated bank does not accept a draft drawn on it or, having accepted a draft drawn on it, does not pay at maturity;
   v. negotiation with a nominated bank and that nominated bank does not negotiate.

b. An issuing bank is irrevocably bound to honour as of the time it issues the credit.

c. An issuing bank undertakes to reimburse a nominated bank that has honoured or negotiated a complying presentation and forwarded the documents to the issuing bank. Reimbursement for the amount of a complying presentation under a credit available by acceptance or deferred payment is due at maturity, whether or not the nominated bank prepaid or purchased before maturity. An issuing bank's undertaking to reimburse a nominated bank is independent of the issuing bank's undertaking to the beneficiary.

Article 8 Confirming Bank Undertaking

a. Provided that the stipulated documents are presented to the confirming bank or to any other nominated bank and that they constitute a complying presentation, the confirming bank must:
   i. honour, if the credit is available by
      a. sight payment, deferred payment or acceptance with the confirming bank;
      b. sight payment with another nominated bank and that nominated bank does not pay;
      c. deferred payment with another nominated bank and that nominated bank does not incur its deferred payment undertaking or, having incurred its deferred payment undertaking, does not pay at maturity;

d. acceptance with another nominated bank and that nominated bank does not accept a draft drawn on it or, having accepted a draft drawn on it, does not pay at maturity;
e. negotiation with another nominated bank and that nominated bank does not negotiate.

ii. negotiate, without recourse, if the credit is available by negotiation with the confirming bank.

b. A confirming bank is irrevocably bound to honour or negotiate as of the time it adds its confirmation to the credit.

c. A confirming bank undertakes to reimburse another nominated bank that has honoured or negotiated a complying presentation and forwarded the documents to the confirming bank. Reimbursement for the amount of a complying presentation under a credit available by acceptance or deferred payment is due at maturity, whether or not another nominated bank prepaid or purchased before maturity. A confirming bank's undertaking to reimburse another nominated bank is independent of the confirming bank's undertaking to the beneficiary.

d. If a bank is authorized or requested by the issuing bank to confirm a credit but is not prepared to do so, it must inform the issuing bank without delay and may advise the credit without confirmation.

Article 9 Advising of Credits and Amendments

a. A credit and any amendment may be advised to a beneficiary through an advising bank. An advising bank that is not a confirming bank advises the credit and any amendment without any undertaking to honour or negotiate.

b. By advising the credit or amendment, the advising bank signifies that it has satisfied itself as to the apparent authenticity of the credit or amendment and that the advice accurately reflects the terms and conditions of the credit or amendment received.

c. An advising bank may utilize the services of another bank("second advising bank") to advise the credit and any amendment to the beneficiary. By advising the credit or amendment, the second advising bank signifies that it has satisfied itself as to the apparent authenticity of the advice it has received and that the advice accurately reflects the terms and conditions of the credit or amendment received.

d. A bank utilizing the services of an advising bank or second advising bank to advise a credit must use the same bank to advise any amendment thereto.

e. If a bank is requested to advise a credit or amendment but elects not to do so, it must so inform, without delay, the bank from which the credit, amendment or advice has been received.

f. If a bank is requested to advise a credit or amendment but cannot satisfy itself as to the apparent authenticity of the credit, the amendment or the advice, it must so inform, without delay, the bank from which the instructions appear to have been received. If the advising bank or second advising bank elects nonetheless to advise the credit or amendment it must inform the beneficiary or second advising bank that it has not been able to satisfy itself as to the apparent authenticity of the credit, the amendment or the advice.

Article 10 Amendments

a. Except as otherwise provided by article 38, a credit can neither be amended nor cancelled without the agreement of the issuing bank, the confirming bank, if any, and the beneficiary.
b. An issuing bank is irrevocably bound by an amendment as of the time it issues the amendment. A confirming bank may extend its confirmation to an amendment and will be irrevocably bound as of the time it advises the amendment. A confirming bank may, however, choose to advise an amendment without extending its confirmation and, if so, it must inform the issuing bank without delay and inform the beneficiary in its advice.
c. The terms and conditions of the original credit(or a credit incorporating previously accepted amendments) will remain in force for the beneficiary until the beneficiary communicates its acceptance of the amendment to the bank that advised such amendment. The beneficiary should give notification of acceptance or rejection of an amendment. If the beneficiary fails to give such notification, a presentation that complies with the credit and to any not yet accepted amendment will be deemed to be notification of acceptance by the beneficiary of such amendment. As of that moment the credit will be amended.
d. A bank that advises an amendment should inform the bank from which it received the amendment of any notification of acceptance or rejection.
e. Partial acceptance of an amendment is not allowed and will be deemed to be notification of rejection of the amendment.
f. A provision in an amendment to the effect that the amendment shall enter into force unless rejected by the beneficiary within a certain time shall be disregarded.

Article 11 Teletransmitted and Pre-Advised Credits and Amendments

a. An authenticated teletransmission of a credit or amendment will be deemed to be the operative credit or amendment, and any subsequent mail confirmation shall be disregarded.
   If a teletransmission states "full details to follow"(or words of similar effect), or states that the mail confirmation is to be the operative credit or amendment, then the teletransmission will not be deemed to be the operative credit or amendment. The issuing bank must then issue the operative credit or amendment without delay in terms not inconsistent with the teletransmission.
b. A preliminary advice of the issuance of a credit or amendment ("pre-advice")

shall only be sent if the issuing bank is prepared to issue the operative credit or amendment. An issuing bank that sends a preadvice is irrevocably committed to issue the operative credit or amendment, without delay, in terms not inconsistent with the pre-advice.

Article 12 Nomination

a. Unless a nominated bank is the confirming bank, an authorization to honour or negotiate does not impose any obligation on that nominated bank to honour or negotiate, except when expressly agreed to by that nominated bank and so communicated to the beneficiary.

b. By nominating a bank to accept a draft or incur a deferred payment undertaking, an issuing bank authorizes that nominated bank to prepay or purchase a draft accepted or a deferred payment undertaking incurred by that nominated bank.

c. Receipt or examination and forwarding of documents by a nominated bank that is not a confirming bank does not make that nominated bank liable to honour or negotiate, nor does it constitute honour or negotiation.

Article 13 Bank-to-Bank Reimbursement Arrangements

a. If a credit states that reimbursement is to be obtained by a nominated bank ("claiming bank") claiming on another party("reimbursing bank"), the credit must state if the reimbursement is subject to the ICC rules for bank-to-bank reimbursements in effect on the date of issuance of the credit.

b. If a credit does not state that reimbursement is subject to the ICC rules for bank-to-bank reimbursements, the following apply:

  i. An issuing bank must provide a reimbursing bank with a reimbursement authorization that conforms with the availability stated in the credit. The reimbursement authorization should not be subject to an expiry date.

  ii. A claiming bank shall not be required to supply a reimbursing bank with a certificate of compliance with the terms and conditions of the credit.

  iii. An issuing bank will be responsible for any loss of interest, together with any expenses incurred, if reimbursement is not provided on first demand by a reimbursing bank in accordance with the terms and conditions of the credit.

  iv. A reimbursing bank's charges are for the account of the issuing bank. However, if the charges are for the account of the beneficiary, it is the responsibility of an issuing bank to so indicate in the credit and in the reimbursement authorization. If a reimbursing bank's charges are for the account of the beneficiary, they shall be deducted from the amount due to a claiming bank when reimbursement is made. If no reimbursement is made, the reimbursing bank's charges remain the obligation of the issuing bank.

c. An issuing bank is not relieved of any of its obligations to provide reimbursement if reimbursement is not made by a reimbursing bank on first demand.

Article 14 Standard for Examination of Documents

a. A nominated bank acting on its nomination, a confirming bank, if any, and the issuing bank must examine a presentation to determine, on the basis of the documents alone, whether or not the documents appear on their face to constitute a complying presentation.
b. A nominated bank acting on its nomination, a confirming bank, if any, and the issuing bank shall each have a maximum of five banking days following the day of presentation to determine if a presentation is complying. This period is not curtailed or otherwise affected by the occurrence on or after the date of presentation of any expiry date or last day for presentation.
c. A presentation including one or more original transport documents subject to articles 19, 20, 21, 22, 23, 24 or 25 must be made by or on behalf of the beneficiary not later than 21 calendar days after the date of shipment as described in these rules, but in any event not later than the expiry date of the credit.
d. Data in a document, when read in context with the credit, the document itself and international standard banking practice, need not be identical to, but must not conflict with, data in that document, any other stipulated document or the credit.
e. In documents other than the commercial invoice, the description of the goods, services or performance, if stated, may be in general terms not conflicting with their description in the credit.
f. If a credit requires presentation of a document other than a transport document, insurance document or commercial invoice, without stipulating by whom the document is to be issued or its data content, banks will accept the document as presented if its content appears to fulfil the function of the required document and otherwise complies with sub-article 14(d).
g. A document presented but not required by the credit will be disregarded and may be returned to the presenter.
h. If a credit contains a condition without stipulating the document to indicate compliance with the condition, banks will deem such condition as not stated and will disregard it.
i. A document may be dated prior to the issuance date of the credit, but must not be dated later than its date of presentation.
j. When the addresses of the beneficiary and the applicant appear in any stipulated document, they need not be the same as those stated in the credit or in any other stipulated document, but must be within the same country as the respective addresses mentioned in the credit. Contact details(telefax, telephone, email and the like) stated as part of the beneficiary's and the applicant's address will be disregarded. However, when the address and contact details of the applicant ap-

pear as part of the consignee or notify party details on a transport document subject to articles 19, 20, 21, 22, 23, 24 or 25, they must be as stated in the credit.

k. The shipper or consignor of the goods indicated on any document need not be the beneficiary of the credit.

l. A transport document may be issued by any party other than a carrier, owner, master or charterer provided that the transport document meets the requirements of articles 19, 20, 21, 22, 23 or 24 of these rules.

Article 15 Complying Presentation

a. When an issuing bank determines that a presentation is complying, it must honour.

b. When a confirming bank determines that a presentation is complying, it must honour or negotiate and forward the documents to the issuing bank.

c. When a nominated bank determines that a presentation is complying and honours or negotiates, it must forward the documents to the confirming bank or issuing bank.

Article 16 Discrepant Documents, Waiver and Notice

a. When a nominated bank acting on its nomination, a confirming bank, if any, or the issuing bank determines that a presentation does not comply, it may refuse to honour or negotiate.

b. When an issuing bank determines that a presentation does not comply, it may in its sole judgement approach the applicant for a waiver of the discrepancies. This does not, however, extend the period mentioned in sub-article 14(b).

c. When a nominated bank acting on its nomination, a confirming bank, if any, or the issuing bank decides to refuse to honour or negotiate, it must give a single notice to that effect to the presenter.

The notice must state:

i. that the bank is refusing to honour or negotiate; and

ii. each discrepancy in respect of which the bank refuses to honour or negotiate; and

iii. a) that the bank is holding the documents pending further instructions from the presenter; or

b) that the issuing bank is holding the documents until it receives a waiver from the applicant and agrees to accept it, or receives further instructions from the presenter prior to agreeing to accept a waiver; or

c) that the bank is returning the documents; or

d) that the bank is acting in accordance with instructions previously received from the presenter.

d. The notice required in sub-article 16(c) must be given by telecommunication or, if that is not possible, by other expeditious means no later than the close of the fifth banking day following the day of presentation.

e. A nominated bank acting on its nomination, a confirming bank, if any, or the issuing bank may, after providing notice required by sub-article 16(c)(iii)(a) or(b), return the documents to the presenter at any time.

f. If an issuing bank or a confirming bank fails to act in accordance with the provisions of this article, it shall be precluded from claiming that the documents do not constitute a complying presentation.

g. When an issuing bank refuses to honour or a confirming bank refuses to honour or negotiate and has given notice to that effect in accordance with this article, it shall then be entitled to claim a refund, with interest, of any reimbursement made.

Article 17 Original Documents and Copies

a. At least one original of each document stipulated in the credit must be presented.

b. A bank shall treat as an original any document bearing an apparently original signature, mark, stamp, or label of the issuer of the document, unless the document itself indicates that it is not an original

c. Unless a document indicates otherwise, a bank will also accept a document as original if it:

  i. appears to be written, typed, perforated or stamped by the document issuer's hand; or

  ii. appears to be on the document issuer's original stationery; or

  iii. states that it is original, unless the statement appears not to apply to the document presented.

d. If a credit requires presentation of copies of documents, presentation of either originals or copies is permitted.

e. If a credit requires presentation of multiple documents by using terms such as “in duplicate”, “in two fold” or “in two copies”, this will be satisfied by the presentation of at least one original and the remaining number in copies, except when the document itself indicates otherwise.

Article 18 Commercial Invoice

a. A commercial invoice:

  i. must appear to have been issued by the beneficiary(except as provided in article 38);

  ii. must be made out in the name of the applicant(except as provided in sub-article 38(g));

  iii. must be made out in the same currency as the credit; and

  iv. need not be signed.

b. A nominated bank acting on its nomination, a confirming bank, if any, or the issuing bank may accept a commercial invoice issued for an amount in excess of the amount permitted by the credit, and its decision will be binding upon all parties, provided the bank in question has not honoured or negotiated for an amount in excess of that permitted by the credit.

c. The description of the goods, services or performance in a commercial invoice must correspond with that appearing in the credit.

Article 19 Transport Document Covering at Least Two Different Modes of Transport

a. A transport document covering at least two different modes of transport(multi-modal or combined transport document), however named, must appear to:
   i. indicate the name of the carrier and be signed by:
      - the carrier or a named agent for or on behalf of the carrier, or
      - the master or a named agent for or on behalf of the master.

      Any signature by the carrier, master or agent must be identified as that of the carrier, master or agent.

      Any signature by an agent must indicate whether the agent has signed for or on behalf of the carrier or for or on behalf of the master.
   ii. indicate that the goods have been dispatched, taken in charge or shipped on board at the place stated in the credit, by:
      - pre-printed wording, or
      - a stamp or notation indicating the date on which the goods have been dispatched, taken in charge or shipped on board.

      The date of issuance of the transport document will be deemed to be the date of dispatch, taking in charge or shipped on board, and the date of shipment. However, if the transport document indicates, by stamp or notation, a date of dispatch, taking in charge or shipped on board, this date will be deemed to be the date of shipment.
   iii. indicate the place of dispatch, taking in charge or shipment and the place of final destination stated in the credit, even if:
      a. the transport document states, in addition, a different place of dispatch, taking in charge or shipment or place of final destination, or
      b. the transport document contains the indication "intended" or similar qualification in relation to the vessel, port of loading or port of discharge.
   iv. be the sole original transport document or, if issued in more than one original, be the full set as indicated on the transport document.
   v. contain terms and conditions of carriage or make reference to another source containing the terms and conditions of carriage(short form or blank back transport document). Contents of terms and conditions of carriage will not be examined.
   vi. contain no indication that it is subject to a charter party.

b. For the purpose of this article, transhipment means unloading from one means of conveyance and reloading to another means of conveyance(whether or not in different modes of transport) during the carriage from the place of dispatch, taking in charge or shipment to the place of final destination stated in the credit.

c. i. A transport document may indicate that the goods will or may be transhipped provided that the entire carriage is covered by one and the same transport document.

ii. A transport document indicating that transhipment will or may take place is acceptable, even if the credit prohibits transhipment.

Article 20 Bill of Lading

a. A bill of lading, however named, must appear to:

i. indicate the name of the carrier and be signed by:

- the carrier or a named agent for or on behalf of the carrier, or
- the master or a named agent for or on behalf of the master.

Any signature by the carrier, master or agent must be identified as that of the carrier, master or agent.

Any signature by an agent must indicate whether the agent has signed for or on behalf of the carrier or for or on behalf of the master.

ii. indicate that the goods have been shipped on board a named vessel at the port of loading stated in the credit by:

- pre-printed wording, or
- an on board notation indicating the date on which the goods have been shipped on board.

The date of issuance of the bill of lading will be deemed to be the date of shipment unless the bill of lading contains an on board notation indicating the date of shipment, in which case the date stated in the on board notation will be deemed to be the date of shipment.

If the bill of lading contains the indication "intended vessel" or similar qualification in relation to the name of the vessel, an on board notation indicating the date of shipment and the name of the actual vessel is required.

iii. indicate shipment from the port of loading to the port of discharge stated in the credit.

If the bill of lading does not indicate the port of loading stated in the credit as the port of loading, or if it contains the indication "intended" or similar qualification in relation to the port of loading, an on board notation indicating the port of loading as stated in the credit, the date of shipment and the name of the vessel is required. This provision applies even when loading on board or shipment on a named vessel is indicated by pre-printed wording on the bill of lading.

iv. be the sole original bill of lading or, if issued in more than one original, be the full set as indicated on the bill of lading.

v. contain terms and conditions of carriage or make reference to another source containing the terms and conditions of carriage(short form or blank back bill of lading). Contents of terms and conditions of carriage will not be examined.

vi. contain no indication that it is subject to a charter party.

b. For the purpose of this article, transhipment means unloading from one vessel and reloading to another vessel during the carriage from the port of loading to the port of discharge stated in the credit.

c. i. A bill of lading may indicate that the goods will or may be transhipped provided that the entire carriage is covered by one and the same bill of lading.

ii. A bill of lading indicating that transhipment will or may take place is acceptable, even if the credit prohibits transhipment, if the goods have been shipped in a container, trailer or LASH barge as evidenced by the bill of lading.

d. Clauses in a bill of lading stating that the carrier reserves the right to tranship will be disregarded.

Article 21 Non-Negotiable Sea Waybill

a. A non-negotiable sea waybill, however named, must appear to:

i. indicate the name of the carrier and be signed by:

- the carrier or a named agent for or on behalf of the carrier, or
- the master or a named agent for or on behalf of the master.

Any signature by the carrier, master or agent must be identified as that of the carrier, master or agent.

Any signature by an agent must indicate whether the agent has signed for or on behalf of the carrier or for or on behalf of the master.

ii. indicate that the goods have been shipped on board a named vessel at the port of loading stated in the credit by:

- pre-printed wording, or
- an on board notation indicating the date on which the goods have been shipped on board.

The date of issuance of the non-negotiable sea waybill will be deemed to be the date of shipment unless the non-negotiable sea waybill contains an on board notation indicating the date of shipment, in which case the date stated in the on board notation will be deemed to be the date of shipment.

If the non-negotiable sea waybill contains the indication "intended vessel" or similar qualification in relation to the name of the vessel, an on board notation indicating the date of shipment and the name of the actual vessel is required.

iii. indicate shipment from the port of loading to the port of discharge stated in the credit.

If the non-negotiable sea waybill does not indicate the port of loading stated in the credit as the port of loading, or if it contains the indication "intended" or similar qualification in relation to the port of loading, an on board notation indicating the port of loading as stated in the credit, the date of shipment and the name of the vessel is required. This provision applies even when loading on board or shipment on a named vessel is indicated by pre-printed wording on the non-negotiable sea waybill.

iv. be the sole original non-negotiable sea waybill or, if issued in more than one original, be the full set as indicated on the non-negotiable sea waybill.

v. contain terms and conditions of carriage or make reference to another source containing the terms and conditions of carriage(short form or blank back non-negotiable sea waybill). Contents of terms and conditions of carriage will not be examined.

vi. contain no indication that it is subject to a charter party.

b. For the purpose of this article, transhipment means unloading from one vessel and reloading to another vessel during the carriage from the port of loading to the port of discharge stated in the credit.

c. i. A non-negotiable sea waybill may indicate that the goods will or may be transhipped provided that the entire carriage is covered by one and the same non-negotiable sea waybill.

ii. A non-negotiable sea waybill indicating that transhipment will or may take place is acceptable, even if the credit prohibits transhipment, if the goods have been shipped in a container, trailer or LASH barge as evidenced by the non-negotiable sea waybill.

d. Clauses in a non-negotiable sea waybill stating that the carrier reserves the right to tranship will be disregarded.

Article 22 Charter Party Bill of Lading

a. A bill of lading, however named, containing an indication that it is subject to a charter party(charter party bill of lading), must appear to:

i. be signed by:

- the master or a named agent for or on behalf of the master, or
- the owner or a named agent for or on behalf of the owner, or
- the charterer or a named agent for or on behalf of the charterer.

Any signature by the master, owner, charterer or agent must be identified as that of the master, owner, charterer or agent.

Any signature by an agent must indicate whether the agent has signed for or on behalf of the master, owner or charterer.

An agent signing for or on behalf of the owner or charterer must indicate the name of the owner or charterer.

ii. indicate that the goods have been shipped on board a named vessel at the port of loading stated in the credit by:

- pre-printed wording, or
- an on board notation indicating the date on which the goods have been shipped on board.

The date of issuance of the charter party bill of lading will be deemed to be the date of shipment unless the charter party bill of lading contains an on board notation indicating the date of shipment, in which case the date stated in the on board notation will be deemed to be the date of shipment.

iii. indicate shipment from the port of loading to the port of discharge stated in the credit. The port of discharge may also be shown as a range of ports or a geographical area, as stated in the credit.

iv. be the sole original charter party bill of lading or, if issued in more than one original, be the full set as indicated on the charter party bill of lading.

b. A bank will not examine charter party contracts, even if they are required to be presented by the terms of the credit.

Article 23 Air Transport Document

a. An air transport document, however named, must appear to:

i. indicate the name of the carrier and be signed by:

- the carrier, or
- a named agent for or on behalf of the carrier.

Any signature by the carrier or agent must be identified as that of the carrier or agent.

Any signature by an agent must indicate that the agent has signed for or on behalf of the carrier.

ii. indicate that the goods have been accepted for carriage.

iii. indicate the date of issuance. This date will be deemed to be the date of shipment unless the air transport document contains a specific notation of the actual date of shipment, in which case the date stated in the notation will be deemed to be the date of shipment.

Any other information appearing on the air transport document relative to the flight number and date will not be considered in determining the date of shipment.

iv. indicate the airport of departure and the airport of destination stated in the credit.

v. be the original for consignor or shipper, even if the credit stipulates a full set of originals.

vi. contain terms and conditions of carriage or make reference to another source containing the terms and conditions of carriage. Contents of terms and conditions of carriage will not be examined.

b. For the purpose of this article, transhipment means unloading from one aircraft and reloading to another aircraft during the carriage from the airport of departure to the airport of destination stated in the credit.

c. i. An air transport document may indicate that the goods will or may be transhipped, provided that the entire carriage is covered by one and the same air transport document.

ii. An air transport document indicating that transhipment will or may take place is acceptable, even if the credit prohibits transhipment.

Article 24 Road, Rail or Inland Waterway Transport Documents

a. A road, rail or inland waterway transport document, however named, must appear to :
   i. indicate the name of the carrier and:
      - be signed by the carrier or a named agent for or on behalf of the carrier, or
      - indicate receipt of the goods by signature, stamp or notation by the carrier or a named agent for or on behalf of the carrier.

      Any signature, stamp or notation of receipt of the goods by the carrier or agent must be identified as that of the carrier or agent.

      Any signature, stamp or notation of receipt of the goods by the agent must indicate that the agent has signed or acted for or on behalf of the carrier.

      If a rail transport document does not identify the carrier, any signature or stamp of the railway company will be accepted as evidence of the document being signed by the carrier.
   ii. indicate the date of shipment or the date the goods have been received for shipment, dispatch or carriage at the place stated in the credit. Unless the transport document contains a dated reception stamp, an indication of the date of receipt or a date of shipment, the date of issuance of the transport document will be deemed to be the date of shipment.
   iii. indicate the place of shipment and the place of destination stated in the credit.

b. i. A road transport document must appear to be the original for consignor or shipper or bear no marking indicating for whom the document has been prepared.
   ii. A rail transport document marked "duplicate" will be accepted as an original.
   iii. A rail or inland waterway transport document will be accepted as an original whether marked as an original or not.

c. In the absence of an indication on the transport document as to the number of originals issued, the number presented will be deemed to constitute a full set.

d. For the purpose of this article, transhipment means unloading from one means of conveyance and reloading to another means of conveyance, within the same mode of transport, during the carriage from the place of shipment, dispatch or carriage to the place of destination stated in the credit.

e. i. A road, rail or inland waterway transport document may indicate that the goods will or may be transhipped provided that the entire carriage is covered by one and the same transport document.
   ii. A road, rail or inland waterway transport document indicating that transhipment will or may take place is acceptable, even if the credit prohibits transhipment.

Article 25 Courier Receipt, Post Receipt or Certificate of Posting

a. A courier receipt, however named, evidencing receipt of goods for transport, must appear to:
   i. indicate the name of the courier service and be stamped or signed by the named courier service at the place from which the credit states the goods are to be shipped; and
   ii. indicate a date of pick-up or of receipt or wording to this effect. This date will be deemed to be the date of shipment.

b. A requirement that courier charges are to be paid or prepaid may be satisfied by a transport document issued by a courier service evidencing that courier charges are for the account of a party other than the consignee.

c. A post receipt or certificate of posting, however named, evidencing receipt of goods for transport, must appear to be stamped or signed and dated at the place from which the credit states the goods are to be shipped. This date will be deemed to be the date of shipment.

Article 26 "On Deck", "Shipper's Load and Count", "Said by Shipper to Contain" and Charges Additional to Freight

a. A transport document must not indicate that the goods are or will be loaded on deck. A clause on a transport document stating that the goods may be loaded on deck is acceptable.

b. A transport document bearing a clause such as "shipper's load and count" and "said by shipper to contain" is acceptable.

c. A transport document may bear a reference, by stamp or otherwise, to charges additional to the freight.

Article 27 Clean Transport Document

A bank will only accept a clean transport document. A clean transport document is one bearing no clause or notation expressly declaring a defective condition of the goods or their packaging. The word "clean" need not appear on a transport document, even if a credit has a requirement for that transport document to be "clean on board".

Article 28 Insurance Document and Coverage

a. An insurance document, such as an insurance policy, an insurance certificate or a declaration under an open cover, must appear to be issued and signed by an insurance company, an underwriter or their agents or their proxies.
   Any signature by an agent or proxy must indicate whether the agent or proxy has signed for or on behalf of the insurance company or underwriter.

b. When the insurance document indicates that it has been issued in more than one original, all originals must be presented.
c. Cover notes will not be accepted.
d. An insurance policy is acceptable in lieu of an insurance certificate or a declaration under an open cover.
e. The date of the insurance document must be no later than the date of shipment, unless it appears from the insurance document that the cover is effective from a date not later than the date of shipment.
f. i. The insurance document must indicate the amount of insurance coverage and be in the same currency as the credit.
   ii. A requirement in the credit for insurance coverage to be for a percentage of the value of the goods, of the invoice value or similar is deemed to be the minimum amount of coverage required.
   If there is no indication in the credit of the insurance coverage required, the amount of insurance coverage must be at least 110% of the CIF or CIP value of the goods.
   When the CIF or CIP value cannot be determined from the documents, the amount of insurance coverage must be calculated on the basis of the amount for which honour or negotiation is requested or the gross value of the goods as shown on the invoice, whichever is greater.
   iii. The insurance document must indicate that risks are covered at least between the place of taking in charge or shipment and the place of discharge or final destination as stated in the credit.
g. A credit should state the type of insurance required and, if any, the additional risks to be covered. An insurance document will be accepted without regard to any risks that are not covered if the credit uses imprecise terms such as "usual risks" or "customary risks".
h. When a credit requires insurance against "all risks" and an insurance document is presented containing any "all risks" notation or clause, whether or not bearing the heading "all risks", the insurance document will be accepted without regard to any risks stated to be excluded.
i. An insurance document may contain reference to any exclusion clause.
j. An insurance document may indicate that the cover is subject to a franchise or excess(deductible).

Article 29 Extension of Expiry Date or Last Day for Presenation

a. If the expiry date of a credit or the last day for presentation falls on a day when the bank to which presentation is to be made is closed for reasons other than those referred to in article 36, the expiry date or the last day for presentation, as the case may be, will be extended to the first following banking day.
b. If presentation is made on the first following banking day, a nominated bank must provide the issuing bank or confirming bank with a statement on its cover-

ing schedule that the presentation was made within the time limits extended in accordance with sub-article 29(a).

c. The latest date for shipment will not be extended as a result of sub-article 29(a).

Article 30 Tolerance in Credit Amount, Quantity and Unit Prices

a. The words "about" or "approximately" used in connection with the amount of the credit or the quantity or the unit price stated in the credit are to be construed as allowing a tolerance not to exceed 10% more or 10% less than the amount, the quantity or the unit price to which they refer.

b. A tolerance not to exceed 5% more or 5% less than the quantity of the goods is allowed, provided the credit does not state the quantity in terms of a stipulated number of packing units or individual items and the total amount of the drawings does not exceed the amount of the credit.

c. Even when partial shipments are not allowed, a tolerance not to exceed 5% less than the amount of the credit is allowed, provided that the quantity of the goods, if stated in the credit, is shipped in full and a unit price, if stated in the credit, is not reduced or that sub-article 30(b) is not applicable. This tolerance does not apply when the credit stipulates a specific tolerance or uses the expressions referred to in sub-article 30(a).

Article 31 Partial Drawings or Shipments

a. Partial drawings or shipments are allowed.

b. A presentation consisting of more than one set of transport documents evidencing shipment commencing on the same means of conveyance and for the same journey, provided they indicate the same destination, will not be regarded as covering a partial shipment, even if they indicate different dates of shipment or different ports of loading, places of taking in charge or dispatch. If the presentation consists of more than one set of transport documents, the latest date of shipment as evidenced on any of the sets of transport documents will be regarded as the date of shipment.

   A presentation consisting of one or more sets of transport documents evidencing shipment on more than one means of conveyance within the same mode of transport will be regarded as covering a partial shipment, even if the means of conveyance leave on the same day for the same destination.

c. A presentation consisting of more than one courier receipt, post receipt or certificate of posting will not be regarded as a partial shipment if the courier receipts, post receipts or certificates of posting appear to have been stamped or signed by the same courier or postal service at the same place and date and for the same destination.

Article 32 Instalment Drawings or Shipments

If a drawing or shipment by instalments within given periods is stipulated in the credit and any instalment is not drawn or shipped within the period allowed for that instalment, the credit ceases to be available for that and any subsequent instalment.

Article 33 Hours of Presentation

A bank has no obligation to accept a presentation outside of its banking hours.

Article 34 Disclaimer on Effectiveness of Documents

A bank assumes no liability or responsibility for the form, sufficiency, accuracy, genuineness, falsification or legal effect of any document, or for the general or particular conditions stipulated in a document or superimposed thereon; nor does it assume any liability or responsibility for the description, quantity, weight, quality, condition, packing, delivery, value or existence of the goods, services or other performance represented by any document, or for the good faith or acts or omissions, solvency, performance or standing of the consignor, the carrier, the forwarder, the consignee or the insurer of the goods or any other person.

Article 35 Disclaimer on Transmission and Translation

A bank assumes no liability or responsibility for the consequences arising out of delay, loss in transit, mutilation or other errors arising in the transmission of any messages or delivery of letters or documents, when such messages, letters or documents are transmitted or sent according to the requirements stated in the credit, or when the bank may have taken the initiative in the choice of the delivery service in the absence of such instructions in the credit.

If a nominated bank determines that a presentation is complying and forwards the documents to the issuing bank or confirming bank, whether or not the nominated bank has honoured or negotiated, an issuing bank or confirming bank must honour or negotiate, or reimburse that nominated bank, even when the documents have been lost in transit between the nominated bank and the issuing bank or confirming bank, or between the confirming bank and the issuing bank.

A bank assumes no liability or responsibility for errors in translation or interpretation of technical terms and may transmit credit terms without translating them.

Article 36 Force Majeure

A bank assumes no liability or responsibility for the consequences arising out of the interruption of its business by Acts of God, riots, civil commotions, insurrections, wars, acts of terrorism, or by any strikes or lockouts or any other causes beyond its control.

A bank will not, upon resumption of its business, honour or negotiate under a credit that expired during such interruption of its business.

Article 37 Disclaimer for Acts of an Instructed Party

a. A bank utilizing the services of another bank for the purpose of giving effect to the instructions of the applicant does so for the account and at the risk of the applicant.

b. An issuing bank or advising bank assumes no liability or responsibility should the instructions it transmits to another bank not be carried out, even if it has taken the initiative in the choice of that other bank.

c. A bank instructing another bank to perform services is liable for any commissions, fees, costs or expenses("charges") incurred by that bank in connection with its instructions.

   If a credit states that charges are for the account of the beneficiary and charges cannot be collected or deducted from proceeds, the issuing bank remains liable for payment of charges.

   A credit or amendment should not stipulate that the advising to a beneficiary is conditional upon the receipt by the advising bank or second advising bank of its charges.

d. The applicant shall be bound by and liable to indemnify a bank against all obligations and responsibilities imposed by foreign laws and usages.

Article 38 Transferable Credits

a. A bank is under no obligation to transfer a credit except to the extent and in the manner expressly consented to by that bank.

b. For the purpose of this article:

   Transferable credit means a credit that specifically states it is "transferable". A transferable credit may be made available in whole or in part to another beneficiary("second beneficiary") at the request of the beneficiary("first beneficiary").

   Transferring bank means a nominated bank that transfers the credit or, in a credit available with any bank, a bank that is specifically authorized by the issuing bank to transfer and that transfers the credit. An issuing bank may be a transferring bank.

   Transferred credit means a credit that has been made available by the transferring bank to a second beneficiary.

c. Unless otherwise agreed at the time of transfer, all charges(such as commissions, fees, costs or expenses) incurred in respect of a transfer must be paid by the first beneficiary.

d. A credit may be transferred in part to more than one second beneficiary provided partial drawings or shipments are allowed.

A transferred credit cannot be transferred at the request of a second beneficiary to any subsequent beneficiary. The first beneficiary is not considered to be a subsequent beneficiary.

e. Any request for transfer must indicate if and under what conditions amendments may be advised to the second beneficiary. The transferred credit must clearly indicate those conditions.

f. If a credit is transferred to more than one second beneficiary, rejection of an amendment by one or more second beneficiary does not invalidate the acceptance by any other second beneficiary, with respect to which the transferred credit will be amended accordingly. For any second beneficiary that rejected the amendment, the transferred credit will remain unamended.

g. The transferred credit must accurately reflect the terms and conditions of the credit, including confirmation, if any, with the exception of:

- the amount of the credit,
- any unit price stated therein,
- the expiry date,
- the period for presentation, or
- the latest shipment date or given period for shipment,

any or all of which may be reduced or curtailed.

The percentage for which insurance cover must be effected may be increased to provide the amount of cover stipulated in the credit or these articles.

The name of the first beneficiary may be substituted for that of the applicant in the credit.

If the name of the applicant is specifically required by the credit to appear in any document other than the invoice, such requirement must be reflected in the transferred credit.

h. The first beneficiary has the right to substitute its own invoice and draft, if any, for those of a second beneficiary for an amount not in excess of that stipulated in the credit, and upon such substitution the first beneficiary can draw under the credit for the difference, if any, between its invoice and the invoice of a second beneficiary.

i. If the first beneficiary is to present its own invoice and draft, if any, but fails to do so on first demand, or if the invoices presented by the first beneficiary create discrepancies that did not exist in the presentation made by the second beneficiary and the first beneficiary fails to correct them on first demand, the transferring bank has the right to present the documents as received from the second beneficiary to the issuing bank, without further responsibility to the first beneficiary.

j. The first beneficiary may, in its request for transfer, indicate that honour or negotiation is to be effected to a second beneficiary at the place to which the credit has been transferred, up to and including the expiry date of the credit. This is without prejudice to the right of the first beneficiary in accordance with sub-article 38(h).

k. Presentation of documents by or on behalf of a second beneficiary must be made to the transferring bank.

Article 39 Assignment of Proceeds

The fact that a credit is not stated to be transferable shall not affect the right of the beneficiary to assign any proceeds to which it may be or may become entitled under the credit, in accordance with the provisions of applicable law. This article relates only to the assignment of proceeds and not to the assignment of the right to perform under the credit.

UCP Supplement for Electronic Presentation(eUCP)

Article e1 : Scope of the eUCP

a. The Supplement to the Uniform Customs and Practice for Documentary Credits for Electronic Presentation("eUCP") supplements the Uniform Customs and Practice for Documentary Credits(2007 Revision ICC Publication No. 600,) ("UCP") in order to accommodate presentation of electronic records alone or in combination with paper documents.
b. The eUCP shall apply as a supplement to the UCP where the credit indicates that it is subject to eUCP.
c. This version is Version 1.1. A credit must indicate the applicable version of the eUCP. If it does not do so, it is subject to the version in effect on the date the credit is issued or, if made subject to eUCP by an amendment accepted by the beneficiary, on the date of that amendment.

Article e2 Relationship of the eUCP to the UCP

a. A credit subject to the eUCP ("eUCP credit") is also subject to the UCP without express incorporation of the UCP.
b. Where the eUCP applies, its provisions shall prevail to the extent that they would produce a result different from the application of the UCP.
c. If an eUCP credit allows the beneficiary to choose between presentation of paper documents or electronic records and it chooses to present only paper documents, the UCP alone shall apply to that presentation. If only paper documents are permitted under an eUCP credit, the UCP alone shall apply.

Article e3 : Definitions

a. Where the following terms are used in the UCP, for the purposes of applying the UCP to an electronic record presented under an eUCP credit, the term:
   i. appear on their face and the like shall apply to examination of the data content of an electronic record.
   ii. document shall include an electronic record.
   iii. place for presentation of electronic records means an electronic address.
   iv. sign and the like shall include an electronic signature.
   v. superimposed, notation or stamped means data content whose supplementary character is apparent in an electronic record.

b. The following terms used in the eUCP shall have the following meanings:
   i. electronic record means
      - data created, generated, sent, communicated, received or stored by electronic means
      - that is capable of being authenticated as to the apparent identity of a sender and the apparent source of the data contained in it, and as to whether it has remained complete and unaltered, and
      - is capable of being examined for compliance with the terms and conditions of the eUCP credit.
   ii. electronic signature means a data process attached to or logically associated with an electronic record and executed or adopted by a person in order to identify that person and to indicate that person's authentication of the electronic record.
   iii. format means the data organization in which the electronic record is expressed or to which it refers.
   iv. paper document means a document in a traditional paper form.
   v. received means the time when an electronic record enters the information system of the applicable recipient in a form capable of being accepted by that system. Any acknowledgement of receipt does not imply acceptance or refusal of the electronic record under an eUCP credit.

Article e4 : Format

An eUCP credit must specify the formats in which electronic records are to be presented. If the format of the electronic record is not so specified, it may be presented in any format

Article e5 : Presentation

a. An eUCP credit allowing presentation of:
   i. electronic records must state a place for presentation of the electronic records.
   ii. Both electronic records and paper documents must also state a place for presentation of the paper documents.
b. Electronic records may be presented separately and need not be presented at the same time.
c. If an eUCP credit allows for presentation of one or more electronic records, the beneficiary is responsible for providing a notice to the bank to which presentation is made signifying when the presentation is complete. The notice of completeness may be given as an electronic record or paper document and must identify the eUCP credit to which it relates. Presentation is deemed not to have been made if the beneficiary's notice is not received.
d. i. Each presentation of an electronic record and the presentation of paper documents under an eUCP credit must identify the eUCP credit under which it is

presented.

ii. A presentation not so identified may be treated as not received.

e. If the bank to which presentation is to be made is open but its system is unable to receive a transmitted electronic record on the stipulated expiry date and/or the last day of the period of time after the date of shipment for presentation, as the case may be, the bank will be deemed to be closed and the date for presentation and/or the expiry date shall be extended to the first following banking day on which such bank is able to receive an electronic record. If the only electronic record remaining to be presented is the notice of completeness, it may be given by telecommunications or by paper document and will be deemed timely, provided that it is sent before the bank is able to receive an electronic record.

f. An electronic record that cannot be authenticated is deemed not to have been presented.

Article e6 : Examination

a. If an electronic record contains a hyperlink to an external system or a presentation indicates that the electronic record may be examined by reference to an external system, the electronic record at the hyperlink or the referenced system shall be deemed to be the electronic record to be examined. The failure of the indicated system to provide access to the required electronic record at the time of examination shall constitute a discrepancy.

b. The forwarding of electronic records by a nominated bank pursuant to its nomination signifies that it has satisfied itself as to the apparent authenticity of the electronic records.

c. The inability of the issuing bank, or confirming bank, if any, to examine an electronic record in a format required by the eUCP credit or, if no format is required, to examine it in the format presented is not a basis for refusal.

Article e7 : Notice of Refusal

a. i. The time period for the examination of documents commences on the banking day following the banking day on which the beneficiary's notice of completeness is received.

ii. If the time for presentation of documents or the notice of completeness is extended, the time for the examination of documents commences on the first following banking day on which such bank is able to receive the notice of completeness.

b. If an issuing bank, the confirming bank, if any, or a nominated bank acting on its nomination, provides a notice of refusal of a presentation which includes electronic records and does not receive instructions from the party to which notice of refusal is given within 30 calendar days from the date the notice of refusal is given for the disposition of the electronic records, the bank shall return any paper documents not previously returned to the presenter but may dispose of the electronic records in any manner deemed appropriate without any responsibility.

Article e8 : Originals and Copies

Any requirement of the UCP or an eUCP credit for presentation of one or more originals or copies of an electronic record is satisfied by the presentation of one electronic record

Article e9 : Date of Issuance

Unless an electronic record contains a specific date of issuance, the date on which it appears to have been sent by the issuer is deemed to be the date of issuance. The date of receipt will be deemed to be the date it was sent if no other date is apparent.

Article e10 : Transport

If an electronic record evidencing transport does not indicate a date of shipment or dispatch, the date of issuance of the electronic record will be deemed to be the date of shipment or dispatch. However, if the electronic record bears a notation that evidences the date of shipment or dispatch, the date of the notation will be deemed to be the date of shipment or dispatch. A notation showing additional data content need not be separately signed or otherwise authenticated.

Article e11 : Corruption of an Electronic Record After Presentation

a. If an electronic record that has been received by the issuing bank, confirming bank, or another nominated bank appears to have been corrupted, the bank may inform the presenter and may request that the electronic record be re-presented.
b. If the bank requests that an electronic record be re-presented:
   i. the time for examination is suspended and resumes when the presenter re-presents the electronic record; and
   ii. if the nominated bank is not the confirming bank, it must provide the issuing bank and any confirming bank with notice of the request for re-presentation and inform it of the suspension; but
   iii. if the same electronic record is not re-presented within thirty (30) calendar days, the bank may treat the electronic record as not presented, and
   iv. any deadlines are not extended.

Article e12 : Additional Disclaimer of Liability for Presentation of Electronic Records under eUCP

By satisfying itself as to the apparent authenticity of an electronic record, banks assume no liability for the identity of the sender, source of the information or its complete and unaltered character other than that which is apparent in the electronic record received by the use of a commercially acceptable data process for the receipt, authentication and identification of electronic records.

Uniform Rules for Collections, 1995 Revision, ICC Publication No. 522(URC)

A. GENERAL PROVISIONS AND DEFINITIONS

Article 1. Application of URC 522

a. The Uniform Rules for Collections, 1995 Revision, ICC Publication No. 522, shall apply to all collections as defined in Article 2 where such rules are incorporated into the text of the "collection instruction" referred to in Article 4 and are binding on all parties thereto unless otherwise expressly agreed or contrary to the provisions of a national, state or local law and/or regulation which cannot be departed from.

b. Banks shall have no obligation to handle either a collection or any collection instruction or subsequent related instructions.

c. If a bank elects, for any reason, not to handle a collection or any related instructions received by it, it must advise the party from whom it received the collection or the instructions by telecommunication or, if that is not possible, by other expeditious means, without delay.

Article 2. Definition of Collection

For the purposes of these Articles :

a. "Collection" means the handling by banks of documents as defined in b below, in accordance with instructions received, in order to :
   1. obtain payment and/or acceptance, or
   2. deliver documents against payment and/or against acceptance, or
   3. deliver documents on other terms and conditions.

b. "Documents" means financial documents and/or commercial documents :
   1. "Financial documents" means bills of exchange, promissory notes, cheques, or other similar instruments used for obtaining the payment of money ;
   2. "Commercial documents" means invoices, transport documents, documents of title or other similar documents, or any other documents whatsoever, not being financial documents.

c. "Clean collection" means collection of financial documents not accompanied by commercial documents.

d. "Documentary collection" means collection of :
   1. Financial documents accompanied by commercial documents ;
   2. Commercial documents not accompanied by financial documents.

Article 3. Parties to a Collection

a. For the purposes of these Articles the "parties thereto" are :
   1. the "principal" who is the party entrusting the handling of a collection to a bank
   2. the "remitting bank" which is the bank to which the principal has entrusted the handling of a collection ;
   3. the "collecting bank" which is any bank, other than the remitting bank, involved in processing the collection ;
   4. the "presenting bank" which is the collecting bank making presentation to the drawee.

b. The "drawee" is the one to whom presentation is to be made according to the collection instruction.

B. FORM AND STRUCTURE OF COLLECTIONS

Article 4. Collection Instruction

a. 1. All documents sent for collection must be accompanied by a collection instruction indicating that the collection is subject to URC 522 and giving complete and precise instructions. Banks are only permitted to act upon the instructions given in such collection instruction, and in accordance with these Rules.
   2. Banks will not examine documents in order to obtain instructions.
   3. Unless otherwise authorized in the collection instruction, banks will disregard any instructions from any party/bank other than the party/bank from whom they received the collection.

b. A collection instruction should contain the following information as appropriate.
   1. Details of the bank from which the collection was received including full name, postal and SWIFT addresses, telex, telephone, facsimile numbers and reference.
   2. Details of the principal including full name, postal address, and if applicable telex, telephone and facsimile numbers.
   3. Details of the drawee including full name, postal address, or the domicile at which presentation is to be made and if applicable telex, telephone and facsimile numbers.
   4. Details of the presenting bank, if any, including full name, postal address, and if applicable telex, telephone and facsimile numbers.
   5. Amount(s) and currency(ies) to be collected.
   6. List of documents enclosed and the numerical count of each document.
   7. a. Terms and conditions upon which payment and/or acceptance is to be obtained.
      b. Terms of delivery of documents against :

1) payment
2) acceptance
3) other terms and conditions

It is the responsibility of the party who sends the collection instruction to ensure that the terms for the delivery of documents are clearly and unambiguously stated, otherwise banks will not be responsible for any consequences arising thereto.

8. Charges to be collected, indicating whether they may be waived or not.
9. Interest to be collected, if applicable, indicating whether it may be waived or not, including :
   a. rate of interest
   b. interest period
   c. basis of calculation(for example 360 or 365 days in a year) as applicable.
10. Method of payment and form of payment advice.
11. Instructions in case of non-payment, non-acceptance and/or non-compliance with other instructions.

c. 1. Collection instructions should bear the complete address of the drawee or of the domicile at which the presentation is to be made. If the address is incomplete or incorrect, the collecting bank may, without any liability and responsibility on its part, endeavour to ascertain the proper address.
   2. The collecting bank will not be liable or responsible for any ensuing delay as a result of the incomplete/incorrect address.

C. FORM OF PRESENTATION

Article 5. Presentation

a. For the purposes of these Articles, presentation is the procedure whereby the presenting bank makes the documents available to the drawee as instructed and in accordance with local banking practice.
b. The collection instruction should state the exact period of time within which any action is to be taken by the drawee. Expressions such as "first", "prompt", "immediate", and the like should not be used in connection with presentation or with reference to any period of time within which documents have to be taken up or for any other action that is to be taken by the drawee. If such terms are used banks will disregard them.
c. Documents are to be presented to the drawee in the form in which they are received, except that banks are authorized to affix any necessary stamps, at the expense of the party from whom they received the collection unless otherwise instructed, and to make any necessary endorsements or place any rubber stamps or other identifying marks or symbols customary to or required for the collection operation.

d. For the purpose of giving effect to the instructions of the principal, the remitting bank will utilize the bank nominated by the principal as the collecting bank. In the absence of such nomination, the remitting bank will utilize any bank of its own, or another bank's choice in the country of payment or acceptance or in the country where other terms and conditions have to be complied with.
e. The documents and collection instruction may be sent directly by the remitting bank to the collecting bank or through another bank as intermediary.
f. If the remitting bank does not nominate a specific presenting bank, the collecting bank may utilize a presenting bank of its choice.

Article 6. Sight/Acceptance

In the case of documents payable at sight the presenting bank must make presentation for payment without delay. In the case of documents payable at a tenor other than sight the presenting bank must, where acceptance is called for, make presentation for acceptance without delay, and where payment is called for, make presentation for payment not later than the appropriate maturity date.

Article 7. Release of Commercial Documents

Documents Against Acceptance(D/A) vs. Documents Against Payment(D/P)

a. Collections should not contain bills of exchange payable at a future date with instructions that commercial documents are to be delivered against payment.
b. If a collection contains a bill of exchange payable at a future date, the collection instruction should state whether the commercial documents are to be released to the drawee against acceptance(D/A) or against payment(D/P). In the absence of such statement commercial documents will be released only against payment and the collecting bank will not be responsible for any consequences arising out of any delay in the delivery of documents.
c. If a collection contains a bill of exchange payable at a future date and the collection instruction indicates that commercial documents are to be released against payment, documents will be released only against such payment and the collecting bank will not be responsible for any consequences arising out of any delay in the delivery of documents.

Article 8. Creation of Documents

Where the remitting bank instructs that either the collecting bank or the drawee is to create documents(bills of exchange, promissory notes, trust receipts, letters of undertaking or other documents) that were not included in the collection, the form and wording of such documents shall be provided by the remitting bank ; otherwise the collecting bank shall not be liable or responsible for the form and wording of any such document provided by the collecting bank and/or the drawee.

D. LIABILITIES AND RESPONSIBILITIES

Article 9. Good Faith and Reasonable Care

Banks will act in good faith and exercise reasonable care.

Article 10. Documents vs. Goods/Services/Performances

a. Goods should not be despatched directly to the address of a bank or consigned to or to the order of a bank without prior agreement on the part of that bank. Nevertheless, in the event that goods are despatched directly to the address of a bank or consigned to or to the order of a bank for release to a drawee against payment or acceptance or upon other terms and conditions without prior agreement on the part of that bank, such banks shall have no obligation to take delivery of the goods, which remain at the risk and responsibility of the party despatching the goods.

b. Banks have no obligation to take any action in respect of the goods to which a documentary collection relates, including storage and insurance of the goods even when specific instructions are given to do so. Banks will only take such action if, when, and to the extent that they agree to do so. Notwithstanding the provisions of sub-Article 1.c. this rule applies even in the absence of any specific advice to this effect by the collecting bank.

c. Nevertheless, in the case that banks take action for the protection of the goods, whether instructed or not, they assume no liability or responsibility with regard to the fate and/or condition of the goods and/or for any acts and/or omissions on the part of any third parties entrusted with the custody and/or protection of the goods. However, the collecting bank must advise without delay the bank from which the collection instruction was received of any such action taken.

d. Any charges and/or expenses incurred by banks in connection with any action taken to protect the goods will be for the account of the party from whom they received the collection.

e. 1. Notwithstanding the provisions of sub-Article 10.a., where the goods are consigned to or to the order of the collecting bank and the drawee has honoured the collection by payment, acceptance or other terms and conditions, and the collecting bank arranges for the release of the goods, the remitting bank shall be deemed to have authorized the collecting bank to do so.

   2. Where a collecting bank on the instructions of the remitting bank or in terms of e.1. above arranges for the release of the goods, the remitting bank shall indemnify such collecting bank for all damages and expenses incurred.

Article 11. Disclaimer for Acts of an Instructed Party

a. Banks utilizing the services of another bank or other banks for the purpose of giving effect to the instructions of the principal, do so for the account and at the risk of such principal.

b. Banks assume no liability or responsibility should the instructions they transmit not be carried out, even if they have themselves taken the initiative in the choice of such other bank(s).

c. A party instructing another party to perform services shall be bound by and liable to indemnify the instructed party against all obligations and responsibilities imposed by foreign laws and usages.

Article 12. Disclaimer on Documents Received

a. Banks must determine that the documents received appear to be as listed in the collection instruction and must advise by telecommunication or, if that is not possible, by other expeditious means, without delay, the party from whom the collection instruction was received of any documents missing, or found to be other than listed. Banks have no further obligation in this respect.

b. If the documents do not appear to be listed, the remitting bank shall be precluded from disputing the type and number of documents received by the collecting bank.

c. Subject to sub-Article 5.c. and sub-Articles a. and b. above, banks will present documents as received without further examination.

Article 13. Disclaimer on Effectiveness of Documents

Banks assume no liability or responsibility for the form, sufficiency, accuracy, genuineness, falsification or legal effect of any document(s), or for the general and/or particular conditions stipulated in the document(s) or superimposed thereon ; nor do they assume any liability or responsibility for the description, quantity, weight, quality, condition, packing, delivery, value or existence of the goods represented by any document(s), or for the good faith or acts and/or omissions, solvency, performance or standing of the consignors, the carriers, the forwarders, the consignees or the insurers of the goods, or any other person whomsoever.

Article 14. Disclaimer on Delays, Loss in Transit and Translation

a. Banks assume no liability or responsibility for the consequences arising out of delay and/or loss in transit of any message(s), letter(s) or document(s), or for delay, mutilation or other error(s) arising in transmission of any telecommunication or for error(s) in translation and/or interpretation of technical terms.

b. Banks will not be responsible for any delays resulting from the need to obtain clarification of any instructions received.

Article 15. Force Majeure

Banks assume no liability or responsibility for consequences arising out of the interruption of their business by Acts of God, riots, civil commotions, insurrections, wars, or any other causes beyond their control or by strikes or lockouts.

E. PAYMENT

Article 16. Payment without Delay

a. Amounts collected(less charges and/or disbursements and/or expenses where applicable) must be made available without delay to the party from whom the collection instruction was received in accordance with the terms and conditions of the collection instruction.

b. Notwithstanding the provisions of sub-Article 1.c. and unless otherwise agreed, the collecting bank will effect payment of the amount collected only in favour of the remitting bank.

Article 17. Payment in Local Currency

In the case of documents payable in the currency of the country of payment(local currency), the presenting bank must, unless otherwise instructed in the collection instruction, release the documents to the drawee against payment in local currency only if such currency is immediately available for disposal in the manner specified in the collection instruction.

Article 18. Payment in Foreign Currency

In the case of documents payable in a currency other than that of the country of payment(foreign currency), the presenting bank must, unless otherwise instructed in the collection instruction, release the documents to the drawee against payment in the relative foreign currency only if such foreign currency can immediately be remitted in accordance with the instructions given in the collection instruction.

Article 19. Partial Payments

a. In respect of clean collections, partial payments may be accepted if and to the extent to which and on the conditions on which partial payments are authorized by the law in force in the place of payment. The financial document(s) will be released to the drawee only when full payment thereof has been received.

b. In respect of documentary collections, partial payments will only be accepted if specifically authorized in the collection instruction. However, unless otherwise instructed, the presenting bank will release the documents to the drawee only after full payment has been received, and the presenting bank will not be responsible for any consequences arising out of any delay in the delivery of documents.

c. In all cases partial payments will be accepted only subject to compliance with the provisions of either Article 17 or Article 18 as appropriate.

Partial payment, if accepted, will be dealt with in accordance with the provisions of Article 16.

F. INTEREST, CHARGES AND EXPENSES

Article 20. Interest

a. If the collection instruction specifies that interest is to be collected and the drawee refuses to pay such interest, the presenting bank may deliver the document(s) against payment or acceptance or on other terms and conditions as the case may be, without collecting such interest, unless sub-Article 20.c. applies.

b. Where such interest is to be collected, the collection instruction must bear an indication of the rate of interest, interest period and basis of calculation.

c. Where the collection instruction expressly states that interest may not be waived and the drawee refuses to pay such interest the presenting bank will not deliver documents and will not be responsible for any consequences arising out of any delay in the delivery of document(s). When payment of interest has been refused, the presenting bank must inform by telecommunication or, if that is not possible, by other expeditious means without delay the bank from whom the collection instruction was received.

Article 21. Charges and Expenses

a. If the collection instruction specifies that collection charges and/or expenses are to be for account of the drawee and the drawee refuses to pay them, the presenting bank may deliver the document(s) against payment or acceptance or on other terms and conditions as the case may be, without collecting charges and/or expenses, unless sub-Article 21.b. applies.
   Whenever collection charges and/or expenses are so waived they will be for the account of the party from whom the collection was received and may be deducted from the proceeds.

b. Where the collection instruction expressly states that charges and/or expenses may not be waived and the drawee refuses to pay such charges and/or expenses, the presenting bank will not deliver documents and will not be responsible for any consequences arising out of any delay in the delivery of the document(s). When payment of collection charges and/or expenses has been refused the presenting bank must inform by telecommunication or if that is not possible by other expeditious means without delay the bank from whom the collection instruction was received.

c. In all cases where in the express terms of a collection instruction or under these Rules, disbursements and/or expenses and/or collection charges are to be borne by the principal, the collecting bank(s) shall be entitled to recover promptly outlays in respect of disbursements, expenses and charges from the bank from whom the collection instruction was received, and the remitting bank shall be entitled to recover promptly from the principal any amount so paid out by it, together with its own disbursements, expenses and charges, regardless of the fate of the collection.

d. Banks reserve the right to demand payment of charges and/or expenses in advance from the party from whom the collection instruction was received to cover costs in attempting to carry out any instructions, and pending receipt of such payment, also reserve the right not to carry out such instructions.

G. OTHER PROVISIONS

Article 22. Acceptance

The presenting bank is responsible for seeing that the form of the acceptance of a bill of exchange appears to be complete and correct, but is not responsible for the genuineness of any signature or for the authority of any signatory to sign the acceptance.

Article 23. Promissory Notes and Other Instruments

The presenting bank is not responsible for the genuineness of any signature or for the authority of any signatory to sign a promissory note, receipt, or other instruments.

Article 24. Protest

The collection instruction should give specific instructions regarding protest(or other legal process in lieu thereof), in the event of non-acceptance or non-payment.

In the absence of such specific instructions, the banks concerned with the collection have no obligation to have the document(s) protested(or subjected to other legal process in lieu thereof) for non-payment or non-acceptance.

Any charges and/or expenses incurred by banks in connection with such protest, or other legal process, will be for the account of the party from whom the collection instruction was received.

Article 25. Case-of-Need

If the principal nominates a representative to act as case-of-need in the event of non-acceptance and/or non-payment the collection instruction should clearly and fully indicate the powers of such case-of-need. In the absence of such indication banks will not accept any instructions from the case-of-need.

Article 26. Advices

Collecting banks are to advise fate in accordance with the following rules :

a. Form of Advice : All advices or information from the collecting bank to the bank from which the collection instruction was received, must bear appropriate details including, in all cases, the latter bank's reference as stated in the collection instruction.

b. Method of advice : It shall be the responsibility of the remitting bank to instruct the collecting bank the method by which the advices detailed in sub-Article c.1., c.2. and c.3. are to be given. In the absence of such instructions, the collecting bank will send the relative advices by the method of its choice at the expense of the bank from which the collection instruction was received.

c. 1. Advice of Payment : The collecting bank must send without delay advice of payment to the bank from which the collection instruction was received, detailing the amount or amounts collected, charges and/or disbursements and/or expenses deducted, where appropriate, and method of disposal of the funds.

2. Advice of Acceptance : The collecting bank must send without delay advice of acceptance to the bank from which the collection instruction was received.

3. Advice of Non-Payment or Non-Acceptance : The presenting bank should endeavour to ascertain the reasons for non-payment or non-acceptance and advise accordingly, without delay, the bank from which the collection instruction was received. The presenting bank must send without delay advice of non-payment or advice of non-acceptance to the bank from which the collection instruction was received. On receipt of such advice the remitting bank must give appropriate instructions as to the further handling of the documents. If such instructions are not received by the presenting bank within 60 days after its advice of non-payment or non-acceptance, the documents may be returned to the bank from which the collection instruction was received without any further responsibility on the part of the presenting bank.

저자 약력

이 신 규

- 건국대학교 대학원 무역학과 졸업(경제학박사)
- (주)아모레퍼시픽 해외사업부 근무
- 부산경상대학교 항공해운무역과 교수
- 청운대학교 국제통상학과 교수
- 관세청 혁신지원단 자문위원
- 관세청 자체제안 심사위원, AEO 심사위원
- 관세사, 물류관리사 시험출제 및 선정위원
- 중앙공무원시험 출제 및 선정위원
- 한국관세학회 부회장
- 한국창업정보학회 회장
- 관세국경관리연수원 외래교수
- 국무조정실 국정과제평가위원
- International Academy for Global Business & Trade(IAGBT) 회장
- University of Nebraska-Lincoln(UNL) U.S.A., Visiting Professor
- 관세국경관리연수원 외래교수
- (현) 배재대학교 무역물류학과 교수

〈주요 저서〉

- 엣센스 무역실무, 도서출판 두남
- 무역실무, 도서출판 두남
- International Trade Practice, 도서출판 두남
- 국제통상론, 도서출판 두남
- 국제물류론, 형설출판사
- e-Logistics시대 운송물류론, 형설출판사
- 무역상담영어, 도서출판 두남
- 국제물류, 형설출판사
- 엣센스 무역영어, 도서출판 두남
- 무역학원론(공저), 도서출판 두남
- 무역영어, 도서출판 두남
- Business English, 도서출판 두남
- 국제무역결제론, 도서출판 두남
- 무역영어회화, 도서출판 두남
- 무역학개론(공저), 도서출판 두남
- 국제무역의 이해(공저), 도서출판 두남

International **Trade Practice**

초 판 1쇄 발행 —— 2014년 8월 5일
초 판 2쇄 발행 —— 2019년 2월 20일
개정판 1쇄 발행 —— 2020년 2월 10일
개정판 2쇄 발행 —— 2022년 1월 15일
지은이 —— 이 신 규
펴낸이 —— 전 두 표
펴낸곳 —— 도서출판 **두남**
서울시 강동구 성내로6길 34-16 두남빌딩
신 고 : 제25100-1988-9호
TEL : 02) 478-2065~7, 2311
FAX : 02) 478-2068
E-mail : dunam1@unitel.co.kr
http://www.dunam.co.kr

정가 30,000원

ISBN 978-89-6414-868-6 93320